V.S. Naipaul and the West Indies

American University Studies

Series XIX
General Literature

Vol. 18

PETER LANG
New York • Bern • Frankfurt am Main • Paris

Dolly Zulakha Hassan

V.S. Naipaul
and the West Indies

PETER LANG
New York • Bern • Frankfurt am Main • Paris

Library of Congress Cataloging-in-Publication Data

Hassan, Dolly Zulakha,
   V.S. Naipaul and the West Indies.
      (American university studies. Series XIX, General
literature ; vol. 18)
      Bibliography: p.
      1. Naipaul, V. S. (Vidiadhar Surajprasad), 1932- –
Knowledge –West Indies.   2. West Indies in literature.
I. Title.   II. Series
PR9272.9.N32Z73   1989   823'.914   88-12733
ISBN 0-8204-0750-X
ISSN 0743-6645

CIP-Titelaufnahme der Deutschen Bibliothek

Hassan, Dolly Zulakha:
V. S. Naipaul and the West Indies / Dolly Zulakha Hassan. –
New York; Bern; Frankfurt am Main; Paris: Lang, 1989
   (American university studies: Ser. 19, General literature; Vol. 18)
   ISBN 0-8204-0750-X
NE: American university studies / 19

17916272

© Peter Lang Publishing, Inc., New York 1989

Printed by Weihert-Druck GmbH, Darmstadt, West Germany

Dedicated to the loving memory of
my late father,
Al-Hajj Shaikh Iklaf Husain (Hassan)

Table of Contents

Acknowledgments

I thank the Andrew Mellon Foundation and Dr. Estelle W. Taylor and Dr. Robert L. Owens of Howard University for the support I received from them to undertake this project.

I shall be eternally grateful to Dr. Judith A. Plotz, who suggested the topic of this work to me. Without her deep interest, scholarly guidance, and kind words, this study would not have been completed. Dr. Christopher W. Sten and Dr. James H. Maddox also made valuable suggestions for the improvement of my work.

I owe special thanks to my dearest friend, His Excellency David D. Karran, Guyana's Deputy Permanent Representative to the UN. He not only assisted me in obtaining sources from the Caribbean, but he also encouraged and comforted me at moments of despair. Even though we share different views on the West Indies and on Naipaul, I found his criticisms stimulating.

I acknowledge the assistance of my family, especially little Jameela, as a source of inspiration. I am deeply indebted to my husband, Mohamad K. Yusuff, who first introduced me to Naipaul's works and who offered unstinting support. His patience and understanding during long hours of sustained pressure will be remembered. My mother and deceased father deserve more credit than I can ever mention.

Finally, I thank my typist, Cres Young, who graciously honored my most unreasonable demands and deadlines.

DZH

Preface

Trinidadian born Vidiadhar Surajprasad Naipaul was already
internationally recognized in the mid 1960's when in
Saraswat High School at West Coast Demerara, Guyana (then
British Guiana), my classmates and I were studying George
Eliot's Silas Marner for our London administered General
Certificate of Education examination (GCE). In colonial
Guiana it was more important to study British history, not
West Indian slavery or indentureship; to speak and write
standard English, not the language of our fore- fathers; and
to know English literature and Eliot, not Caribbean
literature and Naipaul. Thus, we could not have conceived
of a West Indian novel written by a local writer. Many of
us who left Guyana to further our studies abroad departed
without ever having heard of Naipaul. Corner bookshops, as
Naipaul himself often mentions, were non-existent;[1] in
addition, the Georgetown Public Library was not easily
accessible to rural residents. It was not until the early
1970's during my undergraduate period at Howard University
in Washington, D.C.--with Naipaul far from his home too in
another foreign capital, London--that I read The Middle
Passage and was introduced to this author, whose writings
have since captured my interest.

My continuing interest in Naipaul's work and my enthusiasm for investigating the West Indian response to this
writer extend beyond my fascination at the late discovery
that there can, after all, be a successful novel with West
Indian characters, written by a West Indian. Unlike
Naipaul's, the end paper of my copy of Kennedy's Revised
Latin Primer contains no written resolution to leave the
West Indies within a certain number of years, but it is a
familiar vow, one that I, too, driven by similar circumstances, repeatedly made orally. For I share with Naipaul
the same social, cultural, and political experiences which
permeate his works, and for this reason he appeals to me.
Although Naipaul hails from a Hindu family in Trinidad and I
from a Moslem one in Guyana, we are both West Indians of
East Indian descent. We grew up in two British multiracial
colonies, which shared a common history and which were beset
by the same problems and tensions. The characters in Miguel
Street are people similar to those that I have known; the
Indian world in the colonial society of Ganesh Ramsumair in
The Mystic Masseur is the world in which I grew up; the
racial and religious maneuverings in Trinidad's elections in
The Suffrage of Elvira are the ploys I witnessed during
general elections in Guyana in the 1960's; the lifestyle of
the Indian enclave in A House for Mr Biswas is one,
although a fading one, with which I have had first hand
experience (my grandmother's house accommodated three other
families with problems similar to those of the Tulsis and

Mr. Biswas); politician Ralph Singh's hardships and the problems of the mixed colonial society in The Mimic Men are similar to the ordeals of ex-Premier Cheddi Jagan and the difficulties which plagued the racially divided Guyana in the 1960's; finally, the black power movement in Guerrillas is every East Indian's secret nightmare. Thus, whether Naipaul refers specifically to Trinidad or vaguely to an unnamed or a fictional island, the background of his novels strikes a responsive chord within me.

A common East Indian West Indian background is not the only experience I share with Naipaul. Having left our respective homes—Naipaul at the age of 18, and I at 19—and having resided abroad since, we have lost our place in the West Indies, and possibly in the world, since internally and externally the East Indian, more than the black or white, finds it impossible to blend with the crowd in London or Washington. This loss may be attributed partly to cultural conflicts but mainly to visible racial difference. Nor, interestingly enough, can the East Indian from the West Indies make a connection with his ancestral roots in India, something that Naipaul realized during his first visit to that country in 1962.

As an East Indian West Indian residing away from the Caribbean, or as a twice displaced individual, I am for another reason in an advantageous position to approach critical reaction to Naipaul. My emotional affinity and at the same time my physical distance place me in a situation in which I have the feelings of an insider and yet the objectivity, or so I believe, of an outsider. I know, for example, that any study of West Indian response to Naipaul must include a study, however brief, of the delicate Indian/black conflict. During the turbulent 1960's in Guyana, I witnessed the development of deep animosity between the two major ethnic groups as racial riots erupted. I understand that even today racial awareness is such that Naipaul is perceived as an East Indian rather than simply as a West Indian, and that such a perception at once divides West Indian readers from him. Because of our political and cultural suppression in the West Indies, East Indians, more than any other ethnic group, are most likely to voice disappointment with conditions there and thus support Naipaul's denunciation of the region. In fact, West Indian response definitely reflects this tendency, for, as this study shows, most of the objections to Naipaul have come primarily from Black West Indians who read him politically. (The ethnic background of a critic can usually be determined by his surname, since blacks have generally adopted Western names, while Indians have maintained Indian ones.) Naipaul does not romanticize the region, nor does he present a cosmetic view of it. Instead, he boldly confronts issues

we are happy to see faced. Thus, he touches my sensibility
and that of many other East Indians in the Caribbean.

On the other hand, my long residence in the United
States distances me from Naipaul, as my discussion of his
persona in Chapter II indicates. Undoubtedly, he is a
controversial writer who compels readers to take a partisan stand. However, my physical distance from the West
Indies enables me to read him dispassionately and to accept
his criticisms of the East Indian community, criticisms
about which many Indians, while embracing Naipaul, are
disturbed. This distance, too, along with my student life
and six years of teaching at a predominantly black university, contributes to my ability to understand and examine in
an unbiased manner West Indian reaction, black or Indian.
In other words, my ethnic origin presents no barrier to
fairness since my emotional affinity to East Indians is
tempered by other comprehensive and enriching experiences.

Many West Indian critics see an urgent need for a West
Indian criticism of Caribbean literature. One popular
argument is that West Indian literature is concerned
particularly with issues of the region and that the works
can be more meaningfully discussed by West Indians themselves than by outsiders.[2] Foreign criticisms, however,
should not be discounted out of hand since some of the
soundest criticisms may indeed be written by a distant
outsider with deep insight into the region. The problem is
that such insight is not easy to acquire. Kenneth Ramchand,
a noted West Indian critic, discusses the difficulties
confronting an alien reader:

> I do not think that a person, born in England and
> fed on English and American Literature and coming
> to Naipaul or any other West Indian writer would
> respond to anything but the universals in his work.
> . . . As an outsider, looking at a foreign
> literature, one can appreciate the major themes and
> universal issues and can recognize human qualities
> and human situations. A lot of difficulties arise
> when the alien critic wants to go beyond that. . .
> . It seems to me that the process of informing
> oneself would include a lot of reading,
> conversation, meeting people from those territories
> and may even include a visit to these territories.
> . . . When an American or British critic tries to
> write as if he were West Indian then problems
> arise.[3]

Readers of Naipaul are at a disadvantage without a clear
understanding of not only the general West Indian scene but
also the East Indian segment of that society. Like
Ramchand, I can assert with confidence that "I know the

region that Naipaul writes about, the raw materials from which his novels are created."[4] I know the Indian community with which many "insiders," black West Indians, are themselves still unfamiliar, and having lived in a mixed neighborhood until I left Guyana at nineteen, I also know the black community well. An American critic has observed that "Naipaul is the kind of artist whose personal outlook and experience merge distinctly with everything he writes, whether fiction or non-fiction."[5] No one understands the truth of this more than an East Indian West Indian who has lived through Naipaul's experiences and who can identify with the background of the books.

My experience, then, as an East Indian in the West Indies and as an East Indian West Indian in a Western society--in short, my ethnic and cultural resemblance to Naipaul himself--places me in a privileged position not only in understanding the thinking of this writer but also in evaluating West Indian reaction to him.

Notes

[1] Shiva Naipaul, <u>Love and Death in a Hot Country</u> (Great Britain: Hamilton Ltd., 1983; rpt. New York: Penguin Books, 1985), is set in a foundering bookstore in a country which resembles Guyana.

[2] Edward Baugh, "Towards a West Indian Criticism," <u>Caribbean Quarterly</u>, 4, Nos. 1&2 (March-June 1968), 140-44.

[3] "V. S. Naipaul and West Indian Writers," <u>Antilia</u> (University of the West Indies), 1 (1983), 15.

[4] "V. S. Naipaul and West Indian Writers," p. 11.

[5] Robert D. Hamner, ed., <u>Critical Perspectives on V.S. Naipaul</u> (Washington, D.C.: Three Continents Press, 1977), p. xv.

Chapter 1

The West Indian Background

Widely considered one of the most talented literary figures
to emerge from the entire English-speaking Caribbean, and
often rated as one of the finest living novelists writing in
English, Vidiadhar Surajprasad Naipaul has dealt
extensively, in both his fiction and his non-fiction, with
the condition of many third world societies. However, it is
his books on his place of origin, the West Indies, which
form the main corpus of his output. Savagely critical in
his depiction of the region, Naipaul has been generally
given a hostile reception by West Indians, whose political
reading of him overshadows their literary one. Behind this
heated controversy, of course, is the important question of
the status and potential of West Indian society. Trinidadian
critic Kenneth Ramchand has observed that Naipaul "moves in
contentious territory because people interpreting his work
judge him from the point of view of whether or not what he
is saying is 'the truth' about society."[1] Obviously, any
study of Naipaul's West Indian works and of West Indian
responses to them--at least any study written for
outsiders--must first include an overview of that society.
This chapter will, therefore, examine the West Indian
milieu, with specific emphasis on the period during which
Naipaul grew up and to which he repeatedly returns for
materials for his writings.
     The West Indies (formerly British West Indies), or the
English-speaking Caribbean, consists of Jamaica; the Leeward
Islands (St. Kitts, Nevis, Anguilla, Antigua, Montserrat,
the British Virgin Islands); the Windward Islands (St.
Vincent, St. Lucia, Dominica, Grenada); Barbados; Trinidad
and Tobago;[2] Belize (formerly British Honduras) and Guyana
(formerly British Guiana).[3] Guyana, although geogra-
phically in South America, is regarded as linguistically,
socially, culturally, and politically West Indian.[4] This
chapter will focus on the West Indies as a whole and on
Trinidad and Guyana in particular. Since West Indians place
themselves, their traditions, and their literatures within
the context of a general West Indian region rather than in
separate countries, it is useful to speak of the whole
Caribbean and to look at its entire East Indian community,
of which Naipaul is a product. Just as important as
Trinidad, therefore, is Guyana because not only does it
share a history of plantation economy, slavery, indentureship, and British colonial rule, but it is also the one
country which ethnically resembles Trinidad in its heavy
concentration of East Indians. In addition, the focus on

Guyana will provide background information central to the interpretation of Naipaul's novel <u>The Mimic Men</u>, which some critics believe is set in Guyana. Finally, the reader will be in a better position to understand the tension within West Indian response--and that includes a large number of Guyanese ones--which is rooted in culture and history.

The West Indies has typically been seen as a microcosm of the entire world containing all types of people, who, regardless of race, creed, and color, enjoy tropical felicity, exuberance, and racial harmony. Nationalists and tourist industries project this paradisiacal image of the region. Trinidad, for example, has been advertised as a "rendezvous of cultures . . . a happy blend of African, Chinese, East Indian, Spanish, French, you name it."[5] Naipaul, however, sees the typical West Indian as a "derelict man in a derelict land," in a place condemned to consist of "half-made societies of a dependent people, the Third World's third world."[6] Bruce King succinctly summarizes the writer's views:

> For Naipaul the West Indies consists of races that have been uprooted from their original society and that have not produced a new culture to replace what was lost. They have been abandoned on Trinidad, with little in common and without the various resources needed to create an energetic new society. There is no creativity, no achievement; the middle classes are parasites, mimicking the ideas and activities of metropolitan societies; each group or race continues to think of foreign lands as 'home'.[7]

The following pages will investigate the accuracy of Naipaul's reading of the West Indies by examining the historical circumstances that brought these different peoples together and the cultural, sociological, and political attitudes responsible for shaping their society. I will argue that, contrary to the judgments of many West Indians, Naipaul is not an eccentric troublemaker but an honest commentator upon a tenuously rooted colonial society.

Located at the northeastern tip of South America, between Venezuela and Surinam, Guyana, a country of approximately 83,000 square miles with a current population of fewer than 800,000, was occupied by the Dutch in 1580.[8] However, in the seventeenth and eighteenth centuries, British, French, and Dutch sporadically fought for control over the territory, which changed hands several times before the British finally prevailed in 1803 and thereafter held undisputed occupation and control until Guyana's independence. The country's indigenous population, the Amerindians (analogous to the native American Indians), escaped enslavement by the new settlers, who needed laborers to work on the sugar plantations. To cope with manpower

3

shortage, the plantation owners imported slaves from Africa;
the first recorded batch arrived in 1672. The whites, or
the descendants of Dutch, British, and European plantation
settlers, eventually established a white oligarchy with
unlimited political and economic power over the rest of the
population.[9] A similar system of white control over black
slaves was implanted in Trinidad.

Situated off the northeastern coast of South America
near Venezuela, Trinidad, an island of approximately 1,980
square miles with a current population of about one million,
was once under the rule of the Spaniards, who, in the 1780's
permitted French planters and their slaves to settle.[10]
The island was captured by the British and integrated into
the British empire in 1797. Subsequently, Venezuelan
political refugees and other immigrants seeking better
opportunities arrived, joined in 1802 and after by economically adventurous British planters and their slaves.
Shortly thereafter, Scots, Irishmen, and Englishmen came as
estate overseers/managers, clerks, businessmen, and professionals.[11] The island's indigenous population, the
Caribs, had been rendered almost extinct by the Spanish
conquistadors before the beginning of the nineteenth
century; therefore, the immigrants, like the planters in
Guyana, solved their growing labor problems by transporting
slaves from Africa to Trinidad. The journey was called the
"middle passage." Again, as in Guyana, the Caucasians, or
the descendants from the various immigrant groups, evolved
as the ruling elite, imposing their culture and controlling
the economy and the administration of the British colony.

In the West Indies slavery was abolished in 1833, and
slaves were emancipated in 1838. Most freed slaves, whose
descendants presently constitute the black population of the
West Indies, deserted the sugar estates and sought an
independent livelihood in an effort to better their condition. This desertion of essential labor predictably created
immense problems for the white settlers and threatened to
destroy the plantations, whose owners were forced to look
for new, cheap manpower in other countries. Thus, after the
1830's recruitment officers, financially supported by the
planters and the colonial government, induced (some say by
dishonest and unscrupulous means) thousands to cross the
Atlantic to become indentured laborers on West Indian
plantations.[12] European yeomen, Portuguese from Madeira,
and Chinese were thus recruited and indentured. The use of
Madeiran contractual labor failed because many of the
Portuguese immigrant laborers were unsuccessful agricul-
turalists, whose problems were compounded when they resented
working together with blacks, former slaves.[13] Because of
physical and emotional problems, Portuguese suffered heavy
mortality. A similar fate befell Chinese immigrants, whose
descendants, along with their Portuguese counterparts,
abandoned the estates and became peddlars, merchants, and
businessmen.[14]

As a last resort to solving plantation problems, colonists recruited Indians, who had proved to be good agrarian farmers and reliable workers in Mauritius. Immigrants, mainly from Madras and the United Provinces, were brought to many West Indian islands, such as Jamaica and Martinique, but the majority were placed in Trinidad and Guyana, where manpower problems were most acute. Terms of indentureship, that is, contractual arrangements between immigrants and their employers, were worked out.[15] Many laborers agreed to a two-year, a five-year, or later a ten-year indentureship, binding them to remain and work on the sugar estates to which they were assigned. Subjected to abominable sanitation facilities and distressing health services, workers lived in poorly constructed, small, barrack-type "ranges" with mud floors, walked miles to and from work, and earned meager wages for long hours of hard labor. They often complained that recruitment officers had misrepresented working and living conditions. During indentureship, they were forbidden, under severe penalty, to leave their employers, live off the estates, and agitate for higher wages or better conditions. At the expiration of indenture, however, they were free to return to India; in fact, return passage home was often an expressed term in the agreement.

Indian immigration, which started in 1838 in Guyana and 1845 in Trinidad, punctuated by intermittent breaks, was banned in 1917 because of strong criticisms from Mahatma Gandhi and other Indian leaders. At that time the total number of Indians imported into Guyana had reached about 239,000 and in Trinidad 134,000.[16] To induce Indians to remain and become permanent residents rather than temporary sojourners, colonists granted them special land privileges in exchange for forfeiting return passage home. Thus, at the termination of their contracts, although some Indians did return home, the majority made the colonies their new home. In the 1960's, when Naipaul wrote The Middle Passage and The Mimic Men, the descendants of Indian immigrants, both Hindus and Moslems (called East Indians to be distinguished from the indigenous Indians), constituted over 51% of the Guyanese and 36% of the Trinidadian population, while blacks made up approximately 31% in Guyana and 43% in Trinidad.[17] In both countries the Indian birth rate is higher than that of any other group. For example, by 1970 there were only two percent more blacks than East Indians in Trinidad.[18] In Jamaica, Martinique, and the Windward Islands Indians comprise no more than two to four percent of the population.[19]

West Indian society, then, is made up of different peoples--an amalgam of whites, blacks, East Indians, Chinese, Portuguese, mixed races, and, especially in Jamaica, Jews and Lebanese--uprooted and displaced from their original cultures. This type of society, notably Guyanese and Trinidadian, has been described as socially and culturally pluralistic. J. S. Furnivall, a British economist, was the first to introduce the concept of "cultural pluralism" in his study of Burma and the Netherlands East Indies. He explains this type of plural society as follows:

> In Burma, as in Java, probably the first thing that strikes the visitor is the medley of peoples--European, Chinese, Indian and native. It is in the strictest sense a medley, for they mix but do not combine. Each group holds by its own religion, its own culture and language, its own ideas and ways. As individuals they meet, but only in the market-place, in buying and selling. There is a plural society, with different sections of the community living side by side, but separately, within the same political unit. Even in the economic sphere, there is a division of labour along racial lines.[20]

With specific application to the Caribbean, this concept has been accepted but somewhat refined by M. G. Smith.[21] A close examination of the cultural habits of the different immigrant groups in the West Indies will reveal some of the problems in the culturally pluralistic Trinidadian and Guyanese societies.

Social scientists frequently use the word "Creole" to describe West Indian societies and their black and white inhabitants. Derived from the Spanish "criollo" meaning "native to locality," "Creole" has different shades of meaning.[22] David Lowenthal points out some variations:

> [Creole] originally denoted Negro slaves born in the New World, as distinct from the African-born. 'Creole' soon came to refer to anyone, black or white, born in the West Indies. It was then extended to things, habits, and ideas; plants grown, goods manufactured, and opinions expressed in the West Indies were all 'Creole'. Recently the term reverted to its earlier association, and in some areas 'Creole' is now a euphemism for coloured or black. But its meaning varies locally. . . . In the Commonwealth Caribbean, where independence and black power now favour national and ethnic appellations, the term 'Creole' is today considered old-fashioned, self-conscious, or 'arty'. . . . As a generic term to distinguish white, coloured, and black West Indians from all others, however, there is no substitute for 'Creole'.[23]

The main point is that the word distinguished what was recently imported from what was aboriginal--hence such expressions as "Creole-music," "Creole-chicken," "Creole-born," and "Creole-culture."[24] Some West Indians currently use the term to include anyone of any ethnic origin born in the West Indies; others restrict the word to blacks only. However, social scientists interpret "Creole" to mean West Indian natives of black, white, or even mixed black-white descent. According to M. G. Smith, Creole society and culture derive from Europe and Africa, and those who maintain their "exclusive identity" are distinguished from Creoles and are referred to in "national terms."[25] East Indians, Chinese, Portuguese, Lebanese, Jews, who were not "original" natives and who were still regarded as transients even decades after their arrival, do not fall within the compass of the definition of "Creole." Creole culture, then, refers to the dominant--white and black--culture, even though the two races were initially distinct, culturally and socially.

Slavery completely emasculated the cultural and social institutions of blacks. Regarded as properties and subjected to inhumane treatment, slaves were not allowed to practice their creed, to marry and to maintain a family life. In fact, they were even encouraged not to have children, since replacements of slaves were no problem and since child-bearing interrupted the mother's labor and caused expenses.[26] Blacks gradually found themselves forced to adopt the language, customs, habits, clothes, and even names of their dominant white masters. Lowenthal explains the psychological motivation behind the conscious imitation of whites:

> When blackness meant slavery and whiteness meant mastery, it was little wonder that blacks wished to be white. Many Caribbean slaves, like colonized people anywhere, sought to improve their lot by copying their masters. . . . To imitate whites was the only path to success in a white-dominated society.[27]

West Indians confess that in order to ameliorate their condition, they had to ape the white man, "do what he did, like what he liked, wear what he wore."[28] The passion to imitate was so strong that some blacks boasted that they were more "cultured" than whites.[29] In addition to undergoing cultural assimilation, most black West Indians accepted conversion by Roman Catholic and Anglican missionaries, who undertook to educate them. Succeeding generations of blacks, especially after the abolition of slavery, remembered less and less of their African heritage and grew to regard white culture as superior and any other, including their own, as inferior. Except in Surinam, where the "Bush Negroes" escaped from the plantations and preserved their African culture and resisted acculturation even to this day, blacks brought to the West Indies gradually lost much, if not all, of their cultural and religious traditions.

On the other hand, the East Indians, the largest non-Creole group in the West Indies, successfully managed to hold on to their culture and to maintain their religious customs intact. Leo Despres offers the most likely explanation:

> The indentures, unlike the slaves, were not pieces of property. They were instruments of production, to be sure, but while their labor could be used, their persons could not be owned. In theory, if not always in practice, the indentures had certain rights. One of these was the right to return to their homeland after completing their contracts. Related to this was the right to maintain their own customs and practices as long as these did not interfere with their obligation to conform to the work routine of the estate. . . . As new indentures arrived in one wave after another for almost three-quarters of a century, they were mixed with those who came earlier. This served to reinforce traditional habits and customs and contributed to a continuity in cultural patterning. Moreover, the indentures were relatively restricted to the estates on which they were placed.[30]

Even if circumstances necessitated more intermingling with all groups, the Indian cultural and religious traditions discouraged socializing with Creoles, whose values and morals the East Indians rejected and scorned.[31] Moreover, many East Indian immigrants initially saw themselves as transients temporarily away from their real homes, thus the continued affinity to India instead of to the West Indies. All of these factors helped foster cultural and religious orthodoxy and ethnic separation.

East Indian immigrants subsequently established in Trinidad and Guyana a miniature India--from the creation of replicas of Indian villages to the perpetuation of all traditional cultural and religious values of Indian life. Not knowing whether their cultural and religious needs would be met, they fetched across the Atlantic as many items as possible to ensure continuity of their life patterns. Either by transplanting or by importing things, Indians have been able to satisfy their wants. Lowenthal mentions rice as one important example: "Rice is the principal Indian food transplanted to the Caribbean. Upland rice had long been grown by Creoles, but Indians were used to and preferred irrigated varieties. Indentured immigrants brought over wet rice, which became the staple crop among East Indian peasant farmers . . . [and] now belongs as much to the Creoles."[32] Both Hindus and Moslems continued to practice their creeds, erecting temples and mosques at their

own expenses. Shopkeepers imported Indian spices, such as
curry and masala; special cooking utensils, especially for
the preparation of <u>roti</u>, curry and <u>dahl</u>; Indian national
attires, such as <u>saris</u> and <u>oronis</u>; and religious parapher-
nalia, for example, Hindu <u>murti</u> (images), Moslem prayer
mats, and holy books. There were thus no inconveniences in
cuisine, clothing and religion. One researcher sums up the
immigrants' practices thus: "[East Indians] built the same
type of houses, wore the same type of clothes, spoke the
same language and worshipped the same Gods in the same kind
of temples."[33] Except for environmental change, daily
routines and habits continued unaltered. The immigrants
even participated in, supported, and identified with India's
struggle for independence. Yogendra Malik notes this
political interest:

> A look at old Indian magazines and newspapers
> shows that the people of Indian origin in Trinidad
> have been taking increasing interest in India
> since the rise of Indian nationalism under the
> leadership of Gandhi. The names of Gandhi,
> Tagore, Nehru thrilled many of the East Indians
> and became objects of national pride.[34]

The same is true of their Guyanese counterparts.
East Indians in the Caribbean also continued to honor
their family structures and to maintain their social
habits. From indentureship to today, little has changed in
this respect. Families are still tightly knit, and familial
relationships are distinctly observed as seen from the
current elaborate kinship terminology, which has specific
words (with no English equivalent) for such relationships as
father's elder brother (<u>barka bap</u>), mother's younger brother
(<u>mamu</u>), and father's younger brother's wife (<u>kaki</u>).
Marriages, which have remained virilocal and patrilineal,
are still being arranged, although the practice has been
steadily declining within the past two decades. It is
generally customary for the bride (<u>doolahin</u>) to reside in
the home of her husband's parents, at least temporarily,
until a separate house is constructed. Some women continue
the tradition of returning to their parents' homes to give
birth. To discipline their children, parents frequently
rely on the belt or whip. (The same is true of Creoles.)
Similar treatment meted out to wives from husbands gave rise
to the saying, "They don't love you 'less they beat
you."[35] For entertainment East Indians still depend
largely on imported Hindi movies and songs and music from
these films. Social activities are somewhat limited. In
rural areas, religious ceremonies, funerals, and weddings
are still important social events where gossip could be
exchanged and acquaintances made and renewed. Both Hindus
and Moslems generally attend each other's social and
religious events. Although mutual distrust and tension

between the two groups are often accentuated during
political campaigns when leaders try to "divide and rule,"
all East Indians see themselves as allies against the
dominant Creoles.[36] Creoles, in turn, have made no
distinction between Hindus and Moslems. The isolation and
cohesiveness of East Indians, caused initially by
restrictions of movement and by fear of the host society,
inevitably sharpened their differences with Creoles, who
greeted them with hostility.

From the beginning Creoles made no effort to understand
or respect the cultures of East Indians. Some sociologists
surmise that the arrival of Indians was seen as an economic
threat to blacks, who also became uneasy about the possibility of being racially dominated by a growing Indian
community.[37] Others point out that blacks had already
deserted the sugar estates after emancipation and that it
was because of the already existing manpower shortage that
Indians were brought to the West Indies. J. A. Froude's
observation in 1888 was thus: "There is no jealousy. The
negro does not regard the coolie [Indian] as a competitor
and interloper who has come to lower his wages. The coolie
comes to work. The negro does not want to work, and both
are satisfied. But if there is no jealousy there is no
friendship."[38] Froude's inflammatory generalization has
been ably refuted by many West Indians, including J. J.
Thomas, who coined the word "Froudacity." The charge of
lack of amity between blacks and Indians, however, has been
fully substantiated. Chandra Jayawardena describes Creole
views on the transient newcomers in Guyana:

> Their language was 'outlandish', they knew no
> English; their clothes were strange and their
> religion was heathen. They lacked the cultural
> characteristics valued in the society, and in
> return the society withheld its rights and
> privileges from them. Indian culture, or 'coolie
> culture', as it was and is [disparagingly] called,
> became a mark of low status in the eyes of the
> white upper status groups as well as of the
> coloured and black lower status group.[39]

Krishna Bahadoorsingh notes that Jayawardena's comments are
also true of Creole reception of East Indians in
Trinidad.[40] Even the press dubbed Hindu and Moslem
ceremonies as "degrading practices," "vile customs,"
"scandalous performances carried on by gangs of
semi-barbarians," "painted devilry."[41] Blacks had been
considered "clay which could easily be moulded into a
Christian and Western shape," while East Indians were like a
"stone that could only be worked painfully and with much
toil."[42] Regarded more or less as culturally intractable,
then, East Indians were left alone. The Chinese and
Portuguese, small in numbers, posed no major problems to the

dominant culture and easily and gradually blended with Creoles.

The hostile reception accorded the arriving East Indians was reciprocated. The Hindu caste system links dark skin pigmentation with low caste. Thus, some sociologists believe that East Indians thought that blacks, like untouchables, were polluted.[43] Others contend that the caste-color explanation is an oversimplification. Selwyn Ryan gives another theory: "It appears that the colour of the Africans led Indians to identify them with the followers of Rawana, the demon king of the Hindu Ramayana epic, and they feared that contact with the Africans would be polluting."[44] (Indians still refer to blacks as "Rawans.") In addition, Charles Kingsley, who predicted that the two races "never will amalgamate," argued that East Indians' first impression of blacks was that they were "awkward, vulgar in manners and savage."[45] The seed of Indian-black hostility, therefore, was sown during the indentureship period, when individual conflicts between Indian and black laborers were frequent, although no serious wide-scale clashes erupted.[46]

In addition to being subjected to humiliation from the host society, East Indians were not granted the benefit of an education. The same had been true of blacks, since whites generally sent their own children "home" to be educated and since the schools which were later established in the islands catered to the elite only. Blacks subsequently gained admission and made immediate use of the opportunities, and, by the first half of the nineteenth century, they had made considerable strides. On the other hand, East Indian children were kept out of the system by their parents and by the establishment. Parents had three main reasons for this decision. First, since all schools were controlled by the church, East Indians had feared, with justification, the proselytizing of their children and, therefore, kept them home.[47] (Up to the 1950's in both Trinidad and Guyana Hindu and Moslem school children were pressured to attend Christian churches for prayers and services conducted during school hours.) Second, East Indians were also afraid that their children would be abused by Creole teachers and students.[48] (Naipaul's uncle, Rudranath Capildeo, who attended Trinidad's Queen's Royal College in the 1930's, claimed that he was not only bullied and humiliated by his Creole classmates but also taunted by his teachers, one of whom held a ruler and asked in class, "Tell me, Capildeo—what is it you worship? Is this what you worship?"[49]) Third, East Indian laborers reared their children to work on the sugar estates, where formal education was not necessary. The Indian community was self-sufficient; therefore, children stayed at home or worked with their parents, who welcomed the assistance.

For selfish and economic reasons, the colonizers fought to keep Indians as uneducated laborers and deliberately encouraged them to maintain their customs and to stay away from Christian schools. In 1868 John Morton, a Canadian Presbyterian missionary, observed that in Trinidad "owing to race prejudice there was scarcely an Indian child to be found in school in the whole island."[50] Appointed in 1869 by the Governor to look into the state of Trinidad's public education, Patrick Keenan found that Indians were the main victims of the system:

> The Coolie's mind was left a blank. No effort was made to induce him, through the awakening intelligence and dawning prospects of his children, to associate the fortune or the future of his family with the colony. It is therefore that--collaterally, and I believe legitimately--I connect the magnitude of the periodical exodus of the Asiatics with the educational system, which fails to provide for their children acceptable schools. I cannot call to mind any other case of a people who, having voluntarily come to a strange land which they enriched by their labour, were--morally and intellectually--so completely neglected as the coolies have been during the past twenty-four years.[51]

But fearing that educated Indians would desert the sugar estates, colonists continued to argue for the status quo. This attitude can be illustrated from a notorious statement made by E. A. Robinson, a Creole sugar planter, before a Select Committee of the Legislative Council appointed in 1926 to investigate labor hours. In response to questionings about the hard labor conditions for children and their lack of education, Robinson argued: "Give them some education in the way of reading and writing, but no more. Even then I would say educate only the bright ones; not the whole mass. If you do educate the whole mass of the agricultural population, you will be deliberately ruining the country."[52]

However, with the self-help projects from Indians themselves and with the aid of the Canadian Presbyterian missionaries, such as Dr. Morton, schools were set up for Indian children in Guyana and Trinidad. The missionaries realized that Indians were reluctant to attend schools with Creoles. Bahadoorsingh reports that in Trinidad "as late as 1914, the Canadian Mission continued to be the principal body interested in the education of the Indian."[53] But there was only so much that the Canadians could have accomplished. Lowenthal reveals these staggering figures:

> Before 1933 most Guyanese Indians never attended school; as recently as 1960 two-fifths of those over fifteen in a solidly Indian section of Chaguanas, Trinidad, had had no education. In

> 1946 almost half the Guyanese Indians over ten
> could not read or write English, and in Trinidad .
> . . Indian illiteracy was at least 60 per cent. .
> . . And since most Indians live in rural areas
> they are even more disadvantaged at higher levels
> of education.[54]

Indians who were fortunate to be sent abroad by their
parents to further their studies preferred independent
professions, such as medicine and law.

Although East Indians were adamant in preserving their
cultural heritage, they found that settling in the West
Indies demanded more and more a modification of their lifestyles. For example, in both Trinidad and Guyana the
complicated rules about food were forgotten, and the Hindu
caste system became almost immediately weakened and subsequently dissolved.[55] From the time the immigrants
arrived, the estate managers ignored caste distinctions;
thus, the people of different castes often shared the same
facilities and worked together. In addition, because of the
initial shortage of women, females assumed greater importance, and religious and caste exogamy was practiced. Today
occupational specialization does not exist, except for
pundits (learned priests), who are still Brahmins. Low
caste appellations, for example "Chamar," have become terms
of common insults and are angrily applied to anyone--blacks,
Moslems, or Brahmins. Although a few traditionalists still
value caste and religious distinctions, most Hindus now see
education and wealth as more important in their Creole-
dominated world, a world in which cultural and religious
sacrifices have become prerequisites to acceptance and
success.

The increasing contact with Creoles in schools (after
East Indians began entering the national system) and in
other places (after residential restrictions were lifted),
the desire to enjoy rights and privileges of the Creole
world, the end of the flow of new immigrants from India--
these are among the factors which have forced East Indians,
willingly or unwillingly, consciously or unconsciously, to
adopt elements of Creole culture. This process of substi-
tution of Creole traditions for Indian ones is called
"creolization." However, many East Indians resent the
expression and prefer instead the words "westernization" or
"Englishification." Malik explains the reason for this
preference:

> East Indians consider the Creole culture as
> inferior to their own and resent the use of terms
> like 'the creolization of Indians'. East Indians
> élites insist very strongly that 'creolization'
> and 'westernization' are two separate processes;
> westernization does not mean the acceptance of the
> 'Creole' moral values, or ways of living. . . .

> In the eyes of East Indians, 'Creole' life lacks
> stability, social virtues, and morality.[56]

The objection is complicated by the fact that since "Creole"
encompasses blacks, "creolization" is sometimes interpreted
as the "imitation of blacks." Most East Indians would not
accept, for example, Arthur Drayton's statement that "it is
the cultural image of the Negro to which the other races
tend to approximate. . . . It is not for nothing that one
meaning of the word 'creole' in Trinidad applies to a
Chinese or an Indian or an Englishman whose manner and
behavior are satisfyingly Negro."[57] In fact, Paul Edwards
and Kenneth Ramchand speak of the creolization of blacks,
and Arthur Niehoff uses creolization to mean a "general
process of westernization which is affecting all folk people
on the island, whether they are Negro or Indian."[58] The
question seems to be whether East Indians adopt European
cultural elements from whites or from blacks who imitate
whites. Whatever the case, the point is that adoption of
the dominant culture took place, while each ethnic group
borrowed extensively from one another. All West Indians are
familiar with Chinese chow-mein, Portuguese stew, Creole
black pudding, and Indian <u>roti</u>.

This process of adoption, which defies dating, has
affected nearly all aspects of East Indian life. Chandra
Jayawardena gives some typical examples:

> In dress, household furniture and decoration,
> secular celebrations and material prestige
> symbols, the Indians have rapidly taken to creole
> patterns. Most important is the transformation of
> Hindi and Urdu into esoteric languages used almost
> solely in religious rituals and in traditional
> wedding songs. . . . The language of daily use is
> the dialect of English.[59]

Generalizations about these cultural traditions, influenced
by rapid westernization, are dangerous, since practices vary
from household to household and since any generalization
made today will have to be revised tomorrow. It is safe to
say, however, that with the passage of time, Indian
languages were lost and clothes modified. The transition
was such that by the end of the first half of the twentieth
century Indians had gone not only from Hindi, to bilingual
in Hindi and English, to English only, but also from saris,
to ankle length skirts and bodices, to western dresses. Yet
even today in the rural areas it is not uncommon to hear
English-speaking individuals intersperse their speech with
Hindi, nor is it unusual to find Indians fluent in Hindi.
Likewise, varieties of dress marking the gradual changes can
still be seen. Up to the 1960's pundits and imams generally
conducted their prayers, rituals and weddings without
English translation or explanation. However, today they are

increasingly pressured not to ignore the fact that Indian languages are no longer understood. It is noteworthy that the changes that have occurred are generally changes of necessity stemming from Creole pressure. For example, Indian languages have not been taught in schools, and the media have used English only. And as Neihoff reports, "Hindu garments, such as the dhoti, were ridiculed when the first Indians came to the island, and this pressure had undoubtedly assisted in some change."[60]

In addition, Creole attitudes have instilled in East Indians the idea that their religious and cultural traditions are "old-fashioned" and "undesirable." Thus, although the majority of East Indians still prepare traditional Indian foods, patronize (now English sub-titled) Indian movies, practice their religions, and select Hindu or Moslem names, a significant number of young people eagerly proclaim a preference for English or American tastes--from food to names--and pretend ignorance of Indian culture, believing that "western" is synonymous with "superior" and "progress." It is not uncommon for some East Indians themselves to belittle Indian culture and language. Although Islam and Hinduism generally remained resistant to strong missionary efforts, converts to Christianity comprised approximately 13% in Guyana and 17% in Trinidad of the Indian population in the 1960's.[61]

It is widely held that most of the Indians who converted to Christianity did so because it was the only way to elevate themselves economically and socially in a society which treated all non-Christians as pagans.[62] Until the early 1960's no one in either Guyana or Trinidad could have become a teacher without converting to Christianity. Researchers have fully documented religious discrimination in both countries. For example, Leo Despres relates a case study in Guyana:

> During the course of field work, depth interviews were obtained from eight Indian teachers in six different villages. Of these, seven complained bitterly that it was necessary for them to become Christians in order to secure teaching positions or in order to make it possible to be considered for promotions. The only Hindu in the group stated that he had refused to become a Christian, and, as a consequence, after thirty years of teaching he had not received a promotion to the position of head teacher. Further checking revealed that this particular individual had passed his teaching examinations with unusual distinction. Moreover, an African informant who served as a member of the governing body at the school where this particular individual taught agreed that he would probably be promoted to the

rank of head teacher almost immediately if he would become a member of the church.[63]

However, conversion to Christianity often meant complete creolization; it meant not only a change in religious beliefs but also a rejection of Indian cultural values. Proud that they did not sacrifice their religious principles for economic opportunities, orthodox Hindus initially regarded converts with contempt.[64] There have been proportionately fewer conversions of Moslems.[65]
Even some of the unconverted felt compelled to be more flexible in their religious attitudes. Indeed, there were cases of orthodox Hindu children who were baptized into Christianity and initiated into Hinduism simultaneously in order to increase their chances of securing an education and a job.[66] To be accommodating meant more and more a sacrifice of all religious and cultural principles, and some traditional Indians saw a link between this sacrifice and complete moral degeneration. Since the 1960's religious conversion and pretense have no longer been necessary; in fact, in both Trinidad and Guyana there has been official recognition of Hinduism and Islam. However, legislation does not eradicate prejudice, and continuing pressures from the Creole-dominated society have still been forcing East Indians who wish to compete for Creole jobs to modify their ways extensively.
The loss of tradition and the parroting of a "superior" culture have contributed to that feeling of isolation and placelessness characteristic of West Indians, especially those of East Indian descent. Even the most creolized East Indians do not wish to see a complete break with their traditional culture.[67] Because of the influence of western-oriented thinking, post-colonial East Indians gradually and reluctantly surrendered any residual attachment to Mother India. Of course, a few Indians never lost contact with their ancestors in India; however, the majority have not bothered to ask the name of their ancestral village. During a visit to India in 1953, Guyana's ex-Premier, Dr. Cheddi Jagan, whose parents were born in that country, was embarrassed when he was asked about his ancestors: "There were many embarrassing moments for me particularly on two questions--language and the birthplace of my grandparents. Actually, I had never taken the trouble to find out. . . . All I knew was that they were from the State of Bihar. . . . The other source of my embarrassment was my inability to speak Hindi or Urdu."[68] Indians have generally not followed the recent trend to trace their ancestry. Lowenthal comments on their alienation from India:

However 'Indian' East Indians in the West Indies may be, they are not much like Indians in India. . . . East Indians who have gone home [to India]

are most keenly aware of being, if not fully West
Indian, at least no longer Indian in any traditional sense. . . . Even as a temporary visitor,
the Caribbean East Indian is now an alien in
India.[69]

Ironically, many East Indians also see themselves as aliens
or are treated as such in their new complicated West Indian
post-colonial societies. Not daring to look back to India
or forward to the West Indies, they remain placeless and
rootless.

Apart from cultural and social problems, West Indians,
to some extent, have not been able to enjoy a politically
stable life or to forge any degree of nationalism. In the
plural Trinidad society, for example, political loyalties
are generally determined by the ethnic origin of a candidate
rather than by serious commitment to an ideology. In a
number of novels, short stories, and much of his
non-fiction, Naipaul presents a sardonic and pessimistic
view of West Indian politics and the West Indian future. As
a result, his critics, as one reviewer notices, "tend to see
him as a patrician, expatriate Indian out of sympathy with
coloured peoples who have won their independence."[70] A
brief look at political attitudes and race politics in the
plural societies of Trinidad and Guyana, especially in the
1960's, will be invaluable in understanding why Naipaul has
become disenchanted and in explaining why his ethnic
identity often features in critical reaction to him. Since
a thorough account of Trinidad's politics encompassing all
its complexities is not within the scope of this study, only
highlights of the political attitudes and divisions within
the society existing at the time of Naipaul's interest in
the region will be scanned.

The struggle for representative government in Trinidad's
colonial political structure was initially carried out by
the European community, but by the beginning of the twentieth century, the black working class began to demonstrate
some degree of political vitality and consciousness.[71]
Many East Indians, fearing that self-government would not
safeguard their rights as minorities, remained apprehensive
of any changes and divided about the type of reform needed.
In 1921, the Colonial Office dispatched to the West Indies
Major E. F. L. Wood, a Member of Parliament, to investigate
the entire issue of representative government. Wood's
report, which noted, among other problems, the heterogeneous
groups in Trinidad's society, did not recommend immediate
implementation of representative government, but, rather, a
modicum of constitutional change. The recommendations were
put into effect, and even though elected members were now
introduced in the legislative body, a privileged oligarchy
still held political power. This period also saw the rise
and influence of a national political leader, surprisingly a
European Creole planter, Captain A. A. Cipriani, as a

champion of the "barefooted." Cipriani's Trinidad Labor
Party (formerly Trinidad Workingmen's Association), which
seriously challenged the old colonial order, was weakened
primarily by economic dissatisfaction of workers, and people
switched loyalty to Grenadian born Uriah Butler.

After all negotiations for home rule failed, in 1937
Butler (who used the Bible as his handbook and saw himself
as a messianic savior of people) organized a strike of oil
workers to dramatize their grievances on several issues,
such as economic problems, bad labor conditions, and poor
constitutional representation. This is an important period
in Trinidad's politics, since it was one of the few times
when blacks and Indians united in a common class struggle.
The West India Royal Commission (Moyne Commission), which
visited the islands in 1938, recommended an increase in the
number of elected members and provided for the appointment
of a Committee to examine the question of adult franchise.
The Franchise Committee's majority report, which was
supported by Captain Cipriani and Albert Gomes, a Portuguese
politician, recommended adult suffrage for every one with a
knowledge of spoken English. The minority report, written
by two East Indian members, Adrian Rienzi and E. E. Abidh,
opposed the language requirement, which was apparently
designed to deprive East Indians of their right to vote.
The Secretary of State for the colonies approved the
Franchise Committee's recommendations on adult suffrage and
dropped the provision that eligibility depended on a
knowledge of spoken English.

During Trinidad's first general elections under
universal suffrage in 1946, East Indians won four of the
nine elected seats in the Council. However, issues were not
central in the campaign. As Selwyn Ryan explains, bribes
and race exploitation were the main ammunition:

> It would seem that election candidates had come to
> feel that only two strategies would mobilize the
> previously inert masses of the population: bribes
> and race. . . . Other commentators . . . felt
> that . . . the campaign was a vast exercise in
> 'obeah', 'voodoo', and other forms of religious
> magic.[72]

Albert Gomes, leader of the Party of Political Progress
Group (POPPG), analyzing the behavior of the electorate,
noted that Trinidadians had not yet begun to think politically and that they needed to eradicate illiteracy and
superstition before democracy and self-government could be
appreciated.[73] In fact, the behavior of the 1946 electorate set the pattern for subsequent elections. Ryan
elaborates on the system as it operated in Trinidad:

> Alliances were made and abandoned as the
> exigencies of electoral politics determined. . . .

> One of his [independent politician's] main
> strategies was to attract to his machine as many
> influential people as possible, who for a
> consideration would contract to deliver a bloc of
> votes to him or to a candidate of his designa-
> tion. Programmes were irrelevant to this type of
> political strategy. Face-to-face contacts and
> bribes were the main implements.[74]

The most common meeting places for the buying and selling of
votes were the rumshops (bars), whose owners, along with
shopkeepers, tailors, butchers, teachers, and religious
leaders, were among the most influential in the community
for such arrangements.

In addition, a system developed, which Morton Klass
called a _praja_ relationship, in which voters received favors
from politicians and thus felt an obligation (or _praja_) to
vote for them.[75] Politicians usually schemed to establish
this relationship:

> The most familiar technique was to become socially
> ubiquitous as the campaign season approached. One
> had to attend rum shops, baptisms, funerals,
> weddings and similar functions, and in this way
> extend one's network of influence. Candidates
> vied with each other in sending gifts and flowers
> to the sick and to those celebrating special
> occasions. In Indian communities rival candidates
> competed with each other to finance funerals and
> to provide cars, public address systems, alcohol,
> or drummers for religious or festive occasions.
> By such acts of 'benevolence' were loyalties
> traded. One minister of government owed his
> political popularity mainly to his widespread
> reputation as a successful 'mystic masseur'.[76]

Thus, only a _nimakharam_ (an ingrate) would fail his bene-
factors and not give his vote.

Following Trinidad's 1946 election a Constitutional
Reform Committee was formed to push for further representation. Ranjit Kumar's minority report did not support the
introduction of immediate responsible government and argued
that the presence of the Crown was still needed, mainly to
protect Indians from the black-dominated majority party.
But the Colonial Office accepted most of the reform measures
recommended by the majority report. The new Constitution
was to be introduced after the 1950 General Election. It
was an election which once again revealed the schism of
Trinidad's electorate. The only successful, though temporary, alliance formed was that between Butler's party and
some Indian politicians. A quasi-ministerial system of five
operated between 1950-1956. In 1955 the constitutional
issue was reopened and a Reform Committee under A. S.

Sinanan appointed. In April that year a motion was passed
to postpone general elections scheduled for September.
Several official reasons were given for the postponement,
but the main problem appeared to be the alarm that an
anti-federationist coalition in the Indian community might
destroy the hope for Federation. (Many Indians feared that
Federation would flood Trinidad with blacks from neighboring
islands.) In addition, there was widespread belief that the
Hindubased People's Democratic Party (PDP) was likely to
win, and non-Indians "considered the prospect of a
Hindu-controlled government intolerable."[77] The
postponement, however, gave the edge not to the old
Legislature but to a new politician, Dr. Eric Williams, who
used the time to organize the People's National Movement
(PNM) for the next general elections scheduled for 1956.
The new 1956 Constitution--based largely on Sinanan's
recommendations on the appointment of a chief minister and
on the composition of the Legislative Council and the
Executive Council--paved the way for a fully responsible
government by a single well-organized party.

As early as 1956, the PNM, under the leadership of
Williams was identified as pro-black and anti-Indian,
although Williams argued for the need for a genuine
multi-racial party and designed a constitution to appeal to
everyone. Ivar Oxaal describes the public perception of
Williams as a messianic leader offering racial redemption:

> For many lower class Negroes, particularly Creole
> women, Dr. Williams was nothing less than a
> messiah come to lead the black children into the
> Promised Land. This messianic tradition had been
> firmly entrenched in the Butler movement and was
> an important basis of the P.N.M.'s mass support as
> well . . . the image of Williams as a racial
> messiah was not limited to the black lower class,
> although it was the strongest there, but could be
> found in the Creole middle class as well.[78]

It was clearly the PNM against the rest of the parties--
Party of Political Progress Groups (POPPG), Trinidad Labor
Party (TLP), Caribbean National Labor Party (CNLP), West
Indian Independence Party (WIIP), Butler Party, and People's
Democratic Party (PDP)--contesting the 1956 elections.
Under the stewardship of the powerful and legendary Bhadase
Maraj, who was also president of the Hindu Sanatan Dharma
Maha Sabha, the PDP with its Indian support paralleled the
black-dominated PNM. One of the wealthiest men on the
island, Maraj generously contributed to building schools and
temples and to organizing important Hindu festivals and
receptions of holy Hindus from India.[79] He became known
as "Nehru of Trinidad," or "rajah," or "babuji." It was the
PDP with its organized Indian following which Williams

perceived as a threat. He tried to divide the Indians and
to discredit the party by suggesting that the PDP was a
Brahmin party and by equating the Sanatan Dharma Maha Sabha
of Trinidad (which supported the PDP) with the fanatic Hindu
Maha Sabha of India, which both Gandhi and Nehru
denounced.[80]
     The controversy, attacks and counter-attacks grew. What
eventually emerged in Trinidad and other countries with a
mixed population is the politics of Apan Jat (Hindi meaning
"each for his own kind or race"). Each ethnic group was
afraid of domination by the other. As Bahadoorsingh puts
it, a PNM victory "was considered by the Negroes as a
victory against the Indians and by the Indians as a threat
to their interest."[81] Both Maraj and Gomes accused the
predominantly black police force of lacking neutrality and
of deliberately failing to protect candidates opposed to
Williams.[82] Racial tension between Indians and blacks was
so high that both races found it impossible to hold meetings
in each other's territory. As expected, the PNM, which won
thirteen out of the twenty-four seats it contested, was
successful in primarily urban areas, where blacks formed the
majority, while the PDP, which won five seats out of the
fourteen it contested, swept the polls in areas such as the
sugar belts, where Indians comprised a majority. It made no
difference that both parties calculatingly chose Indian
candidates to run in Indian areas and black candidates to
run in black areas. Multiracial slates were merely
political "window-dressing." Gomes analyzed the results as
follows: "William's [sic] 'Peoples' National Movement' had
featured anti-Indian propaganda as a major factor of
electoral success. Indeed, the negro vote had rallied to an
essentially racist appeal based largely on the alleged
threat of Indian domination."[83]
     Since the Legislative Council consisted of thirty-one
members, the PNM with its thirteen seats did not have a
working majority. However, through questionable constitutional maneuverings by the Governor, the PNM was assured a
"conditional" majority and formed the government without a
coalition. Yogendra Malik argues that the PNM's "unwilling-
ness to share power with the minority group, led to further
division and consolidation of forces on racial lines."[84]
Divisions were so sharp that even inside the House, members
of the opposition were routinely insulted and heckled by
those in the public gallery. The Trinidad Guardian
commented: "We cannot conceive of any enlightened West
Indian Government in the mid-twentieth century deliberately
encouraging such behaviour, far less bringing into the
public gallery of the Legislative Council a group of rowdies
schooled in insulting tactics intended to embarrass the
opposition."[85]
     After 1956, racial tension in Trinidad rose notably.
The years 1956-62 saw much conflict as the PNM consolidated
its black-dominated party against the Hindu and European

political base. Ryan notes that the conflict between the
PNM and the opposition was "fierce and hysterical, and at
times the community seemed on the brink of racial war."[86]
The several parties saw the need for a strong, united
opposition to the PNM. In 1957 the PDP, TLP, and the POPPG
merged and formed the Democratic Labor Party (DLP), and in
1958 Maraj was elected its leader. Thus, two major parties
relying on ethnic loyalties represented the electorate--the
PNM was identified as pro-black and the DLP, in spite of the
recent coalition, as pro-Indian.

In July 1957, the British Parliament approved an Order
in Council establishing the Federation of the West Indies.
The election to the first Parliament of the West Indies
provided the first opportunity for a national confrontation
between the two groups, and race became the issue:

> The campaign in Trinidad, though on the whole not
> as fierce as in 1956, was much more racially
> tinged. Every issue was twisted to fit the racial
> cleavages in the society. Each party nevertheless
> strove to buttress its claim of being genuinely
> multiracial. . . .[87]

The DLP won six of the ten seats allocated to Trinidad, a
result which shocked the seemingly invincible PNM. As was
expected, both blacks and Indians voted in terms of race.
Williams, angered by the DLP's success, delivered in April
1958 a historic address in which he analyzed the results and
explained the PNM's loss, which he attributed to "race,
pure, and unadulterated." Addressing a predominantly black
audience, he accused the DLP of campaigning to secure an
Indian Governor and an Indian Prime Minister, and angrily
denounced East Indians as a "recalcitrant and hostile
minority." He charged: "Religion figured prominently in
the DLP campaign. By hook or crook they brought out the
Indian vote." His fellow blacks were also scolded:

> We sympathize deeply with these misguided
> unfortunates who, having ears to hear, heard not,
> having eyes to see, saw not, who were complacent
> for whom everything was in the bag, who had the
> DLP covered, who were too tired or busy to vote,
> who wanted a car to take them to the polling
> station around the corner.[88]

Historians read in Williams' address hidden propaganda
appeals to the black population of Trinidad and the West
Indies. Bridget Brereton interprets the speech as "an
appeal for racial counter-mobilization," and Selwyn Ryan
concludes, "Even if one were to be charitable and absolve
the PNM elite from the charge of openly inciting racial
counter-mobilization, one cannot condone the tactlessness of
the address--especially when racial passions were already so

inflamed."[89]   Moreover, while the entire electorate voted
in terms of race, it was only the Indians whom Williams
castigated. Malik, interpreting Williams' speech as an
indication of the working mind of the black middle class
bothered by the prospect of Indians in political power,
notes the exploitation of race by both political parties:
"Williams' accusation of the use of race by the D.L.P. for
getting votes did not make any sense, as both parties were
fundamentally based upon the support of one or the other of
the ethnic groups."[90]   The election results promised that
race, not issues, would be a continuing factor in Trinidadian politics.

     The next national election, scheduled for 1961, after
which constitutional reform granting full internal self-
government would be implemented, was primarily a heated,
tense political struggle between the two major ethnic
groups. Although both major parties chose a multiracial
slate of candidates, such a move did not change the public
perception that the PNM and the DLP represented black and
Indian interests respectively. Indeed, both parties, Malik
noted, "used ethnicity as their major support."[91]
Naipaul's uncle, Dr. Rudranath Capildeo, reputed to be
"Trinidad's most educated man," replaced Maraj as leader of
the DLP. Capildeo was a brilliant intellectual and
scientist (his pioneering work on the theory of Relativity
has been internationally recognized), but he was no
politician. His candor, spontaneity, and impatience often
embarrassed the party. When PNM hecklers disrupted DLP's
meetings, he often called for retaliation by the use of
violence. At one meeting, after the DLP banner was torn and
members were abused, his famous words were, "Arm yourselves
to take over this country. We can no longer stand up and
allow people to trample us anymore."[92]   Williams attacked
the European Creoles and accused them of supporting the
DLP's call for violence and of opposing him because he was
black.[93]

     Capildeo, however, was provoked by the PNM itself and
became frustrated and desperate. The PNM government, with
its monopoly of the radio, exercised its control of the air
waves and denied the opposition equal radio time.[94]   The
newspapers carried a PNM bias and played down the disturbances.[95]   Malik reports that organized heckling and
hooliganism were seen only at DLP meetings, and the black-
dominated police offered no protection to DLP
candidates.[96]   Williams, in fact, subtly called for this
type of harassment and suppression by telling his supporters
not to treat Butler (a black) as they did the DLP and to
"march where the hell you like," that is, presumably in
Indian areas.[97]   At San Juan black workers raided and
looted gas stations, shops, DLP offices and candidates'
homes. Indians frequently became targets of black vandalism:

          Items on the catalogue of woes related by the DLP
          press included the stoning of mosques and temples,

> the looting of Indian homes and retail establish-
> ments, the beating of Indian vendors, the slashing
> of tires on the cars of Europeans, the pulling
> down of DLP streamers, the breaking-up of DLP
> election meetings, police brutality, the use of
> insulting expressions, for example, 'We don't want
> no roti [Indian bread] government', and 'Coolie
> must feed nigger'.[98]

The DLP office was raided by the government for seditious
literature. A state of emergency was declared in troubled
areas, and the DLP was finally forced to suspend all public
meetings until after the elections. Brereton concludes that
it "seems fair to say that the campaign was marked by an
aggressive determination by the PNM to defeat the DLP by any
means."[99]

The PNM has been accused of taking other measures to
eliminate the pro-Indian/white DLP challenge in the 1961
elections. A controversy arose over the establishment of a
Boundaries Commission of mainly pro-PNM supporters (some
sitting illegitimately) to redraft and increase the twenty-
four political constituencies to thirty, most of which now
contained black majorities.[100] Asked by the opposition
whether the Committee was independent, Williams replied, "I
have no responsibility for clarifying matters for people who
are too dense to understand. Get your clarification elsewhere. That is the Commission."[101] Seeing the redrafting
as a "death blow to democracy" and as a ploy of the predominantly black PNM to ensure victory in a general election,
the DLP examined and produced figures to show that the constituencies were gerrymandered and the country was divided
ethnologically, a charge the PNM denied.[102] Historian
Ryan, however, finds that the charges were well-founded:

> The PNM took no chances even in Port of Spain,
> where the boundaries were redrafted to make sure
> that all potential DLP areas . . . were attached
> to heavily working class areas where the PNM had
> been consistently strong. . . . In the country-
> side there was strong evidence to substantiate the
> DLP's claim that the PNM had herded as many Indian
> voters as was possible into constituencies which
> they could not possibly win, and had extracted
> from such areas large blocks of Negro voters who
> were then recombined into new constituencies . . .
> the evidence certainly suggests that the carto-
> graphy was undertaken with the electoral returns
> of the previous elections in mind.[103]

Ryan states that "There is no doubt whatsoever in the
writer's mind that the constituencies were
gerrymandered."[104] Brereton essentially agrees: "There
can be little doubt that the boundaries were systematically

gerrymandered to favour the PNM, and to give the ruling party an excellent chance of winning all the seats except ten where Indians were in the majority and which the PNM in effect abandoned."[105] The DLP's proposed amendment to void the Commission's report and to establish a neutral body was not passed.

The other controversial measures taken by the PNM government were the establishment of a permanent voter registration and the introduction of voting machines for the elections. The DLP bitterly objected to a system whereby citizens were required to carry photographed identification cards with extensive personal data, and the party also argued that too many powers were given to registration officers, who were mostly blacks and, therefore, probably PNM supporters.[106] The government did try to allay some of these anxieties--for example, by enacting penalties for unfair practices of officers and by permitting witnesses to be present when enumerators interviewed illiterates.[107] The voting machines (purchased from Shoup, the same company responsible for padding neighboring Guyana's electoral list) presented a more serious problem. Knowing that the complicated voting machines would work to the disadvantage of many Indians who could not read, the DLP sought permission to inspect, or import, or purchase, or borrow a machine for demonstration purposes, but the request was denied.[108] The machines were totally--the DLP claimed suspiciously--in the protective hands of the PNM government at all times. Whether the machines were rigged or not, historians argue that the PNM dealt with the issue in an unreasonable manner and deepened the rift in the society.[109] On election day many of the delays and instances of malfunctioning occurred in predominantly Indian areas, something that confirmed the suspicions of the DLP. In addition to these problems the PNM, according to Ryan, "introduced rather stringent limitations on the use of motor and animal-drawn vehicles on election day," which made transportation to voting polls difficult in rural (Indian) areas.[110]

The DLP won only ten out of thirty seats. Calling attention to widespread irregularities and noting that the PNM's pre-election prediction was too close to the actual results to be coincidental, the DLP was convinced that the machines were rigged and the election, therefore, fraudulent. To the DLP the PNM had found a way to entrench itself in power without popular support. Even Dennis Mohabir, an East Indian supporter of the PNM and former PNM mayor of Port-of-Spain, said that the DLP lost the elections because of gerrymandering by the Boundaries Committee and because of the voting machines.[111] When the PNM formed its government, it paid little attention to Hindus, who remained unrepresented.[112] Tension was increased when, after the collapse of the West Indian Federation in 1962, the PNM proposed the idea of a Unitary State with other

small interested West Indian islands, Grenada in
particular. H. B. Singh expressed the sentiments of the
Indian community:

> The sole reason for the agitation to incorporate
> Grenada and other West Indian islands with
> Trinidad is founded on P.N.M. racialism against
> the Indians. It is the means that the P.N.M. have
> decided to implement in order to nullify Indian
> voting strength twenty years hence. In a
> Federation, Grenadian votes cannot assist any
> party in Trinidad. In a unitary state, Grenada is
> likely to receive five seats in the Trinidad
> Parliament! Because Grenada is mainly Negro,
> P.N.M. are hoping they will all vote for
> P.N.M.[113]

Indians were convinced that blacks feared the higher birth
rate of the Indian population and wanted to ensure that
blacks from the other islands would give the PNM voting
strength to establish a one-party racial dictatorship.
     The PNM made its decision to take Trinidad to
Independence and published a draft constitution for
independence. In April 1962 the constitutional conference
(Queen's Hall Conference) was held. Some Hindu groups
refused to participate. The DLP and other opposition
forces, after heated exchanges with the PNM, walked out
during the proceedings. While many praised the conference,
opposition elements described it as a "citizen's committee
to cover a dirty dictatorship," and there were already
rumblings that the "new Premier was but old Governor writ
large."[114] In London, the famous Marlborough House
Conference on Independence, with Capildeo representing the
DLP and Williams representing the PNM, opened in May 1962.
Dr. Capildeo wanted a moratorium on independence for five
years; elimination of voting machines; elections before
Independence; guarantee that the police, civil service, and
national guard would be more representative of the ethnic
physiognomy of Trinidad; consultations between the Prime
Minister and the Leader of the Opposition; and three-fourths
majority in both Houses for amendment. The Hindu Youth
Association quoted statistics to show discrimination against
Indians in employment and education. The Indian National
Association declared that if adequate safeguards for East
Indians were not considered, the country should be
partitioned into black and Indian states, in short, "parity
or partition." The PNM and the Colonial Office rejected
many of the opposition's demands. With the conference
deadlocked, racial tension in Trinidad escalated. However,
both parties eventually compromised and averted racial
strife and bloodshed. Trinidad and Tobago became
independent in 1962, ending 165 years of British rule. With

the so-called "spirit of Marlborough House," racial tension, always at its height during political activity, lessened.

However, in spite of decreased tension, there were complaints of blatant racial discrimination, primarily against Hindus. For many years the PNM included a few Moslem Cabinet members but no Hindus. Although Moslems generally follow Hindu social patterns and attitudes and are perceived by Creoles as being culturally the same as Hindus, they have often become more creolized and have had a better relationship with the PNM.[115] A Moslem PNM minister, for example, argued for closer ties between Moslems and people of African origin, pointing out that 50% of the world's Moslems are of African origin.[116] During periods of stress, both Indian Christians and Hindus claim that Moslems who have united with the PNM used the alliance to their own advantage and betrayed the Indian community. The widest rift, though, has remained not between Hindus and Moslems but between Indians on the whole and blacks. Firmly established in power, Williams, according to Ryan, "became a strict and uncompromising majoritarian; any ethnic group which did not rally behind the PNM was either recalcitrant, treasonable, or obscurantist," and he distrusted any cabinet member who advocated cooperation with the opposition.[117] C. L. R. James, once an activist of the PNM, accused the ruling party of "fanaticism and gangsterism" on the racial question.[118]

Since blacks now became the ruling elite, East Indians developed a feeling of helplessness and apathy towards the political system, which isolated and ignored them. Dr. Capildeo himself, disillusioned, left Trinidad in 1963 and accepted a teaching position at the University of London; however, he did not resign the leadership of the opposition but ran it from London and returned to Trinidad during his school vacation only. In addition, he changed his political strategy and stopped criticizing the government, hoping merely to gain concessions from the ruling PNM. His argument was that he was afraid of being perceived as a racist. Indian leadership was, therefore, weakened and people's political spirit broken. In the 1966 election many Indians switched to the Liberal Party, which they helped to form after breaking with the DLP. The DLP won only in predominantly Indian areas, confirming again the importance of race as a main determinant in voting behavior. A defeated Capildeo was pressured to resign, leaving the DLP leadership divided between boss-type politician Bhadase Maraj and radical Vernon Jamadar. To contest the 1971 elections, a faction of the DLP led by Jamadar formed an alliance with a faction of the PNM led by A. N. R. Robinson. The avowed purpose was simply to achieve racial unity; however, because of deeply embedded racial insecurities and distrust, the movement failed to generate mass support and soon collapsed with the withdrawal and boycott of Robinson two weeks before polling day. Jamadar subsequently boycotted the elections also. The PNM was returned to power and has remained in office until its defeat in 1986.

Trinidad's East Indians took a deep interest in the more serious rivalry in Guyana between the black minority and the Indian majority. In Trinidad, it is remembered, Indians and blacks joined forces in the 1940's, but the unity soon collapsed. A similar situation occurred in the 1950's in Guyana under the People's Progressive Party (PPP) led by Dr. Cheddi Jagan, an East Indian, when the two major ethnic groups were united in opposition to British colonialism. This unity was achievable since Dr. Jagan commanded the confidence of the East Indians, while his very close associate, Forbes Burnham, a black lawyer, had the full support of blacks. The PPP's victory at the polls in 1953 was short-lived, since the British suspended the constitution within six months of the elections and sent in troops, contending that the PPP government was hatching a communist "plot." Historian Gordon Lewis has noted that, "So fictitious, indeed, was the 'plot' attributed to the elected majority members, and the atmosphere of 'violence' it was supposed to have engendered, that when British combat troops disembarked to put an end to it all they found nothing more insurrectionary than an inter-island cricket match."[119] In 1955 Burnham split from Jagan but continued to call his faction the PPP. The 1957 General Elections were held over a British devised constitution that provided for a Legislative Council of fourteen elected seats, the constituencies having been gerrymandered to work against Jagan and in favor of Burnham.[120] However, Jagan was victorious, gaining nine of the seats, while Burnham only three.

In 1958 Burnham's faction, organizing itself, adopted the name People's National Congress (PNC). The division was effectively along racial rather than ideological lines, since Jagan's group attracted primarily Indians and Burnham's mainly blacks. The other significant party, the United Force (UF), led by a Portuguese businessman, Peter D'Aguiar, attracted a small number of Indian businessmen and conservative Portuguese. Like the PNM in Trinidad, the PNC waged in 1961 a campaign of race and violence. Burnham hinted to blacks what Jagan's agricultural plan meant for their "ancestral land."[121] The PPP had difficulty holding meetings in black areas; so did the PNC in Indian quarters. Leo Despres reported that the "final months of the election campaign were marked by increased racial tension, threats of intimidation, and sporadic outbreaks of physical violence."[122] Few voters crossed racial lines, and despite the fact that the Colonial Office had again rearranged some boundaries to hurt the PPP at the polls, out of the thirty-five seats, Jagan captured twenty, while Burnham only eleven and D'Aguiar four.

Jagan's victory was unpalatable not only to the internal opposition but also to the United States and Great Britain, which feared the PPP's Marxist ideology. The PNC encouraged demonstrations and implemented a system of organized violence designed to topple the government before it could negotiate for Independence. General strikes, called by black-dominated unions and financed by Jagan's outside enemies, crippled the country. Large scale racial confrontations erupted, and with one segment of the population armed against the other, some of the grossest crimes in Guyana's history were committed. Most of Georgetown was looted and set afire. Leo Despres observed that "practically every East Indian shop had been gutted, several lives had been lost, and the country's economy was seriously disrupted."[123] Indians were physically attacked, and many killed, in black areas, and vice versa in retaliation. As in Trinidad, the Creole-dominated media took a clear anti-Indian (in this case anti-PPP) stand, and the predominantly black police force committed injustices with absolute impunity. David Lowenthal reported that the race conflict in Guyana "took more lives than did all the West Indian labor clashes of the 1930's."[124] Arthur Schlesinger explains the American policy, which preferred Burnham's accommodationist attitude to Jagan's communist leanings: "An independent British Guiana under Burnham . . . would cause us many fewer problems than an independent British Guiana under Jagan."[125]

Both Burnham's PNC and D'Aguiar's UF insisted that elections be held under a proportional representation system (PR) before Independence. Under PR, the entire country is treated as one constituency, and each party is given a number of seats in proportion to the votes received; thus, the opposition strategically planned to take power by winning altogether more votes, and, thus, more seats. The British Colonial Office imposed the PR electoral system much to the displeasure of Jagan's PPP. At the 1964 elections under PR, Burnham's PNC and D'Aguiar's UF joined in a coalition and took power under the guise of consti-tutionalism, thus preventing Jagan from forming a government. Guyana became independent in 1966, but so polarized had the nation become that on Independence Day, blacks hoisted the flag of Ghana, and East Indians the flag of India. Once in power, the PNC ousted D'Aguiar and, with the support of the predominantly black military and para-military forces and with cleverly executed electoral frauds and rigged overseas voting, has remained in office to date. The 1982 Country Reports on Human Rights, prepared by the United States State Department, asserts that the PNC and Burnham "have imposed a racially oriented minority government" on the nation. Thus, the history of Guyana parallels that of Trinidad in terms of ethnic struggle for political power.

East Indians in Trinidad reacted emotionally to the
development in Guyana and have learned not to use the PPP as
a model for the DLP. Condemning Burnham's dishonesty and
quest for unlimited power, they concluded that Jagan was too
naive, honest, idealistic, and trusting of blacks, whom he
tried to placate. Malik elaborates on the sentiments of
Trinidadian East Indian elites:

> They praise him [Jagan] for his non-racial
> attitude, while a majority term Burnham a
> 'racist'. They regard Jagan as an honest
> politician. . . . Many of those who express
> hostility towards Jagan argue that Jagan foolishly
> betrayed East Indian interests in British Guiana
> by placing too much emphasis on ideology. . . .
> [They] throw the entire blame on Great Britain and
> to lesser extent on the United States for imposing
> the minority rule over the majority. . . . Many
> people among the East Indian élites hold . . .
> that British and Americans distrust Indians. They
> know that the Negro can be manipulated whereas it
> is difficult to manipulate Indians. . . . They
> argue that the Negro has no business sense . . .
> and therefore he would never be a challenge to
> British and American interests in the West
> Indies.[126]

However, some do concede that the United States and Britain
intervened because they saw Jagan as a communist threat in
the Caribbean.
From the foregoing discussion, it is clear that East
Indians in the Caribbean have not fared well politically.
Trinidad's Indians almost equal blacks numerically, and
Guyana's Indians far outnumber blacks, yet blacks have
succeeded in controlling the political scene since the
1960's. Lowenthal neatly sums up how blacks have managed to
dominate political life: "By means of proportional
representation in Guyana, gerrymandering in Trinidad, and
spoils sharing in Surinam, Creoles still (or again) dominate
governments in all three territories."[127] In both Guyana
and Trinidad East Indians have generally been excluded not
only from major roles in politics but also from social
programs, and from employment in such key positions as the
civil and foreign services and the police and military
forces. In 1964 only one-fifth and one-fortieth of the
police force in Guyana and Trinidad respectively were
Indians; recruiting officers have usually been
Creoles.[128] In the same year Justice Trinidad, an
organization responsible for ensuring freedom, called
attention to ethnic imbalances in the police force, civil
service, and judiciary. In Guyana, the International
Commission of Jurists made the same observations, but since
then the margin has widened, with blacks making up more than

95% of all armed forces. Studying the problem in Trinidad,
Neihoff attributes the imbalances in the civil service to
discriminatory practices.[129] After Trinidad's
Independence there were legitimate complaints that Indian
sugar workers were discriminated against in housing and
agricultural projects, in secondary schools, and in
allocation of public resources.[130] A similar situation
has occurred in Guyana, and conditions have worsened over
the years in both countries.

East Indians also complain that in addition to political
and economic suppression, they are victims of Creole
cultural dominance. The lack of understanding of cultural
patterns and the hostility between the two groups during
indentureship have continued in the Caribbean to the present
day. Blacks do not, as a rule, participate in Indian
cultural affairs, play Indian musical instruments, know the
significance of Hindu and Moslem festivals, or even bother
with the correct spelling of Indian names. Likewise, few
Indians attend fetes, play in a steelband, sing calypsos, or
participate in Carnival--all staples of black culture. But,
being politically impotent, Indians, not Creoles, are
pressured to shed their cultural heritage. Ivar Oxaal,
describing the attitude of the two groups to each other in
Trinidad as one of "negative indifference," asserts that
"Creole ideology . . . tends to regard the existing
alienation of a large percentage of the East Indian
population from the Creole majority as an aberration. It
is, moreover, an ideology expressed in the tendency to
regard Carnival as a 'national' festival when in fact it is
almost exclusively a Creole event."[131] Gordon Lewis
observes that although the "official theory of Carnival is
that it is a national festival a large percentage of East
Indians do not so regard it and, in fact, hold it in
disdain."[132] In an effort to project an image of one
society, some intellectuals deny the existence of Indian
cultural patterns. The classic example often cited, of
course, is Prime Minister Eric Williams' criticism of Morton
Klass' East Indians in Trinidad, a work regarded by informed
West Indians as the best on the subject. Klass concluded
that the village he studied was "in basic structure . . . an
'Indian' community, and not a West Indian community," a
conclusion which drew the following reprimand from
Williams: "A foreign student, with all the impetuosity of
youth rushing in where angels fear to tread, may talk glibly
of an Indian village in Trinidad not being West
Indian."[133] One interpretation is that Williams was
provoked because Klass' study confirmed the existence of a
"two-nations" theory and of a community which blacks feel
"ought not to exist."[134] Depending on the circumstance
and event, politicians issue different statements on the
oneness or plurality of the society.[135]

In all West Indian societies, even in Guyana where
Indians form a majority, it is the Creole culture which is

projected as the national culture. Overseas cultural
displays omit Chinese, Portuguese, and Indian elements. For
example, Lowenthal notes that "Trinidad's Expo '67 pavilion
in Montreal presented a predominantly Creole image of
Trinidad."[136] He finds that this attitude still prevails:

> [Creoles] take for granted that East Indians
> should become West Indian by adopting Creole ways,
> never the reverse. . . . A black Trinidadian
> confirms that 'creole elements on the whole still
> do not consider the Indian subculture to be legit-
> imate and worthy of promotion'. Indeed, the
> Trinidad Government tends to regard Creole as the
> culture and Indian separation as refractory if not
> treasonable.[137]

Again, the same holds true of Guyana, where the black
minority government ignores Indian tradition and mores. A
Trinidadian writer's list of grievances is equally
applicable to Guyana:

> Radio stations give only two hours Indian music a
> day. Neither newspaper pays more than token
> attention to them, and a casual reading of the
> newspapers would never show a stranger that
> Indians form one third of the population. . . .
> The Ministry of Culture has conveniently forgotten
> to encourage Indian cultural activities, but it
> has pushed the Creole version. And Indians are
> angry about . . . the unequal expenditure, the
> unequal radio time, and the obvious ignoring of
> their interests as a group.[138]

Any attempt to refer to Indian cultural heritage is met
with strong hostility and suspicion. For example, Sydney
King (now Eusi Kwayana) saw Peter Ruhoman's centennial
history of Indians in Guyana as an Indian "plan of
conquest," whereas the book, as Gordon Lewis states,
"evinced not a separatist tendency but, rather, a search for
Indian equality within a Guyanese universe."[139] Many will
agree with K. V. Parmasad that West Indian society is closed
to the Indian unless he is "prepared to strip himself of his
name, his religion, his culture, his language, his history
and become . . . Christianized, Westernized, colonized,
dehumanized . . . [but] the new society will only come when
Indians are recognized and accepted for what they are rather
than for what others would want to make of them."[140]
Nonetheless, Creoles continue to believe that the creation
of an assimilated West Indian society is possible only if
East Indians forget their cultural and religious heritage
and try to adapt to or blend with Creole culture.

The problem, however, is that the recent preoccupation
with ancestral roots led black West Indians to an African
past--a past which East Indians do not share. So much has
the society pushed the consciousness of blacks and Africa
that Parmasad made this observation: "There are Indians . .
. who are possessed by the erroneous conviction that being
as little Indian as possible and being as much Afro-Saxon,
Afro-American or any other thing is being 'Trinidadian'.
But this blatant denial of self is what creates the 'mimic-
man'."[141] Such Indians, however, are in the minority.
Most contend that it is unreasonable to be asked to trade
interest in their heritage for an unknown, African one. As
Parmasad suggests, a trade off--by either side--should not
be demanded: "Africans in the West are engaged in the
frantic but the vitally necessary quest for their forgotten
roots. . . . Who can rightly demand of us what they would
not demand of themselves?"[142] It might be thought that
the growing consciousness of Africa and the emphasis on
African culture in the West Indies would have effected a
more tolerant attitude towards the Indian subculture. But
in spite of professed tolerance and official proclamations,
what has taken place instead, much to the disappointment of
East Indians, is the projection of a completely African
cultural image of both Guyana and Trinidad. The formation
of a West Indian national identity will remain elusive as
long as this attitude persists.

East Indians in the Caribbean are disappointed at being
treated as second-class citizens by people who were
themselves once brutalized and, therefore, it is believed,
should be more sensitive and understanding. Malik explains
the thinking of East Indians in Trinidad:

> [People claim] 'Earlier Negroes were the victims
> of the race prejudices, now those victims of the
> past have become the aggressors of the present
> day'. Even Dr. Winston Mohabir who had held
> office in the P.N.M.'s Government warned against
> the introduction of 'apartheid in reverse' and
> against the propagation of a nationalism which
> excludes a particular ethnic group.[143]

The same holds for Guyana, where white domination has given
way to black domination. As an example of the oppressed
becoming the oppressors, Indians point to the West Indian
cricket team, which, in early colonial days, was exclusively
white but is now predominantly black. Such exclusion
undoubtedly encourages racial division, for during the 1983
cricket match in England East Indians from the West Indies
rooted for the Indian team, not the West Indian one. East
Indians point out that blacks view them as Indians, not as
West Indians: "When a Negro does or says something, he is
Trinidadian, or a West Indian. When an Indian does or says
something, he is Indian."[144] Indians claim that their

contribution to the West Indian economy has never been recognized. They have been ignored so much that politicians, according to one observer, have described "the question of the West Indies to be that of the Negroes and the whites as if the East Indians did not live in these parts at all."[145]

Indians attribute their lot to both black aggressiveness and Indian passivity. The West Indian black-white race issue has been summed up as follows: "Just as all issues may be judged as racial, so any criticism may be imputed to prejudice. To avoid saying anything that might be felt as a racial slur, West Indians often refrain from any comment whatever."[146] This statement is especially applicable to the Indian-black conflict in that Indians are generally afraid to challenge the status quo, and Indian politicians are extremely cautious lest their statements about inequality be construed as racist. Parmasad takes the black West Indian leadership to task with this blistering indictment:

> When Indians stand up and demand their rights they are branded "racists" . . . they have been totally neglected by the government, yet, whenever an attempt is made by Indians to help alleviate the sufferings of Indians we are branded "separatists". But anyone can speak about bettering the lot of the "black man" . . . without being a racist. But the moment one speaks in favour of the Indian he is confronted with a wall of hate, suspicion, indifference, contempt, hostility, antagonism and open, brass-faced racism and discrimination.[147]

This attitude, coupled with Indians' self-imposed reticence, has frustrated efforts to effect change.

Creoles often blame racial stress on Indian isolation and exclusiveness, but evidence indicates that increased contact between the two groups exacerbates rather than alleviates the tension. When Indians first arrived in the West Indies, they were deliberately segregated in clusters of barracks on the plantations, which were the only places they were legally permitted to be. Curtailment of movement restricted contact with Creoles; in fact, the government even prescribed separate latrine accommodations to ensure complete segregation.[148] Thus, isolation was initially not self-imposed, though East Indians undoubtedly preferred it because they were protected from the hostility of Creoles. After the end of indentureship most Indians continued to work on the estates and constructed their permanent homes, called "housing schemes" nearby. Keeping to agriculture, Indians have generally remained rural. On the other hand, most blacks continued to abandon the estates and the rural areas for the cities or the mines in Guyana and oil fields in Trinidad. Occupational division, therefore, kept the two races apart after restrictions on the movement of Indians were lifted.

Referring specifically to Guyana, Gordon Lewis notes that it was the "breakdown of that separatism, increasingly evident after 1945, under the pressure of new occupational and geographical mobilities that set the stage for the present-day ordeal."[149] For when Indians in the West Indies became more and more economically competitive and politically conscious and sought fuller participation in all walks of life, they inevitably came into close contact with blacks, who feared competition and became uneasy. Lowenthal confirms this phenomenon:

> Residential mixing is no guarantee of ethnic amity. . . . The chief cause of ethnic conflict today is not the paucity of contact but its increasing frequency. . . . Creoles and Indians now compete for the power and status formerly held by expatriates and local whites. . . . In all territories tension accompanies increased East Indian participation in many walks of life. . . . Creoles misread separatism as jealousy and regard Indian ways as useless relics of the dead past.[150]

Leo Despres also finds that "when large numbers of both groups live together in the same village, the community is usually riven by hostile factionalism."[151] The Guyanese race riots of the 1960's forced "house swapping" and reduced mixed villages, since both black and Indian minorities were forced to flee to segregated villages where their own ethnic group dominated. The main point is that residential inter-mixing and increased contact have not worked. In mixed villages East Indians and blacks have continued to keep socially apart, rarely attending each other's social events, such as weddings and religious ceremonies.

Because of political maneuverings, racial discrimi-nation, and the hostility of Creoles, Guyanese and Trinidadian Indians have generally developed a strong feeling of alienation towards the political system.[152] In fact, in the entire region many countries have become one-party states, and their small size has bred corruption, nepotism, authoritarianism, personalization, and government involvement in every aspect of life.[153] Several remedies have been proposed to revive the spirit of East Indians. Some of these (all of which have failed to materialize), include the provision of equal opportunities and fair treatment of East Indians; increased social and cultural intermixing; and a coalition government representing the two races. Frustrated by existing conditions, Indian extremists in both countries have called for the creation of a separate homeland for East Indians. One leader explains his position:

> Partition of British Guiana is the only solution.
> . . . Jagan will oppose this solution. . . . The
> Indian community in the West Indies lives under
> constant fear of molestation and even physical
> destruction. . . . Had they pressed, like the
> Negroes in British Guiana, for introduction of
> proportional representation in Trinidad or asked
> for some type of parity in the formation of
> governments or in the civil services, before
> independence of the country, Negroes would have
> resorted to the use of violence against East
> Indians in Trinidad, as they did in British
> Guiana.[154]

Thus far, no solution has been found to the mutual fear
existing between the two ethnic groups.

The struggle for political power and economic opportunities, then, has left a legacy of racial division and
animosity between blacks and Indians in the Caribbean. J.
A. Froude's remarks in 1888 that the "two races are more
absolutely apart than the white and black" is an observation
that most modern-day sociologists, including M. G. Smith,
confirm.[155] Guyana's coat of arms, "One People, One
Nation, One Destiny" and Trinidad's "Together We Aspire--
Together We Achieve" represent the ideal, not reality. So
does the PNM's slogan "All a' we is one." The derogatory
names used by both groups--"nigger" and "kaphar" (dis-
believer) for black and "coolie" for Indian--indicate this
antipathy. Both groups, isolated from each other's social
structure, apply stereotypes to disparage each other not
only in Trinidad and Guyana but also in other islands
wherever the two groups reside. Indians often allude to
blacks' permissiveness and promiscuity, tendency to cohabit,
love of fete, rum, dance, expensive clothes, and carnival,
and prodigality. Blacks, on the other hand, often refer to
Indians' secrecy, clannishness, parsimoniousness, and love
of land. Despres discusses these stereotypes:

> Africans tend to think of East Indians as a
> miserly people who devote all of their time and
> energy to work and who are so bent upon accumu-
> lating land and money that they are not able to
> enjoy the fruits of their labor. East Indians, on
> the other hand, view Africans as a people without
> ambition, lazy, wasteful, and so preoccupied with
> sporting that they are unable to put anything
> aside. . . . On the surface, there would appear
> to be some truth to these stereotypes. . . .
> Africans, when they have money, consume conspic-
> uously. . . . Considerable money is spent on rum,
> clothing, and weekly dances. . . . The values
> which tend to regulate East Indian consumption are

derived, in large part, from the deeply rooted
beliefs which Indians hold with respect to their
religious practices.[156]

Morris Freilich, who studied both groups, has concluded the
same about their respective philosophies.[157] Blacks
admit, "With us it is a good time and a fete for everything
imaginable. . . ."[158] So deeply embedded are the stereotypes that as early as 1927 one British agricultural expert
thought that "contact with the African races has led to a
more thriftless and indolent mode of life (in the East
Indians) and the temperate habits enforced in India by the
struggle for existence, the joint family system and caste
scruples no longer exist."[159] The premise and conclusion,
however, are questionable since the two races never mixed to
the extent suggested by the statement.

Many West Indians, however, tend to ignore racial
uneasiness and to deny that harmony remains an aspiration,
not a reality. This interracial image is projected
especially by the tourist industry and by promoters of
foreign investment. But some intellectuals agree that "one
of the prime obstacles in the way of better relationships
and greater social justice is the stubborn belief on the
part of the majority that race relations are ideal, and that
these Indians who protest are mischievous and misguided
professional racialists."[160] C. L. R. James, a renowned
black West Indian and one-time adviser of Eric Williams,
calls the image of racial harmony one of the "greatest lies
of our society":

> Everybody in public life pretends that [racialist
> practices] do not exist; they talk about them only
> to one another and in whispers. . . . Let us face
> the fact; middle-class West Indians of African
> descent feel that this island . . . . is
> predominantly their field of operation.[161]

After 1966 Trinidadian radicals began to challenge the
"racial détente" which existed after Independence.[162]
Yet, as Lowenthal points out, "Overt ethnic conflict is rare
in Trinidad owing not to acculturation but rather to
disassociation, a live-and-let live propensity to mind one's
affairs"; the relationship between the two groups is often
described as one of passive coexistence.[163] If any one
group remains excluded from positions of influence, however,
the potential for racial confrontation would be present.
Parmasad argues: "To boast of a national identity here, is
to live in a world of make-believe. To claim that we are
all one is to ignore the stark realities of the present. To
ignore the presence of any one group is to sow the seeds of
future conflict, discord and chaos."[164] Some observers
have even predicted serious clashes.[165]

Sharply differing lifestyles and values, together with
geographical and occupational separation, have added to
mutual contempt and misunderstandings between the two
races. If intermarriage is an indication of group
acceptance, then the society has not reached that stage.
Given the climate of race relations from the period of the
arrival of East Indians, it is not surprising that despite
the initial shortage of women, there were no known cases of
intermarriage between Indians and blacks in Trinidad up to
1900.[166] Miscegenation is somewhat common today, but
Indians generally disapprove of it, and those who defy
tradition and intermarry are often threatened with dis-
inheritance and ostracism by their families. Children of
Indian-black parents are called "dogla" and are more
acceptable to blacks than to Indians.[167] In a survey
conducted in the 1960's on the issue, East Indian political
and social leaders and top professionals all generally rejected intermarriage with blacks but not necessarily with
whites. The rationale the informants offered was that
physiognomical and physical differences between whites and
East Indians are negligible; moreover, while black physical
traits are regarded as undesirable by everyone, the opposite
is true of white.[168] And as Indians are beginning to
compete for jobs in the Creole-dominated world and are drawn
further into the mainstream of West Indian society, they,
like blacks, tend to strive for white ideals and manners.
Thus, the major ethnic groups, both victims of colonialism,
have become polarized, but ironically they have idealized
their former masters.

In West Indian societies, up to the late 1960's, both
blacks and Indians showed an open preference for white
physical features. During the early days of colonialism,
color was central in the social hierarchy, as Cheddi Jagan
explains:

> The colour of the person generally determined his
> social status--the whiter the colour of skin, the
> higher the social status. At the top were the
> white planters; at the bottom were the African
> slaves; in the middle were the "men of colour". .
> . . The Indians, although "brown" in colour, were
> not accommodated within the social hierarchy.[169]

After Emancipation, color, instead of diminishing in
importance, assumed a greater role. Despres found that
Georgetown's public places--shops, banks, travel
agencies--employed light-skinned blacks.[170] But the
prejudice went deeper than just skin pigmentation; it also
encompassed a constellation of physical traits--straight
hair, thin lips, narrow nose were considered "good."
Mothers pulled and annointed their children's noses to make
them narrow and long, and some people sought to marry
"light" to produce desirable children.[171] Even

politicians were sensitive about their blackness in official pictures, and photographers learned to "lighten" their subjects.[172] The black-is-beautiful revolutionary thinking of recent years has had some, though not much, impact in the West Indies:

> Despising blackness, West Indians seek to expunge it from their features. . . . Almost every West Indian woman 'fixes' her hair with a hot comb. . . . The 'Afro' style popular in Black America is much less known in the Caribbean and is viewed askance by West Indians embarrassed by the exposure of 'bad' hair.
> Skin bleaching creams and lotions, introduced from America during the Second World War, are widely used, as are peroxide and face powder. . . . Rural women visiting town are often so heavily powdered they appear ghost-like. . . . Few West Indians profess to admire the 'natural' look; their ideal types are avowedly whiteoriented . . .
> In the West Indies black is not yet thought beautiful. . . . 'We like to say that colour does not matter to us', a friend of mine told me in 1960. 'We know very well that this is not true. But we do not want to admit it to an outsider or to have anyone else suggest it to us.'[173]

In __Black Skin, White Masks__ Frantz Fanon, a noted Martinician psychologist, puts forth the theory that "The black man wants to be white. The white man slaves to reach a human level. . . . For the black man there is only one destiny. And it is white."[174] West Indians of East Indian descent also favored light skin. They, too, bought the popular "skin-bleaching" cream, falsely advertised to lighten complexions, and they compared the dark-skinned Madrasis with blacks. West Indian preoccupation with color and appearance declined somewhat with the importation of the Black Power Movement in the late 1960's, but deeply embedded prejudices remain.

The adoption and gradual idolization of white standards assumed new dimensions after Independence when West Indian politicians, while decrying the trappings of colonialism, became replacements and mimics of their colonial masters. "Feudal lords," "barons," "imperialist overlords," "slave masters," "mimic men"--these are all labels West Indians apply to their politicians. One writer complains, for example, that the leaders are often seen "proper in dress and formal in mien, . . . sitting in the back of large cars, preceded by outriders. . . . This style is derived from the bad colonial days and is meant both to emphasize and hallow the power they wield."[175] Local politicians continue to relish their new prestige by delightedly mimicking the

authoritarian style of their former colonial rulers. Their
behavior and actions, in the words of Sparrow, the popular
calypso singer, say, "Who gave the privilege to object? Pay
your taxes, shut up and have respect." Politicians consider
themselves above the law and expect and demand subservience,
while they treat their opposition as "anti-nationalist"
mischief makers.[176] Decolonization has become
neocolonization, with the gaps between classes and between
ethnic groups becoming wider.[177] West Indians lament that
their leaders have "become carbon copies of the European
slave master. But what they have retained are his worst
vices."[178] Many West Indians, cynical about Eric
Williams' boast, "Massa day done," know well that "massa"
can be black too.

Counteracting this imitation of white attitudes was the
protest of the West Indian Black Power Movement in the late
1960's and early 1970's. Historian Ryan notes that the
"clenched fist salute, 'Afro'-hair styles, and African dress
had suddenly become the 'in' fashion (even among the
government ministers) in a country where only a few years
before an African student in traditional dress was
derisively dismissed as a 'Congo man'."[179] Proponents of
the movement in the West Indies argued that the system of
colonial values must be eliminated, that black racial pride
and an indentification with Africa must be developed, that
the gap between the black elite and the ordinary masses must
be closed, that the industries and businesses, which are
owned and controlled by foreigners (mainly white)
corporations, must be transferred to the hands of the
people, and, most of all, that West Indian governments,
betrayers of their people, must cease being collaborators in
the oppression of blacks. Only then, it was thought, could
the political, social, economic uplifting of blacks be
accelerated. Political activist James Millette articulated
the main issue of the movement:

> The governments of the West Indies have been faced
> in our time with an unceasing dilemma. . . .
> Either they have to adopt policies which are
> increasingly unpalatable for many of them since
> they have become part of the vested interest them-
> selves, or they have to oppress the people. . . .
> This is what, in essence, is the cause of the
> basic conflict which has developed in recent times
> in a black power movement in Trinidad and Tobago.
> . . . West Indian people [are saddled] with a
> very fundamental experience of poverty, dispos-
> session, and oppression. All in all, West Indians
> own and control nothing. . . . The road forward
> must begin in one way or the other with a
> reckoning with those international corporations
> operating in our midst and exploiting us. But
> between the population and the corporations stand

the governments concerned. Remove the governments
and you will have a reckoning in the West
Indies.[180]

Leaders organized street demonstration and directed their
protest primarily against the middle class and governments
in order to effect an immediate change.
    West Indians, however, have not reacted with unanimity
to the call for solidarity to the movement. Some saw in it
a manifestation of what has been called the West Indian
"amazing predilection for imported sloganry."[181]
Lowenthal shows that West Indians themselves discuss the
pattern of imported imitation:

>   In black power as in so much else, the West Indian
>   intellectual tradition is to emulate and imitate.
>   'The present rash of African sentiments contains a
>   fair proportion of the West Indian tendency to
>   look everywhere but at the West Indies.' The
>   minutest details of Caribbean black power reflect
>   Africa, if at all, by way of the United States.
>   Malcolm X begets Michael X, Black Panthers
>   generate Black Eagles. 'Leaders of the protest
>   movement are apparently so deficient in
>   innovation', charges a Trinidadian, 'that they
>   find it necessary to copy their nomenclature,
>   syllable by syllable, and their ornamentation
>   (beards, black jerseys, clenched fist salute,
>   etc.) from the American "black power"
>   movement'.[182]

The middle-class blacks, whites, and East Indians reacted to
the movement by accusing the militants of envying their
successes and of aping American styles and politics which
are irrelevant, since in the West Indies "power is
black."[183] Answering this charge, Millette stated that
"Black men in power do not connote black power. . . . The
rewards of the society are very obviously going to those in
the society who are not black."[184]
    Indeed, the issue of the relevance of the Black Power
Movement in multiracial West Indian societies, already
governed by blacks, became the center of controversy. Black
Power activists such as Trinidad-born Stokely Carmichael
and Guyanese Walter Rodney were banned in Jamaica, where the
official position was that the movement had no relevance to
the West Indies. In Trinidad, Eric Williams hoped that the
movement would evaporate, and he took a cautious stand:

>   It is immediately obvious that the issue of the
>   constitutional inequality of the blacks has no
>   relevance for the West Indies. But it is absurd

>   to expect black West Indians not to sympathize
>   with and feel part of black American movements for
>   the achievement of human rights by black Americans
>   . . . or the emancipation of black Africans from
>   white tyranny. . . .[185]

Williams welcomed the recognition of African culture, but he
argued that "it has its possible dangers if it is
overplayed, if it seeks to impose the very apartheid of
which it has been a victim in the past, and if it seeks to
dominate and denigrate other cultures which have contributed to Trinidad and Tobago."[186]

Recognizing the problems black power poses in a
multiracial society, some leaders attempted to recruit
Indians by suggesting that the term "black" includes
Indian. But the movement, which stressed the concept of
negritude and things African, succeeded in rekindling East
Indian racial consciousness. For Caribbean East Indians
vehemently reject any suggestion that they could be included
in the broad definition of black, as Ramdath Jagessar writes:

>   New World Negroes can talk at length of their
>   growing consciousness because they never had any
>   before. They lost it in the Middle Passage. . .
>   . [Indians] do not have to argue, to shout aloud
>   that Indians are beautiful. . . .
>   If you talk of black people you cannot mean
>   Indians. Physically they are not black; emo-
>   tionally they do not feel the Negro stigma of
>   blackness, or of colonialism. Indians are
>   insulted at being considered black in the Negro
>   sense of the word. . . . There is no active race
>   hatred against Negroes. Indians are not that
>   concerned. . . . Indians do not identify with the
>   flag or the tourist brochure idea of Trinidad. . .
>   . Most care little for calypso, carnival,
>   steelband and other forms of Negro cultural
>   life.[187]

Ryan concludes that Jagessar's statement is "fundamentally
correct for about 90 percent of the Indian population" in
Trinidad.[188] During the regular massive street demonstrations of 1970 in Trinidad, considerable damage was done
to Indian-owned businesses and establishments, and Indian
properties were destroyed and burned.[189] One Indian
angrily protested: "We want no part of your struggle
because you talk nothing but destruction."[190] In fact,
many felt that the movement was another step in the
direction of further black domination.

Thus, instead of uniting the two groups, the movement
caused confusion and conflict. It also revived latent
hostility between blacks and whites. Stokely Carmichael,

who visited Guyana during this turbulent period, insisted
that Black Power excluded Indians. Burnham subsequently
welcomed Carmichael, but Jagan chided: "If the struggle is
economic, political and ideological and is against
imperialism, there is no necessity for expressing it in
racial terminology. This is emotional and unscientific and
causes confusion."[191] Blacks themselves were divided.
One writer suggested that the term "Majority Power" would be
a more appropriate replacement for the racist content
suggested by "Black Power," a term suitable in South Africa
and the United States; another argued that "black
neo-colonialism is as real a threat as the white exploiting
organization [and] . . . appears to be another emotional
'cop out.'"[192] The movement was crushed, but not until it
caused a mutiny of the Trinidad Defense Force and a
declaration of a State of Emergency on April 21, 1970. More
important, though, the Black Power Movement added to the
confusion about West Indian identity to such an extent that
there is still an ongoing debate as to whether West Indians
should study only things West Indian.
     The importation of the Black Power Movement reveals the
region's external cultural dependence. West Indians grew to
realize that political autonomy does not end economic and
cultural dependence. Caribbean economic institutions are
still owned and operated by international corporations and
foreign investors. Technology is still something that has
to be imported from abroad. Even with imported technology,
locally produced items suffer the set-back of not being
easily marketable, since consumers have conditioned
themselves to prefer imported products over local ones.
Lowenthal notes this inclination:

          Caribbean products have yet to gain general
          respect, let alone popular esteem. Businessmen do
          not stock local goods of equal or better quality
          than the foreign-made for fear of losing
          customers. European-oriented culture at school
          persuades West Indians that it is better to ignore
          most aspects of local life.[193]

Everything foreign is admired, everything local eschewed.
Although attempts are now being made to decolonize the
educational system, to use books and other materials
relevant to the West Indies, and to promote local culture,
West Indians, to a great extent, still rely on overseas
books and films and pattern their lives after European and
American values and tempo.
     Politicians and commentators, recognizing this curse of
dependence, express cynicism towards nations that have
achieved independence and sovereignty. For example, one
writer declares that "Independence for each island is really
nothing more than a flag, an anthem, a diplomatic corps that

gets rich and ever more pretentious."[194] Even Cheddi
Jagan notes that "nominal political independence [may] sever
the formal ties of colonialism with the 'mother' country,"
but despite all "the trappings of national sovereignty [we]
still remain a colony."[195] Some West Indians frequently
suggest that the post-colonial societies of the region are
in a worse predicament than they were before their
independence, an indication of the extent of people's
disillusionment. The Trinidadian journal Moko puts it this
way:

> The old colonial days were much better than now.
> At least bones used to shake the branches and some
> leaves used to fall in our pockets, although he
> [the colonizer] took all the fruits. Since . . .
> [self-government], fruits, leaves, branches, tree
> trunks, everything go in the big boys pockets.
> Nothing comes to us, the poor people.[196]

Nowhere is this statement more frequently heard than in
Guyana, in which the colonial white elite has been replaced
by the local privileged clique, headed by a President, a
Prime Minister, four vice-Presidents, and several
"technocrats." At the same time West Indian politicians
tend to shower blame on colonialism for every ill in the
society, a tendency appropriately referred to as "the most
comforting discovery of the age."[197] Observers continue
to project a grim picture for the region.

After World War II, West Indians generally became
obsessed with migration as a solution to their political and
economic problems. West Indian emigraton to England during
the 1950's and 1960's has been called "the largest net
outward movement of population to take place from . . . the
British Caribbean."[198] It has been estimated that in the
early 1970's about 10,000 to 15,000 skilled and professional
Trinidadians (out of a population of about 1,100,000)
emigrated yearly.[199] During Naipaul's time, as Patrick
Parrinder states, it was fashionable to go overseas to
secure a well-rounded education and a career.[200] Today,
even those who do not seek an education or a career, or
those who have already acquired both, are convinced that the
only way to improve their economic, social, and
psychological condition and to ensure better educational
opportunities for their children is to reside abroad and
accept any type of employment. Willingness to sell anything
to secure passage led one observer to conclude that "tens of
thousands of West Indians would prefer to live anywhere
rather than in the West Indies."[201] The "brain-drain,"
that is, the exodus of all skilled workers, has had a
detrimental effect on the small countries. This is
especially true of Guyana, where everyone, including the
children of the ruling class, abandons the country at the

earliest opportunity. (Emigration, though, rids the governments of potential agitators.) West Indians who earn their degrees and return home hoping to serve their country soon become afflicted with "culture shock" and quickly abandon the slow tempo and insularity of West Indian life. Thus, the majority of foreign-educated West Indians, including artists and writers, choose to live abroad, visiting the region periodically. This has been the case with Naipaul, who, having spent his formative years in Trinidad, has been residing in London since 1950.

Thus, characterized by political and racial division, by social and cultural confusion, and by economic and educational dependence, West Indian societies have not been able to appeal to the intellectually and socially ambitious within them. East Indians in particular have not developed a sense of belonging in the West Indies. Having been forced to become culturally alienated from India, they have found nothing to replace this loss. In addition, the political machinery has worked to condemn them to the state of a large, silent minority. To survive, they feel pressured to become mimic men and to play the game, not "play the fool." It is against this background that Naipaul's fictional and non-fictional West Indian works are set.

Notes

1 "V. S. Naipaul and the West Indian Writers,"
Antilia, 1 (1983), 9.

2 Tobago is a separate island of about 116 square
miles and forms part of the government of Trinidad.

3 For a detailed discussion of the complicated system
of inclusion and exclusion of countries belonging to the
West Indies, see David Lowenthal, West Indian Societies
(London: Oxford University Press, 1972), pp. 2-3.

4 Lowenthal, West Indian Societies, p. 3; see also M.
G. Smith, The Plural Society in the British West Indies (Los
Angeles: University of California Press, 1965), p. 3.

5 Lowenthal, West Indian Societies, p. 23.

6 The Middle Passage (London: André Deutsch, 1962;
rpt. New York: Vintage Books, 1981), p. 190; "Power?" in
The Overcrowded Barracoon (London: André Deutsch, 1972;
rpt. New York: Penguin Books, 1976), p. 271.

7 The New English Literature (New York: St. Martin's
Press, 1979), p. 103.

8 Some historians contend that Dutch occupation began
at the beginning of the seventeenth century. See Cheddi
Jagan, The West on Trial (London: Michael Joseph Ltd.,
1966), p. 25; for historical details on Guyana, see Raymond
Smith, British Guiana (London: Oxford University Press,
1962).

9 Jagan, p. 27.

10 For historical details on Trinidad, see Eric
Williams, History of the People of Trinidad and Tobago (New
York: Frederick A. Praeger, 1962).

11 Yogendra Malik, East Indians in Trinidad: A Study
in Minority Politics (London: Oxford University Press,
1971), p. 5; Bridget Brereton, Race Relations in Colonial
Trinidad (London: Cambridge University Press, 1979), pp.
7-8.

12 Lowenthal, West Indian Societies, pp. 61-62; Morton
Klass, East Indians in Trinidad (Columbia: Columbia
University Press, 1961), pp. 10 ff. discusses the claims of
deceit.

13 Jagan, p. 39.

[14] Jagan, p. 39; Lowenthal, West Indian Societies, pp. 202-08. For more information on Portuguese and Chinese immigration, see Williams, p. 76; Raymond Smith, pp. 42-46; F. R. Augier et al., The Making of the West Indies (London: Longmans, Green & Co. Ltd., 1960), pp. 195-98.

[15] For more detailed information concerning the terms of indentureship, see Dwarka Nath, A History of Indians in Guyana (London: Thomas Nelson & Sons Ltd., 1950), pp. 173-76.

[16] Figures are taken from Augier, p. 210; Williams, p. 118; and Nath, pp. 179 ff.

[17] Jagan, p. 422; Malik, p. 5. Hindus far outnumber Moslems in both Guyana and Trinidad.

[18] Since the 1960's the Guyana Government has made no official figures available.

[19] Lowenthal, West Indian Societies, p. 146.

[20] J. S. Furnivall, Colonial Policy and Practice (London: Cambridge University Press, 1948), p. 304.

[21] M. G. Smith, pp. 75-91.

[22] Brereton, Race Relations in Colonial Trinidad, pp. 1-3.

[23] Lowenthal, West Indian Societies, pp. 32-33.

[24] Conflict and Solidarity in a Guianese Plantation (London: The Athlone Press, 1963), p. 3, note 1.

[25] M. G. Smith, p. 13 and p. 307; see also Brereton, Race Relations in Colonial Trinidad, p. 12.

[26] Lowenthal, West Indian Societies, p. 42.

[27] Lowenthal, West Indian Societies, p. 250.

[28] Lowenthal, West Indian Societies, p. 251.

[29] Brereton, Race Relations in Colonial Trinidad, p. 5.

[30] Cultural Pluralism and Nationalist Politics in British Guiana (Chicago: Rand Mc Nally & Co. 1967), p. 58.

[31] Despres, p. 103; Selwyn D. Ryan, Race and Nationalism in Trinidad (Toronto: University of Toronto Press, 1972), p. 22.

[32] Lowenthal, West Indian Societies, p. 154.

[33] H. Sampath, as quoted by Krishna Bahadoorsingh, Trinidad Electoral Politics (London: Headley Brothers, Ltd., 1968), p. 7.

[34] Malik, pp. 9-10.

[35] Lowenthal, West Indian Societies, p. 107.

[36] Malik discusses relations between Hindus and Moslems, for example, during the time of India's Independence and during Trinidad's political campaigns, pp. 35-40.

[37] Lowenthal, West Indian Societies, p. 63; Brereton, Race Relations in Colonial Trinidad, pp. 189-90.

[38] The English in the West Indies (London: Charles Scribner's Sons, 1888; rpt. New York: Negro University Press, 1969), p. 76.

[39] Jayawardena, p. 17. Hindu and Moslem marriages were not considered legally binding unless performed by a Christian minister. See Nath, p. 126.

[40] Bahadoorsingh, p. 6.

[41] Brereton, Race Relations in Colonial Trinidad, p. 187; see also Gordon Lewis, The Growth of the Modern West Indies (New York: Monthly Review Press, 1968), p. 202.

[42] Donald Wood, Trinidad in Transition (London: Oxford University Press, 1968), p. 110.

[43] Brereton, Race Relations in Colonial Trinidad, pp. 188-89.

[44] Ryan, pp. 21-22.

[45] Charles Kingsley, as quoted by Ryan, p. 21 and by Brereton, p. 190.

[46] Ryan, p. 23; Brereton, p. 189.

[47] Bahadoorsingh, p. 10; see also Arthur and Juanita Niehoff, East Indians in the West Indies (Wisconsin: Milwaukee Public Museum Publications in Anthropology #6, 1960), pp. 77-78.

[48] Bahadoorsingh, p. 10; Malik, p. 4.

[49] Ivar Oxaal, Black Intellectuals Come to Power (Cambridge, Mass.: Schenkman Pub. Co., Inc., 1968), p. 162.

[50] As quoted by Bahadoorsingh, p. 10.

[51] As quoted by Williams, p. 211.

[52] As quoted by Williams, p. 213.

[53] Bahadoorsingh, p. 10.

[54] Lowenthal, West Indian Societies, p. 169; see also Niehoff and Niehoff, pp. 77 ff.

[55] Lowenthal, West Indian Societies, p. 148; Brereton, Race Relations in Colonial Trinidad, p. 186; Niehoff and Niehoff, pp. 88-89. The four castes of Hindu social life are the Brahmins (priests and teachers); the Khshatriyas (warriors and rulers); the Vaish (traders); and the Sudras (menials). See Malik, p. 31.

[56] Malik, p. 21.

[57] "West Indian Fiction and West Indian Society," Kenyon Review, 25 (Winter 1963), 133.

[58] Paul Edwards and Kenneth Ramchand, intro., The Mystic Masseur (London: André Deutsch, 1957; rpt. London: Heinemann Educational Books Ltd., 1978), p. viii; Niehoff and Niehoff, p. 73.

[59] Jayawardena, p. 24.

[60] Niehoff and Niehoff, p. 74.

[61] Niehoff and Niehoff, pp. 136 and 187; Despres, p. 96.

[62] Niehoff and Niehoff, p. 150; Malik, p. 40.

[63] Despres, pp. 101-02.

[64] Some people believe that only Hindus of low caste converted as an escape from the caste system, see Malik, pp. 39-40.

[65] Niehoff and Niehoff, p. 136.

[66] Niehoff and Niehoff, p. 150.

[67] Malik, p. 51.

[68] Jagan, pp. 150-51.

[69] Lowenthal, West Indian Societies, pp. 146-56; see also John Gaffar La Guerre, "The East Indian Middle Class

Today," in <u>Calcutta to Caroni</u>, ed. John La Guerre (London: Longman Group Ltd., 1974), p. 103.

70 "An Area of Brilliance," <u>Weekly Observer</u>, 28 November 1971, p. 8.

71 I am indebted to the following sources for information concerning Trinidad's history: Eric Williams; Selwyn Ryan; and Albert Gomes, <u>Through a Maze of Colour</u> (Trinidad: Key Caribbean Publications Ltd., 1974).

72 Ryan, pp. 76-77.

73 Ryan, pp. 77-78.

74 Ryan, p. 146.

75 Klass, pp. 199-201.

76 Ryan, p. 147.

77 Ryan, pp. 100-101.

78 Oxaal, <u>Black Intellectuals Come to Power</u>, pp. 100-1.

79 Malik, p. 83.

80 Malik, p. 93; Ryan, pp. 140-42.

81 Bahadoorsingh, p. 13.

82 Gomes, p. 237; Malik, p. 94.

83 Gomes, p. 237.

84 Malik, p. 95.

85 As quoted by Malik, p. 96.

86 Ryan, p. 171.

87 Ryan, p. 185.

88 Ryan, pp. 191-93; Malik, p. 103. Morton Klass, who observed the 1958 elections, mentions a rumor that the Maha Sabha members went to houses and asked East Indians to swear on the lota (a ceremonial vase) that they will vote for the East Indian candidate. See p. 222.

89 <u>A History of Modern Trinidad, 1783-1962</u> (London: Heinemann Educational Books Inc., 1981), p. 239; Ryan, p. 193.

90 Malik, p. 103; Morley Ayearst, "A Note on Some Characteristics of West Indian Political Parties," in The Aftermath of Sovereignty, ed. David Lowenthal and Lambros Comitas (New York: Anchor Press, 1973), p. 79 casually and generally refers to the "tendency of the East Indian elector to vote only for one of his own race," thus ignoring the fact that the same is largely true of blacks.

91 Malik, p. 116.

92 As quoted by Bahadoorsingh, pp. 16–17.

93 Ryan, pp. 272–73.

94 Malik, p. 118; see also Ryan, p. 266, note 11.

95 Ryan, p. 269, note 17.

96 Malik, pp. 116–17. Malik states that the Vice-President of the PNM once noted that she saw few "DLP faces [Indians]" at her meeting.

97 Malik, p. 117; Ryan, p. 258.

98 Ryan, pp. 266–7.

99 Brereton, A History of Modern Trinidad, p. 246.

100 Bahadoorsingh, pp. 20–23; Malik, p. 111; Ryan, p. 243.

101 As quoted by Bahadoorsingh, p. 23.

102 See, for example, Bahadoorsingh, p. 22.

103 Ryan, pp. 244–45.

104 Ryan, p. 245, note 14.

105 Brereton, A History of Modern Trinidad, p. 245.

106 Malik, pp. 110-11; Ryan, pp. 238–40.

107 Ryan, p. 240, note 3.

108 Ryan, p. 266; Bahadoorsingh, pp. 23–24; Malik, p. 112.

109 See, for example, Ryan, p. 241 and p. 289, note 56; Brereton, p. 245.

110 Ryan, pp. 241–42.

111 Malik, p. 123.

112 See, for example, Lowenthal, West Indian Societies, p. 171.

113 H. P. Singh, as quoted by Bahadoorsingh, p. 19; see also Ryan, pp. 290-91.

114 Ryan, p. 328.

115 Lowenthal, West Indian Societies, p. 151 and 172.

116 Malik, p. 36.

117 Ryan, pp. 375-77.

118 Ryan, p. 377, note 29.

119 Lewis, p. 272.

120 Jagan, pp. 182-83.

121 Despres, p. 261.

122 Despres, p. 263.

123 Despres, p. 265. See also Lewis, p. 106.

124 Lowenthal, West Indian Societies, p. 145.

125 As quoted by Lowenthal, West Indian Societies, p. 235, note 4.

126 Malik, pp. 63-67.

127 Lowenthal, West Indian Societies, p. 171.

128 Lowenthal, West Indian Societies, pp. 168-69; see also Bahadoorsingh, pp. 24-25.

129 Niehoff and Niehoff, p. 52.

130 Lowenthal, West Indian Societies, p. 166 and 171; Ryan, pp. 378-79. To Trinidadian Indians, 1969 was known as "Black Agricultural Year." Indian rural areas still remain undeveloped, see Kelvin Singh, "East Indians and the Larger Society," in Calcutta to Caroni, ed. John La Guerre, pp. 65-66.

131 Oxaal, Black Intellectuals Come to Power, p. 23.

132 Lewis, p. 225.

133 Williams, p. 278.

134 Oxaal, <u>Black Intellectuals Come to Power</u>, p. 26. La Guerre, <u>Calcutta to Caroni</u>, p. 102, believes that the early reformers failed because they refused to accept Trinidad as a plural society.

135 Williams himself, for example, has stated that "The task facing the people of Trinidad and Tobago after their Independence is to create a nation out of the discordant elements and antagonistic principles and competing faiths and rival colours," p. 278.

136 Lowenthal, <u>West Indian Societies</u>, p. 166.

137 Lowenthal, <u>West Indian Societies</u>, pp. 174-75.

138 Ramdath Jagessar, as quoted by Lowenthal, <u>West Indian Societies</u>, p. 171.

139 Lewis, pp. 279-80.

140 "By the light of a Deya," in <u>The Aftermath of Sovereignty</u>, ed. Lowenthal and Comitas, p. 285.

141 Parmasad, pp. 286-87.

142 Parmasad, p. 291.

143 Malik, pp. 58-59.

144 As quoted by Lowenthal, p. 175.

145 La Guerre, p. 102.

146 Lowenthal, <u>West Indian Societies</u>, pp. 262-63.

147 Parmasad, p. 286.

148 Williams, p. 212.

149 Lewis, p. 261. See also Roy A. Glasgow, <u>Guyana</u> (The Hague: Martinus Nijhoff, 1970), p. 97.

150 Lowenthal, pp. 165-74.

151 Despres, p. 86.

152 Malik, p. 58. He suggests that apathy is more common among Hindu elites and Indian Christians.

153 <u>The Aftermath of Sovereignty</u>, ed. David Lowenthal and Lambros Comitas, p. xiv.

[154] As quoted by Malik, pp. 62-63.

[155] M. G. Smith, p. 12.

[156] Despres, pp. 93-95; see also Klass, p. 244; Lowenthal, West Indian Societies, pp. 160-62.

[157] Malik, p. 30.

[158] As quoted by Lowenthal, West Indian Societies, p. 161.

[159] As quoted by Lewis, p. 276.

[160] Ryan, p. 381.

[161] As quoted by Ryan, p. 381; Lowenthal, West Indian Societies, p. 22.

[162] Ryan, p. 363.

[163] Lowenthal, West Indian Societies, p. 174. See also Ryan, pp. 381-83 and Malik, p. 24.

[164] Parmasad, p. 284.

[165] Malik, p. 168; Lewis, p. 225.

[166] Brereton, Race Relations in Colonial Trinidad, p. 183.

[167] Niehoff and Niehoff, pp. 65-6. See also Lowenthal, West Indian Societies, p. 162.

[168] Malik, pp. 53-54; Niehoff and Niehoff, p. 67; Oxaal, Black Intellectuals Come to Power, p. 179. Lowenthal, West Indian Societies, p. 176, cites another survey in which East Indian high school students in Trinidad admit white bias.

[169] Jagan, pp. 291-92.

[170] Despres, p. 147.

[171] Lowenthal, West Indian Societies, p. 97, pp. 257-60.

[172] Lowenthal, West Indian Societies, p. 255.

[173] Lowenthal, West Indian Societies, pp. 255-61. See also David Lowenthal and Lambros Comitas, ed. Consequences of Class and Color (New York: Anchor Press, 1973), p. xvi.

54

174 *Black Skin, White Masks* (New York: Grove Press, Inc., 1967), pp. 9-10.

175 As quoted by Lowenthal, *West Indian Societies*, p. 312. In 1969 Eric Williams was widely criticized for accepting a Companion of Honor from the queen, see Ryan, p. 340.

176 Lowenthal, *West Indian Societies*, pp. 311-13.

177 Ryan, p. 7; Malik, p. 137.

178 As quoted by Lowenthal, *West Indian Societies*, p. 253. See also Orde Coombs, ed. *Is Massa Day Dead?* (New York: Anchor Press, 1974), p. xiv.

179 Ryan, p. 367.

180 Millette, "The Black Revolution in the Caribbean," in *Is Massa Day Dead?* ed. Orde Coombs, pp. 54-56.

181 Glasgow, p. 100.

182 Lowenthal, *West Indian Societies*, p. 291. Ryan, p. 456 notes that words such as "pig" and "police brutality," long popular in the American Black Power Movement, became part of the Trinidad vocabulary.

183 Ryan, pp. 367-69.

184 Millette, p. 64.

185 As quoted by Ryan, p. 369.

186 As quoted by Ryan, p. 370.

187 As quoted by Ryan, p. 380.

188 Ryan, p. 380.

189 Ivar Oxaal, *Race and Revolutionary Consciousness* (Mass.: Schenkman Publishing Co., 1971), pp. 33-41.

190 As quoted by Lowenthal, *West Indian Societies*, p. 161.

191 As quoted by Oxaal, *Race and Revolutionary Consciousness*, p. 41.

192 R. K. Richardson, "Majority Power Would Be Better," *Trinidad Guardian*, 26 March 1970, p. 10; Timothy O. McCartney, "What is the Relevance of Black Power to the Bahamas?" in *Is Massa Day Dead?* p. 186.

[193] Lowenthal, West Indian Societies, p. 279.

[194] As quoted by Lowenthal, West Indian Societies, p. 233.

[195] Jagan, p. 362.

[196] As quoted by Lowenthal, West Indian Societies, p. 310.

[197] As quoted by Ryan, p. 349, note 13.

[198] Ceri Peach, West Indian Migration to Britain (London: Oxford University Press, 1968), p. 1.

[199] James Millette, "The Black Revolution in the Caribbean," p. 63.

[200] "V. S. Naipaul and the Uses of Literacy," Critical Quarterly, 21, No. 2 (Summer 1979), 6.

[201] Lowenthal, West Indian Societies, pp. 216-17.

Chapter II

Constraints of a West Indian Artist

"The most significant feature of West Indian life and imagination since Emancipation has been its sense of root-lessness, of not belonging to the landscape," complained the black West Indian poet Edward Brathwaite. He also declared that he and many other West Indian artists in London in the 1960's felt "rootless," having been born in a society characterized by fragmentation rather than by wholeness.[1] While West Indians of both African and Indian origin are born into a type of exile, Indians, more than blacks, are harrowed by the condition of placelessness. This is so because East Indians are not _fully_ assimilated into the mainstream of West Indian society and because they are denied any significant political voice in the system. As a member of the East Indian community in the West Indian island of Trinidad, V. S. Naipaul, who imposed a "second exile" on himself by moving to London, is saddled with the problems and responsibilities of being an <u>East Indian</u> West Indian artist writing for a foreign audience. Naipaul is alienated from many West Indians at home and abroad primarily because his works are perceived as "anti-West Indian," his standards Euro-centered, and his sensibility Brahmin/Indian. After scanning his biography, this chapter will examine this perception of Naipaul, the doubly exiled Caribbean writer from whom his fellow West Indians demand a specific philosophical commitment to the region.

In 1972 Paul Theroux categorized Naipaul as an extremely private person about whom very little is known, despite some recorded autobiographical references in The Middle Passage, An Area of Darkness, and a few articles.[2] Since that date, however, many interesting details about Naipaul's life and development as an artist have come to light, especially with the appearance of a number of pub-lished interviews and a recent autobiographical piece.[3] Born on August 17, 1932 to Brahmin Hindu parents in Chaguanas, a small predominantly Indian sugar belt area in central Trinidad, Naipaul is the grandson of an adventurous pundit (that is, a learned priest of Hinduism) who indentured himself as a teacher from Utar Pradesh, India, to work in Trinidad. Naipaul was born in the magnificent North Indian style house, or "Lion House" (so called because its terrace was decorated with a Lion statue) of the wealthy and influential Capildeo family. In 1929 Capildeo's seventh daughter, Bropatie, had married Seepersad Naipaul, a poor Brahmin sign-painter. Within a few months after his marriage, Mr. Naipaul, with no fixed profession or address, became a regular contributor of controversial articles on Indian subjects to the <u>Trinidad Guardian</u>, then under the

editorship of Gault MacGowan, who had come from the <u>London</u>
<u>Times</u> to modernize the paper. MacGowan catered to the
interests of the ignored rural Indian population and offered
fatherly advice to Mr. Naipaul, the aspiring writer. Given
the educational handicaps and discriminatory practices in
West Indian societies, entering the field of journalism was
quite an accomplishment for an East Indian at that time. In
1932, when his son V. S. Naipaul was born, Mr. Naipaul
returned to Chaguanas as the paper's local correspondent.

Seepersad Naipaul seemed to prosper, but he underwent a
tumultuous period, recounted by V. S. Naipaul in his recent
autobiography. Established in the Trinidadian East Indian
community in the 1920's was the Arya Samaj Movement, an
Indian missionary sect which proposed radical reforms, such
as the elimination of caste and of animistic practices. Mr.
Naipaul symphatized with this reformist group and wrote
good, lively stories about various controversial subjects.
The articles, however, continually antagonized conservative
Hindus, especially the Capildeos, who defended orthodox
Hinduism against this movement and against Presbyterianism.
The family was run by the two eldest sons-in-law, brothers,
who aggressively, and sometimes violently, fought for
religious preservation, political strength, and improved
facilities in the Indian community. V. S. Naipaul later
analyzed his father's role as a Chaguanas correspondent and
as a member of a close-knit family, a "totalitarian
organization":

> To belong to the family was to be in touch with
> much that was important in Indian life; or so my
> father made it. And in MacGowan's <u>Guardian</u>, Indian
> news became mainly Chaguanas news, and Chaguanas
> news was often family news. 600 AT MASS MEETING TO
> PROTEST THE ATTITUDE OF CIPRIANI. That was news,
> but it was also a family occasion: the meeting had
> been convened by the two senior sons-in-law. And
> when three days later the Chaguanas correspondent
> reported that feeling against Cipriani . . . was
> still so strong that an eleven-year-old boy had
> been moved to speak "pathetically" at another
> public gathering, MacGowan couldn't have known that
> the boy in question was my mother's younger brother
> . . . [who] became the first leader of the
> opposition in independent Trinidad. . . .
> But this closeness to the newsmakers of
> Chaguanas had its strains . . . what could be asked
> of a member of the family couldn't be asked of the
> reporter. . . . My father had to report that the
> two sons-in-law had been charged with uttering
> menaces (allegedly, a "death threat") against
> someone on the other side. . . . From being the
> reporter who could act as family herald, he became
> the reporter who got people into the paper whether

they wanted it or not; he became a man on the other side.[4]

In 1933 Mr. Naipaul gained national attention when he criticized the Hindu system of combating cattle disease, a system which recommended a superstitious goat sacrifice to the goddess Kali instead of a government-sponsored vaccination. He received an anonymous letter which predicted his death unless he performed the very ritual he had ridiculed. After much journalistic exploitation of this sensational story, he quietly yielded (perhaps because he saw the letter as a murder threat from a family member), and the sacrifice was performed on June 23 that year. (It was not until the 1970's that Naipaul learned about the incident and investigated it.) In 1934, coincidentally the year when MacGowan left the Guardian, Mr. Naipaul suffered a nervous breakdown at Montrose in his wooden house, and he resigned from the paper. Reviewing this period, Naipaul noted that his father "dangled all his life in a half dependence and half esteem" between a rich uncle by marriage and the Capildeos.[5]

The jobless correspondent, dependent on these two families, underwent a difficult and uncertain period, some of which he spent as an overseer in Cunupia and as a shopkeeper in Chase village. But in 1938 he returned to Port-of-Spain, rejoining the Guardian and later administering the Neediest Cases Fund, a Christmas project which entailed visiting the destitute and writing case histories. For several years he shifted away from and back to Port-of-Spain, from house to house belonging to the Capildeos (he was not destined to own his own until 1946). In the summer of 1943 his small book of seven short stories, Gurudeva and Other Indian Tales, was issued by Trinidad Publications. Two years later he left the Guardian for a better paying job as a social surveyor at the government's new Department of Social Welfare, but when that ministry became defunct in 1948, he once more rejoined the Guardian. He continued to write stories, but now for the B.B.C. program, Caribbean Voices. In October 1953 he died from a heart attack. His second son, V. S. Naipaul, had left Trinidad three years earlier, but already had the blueprint of his father's life to create a fictional Mr. Biswas later. More importantly, though, he had taken with him the lasting effects not only of his chaotic Trinidad childhood but also of his father's literary and journalistic influence.

"My relationship with my father is the big relationship in my life," recalls Naipaul. "When he died . . . for a time it rather broke the links with my family, largely because there was no one to write to. My father was extremely important in my childhood."[6] Growing up with a large extended family--five sisters, a brother (writer Shiva Naipaul), and an estimated fifty cousins--and constantly moving, Naipaul has confessed that for a long time he had been unwilling to face this disordered childhood, which, he later realized, was an unhappy one. His memory of his father at the family Lion House has remained vague, but he still owns one important gift from him: a small anthology, The School of Poetry, edited by Alice Meynell, with the inscription, "To Vidyadhar, From his father. Today you have reached the span of 3 years 10 months and 15 days. And I make this present to you with this counsel in addition. Live up to the estate of man, follow truth, be kind and gentle and trust God."[7] Having been taught by his father, Naipaul went to school able to read. In 1936 he started his formal education at Chaguanas Government School, formerly the Canadian Mission School, which Mr. Naipaul himself had attended. With the move to Port-of-Spain in 1938, Naipaul transferred to the Tranquility Boys' School, and, most importantly, got to know his father better. By that time, according to his count he had lived in about seven or eight different houses, all within a small area.[8] He had no special attachment to or dislike for Lion House and looked forward to the move to the city since it promised more space and new sights.[9] The move also meant possibly more exposure to the Creole world, but Naipaul remained generally confined to his own ethnic group. He explains his impressions: "The child simply understood that what was outside the large clan was somehow not 'it': it was outside; it was something else, the food would be different, the manners would be different. That was all—a sense of great difference."[10]

The pressures of the Capildeo family, the upheavals, and the battle for space followed Naipaul. He describes the disorder of each move:

> My mother's mother decided to leave Chaguanas. She bought a cocoa estate of 350 acres in the hills to the north-west of Port of Spain, and it was decided—by the people in the family who decided on such matters—that the whole family, or all its dependent branches, should move there. My mother was willing enough to be with her family again. The rest of us were not so willing. But we had to go. We had to leave the house in Port of Spain. After the quiet and order of our two years as a separate unit we were returned to the hubbub of the extended family and our scattered nonentity with it. . . .
>
> After two years we moved back to the house in Port of Spain, but only to some rooms in it. There was a period of calm, especially after my father got a job with the government and left the Guardian. But we were under pressure. More and more people from my mother's family were coming to Port of Spain, and we were squeezed into less and less space. The street itself had changed. . . .

> Disorder within, disorder without. Only my
> school life was ordered. . . .[11]

But Naipaul hated school too and found it difficult to
associate with people. He attributes this problem to an
attitude of being "always very critical, liable to too easy
a contempt," a temperament which he claims he developed from
his "defeated" father. He insists that this attitude arises
from the experience of life within a large clan: "That was
a crash course in the world. You learned about cruelty,
about propaganda, about the destructions of reputations.
You learned about forming allies. It was that kind of
background, I think, to which my father was reacting."[12]
Naipaul's temperament and personality, as reflected in his
fiction and non-fiction, will be discussed later in this
chapter.

Despite problems at home and at school, Naipaul did
well academically, although he has modestly claimed slow
development and no high marks, for example, in composition.[13] At Tranquility Boys' School his performance
earned him one of the coveted free places at the presti-
gious Queen's Royal College, which he attended from January
1942 to April 1949, specializing in French and Spanish.
Wanting to be a writer, he felt stifled in the small island,
and he was in the fourth form when he wrote a resolution to
go abroad within five years. In January 1950 he returned to
Queen's Royal as a student-teacher but left Trinidad after
six months (a year later than he had vowed), having accepted
from the government a scholarship to further his studies
abroad. Under the conditions, Naipaul could have selected
any university, but he chose Oxford and decided on a degree
in English. He has admitted that he was really not
interested in the degree but in the hope that at Oxford his
talent would be developed and discovered: "Really I went to
Oxford in order at last to write. Or more correctly, to
allow writing to come to me. . . . I had no gift. At least,
I was aware of none. . . . But I began to build my life
around the writing ambition."[14]

"The ambition of a writer," recalls Naipaul, "was given
me by my father."[15] Seepersad Naipaul not only instilled
in his son the idea that writing was a noble and worthwhile
profession but he also provided him with his first models.
At an early age Naipaul was fascinated by the contents of
his father's "bookcase-and-desk," which he curiously and
carefully inspected and soon discovered that his father was
writing stories with local setting and characters. Naipaul
asserts that the "greatest imaginative experience" of his
life occurred when he was actually involved in the process
of creating one of these comic stories, "Gurudeva," the
longest one, which his father read to him as changes were
made and as the story developed.[16] The narrative relates
the life of a Hindu youth, Gurudeva, who leaves the
Presbyterian mission school at fourteen to marry, and who,

ending up in prison, asserts his manhood: "Is orright, Bap
[Dad]. I is a man."[17] (It is a line that Naipaul will
echo in one of his own stories, "Bogart.") From his father
Naipaul received a lesson in comedy: "It ['Gurudeva'] was
comic; yet it dealt with cruelty. . . . The world of this
story of my father's was something I knew. To the pastoral
beauty of his other stories it added cruelty, and comedy
that made the cruelty just bearable."[18] Naipaul himself
describes the subjects of the seven stories, collected under
the title Gurudeva and Other Indian Tales:

> These stories celebrated Indian village life, and
> the Hindu rituals that gave grace and completeness
> to that life. They also celebrated elemental
> things, the order of the working day, the labor of
> the rice fields, the lighting of the cooking fire
> in the half-walled gallery of a thatched hut, the
> preparation and eating of food. . . . And when we
> went to the country to visit my father's own
> relations, who were the characters in these
> stories, it was like a fairy tale come to life.[19]

Indeed, Mr. Naipaul admitted to his son that the principal
characters in nearly every story were members of his own
family.[20] This close association with his father taught
Naipaul a great deal about the craft of writing comedy. A
number of studies have detailed the innumerable resemblances in characterization, plot, theme, dialogue, and
technique between Gurudeva and Naipaul's works set in
Trinidad.[21] Naipaul himself confessed that he
"cannibalized" one of this father's story, "They Named Him
Mohun," for the beginning of one of his own books.[22] But
the most important lessons were on the value of local
material and the importance of honesty.

In 1976 Naipaul convinced his London publishers to
reprint his father's stories, and in the "Foreword" which he
himself wrote, he acknowledges the work as a "valuable part
of the literature of the region," "a unique record of the
life of the Indian or Hindu community in Trinidad in the
first fifty years of the century."[23] To Naipaul the
stories show how a literature can grow from local material.
Throughout his career he has repeatedly stressed the
importance of an artist to find a "center" and to work in a
society which can stimulate him. Coming from a transplanted culture and not a rooted one, he felt handicapped
with the tradition of English literature and with a mentality which prevented him from using the name of a local
Port-of-Spain street. Referring implicity to Gurudeva,
Naipaul then acknowledges its influence in getting him
started:

Something of a more pertinent virtue was needed, and this was provided by some local short stories. These stories, perhaps a dozen in all, never published outside Trinidad, converted what I saw into 'writing'. It was through them that I began to appreciate the distorting, distilling power of the writer's art. . . . They provided a starting point for further observation; they did not trigger off fantasy.[24]

He made a more direct reference to his indebtness to his father in a 1963 interview for the Times Literary Supplement: "A great deal of my vision of Trinidad has come straight from my father. Other writers are aware that they are writing about rooted societies; his work showed me that one could write about another kind of society."[25] Above all, Mr. Naipaul showed his son how to be honest in the depiction of that society.

Naipaul learned to be courageously provocative from his father. He noted that his father wrote for and from within a Hindu community, which he sees "as a whole" and "can at times make romantic and at other times satirize." Commenting on the technique in Gurudeva, Naipaul points out its influence on him: "There is reformist passion; but even when there is shock . . . there is nothing of the protest--common in early colonial writing--that implies an outside audience; the barbs are all turned inwards. . . . I stress it because this way of looking, from being my father's, became mine: my father's early stories created my background from me."[26] The recurring theme in the stories, addressed to the Hindu community, is the limitation of the Indian world, already a decaying society, which, faced with pressure from the Creole world, cannot fulfill the dreams and satisfy the aspirations of the ambitious young. Landeg White comments on Mr. Naipaul's perception and its effect on Naipaul:

The vision of Trinidad that emerges from these stories . . . is of a place where custom and ambition, opportunity and talent, ritual and imagination, are in direct conflict; a place where ability is squandered for the sake of ancient prejudices, and where romance is finally accommodated with the dreams of escape. The ultimate effect of these stories on V. S. Naipaul was . . . to demonstrate the value of the material at hand. Their immediate influence, and of the personality behind them, was to teach him the urgency of getting away.[27]

Naipaul reported that a few abusive letters his father received complained of the damage allegedly done to the Indian community.[28] Mr. Naipaul, however, did anticipate

this hostile reaction from his readers: "I wrote what I
saw--what, in fact, I see everyday, and what I know. . . .
Perhaps many will criticize me for writing on what they may
call the ugly side of life. Well, I certainly did not set
out purposely to write on the ugly side of life."[29]   It is
a defense that Naipaul will need when his turn comes.

      After taking his B.A. degree in English at Oxford,
Naipaul went to London in 1954 and embarked seriously upon a
literary   career.   Financially   unsupported,   he   briefly
considered entering business or going to India to work, but
with no prospects, he, like several West Indian writers
before him, settled for a part-time job of editing and
broadcasting a literary program for the B.B.C. Caribbean
Service.[30]   The   Caribbean   Service   was   located   on   the
second floor of the former Langham Hotel, and Room 235,
called the Freelancer's Room, was reserved for writers, who
used the space to socialize and confer.   In this room,
enjoying the camaraderie, Naipaul wrote a story about an old
family acquaintance, Bogart, whom he had known in Trinidad.
In fact, his Trinidadian memories provided him with an
endless supply of fresh materials: "I had trained my memory
and developed a faculty of recall. . . .   I had trained
myself to an acute feeling for human character as expressed
in words and faces, gestures and the shape of bodies. . . .
I discovered I had processed and stored a great deal."[31]
Encouraged by friends who saw the Bogart manuscript, he
composed more stories with familiar Trinidadians, whom he
placed on a fictional Miguel Street in the same atmosphere
of fellowship he was then enjoying.[32]   The result, Miguel
Street (1959), which won the Somerset Maugham Award, was
completed as early as 1955.   It was in that year, too, that
Naipaul married an Englishwoman, Patricia Hale (they have
had no children).

      The period from the completion to the publication of
Miguel Street was an active and productive one for Naipaul,
who lived a part of this time on an attic floor of a large
Edwardian   house   in   Muswell   Street,   London.   The   Mystic
Masseur, which traces the rise of an ordinary man to an M.
B. E. (Member of the British Empire) in colonial Trinidad,
was published in 1957 and won the John Llewelyn Rhys
Memorial Prize. This work was followed the next year by The
Suffrage of Elvira (completed in 1955), organized around
Trinidad's 1950 elections.   Naipaul has referred to these
three light satirical comedies as his "apprenticeship"
works.   To support himself, he was simultaneously working as
a reviewer for the New Statesman and as a feature writer for
other journals.   In addition, he was well on his way with
his masterpiece, A House for Mr Biswas, a book to which he
feels the "closest."   A great part of the novel was written
during the calm period at a new address, the upper floor of
a semi-detached house at Streatham Hill.   Naipaul recalls
the serenity: "The two years spent on this novel remain the
most fulfilled, the happiest years of my life. . . .   I

thought: If someone were to offer me a million pounds on condition that I leave the book unfinished, I would turn the money down."[33] (Seven years later he would have stopped writing for much less.[34])

Despite his isolation in London, Naipaul liked the city; however, his contentment was mixed with some concern. Reviewing the first eight years in his adopted country, he found that he achieved the "Buddhist ideal of non-attachment": "I am never disturbed by national or international issues. I do not sign petitions. I do not vote. I do not march. And I never cease to feel that this lack of interest is all wrong."[35] But he was also concerned about his position as a regional writer not understood by the audience for whom he writes. More importantly, though, was his fear that he might become sterile in London unless he refreshed himself "by travel--to Trinidad, to India."[36]

Not surprisingly, then, Naipaul became a traveler. In 1960 he accepted a grant from the Trinidad government to visit the West Indies. While on that eight-month tour, he completed A House for Mr Biswas (1961), which ends the early phase of his career. He took Dr. Eric Williams' advice to write a non-fiction book about the region. The Middle Passage, severely critical of several West Indian societies, was published in 1962, the year that Naipaul made his first trip to India in search of his ancestral roots. He had come to realize that London was not the "center" he had been seeking. During his serene stay at a lakeside Kashmir hotel, he wrote, in his own words, "a compressionist novel pared to the bone,"[37] Mr Stone and the Knights Companion (1963), which won him the Hawthornden Prize. Set in England and with English characters, this short novel, using the Naipaulian theme of isolation, focuses on Mr. Stone, a sixty-two year old bachelor who marries and works on a scheme, whereby retired employees of the company, Excal, are organized to perform good deeds for their fellows, now abandoned by society. It had appeared that the work represented a permanent break from the West Indies, but after the publication of his account of his disquieting experiences in India in An Area of Darkness (1964), for which he received the Phoenix Trust Award, Naipaul returned to the familiar West Indian background.

The three books that followed are all set in the West Indies, and a note of despair becomes strong in them. In 1967 The Mimic Men was published, followed in the same year by a collection of short stories and a novella, whose name, "A Flag on the Island," is the title for the entire volume. With the setting and characters varying from English to Trinidadian, the short stories, written in the fifties and sixties, resemble the Miguel Street sketches. However, "A Flag," completed in 1965, is unlike anything Naipaul had ever done, since he was writing a story for the screen and was complying with the film company's request for a leading

66

American character, much sex and dialogue. The American, whose ship is forced to anchor off an island where he had been previously stationed, surveys the disturbing changes and colonial mimicry in the newly independent place. In The Mimic Men, written between August 1964 and July 1966, Naipaul elaborates on these problems and focuses on the familiar theme of isolation and placelessness. Well received in England, the book won the W.H. Smith Annual Literary Award, but Naipaul, much to his disappointment, had not built a wide American readership. In an interview in 1968 he speculated on the cause: "It is because the moment people hear of the Caribbean--as one publisher told me--they think of 'those crazy resort places.' . . . This is very damaging to a writer . . . to be purely regional is in fact to sink."38 During the same interview Naipaul made a premature announcement that he would write more about England, which he had grown to know better than Trinidad.

Increasingly, Naipaul was beginning to concentrate on journalism and on travel. He had written two non-fiction books, and to these he now added several short journalistic pieces for various magazines. This shift was a practical action, as he explains: "I came to the conclusion that, considering the nature of the society I come from, considering the world I have stepped into and the world which I have to look at, I could not be a professional novelist in the old sense. I realized then that my response to the world could be expressed equally imaginatively in non-fiction, in journalism: and I take my journalism extremely seriously. . . ."39 The Loss of El Dorado (1969), originally planned as a simple journalistic venture, turned out to be a remarkable construction of four centuries of West Indian history told through two seemingly unconnected yet relevant episodes. In 1970 the book was named among Time's best non-fiction works.

After completing The Loss of El Dorado, Naipaul, still afflicted with a sense of rootlessness, sold his house and said that he was leaving London permanently. However, after traveling, he returned shortly afterwards, though not entirely satisfied: "Well, I come back to England because I have all my friends here now, in London. It's the place where I operate, and my publishers are here, the magazines for which I write are here. But again I must make the point that it's not a place where I can flourish completely. It doesn't feed me."40 As subsequent chapters in this book will show, West Indians have labeled Naipaul as Euro-centered. Despite charges of his Anglophilia, however, England has been only a "commercial center" to him, or so he has claimed. His next publication, In a Free State (1971), which won the Booker Prize, shows that he continues to be concerned with the theme of restlessness and that he feels that the concept of freedom is illusory. In addition to the title novella, the work contains two stories (one involving West Indian characters in London and the other an Indian character in Washington) and two journal entries (a prologue and an epilogue). Pointing out that "In a Free State" is set primarily in Uganda with "touches of Kenya and one or two other countries," Naipaul later said that he wrote the novella before "our African 'strong man' [Idi Amin] had shown his hand," adding that he got a "fabulous roasting" since the accuracy of his predictions were not foreseen at that time.[41]

Even while steadily publishing his books, Naipaul has been traveling internationally and writing occasional journalistic pieces for such publications as the Daily Telegraph, Sunday Times Magazine and the New York Review of Books. Collected in The Overcrowded Barracoon (1972) are many of these interviews and articles, which have taken Naipaul to both familiar and new places--India, West Indies, New York, California, Tokyo, and Mauritius, the overcrowded barracoon itself. In addition, he kept in touch with home by making periodic visits, for example, to Trinidad in 1972 to his father's unhappy brother and sister. And in spite of the controversy he stirred in the Caribbean, in 1975 the University of West Indies conferred on him an honorary doctorate in literature.[42]

While his reportage and travelogues have dominated his later works, Naipaul has continued to intersperse his output with fiction. His next novel, Guerrillas (1975), returned to the West Indian scene and its politics, specifically the irrelevance of the Black Power revolutionary movement. The work won its author a wide American readership: 15,000 hard-bound copies were sold, four times as many as any one of his other books.[43] Naipaul had done a Sunday Times article, "The Killings in Trinidad," on the career of Trinidadian Black Power leader, Abdul Malik, or Michael X, on whom the fictional story of Guerrillas is based. Similarly, an article, "A New King for the Congo," on Mobutu appears to be the germ for Naipaul's latest novel A Bend in the River (1979), a work in which he manages to express all his major concerns, from rootlessness as seen in the Indian character Salim to the conditions of ex-colonial societies. Between Guerrillas and A Bend in the River is sandwiched India: A Wounded Civilization (1977), a collection of related essays which grew from Naipaul's visit to India from August 1975 to October 1976, the time of Indira Gandhi's Emergency rule. "The Killings" and "A New King," along with "Conrad's Darkness" and "The Return of Eva Peron," all written in 1972 and 1973, were collected in one volume in 1980. (Except for "The Killings," these essays previously appeared in the New York Review of Books.)

Increasingly, then, Naipaul has become a world patrolman, who has gained a correspondingly wide audience. In 1980 he won the Bennett Award for his "outstanding accomplishments as a novelist and man of letters."[44] Among the Believers (1981), which records his impressions of a seven-month tour of four Islamic countries--Iran,

Pakistan, Malaysia, and Indonesia--and <u>Finding the Center</u>
(1984), which contains a report on his visit to the Ivory
Coast, expanded his territory even further. In 1983 to his
innumerable prizes and awards collected thus far, he
received the Jerusalem Prize and an honorary doctorate from
Cambridge University.[45] In a 1979 interview he said
again: "I began as a comic writer and still consider myself
one. In middle age now, I have no higher literary ambition
than to write a piece of comedy that might complement or
match this early book [<u>A House</u>]."[46] His literary career
still in progress, Naipaul remains journalistically active.
     In spite of the broadening scope of his work, however,
Naipaul's specialty has always been the West Indies, a place
which has found its way into most of his fiction and
non-fiction. Even those who contend that it is no longer
possible to view him as a Caribbean writer admit that his
sensibility is saturated with the West Indies.[47] Naipaul
himself has acknowledged the influence of his background:
"I imagine that one is really shaped by everything that
occurs when one is young. I think I was greatly made by my
childhood and by my background and naturally therefore by
Trinidad."[48] In 1975 Landeg White observed that Naipaul
is "still a writer from the West Indies writing largely
about the West Indies for an audience abroad."[49] Although
Naipaul has since added several non-West Indian books to his
<u>oeuvre</u>, the statement still holds. St. Lucian born Anthony
Boxill has also stressed Naipaul's closeness to West Indian
rather than to Indian, British or European tradition.
Boxill concludes: "Far from being clearly 'extra-
Caribbean'. . . . Naipaul's sources can roughly speaking be
divided into two categories: those from his general reading
which he often uses ironically to help him make a point, and
those from the West Indies, notably his father, West-Indian
history, and the calypso, which have both shaped and
inspired his vision."[50] Naipaul, for his part, has put a
distance between himself and the British literary scene--for
example, by saying, "I can't be interested in the latest
English extravaganza. I can't be interested in a novel
about the men in London. I can't--it's too far from me."[51]
     Whatever the West Indian region is to Naipaul, however,
it is not home. Nor can any other place be, he has
eventually learned. Bruce King has argued that Naipaul
initially thought of India, not England as home, and
Consuelo Lopez de Villegas has called attention to a growing
obsession with the theme of exile after Naipaul's
disappointment with India.[52] As an East Indian in
Trinidad, or as an East Indian West Indian Englishman in
India, or an East Indian West Indian in England, Naipaul has
always been displaced and restless, a condition which the
unique East Indian West Indian background can explain.
Currently keeping two residences--a small London flat and a
house in the countryside near Salisbury--he continues,

through necessity, not choice, to use London as his base.
He lives in isolation, stoically accepting the sad fact that
his relationships with friends have all "withered."[53]
Thus, twice displaced--from India and from the West
Indies--Naipaul remains a citizen of the world, belonging to
no land and every land. A. J. Gurr's assessment is accurate
when he suggests that Naipaul's "present identity is not so
much that of an exile, which would presume a home to be
exiled from, as a permanent alien."[54]

As a lonely exiled artist in London, Naipaul found a
parallel between his life and that of another exiled artist,
Polish born Joseph Conrad, who had used that city as his
base more than half a century ago. In an appreciative
essay, "Conrad's Darkness" (1974), Naipaul related that his
father introduced him early to Conrad and to such stories as
"The Lagoon" and "Karain," which he admired.[55] Even
though he found Conrad generally difficult and even though
he complained that Conrad lacked the "true fantasy of a
novelist," Naipaul learned as much from Conrad as he did
from Mr. Naipaul.[56] Like Naipaul, Conrad also experienced
a traumatic childhood. Spending some of his early years in
Russia in exile with his politically active parents, he was
orphaned at eleven and placed under the guardianship of his
maternal uncle. He chose not to follow the route of his
relatives in the seemingly futile struggle for Polish
independence; rather, he found escape in books, in France,
in the sea and subsequently in England, where after
contemplating a number of professions, he eventually settled
as an introspective writer. Conrad, like Naipaul, was not
only a late bloomer but also a secluded alien. Both
remained detached from the political struggle at home and
from the mainstream of English intellectual life. In
addition, when they established themselves as writers, they
were reviled in their respective countries as betrayers who
abandoned their motherland in favor of their adopted
country. It is, however, in the practice of his craft that
Naipaul saw Conrad as his guru.

Conrad and Naipaul had to overcome the hindrances of
their limited background and the difficulties of launching
their literary careers. Naipaul has repeatedly echoed
Conrad's complaint that

> Other writers have some starting point. Some-
> thing to catch hold of. . . . They lean on
> dialect--or on tradition--or on history--or on the
> prejudice or fad of the hour; they trade upon some
> tie or conviction of their time--or upon the
> absence of these things--which they can abuse or
> praise. But at any rate they know something to
> begin with--while I don't.[57]

Experiencing and understanding this problem, Naipaul
observed that "It is the complaint of a writer who is
missing a society, and is beginning to understand that
fantasy or imagination can move freely with a closed and
ordered world."[58] As he explained, he himself has had to
grapple with the shortcomings of his origin: "It came to me
that the great novelists wrote about highly organized
societies. I had no such society; I couldn't share the
assumptions of the writers; I didn't see my world reflected
in theirs. My colonial world was more mixed and secondhand,
and more restricted."[59] And although he mentally pictured
the setting of "The Lagoon" in some distant place rather
than Trinidad, he later found his sensations captured in a
landscape description in Conrad's "Karain." In fact,
Naipaul gradually discovered himself and his vision of the
world in Conrad:

> I found that Conrad . . . had been everywhere
> before me. Not as a man with a cause, but a man
> offering . . . a vision of the world's half-made
> societies as places which continuously made and
> unmade themselves, where there was no goal. . . .
> Conrad's value to me is that he is someone who
> sixty or seventy years ago meditated on my world, a
> world I recognize today. I feel this about no
> other writer of the century.[60]

He is especially touched that Conrad, unlike other contemporary writers, was able to view the Third World with
seriousness and to treat Asiatics with understanding and
sympathy.[61]

When Naipaul commenced writing in the 1950's, there was
no established West Indian writer who was able to offer him
the type of inspiration he received from Conrad's works.
Most Caribbean writers were in self-imposed exile trying to
cope with problems similar to Naipaul's. It is useful to
understand the climate of the West Indian literary scene in
order to place Naipaul within its context; hence, the
following pages will focus on the burdens and
responsibilities of a West Indian writer.

West Indian literature is young. In fact, it was only
in the late 1930's that the true West Indian novel, written
by a West Indian about West Indian scenes, emerged, and only
in the 1950's that West Indian literature as a body of work
was identified.[62] The literature of the eighteenth and
nineteenth centuries appeared mainly in the form of either
journals and diaries (written by foreigners) and stilted
verses imitative of old English forms. After the Second
World War, a type of West Indian literature developed,
influenced by the rise of nationalism, the West Indian
Federation movement, the rejection of colonialism and the
struggle for political independence.[63] In addition,
during the 1940's and 1950's, several literary magazines and

programs (for example, the publications <u>Bim</u> in Barbados, <u>Focus</u> in Jamaica, and <u>Kyk-over-al</u> in Guyana, and the B.B.C. radio program "Caribbean Voices") contributed to a growing interest in local literature.[64] In spite of this surge, however, the West Indian artist, intent on making writing his profession, was, and still is, faced with several discouraging, even insurmountable obstacles.

Because of the smallness and poverty of the region, the local market is economically discouraging to writers who have no other source of income. The serious reading public is proportionally much smaller than that, for example, in the United States or England. Mervyn Morris, a Jamaican poet and critic, blames the region's high illiteracy rate and suggests that the institution of slavery taught blacks to copy the materialistic values of the idle white elite society, whose major concern was to make money and enjoy sensual pleasures in the warm islands.[65] Whether this is so or not, it appears that West Indians have conditioned themselves to believe that literature is a subject to be studied for examinations only. At any rate, with the total Caribbean population only about three to five million and with an estimated 30% unemployed, the readership is naturally too small to sustain a full-time artist.[66] Barbadian poet and novelist George Lamming observes that the common people are preoccupied with making a living and "when a man is really rummaging for bread, you can't be too hard on him when he says, 'I haven't the time for books.'"[67] Since very few individuals purchase books for mere pleasure, a writer can expect his books to be sold in the West Indies primarily to libraries and to students whose curriculum specifies his works.

West Indians generally turn to movie theaters, radio serials, and to popular culture instead of books to engage their free time. From African culture arose a stong oral tradition as evident in story-telling (especially of yarns involving the Ashanti spidergod, Anansi) and in calypsos. In these forms of entertainment English dialect became a staple. For decades the folk poetry of Louise Bennett and the calypsos of Francisco Slinger ("The Mighty Sparrow"), both capitalizing on social issues and natural speech idiom, have been providing oral entertainment regionally. And even though held only once a year, Carnival has become one of the most important forms of cultural expression for black West Indians. It has been surmised that books suggest "the lonely act of reading," and that West Indians choose to enjoy their art as a "communal activity."[68] In fact, Naipaul himself has scoffed at West Indians who "prefer their reggae a thousand times over" his books.[69] Generally, Caribbean artists supplement their income by working as teachers, journalists, broadcasters or panelists on television talk shows.[70] This circumstance, in turn, restricts the creative growth of writers.

In addition to the problem of small readership, writers
in the West Indies are not treated respectably or seriously
unless they have the stamp of foreign, preferably English,
approbation. This propensity to regard anything local as
inferior has been noted by several commentators, even by
Naipaul. West Indian literature (especially West Indian
dialect) and local music (for example, the calypso) did not
receive middle-class endorsement until recently. Edward
Baugh comments on this attitude, which has its roots in
self-contempt taught during colonialism: "There are still
'educated' people among us who believe that literature, like
history ('real' literature, 'real' history), must be
British; and even the most enlightened of us find it hard to
reject beliefs fed into us from birth."[71] Although there
is now a tendency in some circles to overrate local talents
or efforts as a form of encouragement, general underrating
continues. Because of these problems--the small percentage
of serious readers and the inferiority complex--publishers
are reluctant to make a commercial investment in literature
in the West Indies.

In frustration West Indian artists are constantly
driven into exile in places such as London, New York, Paris,
making the bulk of West Indian literature a literature of
exile written by "absentee West Indians."[72] It was
natural, therefore, for Naipaul to leave Trinidad, where, as
he reflectively wrote in The Middle Passage, the only
lucrative professions were those of law and medicine, and
the most successful men were in finance and commerce.[73]
All of his works, of course, have been written and published
away from home, making him, so to speak, a writer in
self-imposed exile. He himself explained the reason for his
emigration to London:

> An artist needs to be nourished, needs an audience
> and a response. . . . A writer like myself has no
> society, because one comes from a very small island
> which hardly provides an audience, and one's books
> are published in London because one of the great
> legacies of imperialism is that the
> English-speaking world is divided between New York
> and London.[74]

Naipaul has claimed that he could not carry on the much-
needed dialogue with his society since the "primitive
island" of Trinidad has "gone back to the bush," and the
bush is "not very propitious to literature."[75] At the
1971 Conference on Commonwealth Literature held in Kingston,
Jamaica, he confessed that he could not be stimulated to
produce in the culturally sterile islands.[76] Delivering
the keynote address at the 1975 Symposium of East Indians in
the Caribbean, he suggested that because of the destitution
of the society, the West Indian writer either becomes dry or
courts political writing.[77]

Arguing that artists emigrate for reasons besides poor
publishing or economic opportunities, some commentators call
attention to the sterile environment about which writers
often express concern. Mervyn Morris has pointed out that
in the islands, films arrive late, play productions are not
as plentiful or as good as those in developed countries,
air-mail subscriptions to scholarly journals are too
expensive, the libraries are inadequate for the needs of the
scholarly, and bookstores do not carry current books.[78]
Under these conditions the creative writer is culturally
isolated from the rest of the world. In <u>Writers in Exile</u>
Andrew Gurr attributes the move of writers from colonies to
the metropolis to the need for artistic freedom and
intellectual expansion:

> In the small community art tends to be
> conservative, traditional, conformist. Artistic
> freedom rules only in the metropolis. . . .
> [Artists] leave the small, static community for the
> metropolis to see what lies on the new horizon, to
> learn more of what they have sampled through the
> media and to create art for themselves in the
> greater freedom of the anonymous darkness away from
> home.[79]

Whatever the reason--economic necessity or artistic or
personal advantages--by the mid-twentienth century there was
a definite pattern of emigration by West Indian writers
seeking their fortunes abroad.

The migration complex did not go unnoticed or unpro-
tested in the islands. As early as 1952, Errol Hill, a
Trinidadian poet and playwright, warned that unless writers
are supported to the same extent that the movement toward
political identity is supported, many of them would continue
to abandon the region.[80] Indeed, in the 1950's London had
become the West Indian literary capital, luring such
talented writers as Edgar Mittelholzer, Samuel Selvon,
George Lamming, Jan Carew, Roger Mais, Wilson Harris, and
Andrew Salkey.[81] Recognizing this phenomenon, Naipaul, in
1960, observed that "It's got so misleading that Angus
Wilson wrote the other day about West Indian writers having
to flee to England, because of racial persecution."[82] In
1966 the Caribbean Artists' Movement (CAM) was launched to
foster closer ties among exiled West Indian artists in
London. In the West Indies, however, as Bill Carr notes,
nationalists frequently have misgivings about artists who
opt for emigration:

> Unfortunately . . . the exile has been greeted with
> only minority sympathy in the West Indies itself.
> Far too much assertive language is heard about
> "sell-out," "betrayal," "doing us an injustice" and
> so on--a purely nationalist reaction, which has

nothing to do with genuinely critical engagement with what the writers have attempted.[83]

Thus, whatever their achievements abroad, West Indian exiled artists are criticized for abandoning their country and shirking their responsibility.

Much to the discouragement of the exiled writers, readers in their adopted country often view them as exotic aliens. The issue seems more complicated when a writer leaves the Third World to reside in a developed country. D. H. Lawrence, Ernest Hemingway, Ezra Pound, James Joyce, and Joseph Conrad were all, for example, exiled writers; however, as Naipaul notices, people "would not ask Hemingway why he left his own provincial town, they would not ask Pound why he left the Middle West, but they will always ask the man from what they accept as an inferior society."[84] So sensitive is Naipaul about this distinction that in 1981 when he was asked about his cultural belonging, he snapped, "Why do you ask _me_ that question? You wouldn't ask Hemingway whether he came from Indiana or Michigan. I left my little island of Trinidad over thirty years ago, and now you decide to hold me up as a provincial, as an exotic. Am I being too abrupt?"[85] Third World artists are aware that discrimination confines them to a separate category and thus limits their marketability.

In the metropolis the exiled writers may be faced with other obstacles. They are more inspired, confident, and secure if they confine themselves to their unique native material. However, because of their dependence on foreign publishers and readers, they soon discover that if they are to carry universal appeal and to have feedback from their audience, they must stop being regional writers. In "London" (1958), Naipaul observed that his early social comedies have not been understood by readers unfamiliar with the West Indies. In addition to the problem of dialect, critics have been accustomed to reading about non-Europeans as depicted by Europeans. The criticisms made about his Trinidadian works, Naipaul complained, would not have been made about a comic French or American novel. He claimed that he could cross the regional barrier by writing about sex, about an English or American character, or about race, but after consideration, he rejected these options—at least at that time.[86] It was in 1963 that Naipaul tried his hand at his first English novel. With specific reference to this work, Andrew Gurr argues that when the exile writes about a foreign environment, the result is weaker and betrays "effort being applied to secondary priorities, with a consequent loss of sensitivity."[87] It is true that in order to accommodate a foreign audience, exiled writers are unfortunately forced to sacrifice the rich local flavor of their West Indian experiences. Sometimes, as is the case with Mittelholzer and Naipaul, after a brief exploration of foreign material, the artists continue to write about a

Caribbean setting for a foreign audience. Or, they may shift their concentration, as Selvon did, to the study of the West Indian immigrant in the adopted country.

West Indian artists may also be handicapped because they have no literary tradition of their own. Naipaul observed that having a tradition helps and that while the English language was his, the tradition was not. The literature was like an "alien mythology." He cited a common West Indian complaint: "There was, for instance, Wordsworth's notorious poem about the daffodil. A pretty little flower, no doubt; but we had never seen it. Could the poem have any meaning for us? . . . [English novels] I set in Trinidad, accepting, rejecting, adapting and peopling in my own way."[88] Convinced that his material was not hallowed by a tradition and embarrassed about using local setting for a foreign audience, Naipaul did not commence writing until he was nearly twenty-three. He compares himself to a French or an English writer of the same age: "He wrote against a background of knowledge. I couldn't be a writer in the same way, because to be colonial, as I was, was to be spared knowledge. It was to live in an intellectually restricted world; it was to accept those restrictions."[89] Naipaul has also explained that a large society permits artists more freedom and possibilities; for example, in giving a character a job, the artist in England or France can select from ten thousand kinds of jobs, whereas in Mauritius from eighty types only.[90]

Opinion is divided as to whether exiled writers, distanced from their backgrounds, are at an advantage or a disadvantage in writing about their homes. West Indian author and political analyst, C. L. R. James, has repeatedly and emotionally called for better conditions to attract Caribbean writers to return home or publish at home. In an article "Home is Where They Want to be," James argues that West Indian artists are desperate for an opportunity to develop their talents at home and that necessary steps must be taken to bring the writers home. "If we don't," James asserts, "they are going to suffer and with them we and the world. It is beginning to happen already. You can see it in the writing of . . . Vidia Naipaul."[91] On the other hand, George Lamming questions the wisdom of repatriation of writers: "They [writers] are not soldiers; and James has not seriously considered the question: what are you bringing them back to?"[92] In another article "The Disorder of Vidia Naipaul," James contends that Naipaul's "disorder" and "sickness" result from absence from home:

> If Vidia were in constant contact with West Indians today, a man so sharp-eyed and so sensitive would be aware of the contending currents in West Indian life. He would write about the contemporary West Indians like one of us, not like an interested and observant stranger.[93]

However, noting that Naipaul composed in London his first
four Trinidadian novels, Andrew Gurr claims that distance
lends the artist perspective and insight.[94] And Mervyn
Morris suggests that migration offers not only greater
objectivity but also a lesser temptation to be documentary.[95]

Admittedly, if exiled artists continue to write about
their homeland, they need constant nourishment; otherwise,
their works would lose freshness. Naipaul's The Mimic Men
and Guerrillas, for example, as Gerald Guinness notices,
lack the "passionately close attention of the insider"[96]
characteristic of the earlier Trinidadian novels, such as
Miguel Street, The Mystic Masseur, The Suffrage of Elvira,
and A House for Mr Biswas. Recognizing the fact that
artists eventually become parched through absence from their
homes, the Trinidadian government, following the Jamaican
practice, offered in 1960 "refresher" fellowships to writers
who have gained international recognition. It was such an
award that Naipaul accepted when he had just finished his
four early works, which are not as critical of his society
as his later writing turned out to be. Derek Walcott, C. L.
R. James, and others applauded the gesture of the
government.[97] Ironically it was during his fellowship
period that Naipaul wrote The Middle Passage (1962), the
work which alienates him most from Caribbean readers.

National consciousness and pride, along with a
rejection of European values, appear to be important West
Indian criteria in assessing a literary work. Kenneth
Ramchand has observed that "in an area of deprivation,
longing and rootlessness, where so many people are
inarticulate, the novelist may find himself tempted into
passionate documentary or criticized for adopting prescribed
stances."[98] As early as the 1950's the controversy about
the role of propagandistic documentary erupted. In 1953,
for example, Kathleen McColgan noted:

> Most writing coming from the West Indies today is
> documentary, and there is nothing wrong with that.
> But in the rather widespread effort to profane all
> that was considered sacred in European civiliza-
> tion, to try to reduce to air all the solid values
> upon which literature has been based for the past
> three thousand years . . . is to rob us of those
> spiritual values that make creative work of any
> kind a positive and personal experience as distinct
> from reporting or propaganda.[99]

McColgan further suggested that "strident nationalism
belongs to the propaganda pamphlet and poster," not to art.
Present-day West Indian assessments of Naipaul show that the
controversy has become even more heated in a post-
Independence atmosphere.

West Indians generally view themselves as underdogs and strongly believe that any criticism, however warranted, could tarnish the international image of their ability to manage their affairs satisfactorily. In his introductory remarks at a panel discussion on Naipaul in 1976, John Figueroa, a Jamaican critic, addressed this problem:

> It is easy to understand, but impossible to accept, why nationalist, leftist, "conservative" and "progressive" critics do not wish to have writers around who will expose, in a devastating way, the real weakness of a society, and the pretentious posturings of those who would hold themselves to be somehow (for the benefit of the nation and the people?) exempt from ridicule.[100]

In dwelling on the negative effects of criticisms, West Indians often fail to realize that honest, constructive criticisms can be equally beneficial.

The writer who ventures to denounce his society is regarded as a disloyal trouble-maker, or in the words of Sparrow's popular Caribbean calypso "Prophet of Doom," "a prophet of doom and gloom," an epithet used in reference to Naipaul.[101] Challenging the writings of C. L. R. James, Naipaul and his brother, Shiva, John Patterson warns of betrayal: "In the final analysis, these three established writers will be held responsible for seeking to discredit their country in its genuine attempt to find an identity in a world which today is being torn apart by man's ego, racial hatred and eternal quest for power."[102] Patterson believes that Naipaul's criticisms of Trinidad could discredit the newly independent island which seeks to establish its identity in an already complicated and unfair world. Many critics see Naipaul as an embarrassment to the region, or as a treacherous, disgruntled family member who unsympathetically "tells the neighbors." Trinidadian poet Eric Roach argues: "He [Naipaul] cannot understand that we accept the facts of our history and the reality of our situation and we are moving out of the wasteland of human degradation into a world of our own ordering."[103] In short, a widely-held view is that the brutal history of the Caribbean and the effort to create a new identity should bring to the criticisms of the region some degree of respectful sensitivity.

This argument, a political one, is based on the premise that all artists ought to be representatives for their nations and should project their society in a favorable manner. Trevor Sudama disagrees: "An artist can have no such limitations. He interprets the world as he sees it. He has license to be savage and brutal or sympathetic and understanding."[104] Similarly, referring specifically to the tendency of academics and politicians to deny the reality of the antagonism between Indians and blacks and to boast of unity during Carnival, a writer from the Trinidadian journal <u>Moko</u> supports the artist's freedom to disagree:

> It is the business of the writer to see what others cannot see, or refuse to see. His prime concern is with things as they are. Where the politician discerns unity or the likelihood of racial harmony, the serious writer cannot help seeing discord, and the continued existence of discord. Naipaul, inspite [sic] of all the antipathy he arouses, and barring a few wild inaccuracies in "The Middle Passage", remains our most honest analyst. . . . What this sick society needs so badly is laceration.[105]

And Bill Carr, a critic of European descent but one who has lived in the West Indies for over twenty years, vehemently denounces the idea that nationalism should prescribe the function and mode of artists. He warns of the danger in having a community which does not safeguard the value of a personal viewpoint.[106] However, there is no question that many Caribbean critics appear to be interested in a one-sided literature.

Naipaul has always rejected the notion that artists are obliged to show a political commitment to their country. As early as 1956 he declared his interest in "honest" writing, and in a 1960 interview with the Jamaican <u>Gleaner</u> he asserted that creative writers should not be caught up in the tide of nationalism.[107] Reviewing the published proceedings of the 1964 ACLALS Conference, Naipaul noted: "Mr. Achebe says that his own purpose is 'to help my society regain its belief in itself and put away the complexes of the years of denigration and self-denigration.' Such drive might produce good novels. But the attitude is political and one's sympathy with it can only be political." To Naipaul, the "writer has his function; the academic or the nationalist has his."[108] He has refused to follow the trend to exalt the West Indian region and to present a cosmetic view of its condition to the world. Australian critic Landeg White notes that Naipaul's refusal to identify with local nationalist fervor seems to his fellow West Indians a betrayal. Naipaul's works, White contends, have always been subjected to political rather than to literary judgments.[109]

West Indian critics used the 1971 Commonwealth Conference as a forum to debate the obligation and responsibilities of artists. Many participants called on exiled writers to shed their Euro-centric outlook and to return home in order to establish their roots among the folk or the illiterate peasantry. Barbadian poet Edward Brathwaite strongly argued that it is the artists' responsibility to focus on social, not aesthetic problems. The goal could not

be accomplished unless writers abandon their ivory towers
and identify with the common people. Naipaul, on the other
hand, rejected as "romantic rubbish" the idea that
writers--already educationally alienated from the ordinary
masses--would improve their work should they return home.
He maintained that it is the destitute society which has
initially driven artists into exile.[110] As Bernth
Lindfors observes, the Conference demonstrated that the
majority of West Indian critics link art to a social and
political purpose and that they reject Naipaul and the few
who argued that art should be divorced from political
commitment:

> Naipaul and his views were energetically attacked
> by West Indians and Afro-Americans . . . but found
> some support among delegates who recoiled from the
> notion that literary art must be socially commit-
> ted to have any validity. . . . This discussion,
> like a lopsided game of ping-pong, ricocheted back
> and forth between the few who favored art for art's
> sake and the many who insisted on art for
> revolution's sake. The revolutionaries were
> clearly not a silent majority.[111]

The debate continues today with the same intensity and is
vividly reflected in West Indian reception to Naipaul.
     Naipaul has referred to the lively 1971 Conference as
"a political demonstration in bad taste."[112] In fact, it
was more than bad taste, for it was here that in the heat of
verbal exchanges an overzealous West Indian nationalist in
the audience threatened to shoot him.[113] Observers at the
Conference attribute Naipaul's hostile reception to the fact
that the people were not in the mood for any Naipaulian
brand of pessimism about their future. Members of the
audience had just been discussing topics such as "the
relevant use of a Creative Arts Centre, socialism, urban
violence, reggae, dread [locks], black power, black resur-
gence. . . ."[114] Moreover, the memory of Naipaul's
denunciation of the black islanders in "Power?" (1970) was
apparently still fresh.
     It is sometimes argued that because of his apparent
lack of sensitivity and his detachment from the Caribbean,
Naipaul has been unfavorably compared with artists who are
of lesser merit but who have sought to romanticize the West
Indies and their people. While a number of West Indian
exiled writers, such as George Lamming, Wilson Harris, and
Samuel Selvon have also criticized the shortcomings of their
society, their works show a strong commitment to and
optimism about the region.[115] The same cannot be said of
Naipaul. Arthur Drayton makes a point of this difference:

> It can be claimed for Lamming and Selvon . . . that
> their criticisms (explicit and implicit) of the
> West Indies have not destroyed their love for and
> attachment to the native land. Indeed, their
> criticisms and concern derive from that love and
> faith. Naipaul's earlier novels suggest that this
> is also true for him. . . . But then comes The
> Middle Passage . . . and in this book he savages
> the Caribbean.[116]

Drayton's implicit contention that Naipaul's blistering
attacks on the Caribbean demonstrates lack of love for the
region is not atypical of West Indian sentiment. For
example, Wayne Brown, who compares Naipaul to other writers,
notes: "Both James and Lamming, writing from England, have
affirmed and reaffirmed . . . that the West Indies remain
the most cherished part of the earth to them."[117] The
question is whether bitterness could not be derived from
concern. In a 1979 interview, Naipaul explained that "it is
not pleasant to see the place where you were born destroyed,
and that is the bottom of it."[118] In the same interview
he emphatically stated that his books grow not out of
contempt, but out of concern."[119]

Naipaul's isolation from fellow West Indians, however,
also stems partly from different approaches in handling
racial issues. In early West Indian literature, East
Indians were merely marginal in fiction, as they were, for
example, in Claude McKay's Banana Bottom (1933). Other West
Indian authors such as Mittelholzer and Harris have focused
on Indians, but Selvon's A Brighter Sun is credited as being
the "earliest West Indian novel to isolate the
Indian-African question as a major theme."[120] However, in
a lecture "West Indian Literature as the Expression of
National Cultures," delivered in 1983 at the John Hopkins
University, Kenneth Ramchand suggested that Selvon papers
over areas of distrust between Indians and blacks and does
not explain what Tiger (the main character) is to do with
his Indianness while he is in the process of becoming a
Trinidadian. The motto "all o' we is one," Ramchand
contended, does not mean that West Indians have to melt into
one; entry into Creole culture should not require
abandonment of Indian culture. Ramchand further noted that
since West Indian writers based their novels on groups known
to them, Indians have remained either peripheral or
unrealistically delineated in the works of non-Indians, for
example, in Lamming's Of Age and Innocence (1958). In
Ramchand's opinion, no West Indian novel, except for Earl
Lovelace's The Dragon Can't Dance (1979), has successfully
handled the issue of racial integration.[121] Naipaul
treats the theme of Indian/Creole relations but not with
optimism, a treatment that disappoints Caribbean readers.
Furthermore, he demonstrates a lack of sympathy with the
movement of black awareness in literature. This attitude

contributes to the hostility many black West Indians feel toward Naipaul.

Because of the exploitation of blacks under slavery and because of the subsequent emaciation of their culture, West Indians expect their literature to recognize African roots and culture. The Jamaican Rastafarians are the group principally responsible for the rise of black consciousness and the apocalyptic vision of a paradisiacal return to Africa. Marcus Garvey's followers and the Rastafarians, who refuse to participate in or cooperate with the social and political structure of "Babylon," read Ethiopian Emperor Selassie's coronation as the fulfillment of their leader's prophecy about the redemption of New World blacks from bondage. Louis James describes this mid-twentieth century movement as creating a "bizarre myth of an Africa that does not exist and that never was."[122] And Naipaul himself disapprovingly writes of the West Indian "vision of the black millennium" and of those who "await crusades and messiahs."[123] This quasi-religious cult, however, which has often sought and received support from the University of the West Indies, has been credited with exerting a significant influence on the literature of the Caribbean.

The creation of the négritude literary movement in the West Indies is often traced to the rise of Haitian nationalism, to Pan-Africanism, to Garvey's movement (the Universal Negro Improvement Association), and to Rastafarianism--all of which were concerned with refashioning the battered image of blacks and Africa.[124] Kenneth Ramchand explains that the literary manifestations which accompanied these movements share the following:

> a celebration of Africa as a cultural matrix; a favourable interpretation of the African past; a pride in Blackness; a contrast between a harmonious way of life and a decadent White civilization lost in materialism; and a joyful proclamation of the sensuous and integrated African or Negro personality. The word 'négritude' has come to imply this complex of facts, attitudes and myths especially as they appear in the works of literature by Negroes throughout the Caribbean.[125]

The négritude approach, or the neo-African theory, found its strongest proponents in Aimé Césaire, the Martinician poet; Léopold Sédhar Senghor, the Senegalese theorist and statesman; and Jahnheinz Jahn, the German theorist.

It is Césaire's famous poem "Cahier d'un retour au pays natal" (circulating in 1938) from which the concept of "négritude" became popularized. Césaire is concerned not with protest against past injustices or revenge against oppressors, but with an affirmation of pride in blackness or an ennobling of African heritage.[126] "Cahier" traces a movement from disillusionment with the Caribbean to a vision

of rebirth and regeneration, a progression which occurs in
Edward Brathwaite's trilogy--<u>Rights of Passage</u> (1967), <u>Masks</u>
(1968), and <u>Islands</u> (1969)--which Césaire's poem may have
influenced and with which it is often compared.[127]

Brathwaite, more than any other writer from the
English-speaking Caribbean, has advocated the négritude
concept. In his trilogy Brathwaite celebrates the discovery of his African heritage and rejects the parroting of
European culture. He employs a unique "black style":

> The style is made up of unusual rhythms, inventive
> stanzaic forms, odd placements of rhymes, many puns
> and other forms of word play associated with black
> speech. References and allusions to New World
> black culture, the use of African words and various
> black dialects, and the parody of expressions
> associated with 'bondage' contribute to the idiom
> of 'black consciousness'.[128]

One critic directly links Brathwaite's stylistic developments to the Rastafarians' speech rhythms and rejection of
European standards.[129] Whatever its exact literary roots,
many black West Indian critics hail the movement of
négritude as a welcome breakthrough since they regard it as
advocating independence from English literary tradition and
values, which are deemed inapplicable in measuring West
Indian characters. West Indians, such as Gordon Rohlehr and
Elizabeth Nunez-Harrell, have charged Naipaul with using
England as the norm in measuring--contemptuously--the
distortions in West Indian society.[130] Referring to
Naipaul's "at once acute and limited perception,"
Nunez-Harrell argues: "Naipaul's emphasis is on the failure of the English literary tradition to impart <u>importance</u>,
that is significance, to his subject matter, and not on its
failure to express the fundamental humanity of the Negro and
to assess the richness of his culture."[131] Many West
Indians see an urgent need to change this orientation.

In his essay "Jazz and the West Indian Novel,"
published in three parts, Brathwaite, using a form of the
neo-African theory, tries to formulate a new aesthetic for
judging West Indian literature, that is, an alternative
critical tool which places emphasis more on the African
expression than on the European cultural tradition.[132]
Defining jazz as "the emancipated Negro's music . . . an
example of a living, active folk expression on easy terms
with all the world," Brathwaite champions the West Indian
jazz novel since jazz has already gained widespread
recognition and since it could be an easy replacement for
European literary forms. Brathwaite theorizes that the jazz
novel will deal with a "specific, clearly-defined folktype
community," and "will try to express the essence of this
community through its form." As an example of the most
successful type of jazz novel, he points to Roger Mais's

Brother Man (1954), but he concedes that the work is "far
from perfect." Moreover, he admits that in the West Indies
there is only one other jazz novel: Andrew Salkey's A
Quality of Violence (1959), and he attributes the scarcity
of the genre to the British orientation of West Indians.
Although Brathwaite acknowledges that Naipaul's A House for
Mr Biswas contains a sense of community, he does not
classify the novel as a jazz novel since it focuses more on
ego exploration. The same, Brathwaite observes, is even
more true of Naipaul's The Mimic Men. Similarly, he
excludes Lamming and Harris as jazz novelists because their
concern lies with individual consciousness and individual
vision respectively.
    The neo-African theory, however, has quite expectedly
met with some West Indian opposition. Kenneth Ramchand
rejects the theory, which sees West Indian literature as a
development from African literature. He argues that the
proponents of the concept are still unclear about its
applications--Jahn, for example, admits that the criteria
for identifying neo-African literature are "still under
consideration," and Brathwaite recognizes the inadequacy of
his paradigm novel, Brother Man. Thus, Ramchand cautiously
concludes: "One must be reluctant to welcome an aesthetic
with [sic] is so useless critically, and which for all its
ceremorial [sic] respect, courtesy and appreciation so
firmly refuses admittance to Naipaul, and then surprisingly
Lamming and Harris."133 In addition, because of its
emphasis on Africa, the neo-African theory has not been able
to attract West Indians of East Indian or of European
descent. (In Trinidad there are now as many East Indians as
there are blacks.) Nunez-Harrell, in supporting the
négritude movement, recognizes this problem, but does not
offer a solution which could accommodate non-blacks.134
    The neo-African approach also presents problems for
black West Indians. Arthur Drayton elaborates on this
apparent contradiction:

        The Caribbean situation is not and never has been a
        Negro situation. . . . It would be pointless to
        expect the English-speaking West Indian writer who
        is a Negro to write from an African point of view.
        He has grown up under conditions that have not
        prepared him for this. . . . Those who have shown
        any recent tendency in the direction of négritude
        have been influenced by contact with those West
        Africans, and those non-English speaking West
        Indians, for whom the matter has been somewhat
        different.135

Indeed, the preoccupation with Africa or things African is
symbolic rather than tangible. Nunez-Harrell notes that
"for English-speaking West Indians, there are few direct
connections with Africa, and it is no wonder that these

writers seek to revive a spiritual rather than material contact with that continent."[136] Some West Indian writers did journey to Africa in search of their roots and identity, but few, if any found a home there. Despite the rise of black consciousness and despite the enthusiastic discussions about settling in Africa, black West Indians find it just as difficult to identify with Africa as East Indian West Indians do with India.

But the insistence on the concept of négritude continues. At the 1971 Commonwealth Conference, one speaker bitterly criticized attempts to judge West Indian literature according to the standards of the English literary tradition. Calling for a strictly West Indian criticism of West Indian literature, he argued for a type of criticism which would examine West Indian use of "our creole language and the facts and notions of our African heritage and oral tradition to construct an alternative to our inherited condition enabling all our people, lettered and unlettered, to sing of the West Indian country-side as home, to assert our West Indian way of life."[137] Naipaul, without doubt, misses the mark. Listening to pleas for the use of local traditions and the rejection of all foreign elements unless they are "indelibly black," some non-black members of the audience were clearly disappointed:

> White and brown delegates . . . grumbled during the coffee breaks about the monotonous "racist rhetoric" of the "militants." Why should West Indian writers resist integration, they asked. Wouldn't it be wiser for them to be eclectic and exploit the manifold possibilities of their various cultural legacies rather than put all their creative eggs into one negritudinous basket? The revolutionaries obviously didn't see it that way.[138]

Referring specifically to the shift in orientation taught in schools, Naipaul recently observed: "The current 'revolutionary' or Africanist overview is not an improvement; it is no more than the old imperialist attitude turned inside out."[139] Undoubtedly, a literary theory devoid of any racial content would have gained wider support.

As early as 1958 Naipaul expressed his impatience with the exploitation of racial issues: "I wonder that no one has yet done a study on the reasons for the perennial popularity of books about racial discrimination. I believe they give a certain sadistic pleasure."[140] In The Middle Passage he observes that a great part of West Indian writing has "little to do with literature, and much to do with race war" (p. 68). He asserts that "the involvement of the Negro with the white world is one of the limitations of West Indian writing," thus robbing the works of any universal appeal. He warns against imitating the literary aims of

black Americans, whose subject of literature is their
"blackness." "This cannot be the basis of any serious
literature," he contends; "once the American Negro has made
his statement, his profitable protest, he has nothing to
say." Naipaul notes that while West Indians have generally
avoided protest literature, their aims have also been
propagandistic in trying "to win acceptance for their
group." Finally, he suggests that by focusing on the
race-color values of their group, West Indian writers
aggravate rather than solve the problem (pp. 69-70).

Naipaul's views on West Indian literature have not gone
unchallenged. Gordon Rohlehr strongly chides the writer for
his lack of understanding:

> The obvious comment is that where one's blackness
> means something very definite, it can become the
> basis of the most serious literature. And much as
> one accepts Naipaul's point that protest litera-
> ture can become a sterile and stereotyped posturing
> in the name of blackness, one also realizes that
> protest against the past is a vital transitional
> stage in the reconstruction of a sense of
> personality. Naipaul does not realize that in
> treating the theme of East Indian acculturation,
> and the reconstruction of the Indian personality in
> the New World, he is at one with Negro writers who
> are also trying to reconstruct personality, and is
> writing a most vital portion of the sensitive
> history of the West Indies.[141]

Rohlehr is supported by Nunez-Harrell, who emphatically
declares that a "black man's expression, if its intention is
to imitate life, must include implicitly or explicitly, his
involvement with the white world."[142] From the foregoing
discussion, it is clear that in practice and in theory
Naipaul stands apart from his fellow West Indian writers.

That Naipaul is of East Indian origin had added enor-
mously to the controversy surrounding him. There is a
feeling among quite a number of blacks that Naipaul the East
Indian cannot understand black West Indian society. They
argue that his vision is impaired because it is restricted
to the East Indian segment of the society.[143] East
Indians in the Caribbean are still regarded by some as
"outsiders" or aliens in a society which they cannot grasp.
For example, explaining the reason for Naipaul's supposed
"jaundiced approach," Rex Nettleford, a Jamaican artist,
argues:

> [Naipaul] belongs to that cultural group of West
> Indians who are decidedly late comers to the
> plantation conflict. By the time East Indians,
> Chinese, and Syrians arrived, the society had
> consolidated itself . . . the value-system had been

> determined. . . . The outsider complex has robbed
> people like Naipaul of a much needed focus and has
> instead offered an area of darkness. . . . The
> Euro-African determinism of the plantation model
> forgets the East Indian Naipauls of this world.[144]

Another related charge is that Naipaul holds all things
black in anathema. Repeating his belief that blacks, who
have shared in the plantation struggle, tend to "claim a
legitimacy" in the Caribbean and isolate those who arrived
after Emancipation, Nettleford in a later interview
asserts: "It is something we have not come to terms with
yet, and we will not discuss it in quite this way . . .
[Naipaul's] contempt for the Caribbean with its indulgence
of things African and things black . . . is quite
understandable."[145] Criticisms such as those suggested by
Nettleford give validity to Figueroa's argument that perhaps
it is the "mixed cultural context which is behind the
controversy which has grown up around Naipual's name."[146]
Indeed, race does surface, sometimes in a subtle way, in
West Indian reaction to Naipaul. For example, a responsible
Caribbean critic remarks: "It is significant to note that
those writers of East Indian birth and heritage who have
made their names as novelists (Selvon and Naipaul) write in
the western tradition."[147] And those who have taught
Caribbean literature often report that students show a
preference for writers of their own race.[148]

East Indians in the Caribbean generally, though not
openly, attribute Naipaul's hostile reception to racial
jealousy, especially since some black West Indians emphasize the writer's East Indian Englishness and his
snobbery which rejects everything black. Most of the
negative West Indian criticisms of Naipaul have come from
blacks. Of course, few East Indians have actually done any
serious writing on Naipaul. This is so mainly because there
are few Indian critics. (And except the Naipauls, Samuel
Selvon and Ismith Khan, there is no other East Indian
novelist regionally known.) It must be remembered that
Indians were late starters in the West Indian educational
system, and when they did enter, they avoided teaching
(which, until recently, was reserved for Christians anyway)
and took to independent professions, such as law and
medicine. Literature was not considered worthwhile or
serious. However, the pattern is changing, though slowly.

Just before Naipaul was scheduled to speak at the 1975
Conference on East Indians in the Caribbean held at the
University of the West Indies, he was given a four-page
typed statement entitled "Naipaul and the Blacks," prepared
by an Indian group called "Mukdah." The statement asserted
that to black academics and writers Naipaul is a serious
problem since he is "the most successful of the writers in
the Caribbean" and has thus upset the "'immediate' yearnings
of the blacks (negroes) to appear to be the leading writers,

and the politicians and sole repository of knowledge and leadership."[149] Interviewed by Selwyn Cudjoe, who wanted to know whether "there is a legitimate sense of Indian grievances which was manifested by the Mukdah group" in its "crude" article, Kenneth Ramchand responded: "Yes. There is a sense of grievance and not without real cause among the East Indians in Trinidad. The Mukdah people are moved at least in part by this sense of grievance."[150] In 1982, when Dr. Ince, Minister of External Affairs in Trinidad, criticized Naipaul for not appreciating his place of origin, Mahabir Maharaj charged:

> If Dr. Williams or Derek Walcott had written the many novels which Naipaul has written, Dr. Ince would have praised them as writers in the class of Aldous Huxley, Ernest Hemingway and others. . . . Please do not let that "gem" wear its ugly head again when others are desperately trying to prop our crumbling home and destroy race politics.[151]

Few East Indians, however, are as candid as Maharaj.
Others attribute the hostility to Naipaul to the professional jealousy of fellow writers. During a panel discussion on Naipaul, John Figueroa points to Naipaul's literary superiority over other Caribbean writers:

> Naipaul very soon had mastered his medium, and it is, perhaps, his utter control of that medium which infuriates some of his literary colleagues. (Gerald Guinness makes a telling, if not to be over-generalized, comparison between the lightness and limpidity of Naipaul on the one hand, and the heaviness and thickness of Wilson Harris and George Lamming, on the other.)[152]

Figueroa's argument is fed by the fact that many West Indian writers have reviled Naipaul. Andrew Johnson has indicated that authors such as Edward Brathwaite, Andrew Salkey, and Jan Carew (who even refused to review a Naipaul book for a publisher) have denounced Naipaul as a spokesperson for neo-colonialism.[153] According to George R. Jones, Guyanese Ivan Van Sertima showed "some resentment over Naipaul's international popularity as against that achieved by Harris," and admitted that as a member of the Nobel Prize Committee he voted for Harris, not Naipaul. Jones concluded that the logical explanation for the belittling of Naipaul by Van Sertima and other West Indians is "pen envy."[154] It is, of course, far-fetched to attribute Naipaul's reception in the West Indies to racial jealousy or professional pique.
Naipaul's personality is such that it is easy for him to be isolated by West Indians, black or Indian. As reported earlier in this chapter Naipaul admits having an

attitude of being "always very critical, liable to too easy
a contempt," and he claims that he inherited this trait from
his father who was reacting against life within an Indian
enclave.[155] Some readers have even assumed that it is
specifically a <u>Brahmin</u> upbringing that molded Naipaul's
temperament.[156] However, such an assumption should be
made with caution. Admittedly, Naipaul has written of his
imitation of his family's prejudice against Moslems, his
development of a "horror of the unclean," his youthful
pleasure at hearing himself referred to as "Brahmin," and
his disappointment that Indian traditions and customs are
fading. However, at the same time, he insists that he was
born an agnostic, and he rejects such important Hindu
practices as rituals and the caste system, a system which
"had no meaning in our day-to-day life."[157] Kenneth
Ramchand, an East Indian Trinidadian critic, responding to a
question about the effect of "Hinduism or East Indianness"
on Naipaul, dismisses any emphasis on his Brahmin upbringing:

> It is not known that he is a Hindu in the orthodox,
> or conventional sense. Those who refer to him as a
> Hindu even specify that he is a Brahmin. If all
> that they wish to indicate is a kind of
> temperament, a certain aloofness, something
> fastidious, then perhaps the term can stand; but I
> think it really does not help to think about him as
> a Hindu or a Brahmin.[158]

There is no conclusive evidence to suggest what specifically
shaped Naipaul's personality. Attributing the source of
influence to a Brahmin background means making a
generalization about Brahmins in the West Indies, where, at
any rate, the caste structure never took root.

What can be said, however, is that in his journalism,
fiction, and interviews, Naipaul invites controversy and
antagonism. As William Walsh points out, the "hostility
shown to Naipaul in the West Indies may seem to some surprising in its intensity, but one cannot overlook a certain
quirk in Naipaul's sensibility that almost certainly has a
part in provoking it."[159] It is obvious that Naipaul the
journalist is easily displeased, bored, fatigued, and
irritated. One writer called attention to his "prickly,
susceptible nature, the rawness of his nerves, his thinness
of skin," evident in <u>The Middle Passage</u>.[160] In this
travelogue, for example, Naipaul listens attentively to some
guests at an Antiguan boarding-house as they exchange views
on different subjects, ranging from the race question to
violence in Western societies, but the atmosphere soon
becomes overbearing to him:

> The older man came over to me and said, 'Excuse me,
> sir. Do you know the doctor?' He indicated the
> lesser Negro patriarch. 'It's his birthday. He's

just coming in and we are going to sing Happy Birthday for him.'
I pushed my coffee cup aside and ran upstairs. (p. 214)

While it may be natural for Naipaul the East Indian to feel alienated and estranged from black West Indian society, it is hard to understand first, why he could not have obliged and, second, why he chose to record the incident. Referring to the scene, Eugene Goodheart notes: "This reader for one finds Naipaul's squeamishness more objectionable than the vulgarity of the scene."[161] The strain from the entire West Indian scene takes its toll at the luxurious holiday resort in Jamaica:

> Within twenty-four hours my interest in food and drink had disappeared. Everything was at the end of the telephone, and it was my duty to have exactly what I wanted. But how could I be sure what I wanted best? . . . No decision couldn't be regretted. I gave up. I left everything to the chef. I never ordered a meal, and the next day I went without dinner. (p. 230)

The persona in The Middle Passage, it appears, presents himself as deliberately unaccommodating.

The later travelogues reveal the same persona, exasperated and aloof. In An Area of Darkness Naipaul complains: "To be in Bombay was to be exhausted. The moist heat sapped energy and will" (p. 19). After a long internal debate about facing the heat, he ventures out and crosses the street. Nissim Ezekiel argues that "from that starting point, nothing can be done; the evidence of Indian bureaucratic stupidity becomes suspect."[162] Some readers contend that the problem is not with the Third World, but, rather, with the journalistic voice which intrudes and takes control of the narrative. An interesting question is sometimes posed: "Does Naipaul see deformity or does his seeing deform?"[163] In the travel books the reader is made conscious of a provocative guide, who refuses to be satisfied.

It has been argued that in Naipaul's works the "intrusion of the observer in the scene" is characteristic not only of the travelogues but also of the fiction.[164] Even in the early comedies and in A House for Mr Biswas, as Goodheart observes, things are imperfect:

> Nothing is ever right with Naipaul's characters. Their incompetence is pervasive: in their speech, their vocations, their bodies, their possessions. In the early books they speak an English patois. . . . Mr. Biswas' muscles are like "hammocks" and the calves of his legs pathetically soft. . . .

90

> His houses are all makeshift affairs. . . . In the
> six hundred pages of <u>A House</u> . . . I can scarcely
> recall an episode in which something is properly
> made or done.[165]

But it is in the later fiction that the persona of Naipaul's
journalism extends. From the non-fictional Gale Benson in
"The Killings" to her counterpart, Jane, in the novel
<u>Guerrillas</u>, Naipaul's women are portrayed mercilessly and
subjected to gross mistreatment. Kerry McSweeney notes that
when Naipaul describes the human body, "the sensitivity
tends to become a fastidiousness which at times, especially
in connection with female sexuality, borders on
revulsion."[166] The frequent, unpleasant references to
women's bodily functions--for example, menstruation--has led
another commentator to observe: "Such fastidiousness
suggests the author's squeamish identification between
menstruation and pollution, an equation confirmed in <u>India</u> .
. . when Naipaul refers to a man serving his crippled wife
'even during the pollution of her periods.'"[167] In
<u>Guerrillas</u> after his brutal sexual assault on Jane, Jimmy
tells her, "You are rotten meat," an echo from Naipaul's
references to Benson. Not surprisingly, Karl Miller notes
that "Ahmed's revulsion from Jane sometimes seems to be
shared by the writer."[168]
Several such parallels between the persona of Naipaul's
journalism and fiction can be found. In <u>The Mimic Men</u>, for
example, the narrator-hero describes in the most revolting
manner the eating pattern of a man, whom he names Garbage:

> His hands are all I can see of him. They are long,
> middle-aged, educated hands; and their primary
> concern appears to be to convert a plate of meat
> and vegetables into a plate of acceptable garbage.
> While chaos comes swiftly and simultaneously to
> other plates; while meat is hacked and pushed
> around and vegetables mangled and scattered on a
> spreading, muddy field of gravy; while knives and
> forks, restlessly preparing fresh, mixed mouthfuls,
> probe the chaos they have created, and cut and
> spear and plaster; those two lands are unhurriedly,
> scientifically, maintaining order, defining
> garbage, separating what is to be eventually eaten
> from what is to be thrown away. What is to be
> thrown away is lifted high and carefully deposited
> on that section of the plate, a growing section,
> which is reserved for garbage. It is only when the
> division is complete--most of the other plates
> abandoned by this time and ready for
> surrender--that the eating begins. This is the
> work of a minute; the plate is ready for surrender.
> . . . After the plate of garbage comes the
> slaughter of the cheese. . . .[169]

This scene, which resembles one in <u>An Area of Darkness</u> (quoted in the Appendix), is conveyed, as Goodheart notes, "without any human interest."[170] Again, in <u>India</u> the journalistic persona makes a point in refuting the "lie" of a woman who insists that the poor are "beautiful" (p. 125), and in <u>The Mimic Men</u>, the narrator echoes: "In this smell of heated sweat . . . I tried to find virtue, the virtue of the poor, the laboring, the oppressed. Such is the vulgarity that mobs generate, in themselves and in their manipulations" (p. 194). It is this passage that prompts Robert Boyers to comment on the "note of disgust, of an offended superiority, [which] resounds through much of Naipaul's fiction."[171] Similar evidence of impatience and revulsion could be gathered from the West Indian novels which fictionalize the sociological findings of <u>The Middle Passage</u>. Goodheart's generous analysis of Naipaul's created persona is that "Naipaul sees the absurd, the grotesque, the deformed, the mechanical in all of life because of an acutely fastidious sense of the unachievable rightness of things."[172] The important point here, though, is that Naipaul's provocative imagery and language account in large part for his antagonistic reception in the West Indies.

Naipaul's tendency to disassociate himself from the Caribbean and to object to being labeled as a "West Indian writer" has served to isolate him further from his countrymen, who view him as contemptuous of them. Before the publication of the controversial <u>The Middle Passage</u>, he rejected the notion that he is a member of a new West Indian school: "I run away from the title. I am a little tired of it. I just like to think of myself as a writer and if you're going to pin me down, it's a writer from Trinidad."[173] Later in a 1968 interview he struck a blow at his fellow West Indians by declaring that he does not consider himself a West Indian writer; that he no longer reads West Indian novels, which "have stopped feeding" him (earlier he had said that the novels abuse the theme of sex); and that he hardly maintains contact with West Indian writers, with whom he has nothing in common. He further asserted:

> I have nothing in common with the people from Jamaica. . . . Or the other islands for that matter. I don't understand them. As a writer I have to make a living and I certainly don't believe I can make a living by being regional.
>
> I hope my work is not regional. One likes to think that what one says would be of interest to the people who read books in various languages.[174]

Naipaul's rejection of a broad West Indian identification, which naturally has produced stormy reaction, could be construed less as contempt for his people and more as, first, an honest admission of his different orientation,

partly due to his East Indian upbringing, and second, his
desire to break away from the regional circle (he has
repeatedly maintained that the term "West Indian writer" is
a political tag).[175] It is curious to note that one
commentator, who refers to Naipaul's "disdainful detachment" from West Indians, has expressed surprise that the
writer "spoke in terms of 'we'" during his keynote address
at the 1975 Commonwealth Conference on East Indians in the
Caribbean, a conference at which three-fourths of the
audience were East Indians.[176]

Some West Indians are ambivalent about whether they
want to regard Naipaul as a Caribbean writer. So isolated
did the West Indian Writers' Association feel from him that
it decided not to invite him to join the group because "he
might laugh at us," a decision the _Trinidad Guardian_ calls
wise.[177] This uneasiness in accepting Naipaul as a West
Indian novelist is reflected in Arthur Drayton's analysis of
the criteria which categorize a writer as West Indian.
Drayton suggests that a writer cannot be determined West
Indian based on questions of citizenship, place of residence
or subject matter; instead, the work must be stamped with a
"West Indian interest." Drayton reluctantly admits Naipaul
as a West Indian:

> Ironically enough, the one writer whose attitude to
> the West Indies constantly threatens to cut him off
> as a West Indian writer is the one who contri-
> butes most vigorously (Wilson Harris apart) to our
> national literature. Vidia Naipaul . . . is a
> curious casualty of the European factor, with
> restricted possibilities of further contribution,
> not technically but philosophically, to West Indian
> literature.[178]

As early as 1968 the _Trinidad Guardian_ saw Naipaul as a
"literary curiosity" and as an elusive eccentric with
evasive answers to questions about his work.[179]

What angers West Indians is that although Naipaul
disclaims territorial and philosophical affinity with the
West Indies, he continues to visit, expose and criticize the
region. Wayne Brown's tirade typifies West Indian
sentiments:

> Having turned one's back on a country in no
> ambiguous terms, one ought not to proceed for the
> next twenty years to make a living by periodically
> kicking that country in the teeth. . . .
> Naipaul, in a very private and terrible way,
> cannot forget the West Indies. . . .
> His constant assaults on the West Indies must be
> seen, partly at least, as sorties against his
> predicament, desperate rationalizations of his
> situation.

> A man who has successfully turned his back on
> his native country simply forgets it. But Naipaul
> has forgotten nothing. . . .[180]

Naipaul's reaction to criticisms such as Brown's is that
"There's a primitive way of approaching a writer. They
[critics] would willingly read attacks by other writers on
their own culture. They would see that as marvelous and
fair-minded. But anyone who probably just writes about the
realities of their own might seem very wrong."[181] However, Naipaul's uncoated criticisms and quick-witted
cynicism inevitably generate hostility. For example, he
speaks to Caribbean readers about their "unimportant,"
"primitive," "inferior," "backward," and "half-made" slave
societies, about their destiny to be dependent on the
metropolis of the developed world, and about their hopelessness as a condemned people. It appears that he
deliberately provokes West Indians by statements such as the
following: "They [Trinidadians] don't understand literature
there. Those chaps are very happy beating their little
drums. It's not a literary culture. I don't think they
know what it's about."[182] Because of such loaded language
and grim prognosis, West Indians are convinced that Naipaul
is ashamed and contemptuous of his background.

Naipaul has always emphasized that he does not detest
his background. Interviewed by the Caribbean Contact in
1973, he was directly asked whether he rejects his origin.
His answer, though in the negative, has the potential to
spark more serious controversies in a never ending circle:

> No. You don't reject your origins. . . . And not
> to be disgusted by the Trinidad of 1950 . . . in
> every way . . . required a man who really believed
> that Carnival and calypso were the height of human
> achievement. . . . I can't understand people who
> talk about the horrors of colonialism and then
> ignore the fact that a kind of inferior human being
> was created. . . . You just can't sing paeans of
> praise to the inferior human being. You have to do
> things to help them.[183]

One of the positive steps Naipaul seems to have in mind
includes education. For example, in answer to another
related charge that he is unsympathetic, Naipaul states that
he finds it difficult to be sympathetic to Trinidad's
uneducated, who, instead of blaming themselves for not
becoming educated, beg for sympathy.[184] Equally provocative is Naipaul's devasting onslaught against critics when
he is told that they view him as contemptuous of his own
people: "You see, this is such an old charge. And it's a
charge made in primitive societies against writers because
primitive societies when they read, have very primitive ways
of reading. And people here, I think, are still at the

primitive state where writers are really perhaps really
writing political things." Naipaul then compared his hostile reception to that of Ibsen and Gogol, showing that
critics always tend to make "absurd" comments and give
writers a "hard time" for the "bad portrayal of their
country."[185] As valid as this point may be, Naipaul's
caustic and acrimonious rebuttal has further alienated him
from his Caribbean readers.

This chapter has shown that the West Indian writer,
born in a culturally sterile society and forced into exile,
has limited artistic freedom. Since it is now fashionable
to romanticize underprivileged young societies trying to
undo the damage of colonialism and exploitation, West Indian
critics expect their writers to assist by glamorizing--or
even distorting--the social and political achievements and
capabilities of their countries. For Naipaul, the problem
is complicated by his fastidiousness. In addition, his
seemingly Euro-centered orientation disturbs some critics,
whose very goal it is to replace all white values and
traditions; however, the Afro-centered alternative presents
more problems in critical approaches to Naipaul, who is East
Indian. Thus, Naipaul is politically and culturally
alienated from most of his Caribbean critics. John Figueroa
suggests that in composing the following lines to exiled
novelists, Derek Walcott, a St. Lucian poet and playwright
residing in Trinidad, may have had Naipaul in mind:

> You spit on your people,
> Your people applaud,
> Your former oppressors
> laurel you.
> The thorns biting your forehead
> are contempt
> disguised as concern,
> still, you can come home, now.[186]

The following chapters, which will examine West Indian
objections to specific works, will determine whether
Naipaul's seeming contempt is really a disguised concern.

Notes

1 "Timehri," in <u>Is Massa Day Dead</u>? ed. Orde Coombs (New York: Anchor Books, 1974), 30-36.

2 <u>V. S. Naipaul</u> (New York: Africana Publishing Co., 1972), p. 7.

3 Naipaul's autobiographical sketch, "Prologue to an Autobiography," <u>Vanity Fair</u>, 46, No. 2 (April 1983), 51-59 and 138-56, was published (along with "The Crocodiles of Yamoussoukro") in <u>Finding the Center</u> (New York: Alfred Knopf, 1984).

4 "Prologue to an Autobiography," p. 154.

5 "Prologue to an Autobiography," p. 59.

6 "The Novelist V. S. Naipaul Talks to Nigel Bingham About his Childhood in Trinidad," <u>Listener</u>, 7 Sept. 1972, p. 306.

7 "Prologue to an Autobiography," p. 156.

8 "The Novelist V. S. Naipaul Talks to Nigel Bingham," p. 306.

9 "Prologue to an Autobiography," p. 59.

10 "The Novelist V. S. Naipaul Talks to Nigel Bingham," p. 306.

11 "Prologue to an Autobiography," pp. 138-40.

12 "The Novelist V. S. Naipaul Talks to Nigel Bingham," p. 306.

13 Ewart Rouse, "Naipaul: An Interview," <u>Trinidad Guardian</u>, 28 Nov. 1968, p. 13.

14 V. S. Naipaul, "Writing 'A House for Mr. Biswas,'" <u>New York Review</u>, 24 Nov. 1983, p. 22.

15 "Prologue to an Autobiography," p. 59.

16 "Prologue to an Autobiography," p. 140.

17 Seepersad Naipaul, <u>Gurudeva and Other Indian Tales</u> (Trinidad: Trinidad Publications, 1943), p. 32.

18 "Prologue to an Autobiography," p. 140.

[19] "Prologue to an Autobiography," p. 140.

[20] V. S. Naipaul, "Foreword," The Adventures of Gurudeva and Other Stories, by Seepersad Naipaul (London: André Deutsch Ltd., 1976), p. 16.

[21] White, pp. 41 ff.; Anthony Boxill, "Mr. Biswas, Mr. Polly and the Problem of V. S. Naipaul's Sources," Ariel, 8, No. 3 (July 1977), 129-41; Bruce Macdonald, "The Birth of Mr. Biswas," Journal of Commonwealth Literature, 11, No. 3 (1977), 50-54.

[22] "Foreword," The Adventures of Gurudeva, p. 19.

[23] "Foreword," The Adventures of Gurudeva, p. 19.

[24] "Jasmine," in The Overcrowded Barracoon (London: André Deutsch, 1972; rpt. New York: Penguin Books, 1976), p. 27.

[25] David Bates, "V. S. Naipaul," Sunday Times Supplement, 26 May 1963, p. 12.

[26] "Foreword," The Adventures of Gurudeva, p. 15.

[27] White, p. 45.

[28] "Foreword," The Adventures of Gurudeva, p. 7.

[29] Seepersad Naipaul, "Foreword," Gurudeva and Other Indian Tales.

[30] "Critics and Criticism," Bim (Barbados), 10, No. 38 (Jan. - June 1964), 74.

[31] Naipaul, "Writing 'A House for Mr. Biswas,'" p. 22.

[32] For details, see "Prologue to an Autobiography," pp. 54 ff.

[33] "Writing 'A House for Mr. Biswas,'" p. 24.

[34] Andrew Dopson, "I'll Stop Writing for Less" (Interview), Trinidad Guardian, 12 Dec. 1971, p. 18.

[35] "London," in The Overcrowded Barracoon, p. 16.

[36] "London," p. 17.

[37] "Speaking of Writing," The Times (London), 2 Jan. 1964, p. 11.

[38] Ewart Rouse, p. 9.

[39] "The Novelist V. S. Naipaul Talks About his Work to Ronald Bryden," Listener, 22 March 1973, p. 367.

[40] "The Novelist V. S. Naipaul Talks About his Work to Ronald Bryden," p. 370.

[41] Bharati Mukherjee and Robert Boyers, "A Conversation with V. S. Naipaul," Salmagundi, 54 (Fall 1981), 18.

[42] "UWI to Honour Naipaul," Sunday Guardian (Trinidad),
29 June 1975, p. 1.

[43] Mel Gussow, "Writer Without Roots, New York Times Magazine, 26 Dec. 1976, p. 19.

[44] "The Bennett Award, 1980" (Announcement), The Hudson Review, 33, No. 3 (Winter 1980-1), 321.

[45] "University News," The Times (London), 21 Feb. 1983, p. 12.

[46] Mukherjee and Boyers, p. 16; V. S. Naipaul, "Writing 'A House for Mr. Biswas,'" p. 22.

[47] William Walsh, "V. S. Naipaul," The Literary Criterion, 10 (Summer 1972), 25.

[48] Keith Hamish, "The Ridiculous Panic Behind V. S. Naipaul" (Interview), Trinidad Guardian, 29 Nov. 1973, p. 9.

[49] White, p. 14.

[50] V. S. Naipaul's Fiction (Canada: York Press, 1983), p. 24.

[51] Mukherjee and Boyers, p. 11.

[52] Bruce King, The New English Literatures (New York: St. Martin's Press, 1980), p. 104; Consuelo Lopez de Villegas, "The Paradox of Freedom in Naipaul's Later Fiction," Revista/Review Interamericana," 6, No. 4 (1976-77), 575.

[53] Gussow, "Writer Without Roots," p. 18.

[54] Writers in Exile (Sussex: The Harvester Press Ltd., 1981), p. 141. See also Lopez de Villegas, p. 574.

55 "Conrad's Darkness," in The Return of Eva Peron (New York: Alfred Knopf, 1980; rpt. New York: Vintage Books, 1981), pp. 223 ff.

56 Mukherjee and Boyers, p. 9.

57 "Conrad's Darkness," pp. 243-44.

58 "Conrad's Darkness," p. 244.

59 "Conrad's Darkness," p. 230.

60 "Conrad's Darkness," pp. 233-36.

61 Mukherjee and Boyers, pp. 9-10.

62 For a concise account of the literary history of the West Indies, see Kenneth Ramchand, The West Indian Novel and Its Background (New York: Barnes and Noble Inc., 1970); Bruce King, ed., West Indian Literature (Connecticut: Archon Books, 1979); and Bruce King, The New English Literatures, pp. 98-139. Bill Carr, "Reflections on the Novel in the British Caribbean," Queen's Quarterly, 70, No. 4 (Winter 1963), 585, dates the British Caribbean novel from Vic Reid's New Day (1949) and Edgar Mittelholzer's Morning at the Office (1950), but most critics regard C. L. R. James' Minty Alley (1936) as the first.

63 Bruce King, ed., West Indian Literature, p. 3.

64 Ramchand, The West Indian Novel and Its Background, pp. 71-73; Bruce King, ed., West Indian Literature, p. 2.

65 "Some West Indian Problems of Audience," English, 16, No. 94 (Spring 1967), 128.

66 Statistics are taken from Ian Muro et al., "Writing and Publishing in the West Indies," World Literature Written in English, 19 (April 1971), 19 and Ramchand, The West Indian Novel and Its Background, p. 74.

67 Ian Muro et al., p. 18.

68 Louis James, Introd., The Islands in Between (London: Oxford University Press, 1968), p. 14.

69 "V. S. Naipaul in Paris," Manchester Guardian Weekly, 26 July 1981, p. 13.

[70] David Lowenthal, West Indian Societies (London: Oxford University Press, 1972), p. 216.

[71] "Towards a West Indian Criticism," Caribbean Quarterly, 14, No. 1 & 2 (March-June 1968), 141. See also George Lamming, The Pleasures of Exile (London: Michael Joseph, 1960), p. 40. For a detailed discussion of the lack of positive interest in local literature, see Bill Carr, "Reflections on the Novel in the British Caribbean," pp. 585-86.

[72] Mervyn Morris, "Some West Indian Problems of Audience," p. 127.

[73] The Middle Passage (London: André Deutsch, 1962; rpt. New York: Vintage Books, 1981), p. 41. Subsequent references will be to this edition and will be indicated in the text.

[74] "V. S. Naipaul: Interview with Israel Shenker," in Critical Perspectives on V. S. Naipaul, ed. Robert Hamner (Washington, D.C.: Three Continents Press, 1977), p. 50.

[75] "V. S. Naipaul in Paris," p. 13.

[76] Bernth Lindfors, "The West Indian Conference on Commonwealth Literature," World Literature Written in English, 19 (April 1971), 10.

[77] "Introduction," in East Indians of the Carribean. Papers Presented to a Symposium of East Indians in the Caribbean, June 1975 (Jamaica: University of the West Indies, 1975), p. 8.

[78] "Some West Indian Problems of Audience," p. 129. Naipaul has also complained about the absence of a general bookshop in Trinidad. See Adrian Rowe-Evans, "The Writer as Colonial" (Interview), Quest, 78 (Sept.- Oct. 1972), 48.

[79] Writers in Exile, p. 7. Bill Carr, "Reflections on the Novel in the British Caribbean," p. 587, agrees that by residing abroad, the writer enriches his experiences.

[80] "The West Indian Artist," The West Indian Review, 9 Aug. 1952, pp. 13-14.

[81] Ramchand, The West Indian Novel and Its Background, p. 63, shows a table of figures for the number of West Indian novels published abroad from 1950-1965.

82 "An Exile Returns," <u>Trinidad Guardian</u>, 25 Sept. 1960, p. 7.

83 "Reflections on the Novel in the British Caribbean," p. 587. For a similar view, see Victor Ramraj, "Diminishing Satire," in <u>Awakened Conscience</u>, ed. C. D. Narasimhaiah (New Delhi: Sterling Publishers, 1978), p. 262.

84 "V. S. Naipaul: Interview with Israel Shenker," p. 50.

85 "V. S. Naipaul in Paris," p. 13.

86 "London," in <u>The Overcrowded Barracoon</u>, pp. 11-13.

87 <u>Writers in Exile</u>, p. 26.

88 "Jasmine," in <u>The Overcrowded Barracoon</u>, pp. 24-25.

89 "Prologue to an Autobiography," p. 58; see also Mukherjee and Boyers, p. 7.

90 "The Novelist V. S. Naipaul Talks About his Work to Ronald Bryden," p. 367.

91 "Home is Where They Want to be," <u>Trinidad Guardian Magazine</u>, 14 Feb. 1965, pp. 4-5.

92 Lamming, <u>The Pleasures of Exile</u>, p. 47.

93 "The Disorder of Vidia Naipaul," <u>Trinidad Guardian Magazine</u>, 21 Feb. 1965, p. 6. See also C. L. R. James, "The Artist in the Caribbean," in <u>The Future in the Present</u> (Connecticut: Lawrence Hill & Co. Publishers, Inc., 1977), pp. 188-89.

94 <u>Writers in Exile</u>, p. 25.

95 Mervyn Morris, p. 128.

96 "Naipaul's Four Early Trinidad Novels," <u>Revista/ Review Interamericana</u>, 6, No. 4 (Winter 1976-77), 564.

97 See, for example, Derek Walcott, "Now Hope for Exiled Artists," <u>Sunday Guardian</u> (Trinidad), 21 Aug. 1960, p. 4.

98 <u>The West Indian Novel and Its Background</u>, p. 6.

99 "Born Yesterday," <u>The West Indian Review</u>, 16 May 1953, p. 16.

100 "Introduction--V. S. Naipaul: A Panel Discussion," Revista/Review Interamericana, 6 (1976-77), 560.

101 Eric Roach, "As Naipaul Sees Us," rev. of The Mimic Men, Trinidad Guardian, 17 May 1967, p. 9.

102 "Challenging CLR and the Naipauls," Sunday Guardian (Trinidad), 18 Oct. 1970, p. 10.

103 "Naipaul's Death Wish is Not Our Bag," rev. of The Overcrowded Barracoon, Trinidad Guardian, 1 Feb. 1973. p. 4.

104 "Walcott-Naipaul," Trinidad Guardian, 20 Aug. 1967, p. 9.

105 Winston Hackett, "The Writer and Society," Moko (Trinidad), 13 Dec. 1968, p. 4.

106 "The West Indian Novelist . . . A Footnote," Sunday Gleaner (Jamaica), 23 April 1961, p. 14.

107 Fitzroy Fraser, "A Talk With Vidia Naipaul," Sunday Gleaner (Jamaica), 26 Dec. 1960, p. 14; V. S. Naipaul, "Honesty Needed in West Indian Writing," Sunday Guardian (Trinidad), 28 Oct. 1956, p. 29.

108 "Images," rev. of Commonwealth Literature, ed. John Press, in Critical Perspectives on V. S. Naipaul, ed. Robert D. Hamner, pp. 28-29.

109 White, p. 11.

110 Lindfors, pp. 10-11.

111 Lindfors, pp. 10-11.

112 V. S. Naipaul, "Introduction," in East Indians of the Caribbean, p. 1.

113 Figueroa, "Introduction," p. 557; Lindfors, p. 10.

114 Lennox Grant, "Naipaul Joins the Chorus," Tapia (Trinidad), 6 July 1975, pp. 6-7.

115 Lowenthal, p. 319.

116 "The European Factor in West Indian Literature," The Literary Half-Yearly (Mysore), 11, No. 2 (July 1970), 80-81.

102

117 "On Exile and the Dialect of the Tribe," _Sunday Guardian_ (Trinidad), 8 Nov. 1970, p. 19.

118 Mukherjee and Boyers, p. 13..

119 Mukherjee and Boyers, p. 13.

120 Rhonda Cobham, "The Background," in _West Indian Literature_, ed. Bruce King, p. 24.

121 "West Indian Literature as the Expression of National Cultures," The Program in Atlantic History, Culture and Society, Johns Hopkins University, Maryland, 9 Nov. 1983.

122 Louis James, ed., _The Islands in Between_, p. 11.

123 "Power?" in _The Overcrowded Barracoon_ (London: André Deutsch, 1972; rpt. New York: Penguin Books, 1976), p. 269.

124 Ramchand, _The West Indian Novel and Its Background_, pp. 132-33.

125 Ramchand, _The West Indian Novel and Its Background_, pp. 133.

126 Elizabeth Nunez-Harrell, "Lamming and Naipaul," _Contemporary Literature_, 19, No. 1 (1978), 41-42.

127 Michael Dash, "Edward Brathwaite," in _West Indian Literature_, ed. Bruce King, pp. 215-6; Louis James, ed., _The Islands in Between_, pp. 28-29.

128 Bruce King, _New English Literatures_, p. 135.

129 Rhonda Cobham, "The Background," in _West Indian Literature_, p. 26.

130 Gordon Rohlehr, "The Ironic Approach," in _The Islands in Between_, p. 124; Nunez-Harrell, pp. 31-32.

131 Nunez-Harrell, p. 41.

132 L. Edward Brathwaite, "Jazz and the West Indian Novel," _Bim_ (Barbados), 11, No. 44 (Jan.-June 1967), 275-84; _Bim_, 12, No. 45 (July-Dec. 1967), 39-51; _Bim_, 12, No. 46 (Jan.-June 1968), 115-25.

133 Kenneth Ramchand, "Concern for Criticism," _The Literary Half-Yearly_, 11, No. 2 (July 1970), 154.

134 Nunez-Harrell, pp. 42-43.

135 "West Indian Fiction and West Indian Society,"
Kenyon Review, 25, No. 1 (Winter 1963), 132.

136 Nunez-Harrell, p. 44.

137 As quoted by Lindfors, p. 11.

138 Lindfors, p. 11.

139 "Prologue to an Autobiography," p. 148.

140 "London," in The Overcrowded Barracoon, p. 13.

141 "The Ironic Approach," in The Islands in Between,
p. 132.

142 Nunez-Harrell, p. 27.

143 See, for example, Donald E. Herdeck, ed.,
Caribbean Writers (Washington, D.C.: Three Continents
Press, Inc., 1979), p. 158.

144 "Caribbean Perspectives," Caribbean Quarterly,
17, Nos. 3 & 4 (1971), 119.

145 Ulric Mentus, "Is There Something Called Black
Art?" Caribbean Contact, 3, No. 11 (Feb. 1976), p. 7.

146 Figueroa, "Introduction," p. 557.

147 Frank Collymore, "Writing in the West Indies,"
Tamarack Review, 14 (Winter 1960), 117.

148 See, for example, Lennox Grant, "For Naipaul
there is a Challenge of Faith," Tapia (Trinidad), 13 July
1975, p. 7.

149 Michael Harris, "Naipaul on Campus," Tapia
(Trinidad), 29 June 1975, p. 2.

150 "V. S. Naipaul and West Indian Writers," Antilia
(University of the West Indies), 1 (1983), 14-15.

151 "Failure to Understand Naipaul," Trinidad
Guardian, 30 Aug. 1982, p. 8.

152 Figueroa, "Introduction," p. 560.

153 "Gunga Din of Caribbean Literature," Trinidad
Express, 3 July 1982.

154 "In Defense of Naipaul," Trinidad Guardian, 22
Aug. 1982, p. 8.

104

155 "The Novelist V. S. Naipaul Talks to Nigel Bingham," p. 306. Paul Theroux, "V. S. Naipaul," _Modern Fiction Studies_, 30, No. 3 (Autumn 1984), 445-54, gives a detailed profile of Naipaul's personality.

156 See, for example, William Walsh, _V. S. Naipaul_ (Edinburgh: Oliver & Boyd, 1973), pp. 22-3; Anniah H. H. Gowda, "Naipaul in India," _The Literary Half-Yearly_ (Mysore), 11, No. 2 (1970), 165-66.

157 _An Area of Darkness_ (London: André Deutsch, 1964; rpt. New York: Vintage Books, 1981), pp. 33-8. Subsequent references will be to this edition and will be indicated in the text.

158 "V. S. Naipaul and West Indian Writers," p. 9.

159 _Commonwealth Literature_ (London: Oxford University Press, 1973), p. 60.

160 D. J. Enright, "Who is India?" rev. of _An Area of Darkness, Encounter_, 23 (Dec. 1964), 60.

161 "Naipaul and the Voices of Negation," _Salmagundi_, 54 (Fall 1981), 50.

162 "Naipaul's India and Mine," in _New Writing in India_, ed. Adil Jussawalla (Baltimore, Maryland: Penguin, 1974), p. 74.

163 Goodheart, p. 52.

164 Goodheart, p. 50.

165 Goodheart, p. 44.

166 "V. S. Naipaul: Sensibility and Schemata," _Critical Quarterly_, 18, No. 3 (Autumn 1976), 75.

167 Robert Hemenway, "Sex and Politics in Naipaul," _Studies in the Novel_, 14, No. 2 (Summer 1982), 193.

168 "In Scorn and Pity," _New York Review of Books_, 11 Dec. 1975, p. 3.

169 _The Mimic Men_ (London: André Deutsch, 1967; rpt. New York: Penguin Books, 1981), pp. 245-46. Subsequent references will be to this edition and will be indicated in the text.

170 Goodheart, p. 53.

171 "V. S. Naipaul," The American Scholar, 50 (Summer 1981), 360.

172 Goodheart, p. 51.

173 Derek Walcott, "Naipaul's New Book," rev. of Mr Stone and the Knights Companion, Trinidad Guardian, 7 July 1963, p. 15.

174 Ewart Rouse, p. 9 and Fraser, p. 14.

175 Charles Michener, "The Dark Visions of V. S. Naipaul," Newsweek, 16 Nov. 1981, p. 108.

176 Lennox Grant, "For Naipaul There is a Challenge of Faith," p. 7.

177 "An Exile Returns," Trinidad Guardian, 25 Sept. 1960, p. 7.

178 "The European Factor in West Indian Literature," p. 80.

179 "Naipaul is a Literary Curiosity," Sunday Guardian (Trinidad), 10 Nov. 1968, p. 4.

180 "On Exile and the Dialect of the Tribe," p. 19.

181 Raoul Pantin, "Portrait of an Artist," Caribbean Contact, 1, No. 6 (May 1973), p. 18.

182 W. J. Weatherby, "Naipaul's Prize?" Sunday Times (London), 21 Sept. 1980, p. 32.

183 Pantin, "Portrait of an Artist," p. 18.

184 Pantin, "Portrait of an Artist," p. 18.

185 Pantin, "Portrait of an Artist," p. 18.

186 Figueroa, "Introduction," p. 557.

Chapter III

West Indian Response to
Naipaul's Early West Indian Fiction

In London in the early 1950's V. S. Naipaul was simply one
more promising but undistinguished expatriate battling
against great odds to establish himself as a writer.
Although philosophically and culturally opposed to the
predominantly black West Indian literary coterie in that
metropolis, he initially sought and received encouragement
and advice from aspiring fellow writers among that group,
such as Andrew Salkey, Ernest Eytle, and Gordon Woolford.
By the 1960's, however, Naipaul had drifted from the company of Caribbean artists with whom, he claimed, he had
nothing in common and whose works had stopped "feeding"
him.[1] With his publication of one award-winning work
after another, expressing an increasingly dark view of West
Indian politics and life, Naipaul's rise to fame in the
North Atlantic was paralleled by his growing notoriety in
the West Indies. Popular and literary opinion on the part
of his countrymen at home and abroad made his name
contemptuously synonymous with "enemy of the Third World"
and "spokesman for neo-colonialism." This chapter will
examine West Indian response to his first three novels
(which he has referred to as his "apprenticeship" works) and
will show that critics have found in the early Naipaul the
germ of his alleged contempt and rejection of everything
West Indian and black.

Naipaul's West Indian writings can be broadly divided
into two phases, with the travelogue The Middle Passage
(1962) serving as the line of demarcation between the early
and late Naipaul. Usually grouped together, The Mystic
Masseur (1957), The Suffrage of Elvira (1958) and Miguel
Street (1959)--listed in order of publication, not composi-
tion--comprise a triad of early social comedies written
before A House for Mr Biswas (1961). These early novels are
set in pre-independence Trinidad, and, with the exception of
Miguel Street, focus primarily on the island's East Indian
community. After The Middle Passage Naipaul shifted his
attention to fictional, post-independence multiracial West
Indian societies in his Caribbean works, The Mimic Men
(1967), A Flag on the Island (1967), Guerrillas (1975), and
he continued his journalistic interest in the region in The
Loss of El Dorado (1969), The Overcrowded Barracoon (1970),
and "The Killings in Trinidad" (1974).

The qualification must be made that not all of these
West Indian books are condemned or dismissed by all West
Indians. In the region Naipaul's reputation rests largely
upon A House for Mr Biswas and The Middle Passage, with West

Indian reaction revealing an ambivalent attitude towards the writer. The former work, generally hailed as an epic and now studied in Guyanese, Trinidadian, and Jamaican schools, has won Naipaul fame as a brilliant novelist; the latter, often condemned as an insult to the West Indies, has gained him notoriety as a dangerous propagandist. Thus, Derek Walcott lauded A House as "great in intention and in range," whereas he dismissed The Middle Passage as an "outrageous work."[2] Appreciation for Naipaul's novelistic and journalistic skill is frequently overshadowed by criticisms of his cynical and pessimistic reading of the Caribbean.

Miguel Street, Naipaul's first book to be written but the third to be published, is really a series of seventeen sketches (resembling John Steinbeck's Cannery Row) about Miguel Street Indian and black residents, drawn from Trinidad's urban lower classes. Set during and after World War II, the stories are related with humor and pathos, through the childhood recollections of a young nameless boy--not to be confused with Naipaul, who was not so much in tune with the street.[3] The narrator describes the world and people of this Port-of-Spain slum section, where a regular group of individuals happen to loiter together and form a club-like atmosphere:

> A stranger could drive through Miguel Street and
> just say 'Slum!' because he could see no more. But
> we, who lived there, saw our street as a world,
> where everybody was quite different from everybody
> else. Man-man was mad; George was stupid; Big Foot
> was a bully; Hat was an adventurer; Popo was a
> philosopher; and Morgan was our comedian.[4]

The discussion in the following pages will not only intro-duce the reader to the flavor of these stories but will also provide the context necessary in understanding West Indian reviews of Miguel Street.

Life in Miguel Street is mainly informal and communal, personal affairs open and public. When the men are not busy giving "blows" to their wives, working on never-ending and fruitless projects, or doing odd jobs, they play cards, swear, hurl harmless insults at each other, smoke, drink rum, sing calypsos, follow cricket scores, discuss their friends' problems, dream about their own plans for career or escape, philosophize about the ongoing war, and condemn their corrupt society. There is a strong spirit of camaraderie among these easy-going inhabitants, who experience together the pains of life--domestic unhappiness, career failures, frustration, depression, poverty--and who discover in the famous words of Hat, the street commentator and adviser: "'Life is a helluva thing. You can see trouble coming and you can't do a damn thing to prevent it coming. You just got to sit and watch and wait.'" (p. 91). Each story focuses on a different personality, who may make a

major or minor appearance in the other sketches. Thus, the
characters themselves provide the work with a unifying
thread and serve as a type of chorus.

Characters are noted for their specific oddities or
memorable actions. Eddoes, the "saga [dandy] boy," brushes
his teeth for hours; Big Foot, a bus driver, stops his
vehicle and orders his passengers out to take a bath;
Morgan, the pyrotechnicist, burns his house and finally
gains an audience to witness his fireworks display; and
Laura, mother of eight children from seven different
fathers, is like "Shakespeare when it comes to using words,"
bad words. Many personalities gain acceptance by asserting
their identity and manhood in strange ways. The tough,
mysterious Bogart, aptly named after the hero of _Casablanca_,
is jailed for bigamy in his effort to be "a man among we
men," a line reminiscent of Gurudeva's "'Is orright, Bap, I
is a man.'"[5] The carpenter, Popo, laboring endlessly to
make "the thing without a name" in order to escape real
work, finds himself the subject of a calypso when he beats
his wife's seducer. Landing in jail for stealing to regain
and impress his wife ("you see the sort of thing woman is"),
Popo, like Bogart, finally wins respect on his return to the
street: "He came back as a hero. He was one of the boys.
He was a better man than either Hat or Bogart" (p. 21).
Since wife-abuse is interpreted as a sign of manhood,
Nathaniel, Laura's current lover, brags that he is a regular
wife-beater, but the street "rabs" know better:

> He [Nathaniel] used to say,
> 'Woman and them like a good dose of blows, you
> know. You know the calypso:
>> Every now and then just knock them down.
>> Every now and then just throw them down.
>> Black up their eye and bruise up their knee
>> And then they love you eternally.
> Is gospel truth about woman.' . . . .
>> Eddoes said, 'I know a helluva lot about
> woman. I think Nathaniel lying like hell. I think
> when he with Laura he got his tail between his legs
> all the time.'
>> We used to hear fights and hear the chidren
> [sic] screaming all over the place, and when we saw
> Nathaniel, he would just say, 'Just been beating
> some sense into that woman. . . . Is only blows
> she really want to keep she happy.'
>> Nathaniel was lying of course. It wasn't he who
> was giving the blows, it was Laura. (p. 87)

The naive narrator sees only the glamor in the "badjohn"
heroes, but occasionally he is touched by pity for the
characters (for example, Laura and Mrs. Hereira) when they
experience pain.

In Miguel Street the men are desperate to prove their manhood because economic opportunities are limited and ambitions aborted. Elias aspires to be a doctor and dreams of doing so well that "'Mr Cambridge go bawl when he read what I write for him,'" but since "litritcher and poultry" turn out to be bothersome, he settles to become a sanitary inspector. Even this new ambition has to be modified because Elias fails the examination each time, concluding, "'What the hell you expect in Trinidad? You got to bribe everybody if you want to get your toenail cut'" (p. 36). His luck does not change in those Caribbean countries where, he is told by Hat, the test is simpler. At any rate, Elias becomes one of the "street aristocrats," "driving the scavenging carts," and he adopts a complacent attitude:" 'No theory here. This is the practical. I really like the work'" (p. 32). The jobless Uncle Bhakcu who fancies himself a "mechanical genius," is convinced to become a pundit since he knows the Ramayana and is a Brahmin. Thus, serious career plans hardly materialize, but people improvise and conceal their disappointments.

Miguel Street derelicts who fail to make it in life become slightly deranged, but such tragedies are cushioned by a narrative technique that accentuates the comic rather than the tragic. The narrator argues that many so-called "sane" Trinidadians are more "mad" than the notorious Man-man, candidate at every election. Man-man finds mental escape by writing one word--one vowel--extending on the surface of several streets, and he gets even with a café owner by breaking into the establishment and leaving "little blobs of excrement . . . on the centre of every stool and top of every table and at regular intervals along the counter" (p. 40). Announcing that he has seen God ("seeing God was quite common in Port of Spain, and, indeed, in Trinidad at that time") and that he is a new Messiah, Man-Man stages his own crucifixion. The crucifixion scene, in which he is brought back to reality, demonstrates not only the dramatic style of the book but also the overshadowing of the pathetic by the comic:

> Man-man began carrying the cross from the road, up the rocky path and then down to the Basin.
> Some men put up the cross, and tied Man-man to it.
> Man-man said, 'Stone me, brethen.'
> The women wept and flung bits of sand and gravel at his feet.
> Man-man groaned and said, 'Father, forgive them. They ain't know what they doing.' Then he screamed out, 'Stone me, brethen!'
> A pebble the size of an egg struck him on the chest.
> Man-man cried, 'Stone, stone, STONE me, brethen! I forgive you.'

Edward said, 'The man really brave.'
People began flinging really big stones at
Man-man, aiming at his face and chest.
Man-man looked hurt and surprised. He
shouted, 'What the hell is this? What the hell you
people think you doing? Look, get me down from
this thing quick . . . and I go settle with that
son of a bitch who pelt a stone at me. . . . Cut
this stupidness out. Cut it out, I tell you. I
finish with this arseness, you hear.' And then he
began cursing so loudly and coarsely that the
people stopped in surprise.
The police took away Man-man.
The authorities kept him for observation.
Then for good. (p. 44)

When another drifter and dreamer, Bolo, makes large invest-
ments in a newspaper game competition and is swindled by an
advertisement, he resolves to flee from Trinidad, a place he
thinks that Hitler should be bombing instead. He pays
someone to take him to Venezuela, but he is ferried around
in the dark and set ashore Trinidad. Failure is such a
predictable way of life in Miguel Street that when Bolo is
told that he eventually wins a sweepstakes, he destroys the
ticket in anger and disbelief: "'These Trinidad people does
only lie, lie. Lie is all they know. They could fool you,
boy, but, they can't fool me'" (p. 137). However, as Landeg
White notes, Miguel Street is "exceedingly funny, and while
one can abstract from it a message of frustration the
overall impression is not of bitterness but of relish and an
infectious nostalgia."[6]

At the end of Miguel Street the narrator arrives at the
conclusion that beneath the mask of glamorous
unconventionality and brutality there lies the grim reality
of waste and futility. Even Hat, usually a level-headed
philosopher and sober commentator on people's business, gets
into trouble with the law and is sentenced to a prison
term. With his departure the Miguel Street informal club is
disbanded. When he is released three years later, changes
have occurred and things cannot return to normal. The
narrator, now eighteen, has matured:

I had grown up and looked critically at the people
around me. I no longer wanted to be like Eddoes.
He was so weak and thin, and I hadn't realized he
was so small. Titus Hoyt was stupid and boring,
and not funny at all. Everything had changed.
When Hat went to jail, part of me had died. (p. 165)

The narrator finds himself inevitably drifting aimlessly,
wasting away: "I had become a little wild. I was drinking
like a fish. . . . I said to my mother, 'Is not my fault
really. Is just Trinidad. What else anybody can do here

except drink?'" (p. 166). Enticed by the image of London, snow, the Thames, big Parliament, the narrator eagerly accepts a scholarship, procured from politician/pundit Ganesh Ramsumair (the hero of Naipaul's The Mystic Masseur) for $100.00. Thus, physical escape is presented as an apparently logical solution to the insularity and stagnation of Trinidadian life. Even after his maturity and his detachment and escape from Miguel Street, the narrator is able to record with tenderness, admiration, and laughter his childhood recollections of the residents.

Miguel Street, then, presents a gallery of people who are frustrated in their efforts to make something of themselves in Trinidad, but who, nevertheless, are characterized by their vitality and resilience and imagination. The following lines from the sketch "B. [Black] Wordsworth" describe a familiar West Indian scene and present the pathetic condition and predicament not only of aspiring and suffering artists but also of the dispossessed and deprived islanders, who must learn patience and endurance:

> [B. Wordsworth] pulled out a printed sheet from his hip-pocket and said, 'On this paper is the greatest poem about mothers and I'm going to sell it to you at a bargain price. For four cents.'
> I went inside and I said, 'Ma, you want to buy a poetry for four cents?'
> My mother said, 'Tell that blasted man to haul his tail away from my yard, you hear.'
> I said to B. Wordsworth, 'My mother say she ain't have four cents.'
> B. Wordsworth said, 'It is the poet's tragedy.'
> And he put the paper back in his pocket. He didn't seem to mind. (pp. 46-47)

Naipaul's accomplishment in this and in all the other sketches is that pathos is never permitted to overshadow comedy, a comedy enhanced by the rich Port-of-Spain dialect. B. Wordsworth despairingly tries to compose the greatest poem, "the past is deep," being a sample line of a whole month's work; yet, like the others, he has learned how to live.

In "Prologue to an Autobiography," Naipaul, working from his own "deep" past, recalled his Trinidadian experiences as he traced the creative process and development of the characters in Miguel Street.[7] A brief look at Naipaul's account will show the reader that, contrary to the belief of some readers, Miguel Street residents are not exaggerations. Naipaul related in detail that with some alteration in story line and characterization, the personalities of his book are generally drawn from people whom he actually knew. Hat, a creolized Madrasi Indian, for example, was Naipaul's Port-of-Spain neighbor, while Bogart, whose father and Naipaul's maternal grandfather journeyed

together from India to Trinidad as indentured laborers,
resided in the "servant room" in the family yard when
Naipaul was a boy. Bogart's mysterious long disappearances,
sometimes to Venezuela, are exploited in the story. His
tailor shop at the seaside village of Carneage, along with
the signboard Naipaul painted for the shop, is also
mentioned in the tale, although the setting is in
Port-of-Spain. (In 1977, after twenty-seven years, Naipaul
found the real, mysterious Bogart, whom he tracked down,
with some difficulty, in Venezuela.[8]) While working on
the story "Bogart," Naipaul recalled that around 1938 or
1939, a black carpenter, who also lived and did his work in
the yard, said that he was "making the thing without a
name." Naipaul described how this memory served him in
composing Miguel Street: "And the scattered memories, my
narrator, the life of the street, and my own childhood sense
. . . of the intensity of the pleasures of the people on the
street, gave the carpenter a story," a story not different
from the real one.[9]

In some cases two people were fused to create one
personality. For example, one of Naipaul's acquaintances,
Gordon Woolford, blended with the figure of a ballad maker:

> Gordon was talking of some early period of his
> life, some period of luxury and promise. Then he
> broke off, said, "But that was a long time ago,"
> and looked down through the reflections of glass
> into the street. That went to my heart. Within a
> few days I was to run it into the memory of a Negro
> ballad maker, disturbed but very gentle, who had
> called at my grandmother's house in Port of Spain
> one day to sell copies of his poems, single printed
> sheets, and had told me a little of his life.[10]

The result, "B. Wordsworth," ranks among the best of the
sketches. The anecdotes of Miguel Street dramatize an
observation Naipaul later made in The Middle Passage that
Trinidad is a "place where the stories were never stories of
success but of failure; brilliant men, scholarship winners,
who had died young, gone mad, or taken to drink."[11] The
important point is that the personalities of Miguel Street
are real people, and "memory provided the material."[12]

Most British and American reviewers have admired
Naipaul's characters as eccentrics but have generally
stopped short of noting that they are authentic eccentrics.
The San Francisco Chronicle's statement that the
personalities are "swift caricatures of humanity" is
balanced by the London Magazine's observation that they are
"eccentrics without being caricatures."[13] Australian
critic Landeg White is among the few non-West Indian critics
to confirm the common existence of Miguel Street characters
and stories:

It is significant that much of the material in
Miguel Street is based on anecdotes which are still
widely current in Trinidad. I myself, for
instance, had heard the adventures ascribed to Bolo
many times before I read Miguel Street, and
'Man-man' exists in other versions . . . and it is
also the subject of the final verse of a splendid
calypso by the Mighty Wonder:
> We had a preacher by de name of Nosegay
> Who say he wan' to die so as to wash our sins
> away;
> He say don' nail but tie me to de cross
> But don' use no big stone, pebble or force;
> Well! Peter hit him with a poui;
> He bawl out, Man, have some sympathy!
> Help! Take me down;
> Help! I ain' do no wrong
> Every niggerman go bear livin'
> I ain' dyin' again.[14]

Since individuals such as Man-man, Bogart, and Elias are
embryonic creations which Naipaul develops in his subsequent
Trinidadian novels, it is important to emphasize that in the
West Indies such personages, who to outsiders appear to be
exaggerations, are actually based on commonly found West
Indian "characters" who have been given tag names by the
community.

Naipaul himself has reminded us--and Guyanese critic
Victor Ramraj agrees[15]--that Trinidadians are "more
recognizably characters than people in England" and are easy
material for a writer. "Only a man's eccentricities can get
him attention," Naipaul writes. "It might also be that in a
society without traditions, without patterns, every man
finds it easier 'to be himself'."[16] One reason why
"characters" are more prevalent and widely known in a place
such as the West Indies as distinct from, say, in England
may be that in the former, life is informal and communal,
while in the latter it is official and private. In
explaining why it is easier for the English to know the West
Indies than vice versa, Naipaul may have found the reason
for the commonality of numerous eccentrics in Trinidad:

> In a warm country life is conducted out of doors.
> Windows are open, doors are open. People sit in
> open verandas and cafés. You know your neighbour's
> business and he knows yours. It is easy for a
> visitor to get to know the country. He is
> continually catching people in off-duty positions.
> In England everything goes on behind closed doors.
> The man from the warm country automatically leaves
> the door open behind him. . . . I have met many
> people [in England] but I know them only in
> official attitudes--the drink, the interview, the
> meal.[17]

It is more likely that in an informal, familiar society, individuals are frequently caught being themselves and do not mind going about unmasked. These "characters" are generally unfamiliar to residents and reviewers in Western metropolises.

A comparison of Western and West Indian reviews of Miguel Street shows a sharp difference in critical emphasis. British and American critics may miss the point that Naipaul's eccentrics are authentic, but they are often enchanted by the "unfamiliar background" and by what has been called the "mangled English" and "fractured accents" of the characters.[18] Caribbean critics, on the other hand, view the book from a different perspective. The rich West Indian dialect and characters are familiar to them, and they have not challenged the authenticity of the personalities. At the same time, they have rarely commented on Naipaul's skill at reproducing local color. Guyanese critic Ivan Van Sertima, instead, acknowledged that the stories and characters show Naipaul's comic inventiveness, but charged that the sketches lack the "sparkling punch and pointed finish that distinguish the short stories" of Selvon.[19] In sharp contrast to this judgment are almost all Western reviews, including the Saturday Review's opinion that "the mantle of Chekov has fallen on Mr. Naipaul's shoulders."[20] And unlike British and American reviewers, Caribbean readers have focused on what they see as traces of Naipaul's Eurocentered view of their region, a charge often leveled against Naipaul, especially in his later works.

To prove this accusation in Miguel Street, Caribbean readers have referred to the characters who generally never achieve success, something which is presented as impossible in Trinidad. Indeed, many men (Bogart, Man-man, and Hat) end up in confinement; others (Edward, Morgan, Bolo) dream of escape; and still others (Popo, Bhakcu, and B. Wordsworth) make feeble and futile attempts to achieve. According to West Indian Anthony Boxill, Naipaul implies that Trinidad is a prison because of its isolation and history of colonialism and slavery, and that since the society lacks standards and stifles creativity, freedom can be secured only by emigrating to a country unretarded by colonialism.[21] Boxill's reading of Miguel Street is more literary than political and is supported by the text. Such is not the case, however, with Guyanese Gordon Rohlehr, who asserted that Naipaul's "ironic awareness"

> manifests itself, rather, in his unconscious acceptance of a typical European view of Third World inferiority, a view which is now being attacked from several quarters. It shows itself in his contemptuous rejection of all things West Indian. . . . The conviction of an anarchic society which the author must reject lies . . . behind Miguel Street.[22]

The issue appears to be whether Naipaul, because of his
alleged Euro-centered outlook, rejects the Caribbean or
simply presents the region as it is.

Australian critic Landeg White, who may have had this
debate in mind, has made an important point: "Whatever
larger conclusions about Trinidad one may have to draw from
the book [Miguel Street], Naipaul's first concern is to
recreate the world in which he grew up, to do justice to
characters he once admired."[23] Faced with unemployment,
the unskilled in the Caribbean know that their opportunities
are limited. As pointed out in Chapter 1, after World War
II, the setting of the book, it was the growing feeling in
the West Indies that migrating to the metropolis, preferably
to secure an education and to take advantages of
opportunities unavailable at home, was the only way of
assuring success. Many who were not even desirous of
pursuing studies were, like the narrator of Miguel Street,
tempted merely by the prospects of escaping the dull island
life. In his autobiographical sketch, Naipaul recalled that
when he was growing up in Trinidad, the island was poor and
that many individuals sought to escape to Venezuela for both
money and adventure.[24] He has simply recorded a migration
pattern, which is a historical fact. Thus, his characters'
rejection of Trinidad's society cannot definitely be tied to
his alleged Euro-centered view.

One issue not debated is Naipaul's sympathetic or
compassionate handling of characters in Miguel Street, a
quality praised by both Western reviewers and Caribbean
readers. Gordon Rohlehr has argued that in his book,
Naipaul rejects Trinidad, not with contempt as in the other
novels but with sympathy.[25] The reviewer for the Jamaican
Gleaner, who did not find the work "wholly satisfying,"
admitted that "perhaps the feeling that the book doesn't
quite certainly come off may be due to prejudice because of
some of Naipaul's unkind humour."[26] However, West Indian
critics are generally in agreement in noting that in spite
of Naipaul's irony and satire, the characters are drawn with
a great deal of compassion. Victor Ramraj, a Guyanese,
reading Miguel Street as the warmest of Naipaul's first
three novels, referred to the "tolerant, sympathetic
laughter" in the sketches, the "commingling of humour and
pathos" and the use of innocuous philosophical irony as the
source of humor.[27] Even A. C. Derrick, an Antiguan, who
charged Naipaul with lack of sympathy and with failure to
show a humane understanding of his characters' weaknesses in
all of his novels, argued that in Miguel Street, "the
characterizations show a human sympathy and understanding
that is rare in Naipaul's satire. . . . The sketches of B.
Wordsworth, Laura and Hat have a rare pathos which Naipaul
succeeds in conveying even through the satiric mode."[28]
It is partly this quality of sympathy that saves Miguel
Street from total rejection by West Indian critics.

Sympathy is what many West Indian critics see as lacking in Naipaul's second novel, The Mystic Masseur, which traces Ganesh Ramsumair's quiet, gradual acceptance and eventual control of a chaotic Trinidadian world, a world genially presented as one of superstition, knavery, quackery, trickery, and chicanery. Divided into twelve chapters and an epilogue, with internal breaks, the story is related by an anonymous, naive black narrator, who occasionally quotes from Ganesh's biography. The book opens in medias res when the narrator, whose foot is swollen, is being taken by his mother to a dull, remote village in Fuente Grove, Trinidad, to see Ganesh, a masseur, for "in those days people went by preference to the unqualified masseur or the quack dentist."[29] And in this world in which the written word draws reverence from people, the depressed narrator is reassured when he notices Ganesh holding a "big book," impressed when he sees about 1,500 books in Ganesh's study, and overwhelmed when he receives a pamphlet 101 Questions and Answers on the Hindu Religion written by the masseur himself. Assuming a bombastic and pretentious manner and using a slightly inflated language, the narrator concludes the chapter with a justification of the importance of Ganesh's life:

> Nineteen forty-six was the turning-point of Ganesh's career; and, as if to underline the fact, in that year he published his autobiography, The Years of Guilt. . . . The wider world has not learnt of Ganesh's early struggles, and Trinidad resents this. I myself believe that the history of Ganesh is, in a way, the history of our times; and there may be people who will welcome this imperfect account of the man Ganesh Ramsumair, masseur, mystic, and since 1953, M.B.E. (p. 14)

This prefatory remark, along with Naipaul's assurance that "all characters, organizations and incidents in this novel are fictitious," prepares us for the typicality of the story in a place such as Trinidad. Throughout the novel Naipaul generally shows, what one reader has called an "amused, poker-faced sophistication."[30]

Ganesh is first presented as a shy, awkward Indian country boy attending a Port-of-Spain school, but there are traces that he has the potential to adjust to his world, for he assumes a more socially acceptable name, Gareth. The description of his Hindu initiation ceremony, which he undergoes during his school vacation, raises the tantalizing question as to whether he is from the start a shrewd charlatan. During the janaywa ceremony—which Naipaul calls, in An Area of Darkness, a "pleasing piece of theatre" and which he refuses to undergo—the initiate announces that he will go to Benares to study; a senior member of the

family pleads with him to change his mind, and he
reluctantly yields and lays down his staff and bundle.[31]
Ganesh's initiation departs from this script:

> They shaved his head, gave him a little saffron
> bundle, and said, 'All right, off you go now. Go
> to Benares and study.'
> He took his staff and began walking away
> briskly from Fourways.
> As arranged, Dookhie the shopkeeper ran after
> him, crying a little and begging in English, 'No
> boy. No. Don't go away to Benares to study.'
> Ganesh kept on walking.
> 'But what happen to the boy?' people asked.
> 'He taking this thing really serious.'
> Dookhie caught Ganesh by the shoulder and
> said, 'Cut out this nonsense, man. Stop behaving
> stupid. You think I have all day to run after you?
> You think you really going to Benares? That is in
> India, you know, and this is Trinidad.' (p. 17)

Is Ganesh protesting against imported Indian rituals in
Trinidad? Or is he still a clumsy country boy? Whatever
the answer, undoubtedly he is his own person, for when his
father orders him to get married or else become an orphan,
Ganesh defiantly becomes an orphan. His academic career as
a substitute teacher in the city is aborted when, insulted
by his predecessor, he spontaneously and angrily leaves
school. So unskilled that he "can't even drive a donkey
cart," he is in a precarious financial position. Coincidentally, however, he is summoned home by the death of his
father and finds that he now enjoys oil royalties.

Throughout the novel, the narrator tries to convince
the reader that things are preordained for Ganesh. He
quotes from Ganesh's The Years of Guilt: "I felt I had
something big ahead of me. For it was indeed a singular
conspiracy of events that pulled me away from the emptiness
of urban life back into the stimulating peace and the quiet
of the country" (p. 27). Among the rural residents is the
wily and lachrymose shopkeeper, Ramlogan--one of the book's
admirable and funny rogues--who is obsessed with modernity
and his "cha'acter and sensa values." He craftily arranges
a match between his daughter, Leela, and Ganesh whom he
convinces to become a masseur. In fact, throughout his
life, Ganesh is accidentally thrown into contact with people
who conspire to shape his career. Mr. Stewart, a deranged
Englishman and Hindu convert, encourages him to read the
Science of Thought Review, to think, to meditate, and to
write. During a visit to Basdeo, the printer, Ganesh is
surprised to find himself talking about a book he will one
day publish, and he unthinkingly makes the same spontaneous
promise to Ramlogan and Leela.

Another important event convinces Ganesh that his life
is preordained: his quarrel with Ramlogan. Ganesh begins
to understand his world when Ramlogan, presenting himself
pathetically as the illiterate and exploited man, dupes him
into an agreement not to prolong the kedgeree-eating wedding
ceremony to elicit a large dowry. (During this carefully
staged ritual the bridegroom eats the rice mixture after
being satisfied with the gifts from the bride's party.) And
when Ganesh's aunt (called The Great Belcher because of her
frequent and impolite burps), her assistant (inexplicably
named King George), and a number of other women manage his
wedding house, charging their expenses to his account with
Ramlogan, Ganesh understands too well: "Oh God! I ain't
even married the man daughter yet, and already he start" (p.
49).

In a scene reminiscent of the initiation ceremony,
Ganesh executes one of his first revenge schemes as he
learns to play the game. Decked in the traditional groom's
outfit of satin robes and bright-colored tasselled head
dress, he is offered the kedgeree:

> Ramlogan was the first to offer money to induce
> Ganesh to eat. He was a little haggard after
> staying awake all night, but he looked pleased and
> happy enough when he placed five twenty-dollar
> bills in the brass plate next to the kedgeree. He
> stepped back, folded his arms, looked from the
> money to Ganesh to the small group standing by, and
> smiled.
> He stood smiling for nearly two minutes; but
> Ganesh didn't even look at the kedgeree.
> 'Give the boy money, man.' Ramlogan cried to
> the people around. . . .'
> Still Ganesh sat, serene and aloof, like an
> over-dressed Buddha.
> A little crowd began to gather. . . .
> [Ramlogan] put down another hundred dollars.
> 'Eat, boy, eat it up. . . .' He laughed, but no
> one laughed with him. Ganesh didn't eat.
> He heard a man saying, 'Well, this thing was
> bound to happen some day. . . .'
> The crowd grew bigger; the laughter grew louder.
> Ramlogan came back and the crowd cheered him.
> He put down two hundred dollars. . . . Ganesh
> didn't move.
> The crowd was beginning to treat him like a hero.
> In the end Ganesh got from Ramlogan: a cow and
> a heifer, fifteen hundred dollars in cash, and a
> house in Fuente Grove. Ramlogan also cancelled the
> bill for the food he had sent to Ganesh's house.
> The ceremony ended at about nine in the morning;
> but Ramlogan was sweating long before then. (pp.
> 50-52)

120

Karl Nyren has argued that Naipaul satirizes Ganesh "most of
the time but occasionally seems to admire him."[32]
Certainly, the kedgeree and janaywa ceremonies are instances
when Naipaul is on Ganesh's side. What makes the kedgeree
scene doubly effective is that by prolonging the charade,
Ganesh dramatically and comically makes a commentary on what
he perceives to be a meaningless theatrical custom, while at
the same time he emerges as an even match for the
calculating Ramlogan. The dowry turns out to be
providential because Ganesh's oil royalties have now dried
up.

Ganesh's life begins to take direction after the
wedding, especially with practical advice and a nudge from
The Great Belcher. One admonition is that "These modern
girls is hell self. . . . All she [Leela] want to make she
straight as a arrow is a little blows every now and then," a
recommendation that Ganesh seriously follows. More
importantly, though, the Belcher implants in him the idea
that in addition to taking up massaging, he should do some
writing because "it go have so much massagers in Trinidad
they go have to start massaging one another" (p. 53). After
endless thinking and unsystematic note-taking, Ganesh
completes the book. However, even with a Trinidad Sentinel
advertisement and with the expertise of salesman Bisoon
(dressed in a three piece suit, tie, and hat but not with
shoes because "they does keep me back"), the book does not
sell. Ganesh reflects in The Years of Guilt: "Everything
happens for the best. If, for instance, my first volume had
been a success, it is likely that I would have become a mere
theologian, writing endless glosses on the Hindu
scriptures. As it was, I found my true path" (p. 107). In
a conversation, which shows Naipaul's ear for local dialect
and dialogue, the Great Belcher opportunely directs Ganesh
to find his natural bent:

'It have a long time now I studying you,
Ganesh. You have the Power all right.'
It was the sort of statement he had grown to
expect from The Great Belcher. 'What Power?'
'To cure people. Cure the mind, cure the
soul--chut! . . .'
Ganesh said acidly, 'You want me to start curing
people soul when you see me cathing good hell to
cure their toenail!'
Leela coaxed, 'Man, the least you could do for
me is to give it a try.' . . .
'All right, then. I have this great Power. How
I go start using it? What I go tell people? "Your
soul a little run down today. Here, take this
prayer three times a day before meals."'
The Great Belcher clapped her hands. 'Is
exactly what I mean. . . .'
Ganesh was interested now. (p. 111)

Thus, Ganesh is persuaded and coached into establishing himself as a mystic masseur and into discarding his Western dress for traditional Indian <u>dhoti</u> and <u>koortah</u>.

Ganesh discovers that he can achieve success simply by going with the flow of things. In a ritualistic ceremony he "exorcises" a spirit from a guilt-ridden black boy who claims that he is about to be devoured by a cloud. Asked whether he used a trick, Ganesh "didn't say." Ironically, it is when he becomes a fraud that he earns the respect of everyone, including Leela. In addition, his tender treatment of the boy and the sincerity of his concern are presented in such a way that he is exonerated from the reader's condemnation. Soon nationally famous, he receives more than enough clients ("he never imagined there were so many people in Trinidad with spiritual problems"). After a while he becomes more flexible--even duplicitous--keeping symbols of Christianity, Hinduism, and Islam. With a refrigerator (placed to be seen from the road), Coca Cola in glasses, a lavatory, and even a musical toilet-paper rack that plays "Yankee Doodle Dandy," Ganesh has started his transformation into a mimic man. Yet his gradual conversion and subsequent prosperity are repeatedly emphasized as events which are beyond his control or which result from his benevolent nature. His take-over of Ramlogan's taxi service, his outfoxing of Narayan, president of the Hindu Association, and his defeat of the affected and pretentious Oxonian Indarsingh are all presented as necessary acts of goodwill he is forced to do in the interest of the people. Ganesh becomes "Hon'ble Ganesh Ramsumair, M.L.C.," convinced that his career was shaped by Providence.

Still learning to adjust in his new world, Ganesh has not yet become a complete mimic man. Accustomed to the informality of West Indian life, he is uncomfortable with formal, Anglicized public etiquette. Before attending his first Government House dinner, he receives a lesson on the use of cutlery, but gives up: "Nah, nah, Fish knife, soup spoon, fruit spoon, tea spoon--who sit down and make up all that?" (p. 201). Such bungled attempts to imitate the cultural patterns of colonizers are a rich source of humor. Again, showing Naipaul's gift for handling individual episodes and scenes, the dinner scene comically and satirically dramatizes the incongruities which follow the aping of a "superior" culture. Most of the members attending the dinner are ridiculously dressed and clumsily lacking in social decorum. The harder they try, the more they fail. They represent a wide cross section of the emerging native West Indian bourgeois society, marked by confused values and uncertainty:

> The dinner was a treat for the photographers. Ganesh came in dhoti and <u>koortah</u> and turban; the member for one of the Port of Spain wards wore a khaki suit and a sun helmet; a third came in

> jodhpurs; a fourth, adhering for the moment to his
> pre-election principles, came in short trousers and
> an open shirt; the blackest M.L.C. wore a
> three-piece suit, yellow woollen gloves and a
> monocle. Everybody else, among the men, looked
> like penguins, sometimes even down to the black
> faces.
>   An elderly Christian Indian member didn't bring
> a wife because he said he never had one; instead he
> brought along a daughter, a bright little thing of
> about four. (pp. 201-02)

Mrs. Primrose ("all of her squeezed into a floriferous print
frock") is not the only one who uses bad grammar and becomes
nervous. Some members, inexperienced in handling cutlery,
agree that they are not hungry after all. The climax of the
scene occurs when Mr. Primrose's monocle falls in his soup:

> The Governor's lady quickly looked away.
>   But Mr Primrose drew her attention to the
> monocle. 'Eh, eh,' he chuckled, 'but see how it
> fall down!'
>   The M.L.C.'s looked on with sympathy.
>   Mr Primrose turned on them. 'What all you
> staring at? All you ain't see nigger before?'
>   The man in jodhpurs whispered to Ganesh, 'But we
> wasn't saying anything.'
>   'Eh!' Mr Primrose snapped. 'Black people don't
> wear monocle?' (p. 203)

Returning home to Fuente Grove after his torturous dinner,
Ganesh, to Leela's surprise, calls for food: "Done dine.
Want to eat now. Going to show them," he mumbled, as his
fingers ploughed through the rice and _dal_ and curry" (pp.
203-4). Ganesh could "show them," that is, get even with
the elites, either by being himself or by joining them.
Apparently, Ganesh realizes that success in his world
can be achieved only by assuming Western norms and by using
subterfuge. In Port-of-Spain his "progress" becomes rapid.
His increased political activities give him less time for
mysticism, a career which embarrassed him now anyway. And
when he is heckled by striking sugar workers, it is a
different Ganesh who calls a press conference to declare
that Providence has opened his eyes and that he will fight
communism. No longer reluctant to don dinner jackets and
attend cocktail parties at Government House, he degenerates
into a darker shade of Indarsingh, who, ironically, is the
one to note the "capitalist mentality inherent in the title"
of Ganesh's new book, _Out of Red_. As an Anglicized
political leader, Ganesh journeys to Lake Success to defend
British colonial rule and later becomes an M.B.E. There is
no question of his transformation when at a London train

station, an impeccably dressed politician disembarks from
the first-class train carriage, and, having been greeted as
Pundit Ganesh, coldly corrects the welcome, "G. Ramsay
Muir." Thus, Ganesh's rise (or fall), presented with
understanding, is not so much a history of the man as it is
a history of the times. The society has made Ganesh, whose
metamorphosis is as understandable as it is reprehensible.
      Except for debates about the use of local color or
about the swiftness of the concluding pages, Western
reviewers have generally given <u>The Mystic Masseur</u> a
favorable rating, singling out in particular the deftness of
individual, satiric scenes, dialogue, and
characterizations. These are also the features admired by
West Indians, including Guyanese Ivan Van Sertima, who,
though no strong admirer of Naipaul, praised the "completely
believable characters and situations" in the novel.[33] In
the same vein the <u>Trinidad Guardian</u> reviewer lauded
Naipaul's talent for creating verisimilitude: "There is,
undoubtedly, the ring of truth in the character and
circumstances of Ganesh Ramsumair. . . . In fact Ganesh is
a composite of persons you will be tempted to believe you
know if you are Trinidadian."[34] The most enthusiastic
review of the novel has come from Frank Collymore, a white
Barbadian critic:

> The "young East Indian" writes suavely, skil-
> fully, and economically, and the dialogue and
> characterisation leave little to be desired; indeed
> some of the episodes, as I heard one crtic remark,
> might be lifted bodily on to the stage.[35]

In his review Frank Collymore touched upon one key controversial issue: Naipaul's attitude toward the characters.
Welcoming the ability to laugh at West Indian foibles and to
look at the society with ironic detachment at a time when
"propaganda and clichés of emergent nationhood are so apt to
occasion all the ill-effects of self-complacency," Collymore
praised Naipaul's approach:

> It must not be inferred that the author has been
> guilty of sneering at the misfortune of the poor
> and ignorant: on the contrary, with his satire is
> mixed not merely humour but fun, and, despite the
> aloofness of his approach, it is not difficult to
> realise that here, not only is there no bitterness,
> but an ever-tolerant understanding and sympathy.[36]

      Collymore's judgment, however, is not typical of West
Indian reaction. Instead, some Caribbean critics have
focused on what they see as the lack of compassion and
sympathy with which the characters are presented and
consequently the destructiveness of the satire.[37] Branded
as done with poor taste, for example, is the scene at the

Government House dinner during which the newly elected members of the legislative Council are culturally embarrassed. Arguing that Naipaul's contempt for the West Indies occasionally "breaks through even the geniality of The Mystic Masseur," Gordon Rohlehr criticized the dinner episode and noted that Naipaul makes a "special point of Mr. Primrose's blackness." Rohlehr then concluded:

> One can accept this as farce intended, in its distorted way, to show the Creole and Indian on the painful and ridiculous road to whiteness. But the suspicion persists that Naipaul himself regards these people with more contempt than compassion. . . . The incongruity of his position here, as Lamming points out, is that while he laughs at his Creoles crudely aping standards of pseudo-whiteness, he can only so do assuming these very norms himself.[38]

(Rohlehr's reference to George Lamming's statement in 1960 that Naipaul is a "colonial, ashamed of his cultural background . . . " is quoted in full below.[39]) Undoubtedly, Naipaul has adopted Western mannerisms; in fact, so have the majority of West Indians. This adoption, however, does not mean that West Indians cannot laugh at themselves, at their bungled efforts to speak, dress, eat, and behave like colonialists. Such humor, common in the West Indies, is innocuous, not contemptuous. It is inconceivable that Naipaul condemns those who are forced by social circumstances to mimic white ways when he himself has had to do the same. Thus, while the dinner scene may offend the sensibility of some readers, such uncomfortable, comical situations did exist when colonizers mixed with the local population, and Naipaul is merely indulging in fun.

Rohlehr's sensitivity to the presentation of Mr. Primrose as the "blackest M.L.C." reflects another concern of many West Indians--that is, that Naipaul may be prejudiced against blacks. Isolated, negative descriptions of blacks in Naipaul's works are often recalled, sometimes out of context, and cited as evidence of racial bias. Selwyn Cudjoe, arguing that Naipaul's black characters are portrayed negatively, and referring to the specific presentation of Mr. Primrose, raised the question as to whether Naipaul is a racist.[40] However, in the Government House dinner scene, non-black characters, such as Oxonian Indarsingh and the elderly Christian Indian (whose conversion to Christianity and whose flaunting of his illegitimate daughter are considered by conservative East Indians to be serious moral transgressions), are equally the butt of Naipaul's satire. Moreover, as the discussion of all his West Indian works, fiction and non-fiction, in subsequent chapters will show, Naipaul is equally savage in his criticisms of East Indians and whites. And since a

racist is someone who believes in the superiority of his own
ethnic group, it cannot be said that Naipaul is a racist, or
that he is even anti-black. Had he limited his criticisms
to blacks only, there would have been valid grounds for
bringing charges of racial prejudice against him.
     Some Caribbean readers are not disturbed by Naipaul's
presentation of West Indian society. Victor Ramraj argued
that there are scenes such as the Government House dinner
with satiric overtones but that such episodes could be
considered "harmlessly farcical" and that Naipaul is "not
wholly lacking in tolerance in his treatment of Ganesh."[41]
In their introduction to the novel, Kenneth Ramchand and
Paul Edwards called the dinner scene "ill-judged" and
"aesthetically unsatisfactory" and noted that such comedy
exposing people's table manners seems "snobbish and
unfeeling." However, they recognized the value of the
episode in ridiculing the pseudo-European grotesqueries of
all West Indian politicians, blacks and Indians: "What
Naipaul seems to be wanting to say is that creolisation in
these islands has proceeded not as growth of a civilisation
original to the area but as a superficial mimicry of models
derived from what is unthinkingly regarded as a superior
European culture."[42] Indeed, the island is establishing a
ridiculous new set of norms, and the narrator's words that
"the history of Ganesh is, in a way, the history of our
times" is significant. It is to the times that Ganesh
learns to adjust. In fact, David Lowenthal, in his
sociological analysis of West Indian societies, quoted from
the Government House dinner scene to demonstrate his point
that bridging race and class gaps could be a mortifying
experience.[43]
     Significantly, at least two of Naipaul's non-West
Indian critics have defended Naipaul against the charges of
lack of sympathy in The Mystic Masseur. William Walsh
argued that if the comedy is satirical, it is because of the
"author's sense of the ridiculous and his eye for
dishonesty" and that it is hard to understand why the work
has been dubbed malicious since Naipaul's attitude is
"neither contemptuous nor patronising."[44] Landeg White,
responding specifically to criticisms of the Government
House dinner scene, justified Naipaul's purpose:

          The whole displaced society is summed up neatly in
          the dinner. . . . The scene has been much
          criticised on the grounds that Naipaul, secure in
          the achievement of having dined at Oxford, thinks
          it funny to ridicule West Indian table manners. If
          this were the point, it would indeed be a very
          cheap triumph. But Naipaul's purpose is to
          complete his picture of the society . . . and to
          show that what has been true of the peasants is
          true also of the new élite. Such are the varieties
          of displacement that it is impossible for the new

> legislators to sit down at table together without
> the most elementary problems arising--problems of
> culture and principle, and only superficially of
> table manners.[45]

Many Western reviewers of The Mystic Masseur agree that
although the Trinidadian world presented is a disordered
one, the characters are attractively and sympathetically
drawn.[46]
    The Trinidadian world with all its shortcomings--
especially superstition, bribery, and chicanery--is repeated
in Naipaul's third novel, The Suffrage of Elvira. With a
Prologue, thirteen short chapters (sprinkled with marked
episodic divisions), and an Epilogue, the author abandons
the first-person narrator employed in his earlier works and
uses a third-person omniscient voice. Again a gentle comic
satire with a predominantly Indian cast, the work is tightly
structured around the second general elections in 1950 in an
unsophisticated, remote and rural part of Trinidad, Elvira,
a place where "things are crazily mixed up."[47] The book
dramatizes Naipaul's own observation made later in The
Middle Passage that "the squalor of the politics . . . came
to Trinidad in 1946 when, after no popular agitation,
universal adult suffrage was declared. The privilege took
the population by surprise. . . . The new politics were
reserved for the enterprising, who had seen their prodigious
commercial possibilities" (p. 72). With 8,000 registered
voters--4,000 Hindu, 2,000 blacks, 1,000 Moslems, and 1,000
Spanish--the Hindu candidate Surujpat (Pat) Harbans' victory
as member of the Legislative Council is almost assured,
since racial prejudice is taken for granted. Yet, because
people have begun to "see possibilities," bargains have to
be struck with Chittaranjan, the goldsmith, who controls the
Hindu vote, and with Baksh, the tailor, who controls the
Moslem vote. In a rich Prologue, a shy but corrupt Harbans,
making his way to visit these men, drives through Elvira's
bad road (which Harbans Transport Service has persuaded the
government to neglect) and passes by an abandoned
cocoa-house, a reminder of the county's brutal and hidden
past. On both occasions when he is forced to hit his brakes
to avoid collisions with two Jehovah's Witnesses and a black
dog, his engine stalls. In spite of his confidence in his
mission in Elvira, Harbans reads the incidents as a bad
sign, a reading he continually confirms as he receives one
lively lesson after another from the several humorously
portrayed characters, who teach him about Elviran
interpretation of democracy.
    Harban's first rough negotiation is with Baksh (known
as a heavy drinker and called "the mouther") and his seventeen year old son, Foam. Foam has an ongoing rivalry with a
Hindu loudspeaking announcer, Lorkhoor, who supports the
candidacy of Harbans' black opponent, Preacher. The meeting
begins awkwardly, but Baksh is adept at playing his game,

which Naipaul reveals through deft handling of dialogue and
dialect:

> Harbans steadied his hands.'. . . In this modern
> world everybody is one. Don't make no difference
> who you is or what you is. You is a Muslim, I is a
> Hindu. Tell me, that matter?' He had begun to coo
> again.
> 'Depending.'
> 'Yes, as you say, depending. Who you for,
> Baksh?'
> 'In the election, you mean?'
> Harbans looked ashamed. . . .
> 'You go want a lot of help. Microphone.
> Loudspeaking van. Fact, you go want a whole
> campaign manager.'
> 'Campaign what? . . .'
> . . . .
> 'You could use my loudspeaker.' He looked
> hard at Harbans. 'And you could use my van.'
> Harbans looked back hard into the darkness.
> 'What you saying, Baksh? You ain't got no
> loudspeaker.'. . .
> Baksh said, 'And you ain't got no Muslim
> vote.'. . .
> Foam said, 'Mr Harbans, Lorkhoor start
> loudspeaking against you, you know.'
> . . . .
> 'But I is a Hindu,' Harbans cried, 'Lorkhoor
> is a Hindu. Preacher is Negro.'
> Baksh saw an opening, 'Preacher giving out
> money hands down. Lorkhoor managing Preacher
> campaign. Hundred dollars a month.' (pp. 17-19)

In the transaction, Baksh secures not only the loudspeaker
and van but also a salaried position of campaign manager for
Foam. Harbans' misery is compounded because he is forced to
endure the company of the domineering Mrs. Baksh and the six
little Bakshes (with alternate Moslem and Christian names as
a "concession to their environment"). But candidate Harbans
has only just begun his torturous educational journey.

Chittaranjan, revered by the Hindus and Spaniards and
respected by blacks and Moslems, is an equally clever and
stubborn force. A reputed stick fighter, he boasts about
his fame at the Supreme Court to his neighbor and enemy
Ramlogan, whose fruits frequently fall on the wrong side of
the fence. In Elvira feud is a natural way of life and a
reputation for violence is cherished. The heated alterca-
tion and Ramlogan's pathetic concession speech, which
Harbans witnesses, do not disturb the calculating
Chittaranjan, who immediately and calmly advises the
candidate to start a rum account for voters at Ramlogan's
rumshop. In fact, the bargain goes more smoothly than

Baksh's, especially when Harbans is introduced to Nelly Chittaranjan:

> 'Daughter?' Harbans asked. As though he didn't know about Nalini, little Nelly; as though all Elvira didn't know that Chittaranjan wanted Nelly married to Harban's son, that this was the bargain to be settled that afternoon. . . .
> 'Taking typing-lesson <u>and</u> shorthand from Teacher Francis, you know. She could take down prescription <u>and</u> type them out. This doctor son you have. . . .'
> 'Oh, he ain't a doctor <u>yet</u>.'
> 'You shoulda bring him with you, you know. I like children with ambition.'
> 'He was learning today. . . . He <u>want</u> to see you.'
> 'I want to see him too.'
> So it was settled. (pp. 30-32)

Reflecting on the sign, his settlements, and Cuffy (Preacher's right hand man), Harbans develops an ominous feeling, but convinces himself--as he does throughout the novel--not to get "down-couraged." An authorial intrusion (one of the few in the novel) informs the reader: "If he only knew, his troubles hadn't started ." However, although a foreboding atmosphere sometimes threatens to take control, the novel remains exceedingly funny, with the emphasis not on Harbans but on the clever maneuvering of the lively, roughish characters.

Harbans is gradually inducted into Elvira's democratic machinery, a system genially presented as being governed by bribes and superstition instead of by issues. Foam abandons painting posters when one of his signs, "Vote Harbans or Die," is mutilated and reads " --TE----N--DIE," a reading that prompts a hysterical Mrs. Baksh to prophesy that this "election sweetness" will turn "sour." Foam concentrates instead on the newly formed enthusiastic Election Committee, which also includes two clumsy members, Mahadeo, an estate driver, and Dhaniram, a Hindu pundit. At a meeting Harbans naively compares Elvira's first, simple 1946 elections to the current complicated one and has to be reminded that "That was only the fust election. . . . Now is different. People learning. You have to spend on them" (p. 46). He loses control when he learns, first, that the Jehovah's Witnesses have convinced the Spanish of Cordoba to abstain from voting since politics is not divine, and second, that Preacher is assisting Hindus and, with Lorkhoor's plea for racial unity, may receive some Hindu votes: "Two or three tears trickled down Harbans' thin old face. . . . I ain't got no friends or helpers or nothing. Everybody only want money, money" (p. 50). This is exactly what Dhaniram's scheme demands, for the black vote must be won at any cost.

The strategy is planned in a comic manner, natural to the characters:

> 'It go take some money. But not much. Here in Elvira the campaign committee must be a sort of social welfare committee. Supposing one of those Negroes fall sick. We go go to them. We go take them to doctor in we taxi. We go pay for their medicine.'
>
> Chittaranjan sucked his teeth. . . . 'Dhaniram, you talking like if you ain't know how hard these Negroes is in Elvira. You ever see any negro fall sick? They just does drop down and dead. And that does only happen when they about eighty or ninety.'
>
> . . . .
> 'Well, if even one dead, we go bury him. We go hold the wake. We go take we coffee and we biscuits.'
>
> Baksh said, 'And you think that go make the Negroes vote for you?'
>
> 'It go make them feel shame if they ain't vote for we,' Dhaniram said.
>
> . . . .
> 'Is a good idea,' Foam said. 'And every one of we could buy just one sweet drink for some Negro child every day until elections. Different child everyday. . . .' (pp. 51-52)

This common Trinidadian practice of praja politics, described in Chapter I, involves a system in which a person of wealth and influence dispenses money and favors to people who pledge loyalty to him. Submitting to unreasonable demands, Harbans realizes that "no one in Elvira was fighting for him. All Elvira . . . were fighting him" (p. 53). Here the writer stimulates interest not by giving an editorial prediction again but by entering Harban's mind: "He thought of the sign he had had. . . . He had seen what the first meant. The women had stalled him in Cordoba. But the dog. What about the dog? Where was that going to stall him?" (p. 53). Yet Harbans remains on the periphery of the action.

Superstition begins to take control of the campaign when Herbert Baksh finds and harbors a dog, Tiger. Since the intoxicated Mr. Baksh spreads the story that the dog was much larger the previous night, it is assumed that Preacher is working obeah (African witchcraft) against those who will vote against him. After Mrs. Baksh's dramatic "key and Bible" trial to determine who brought home the dog, Herbert is fumigated by a mystic and Tiger is given to Foam to be taken away. But soon the incident is known throughout Elvira, affecting voters' decisions. The unpopular Lorkhoor (who speaks English in a "deliberate way, as though he has

130

to weigh and check the grammar before hand"), reports the
matter to Cuffy. And Mahadeo, making suspicious queries as
he compiles the list of sick blacks, leads Cuffy to
conclude: "Obeah! Lorkhoor was right. You people trying to
work some obeah" (p. 17). With each side accusing the
other, voters are reluctant to make commitments.
Chittaranjan, dressed in his one "visiting outfit," which
Naipaul itemizes in detail, has the task of allaying the
people's anxieties. When he is cornered into bribing a sick
man (named "Rampiari's husband") who exploits the situation,
"Chittaranjan smiled; the sick man smiled back; but when he
was outside Chittaranjan muttered, 'Blasted son of a bitch'"
(p. 79). These are the details that provide much of the fun
and laughter in the novel. Plots and counter plots have to
be hatched continually. The Committee decides that it must
discredit the Witnessess by spreading the rumor that they
are practicing obeah. The plan is facilitated by Tiger,
whom Foam had given to Nelly. Thrown out of Chittaranjan's
house, Tiger, in a memorable scene, slowly makes his way
back to the Bakshes, while the superstitious, terrified men,
women, and children of Elvira stare. To the abandoned
cocoa-house (the place where the mistress of the old Elvira
estate had buried her child fathered by a black slave), Foam
takes Tiger and discovers five dead puppies. These he lays
out in the shape of a cross and writes AWAKE below, thus
incriminating the Witnesses and expelling them from Elvira.

But while one problem is solved, another arises, as the
new electoral system is fully tested and political
realignment made. When an angry Chittaranjan, concerned
about a scandal, warns Baksh to have Foam stay away from
Nelly, slurs are traded and latent religious prejudice is
revived:

> 'Foam chasing your daughter? . . . Let me tell
> you, eh, every Hindu girl think they in paradise if
> they get a Muslim boy.'
> 'What is Muslim?' Chittaranjan asked. . . .
> 'Muslim is everything and Muslim is nothing.' He
> paused. 'Even Negro is Muslim.'
> That hurt Baksh. . . . He looked hard at him
> and long. Then he shouted, 'Good! Good! I glad!
> Harbans ain't going to get no Muslim vote. You say
> it yourself. Negro and Muslim is one. All right,
> Preacher getting every Muslim vote in Elvira.'
> Baksh's rage relaxed Chittaranjan. . . . 'We
> could do without the Muslim vote. . . . This is
> pure blood. Every Hindu blood is pure blood.
> Nothing mix up with it. Is pure Aryan blood.'
> Basksh snorted, 'All-you is just a pack of
> kaffir [unbeliever], if you ask me.' (p. 114)

Teacher Francis' observation that the "election bring out
all sort of prejudice to the surface" has turned out

prophetic. But Baksh had well thought out his seemingly
spontaneously outburst, for he tells Foam: "It ain't
Preacher who going to give me anything. Don't worry, you.
I calculate everything already. Everything" (p. 122).
Baksh subtly hints that he himself intends to stand as a
candidate, thus inducing Harbans to bribe him to do it in
order to ensure that no Moslem votes for Preacher. In
another strained bargaining session, Harbans offers the
Moslem leader $2,500, the deposit money, and campaign
posters.

With election day approaching and with Harbans' rum
flowing at Ramlogan's shop, the nervous Committee repeatedly recalculates expected votes, but there is still no
talk of any issue. Candidate Harbans' presence is not
needed; in fact, he is told that he could be in Port-
of-Spain and win the election in Elvira. His checkbook,
however, is important for every minor community project.
Lorkhoor warns that a man "who gives bribes is also capable
of taking bribes," but Chittaranjan knows that in Trinidad
"people like to know they could get a man to do little
things for them every now and then." To Elvirans, bribe is
a tested and an efficient system, and it is hardly surprising when Lorkhoor himself sells out to Harbans for
$500. In addition, Baksh tries to solicit yet a third bribe
when he threatens to join Preacher, but his plan is averted
by the unexpected death of Cuffy. Harbans finds himself
financing Cuffy's funeral, signing numerous rum and petrol
vouchers, paying for slogan buttons. In addition, as a
final touch to a modern campaign, the Committee throws an
elaborate pre-election day motor parade, equipped with soft
drinks, rum, _dalpuri_, _roti_, and goat curry--all at Harban's
expense but without his permission. Even on polling day,
clerks have to be bribed to do their jobs. Thus, with such
heavy prices, Harbans becomes "'noble member of the
legislative council," and "democracy" takes "root in Elvira."
In the Epilogue, reminiscent of Ganesh's last
appearance in _The Mystic Masseur_, a formal Harbans, donning
a double-breasted grey suit and freshly-ironed handkerchief
(with which he meticulously "patted," not "wiped," his
lips), makes a final visit to Elvira. Elvirans, hurt at his
new image, get him to spend lavishly on them, and he has to
be ushered out of the village when a still disgruntled mob
burns his new car (fortunately insured). It is an
exasperated Harbans who gives up: "'Elvira, Elvira.'
Harbans shook his head and spoke to the back of his hands. .
. . 'Elvira, you is a bitch'" (p. 206). Having no use now
for his constituency, he is free to renege on his promise to
Chittaranjan: "We can't let our children marry people who
does run about late at night with Muslim boys" (p. 207).
In the _Suffrage of Elvira_ we are transported essentially to the same world of _The Mystic Masseur_ and, to some
extent, _Miguel Street_. Innumerable bribes, empty _obeah_
threats, petty quarrels among neighbors, trivial disputes

over rum and petrol vouchers, clever revenge schemes--these
are all commonplace in Elvira, where an excited people
easily find themselves mastering the stratagems as democracy is thrown at them and as they learn the real "value"
of their vote. Yet the characters turn out to be admirable,
amusing knaves, tenderly and compassionately presented by
the writer. Although Harbans is mercilessly exploited by
voters, he does not win the reader's sympathy, because he is
of the same clay as Elvirans and because he never emerges as
a full blown character as Ramlogan, Chittaranjan, and the
others do. His distress does not stop the story from
becoming anything other than a comic satire on rural
electioneering as it existed then. The novel focuses on the
system with its schemes and counter schemes, not on the
characters. The question appears to be whether the people
of Elvira are ready for democracy. With a history of racial
and religious division (the buried baby being a symbol of
disunity), they have a unique understanding of the concept
of democracy. Dhaniram explains: "Is not as though you
giving things to we pussonal, Mr. Harbans. You must try and
feel that you giving to the people. After all, is the
meaning of this democracy" (p. 50). Harbans is ahead of his
times when he observes, "They should pass some sort of law
to prevent candidates spending too much money" (p. 205).

Of all Naipaul's books The Suffrage of Elvira has drawn
the fewest reviews and attracted comparatively little
critical attention from Naipaul's non-West Indian readers.
Robert Hamner has argued that the novel betrays an "uneven
artistry" and a "faint touch of immaturity," evident, for
example, in the distracting intrusions of the author's
voice, the incomplete treatment of a suggested affair
between Foam and Nelly, and the undeveloped personality of
Harbans, who is mostly seen from the outside. Hamner,
however, saw any problem with prolonged consistency as being
overshadowed by Naipaul's "felicitious handling" of
characters and actions.[48] Harriet Blodgett praised
Naipaul's comic inventiveness, idiosyncratic figures, and
humor through dialogue but noted that the novel lacks "any
well-developed characters or special richness of theme."
Concerning the actual political events, Blodgett was
ambivalent:

> The Suffrage is a farce, not a realistic novel.
> Elviran affairs are too exaggerated to be true as
> presented, but contain too much truth to be
> discounted . . . change a few incidental details
> and what goes on in Elivira could just as well be
> set in, say, any of the boroughs of New York.[49]

With mixed Western reaction--the book has been called by one
reviewer Naipaul's "least satisfying novel" and by another
"a perfect novel"--many critics appear to be unclear about
Naipaul's purpose and theme.[50] The London Magazine

suggested that the work would have been superior if
Naipaul's attitude to the election had been clearer, but
admitted that "there is probably more irony in the book than
comes through to the uninitiated."[51] Landeg White, though
not exactly among the uninitiated, expressed doubt about
whether Naipaul has decided that he "is writing a farce
about Trinidad elections or whether he is saying that
Trinidad elections are a farce."[52] Even the Times
Literary Supplement reviewer, who praised Naipaul's comic
gift and dialogue, felt that the writer's joke wears thin
before the end of the novel because democracy "is becoming
rather an old joke anyway."[53] Thus, each critic offers
his own reason for his reservation about the novel.

West Indian comments on The Suffrage are also few and
divided, but here the main questions are about the reality
and seriousness of the events described. A. C. Derrick
argued that "so high is the level of comic exaggeration that
one cannot take the book as a serious, realistic indictment
of a colonial society."[54] In a similar vein, Sylvia
Wynter, a Jamaican novelist, complained of the "too
deliberately eccentric" element of the novel, while Van
Sertima, praising the plausibility of plot and characters,
referred to the "exaggerations of the social reality."[55]
However, neither Wynter nor Van Sertima is a Caribbean East
Indian familiar with the electoral process in rural areas.
Although the Jamaican Gleaner's reviewer assumed that the
incidents in Elvira are intended to be received as
exaggerated, he implied that they may be based on reality:
"Presumably the author means his readers to take his
comments as an exaggerated humorous portrayal of conditions
and not to regard them as an indictment of Trinidadian
morals, whatever tales we in Jamaica may have heard which
seem to be just the sort of dishonesty portrayed here."[56]

West Indian social scientists who studied Trinidad's
political attitudes, however, have definitely confirmed the
reality of events in The Suffrage. In East Indians in
Trinidad Yogendra Malik asserted that Trinidad's "old-style
electioneering was based upon rum and roti" and that
Naipaul's The Suffrage "gives a very good account of
old-style electioneering."[57] Likewise, in his essay on
the practices of Trinidad's constituents, Gordon Lewis
argued that "the bad habits of Trinidad politics, described
in Mr. Naipaul's novel, The Suffrage of Elvira, were perhaps
too strongly entrenched in local culture and personality. .
. ."[58] And in his book The Growth of the Modern West
Indies, Lewis noted:

> The Suffrage of Elvira . . . describes the grim
> price paid . . . by a community ignorant of the
> true nature of democracy. . . . West Indian
> scholarship has yet to document all this. But . .
> . Albert Gomes . . . has recently described . . .
> how he first learned the deadly arts of Trinidad

> politics . . . including the necessity for any
> candidate who was anxious to win to accept the paid
> services of professional canvassers who by reason
> of an illogical voting system had the vote and the
> voter in their possession. . . . The political
> charlatan was simply the social climber of the
> Trinidad picaroon society operating in the
> political field.[59]

In addition, as pointed out in Chapter I, there were charges
that in Trinidad's first election, obeah, bribes and race
featured significantly. The events in The Suffrage of
Elvira are not far removed from the reality of Trinidad's
rural electioneering, a system in which candidates court
religious and community leaders who have a great deal of
influence over the voters.

Even those West Indians who do not question the reality
of events in The Suffrage hold divergent views about
Naipaul's purpose. In his analysis of the novel, Anthony
Boxill rejected any reading which questions the plausibility
of events and which sees the novel as "a comedy of errors"
with the action controlled by hilarious events. Such an
interpretation, he claimed, "loses sight of Naipaul's basic
premise that what is termed accidental in certain societies,
can be logical and inevitable in others"; the turns in the
plot are the result of the mentality of the people of
Elvira, a place affected by its unsavory history. To
Boxill, the novel presents a microcosm of the West Indies in
which environment and history "have created standards so far
from the norm of Western standards that it is ridiculous to
expect democracy to work there as it does in Europe"--the
same theme he noted, presented in The Mystic Masseur but
made richer and superior in The Suffrage.[60] Victor Ramraj
also argued that Naipaul apparently suggests that the
problem is not with the roguish Elvirans, though their
crooked electioneering is exposed, but with those who
prematurely introduce suffrage into a community not prepared
for it. But Ramraj maintained that the emphasis is not on
satire:

> When the political activities are considered, we
> get a rollicking picture of the rogues battling
> rogues. The novel is all one huge joke, narrated
> in a fast-paced, pervasively dramatic style. It
> does reflect Naipaul's awareness of the absurdity
> of the Elvirans, and his preference to see the fun
> that is in it rather than the satirical
> possibilities.[61]

Gordon Rohlehr, however, warned about being misled by the
geniality in both The Mystic Masseur and The Suffrage and
censured Naipaul for assuming that the West Indies have no

true standards and for accepting anarchy and absurdity as
the norms of Trinidad's social and political life.[62]
   The Suffrage of Elvira marks the completion of
Naipaul's "apprenticeship" works. The three short, gentle
satires share common features of a picturesque Trinidadian
setting, rich local dialect, and memorable characters,
mostly drawn from the East Indian population. According to
Robert Hamner, an American critic, Naipaul's motive is "not
unlike that of most satirists of the past who claim a
serious purpose, but also as with some of his predecessors
the weight of humor indicates that at least at times he is
simply indulging in sheer fun." This impulse, as Hamner
noted, is especially true of the lighter, early novels.[63]
The author's genial voice accepts Trinidad's society as a
"picaroon" one and treats with tenderness and gaiety the
inhabitants who are bred by an environment in which trickery
and subterfuge are natural and necessary for economic
survival. From Miguel Street to The Suffrage of Elvira, we
are made to believe that things operate differently in
Trinidad, where ambitions are fruitless, superstition is
common, hoodwinking is widely accepted, bribes are
efficient, politics is nonfunctional, and island life is
insulated and backward. Only the charlatan survives, and
much of the comedy results when one trickster tries to
outfox another. The comedies have been considered by some
to be exaggeratedly satirical and have been criticized for
relying "more than they should on eccentric character
profiles and on quaint native dialects."[64] However, this
is generally not the judgment of informed Western critics or
West Indians. Francis Wyndham, reviewer for the London
Magazine, has argued that there is no distortion of reality
in the first three books:

> [They] have often been described as satires, with
> the accompanying suggestion of heartlessness and
> exaggeration. In fact, Mr. Naipaul never distorts
> reality: he acknowledges the farcical aspects of
> West Indian life but these are played down rather
> than heightened in his work, and . . . his sober
> respect for truth has been mistakenly interpreted
> as high-spirited caricature.[65]

Assessing Western reaction to his three light, satiric
comedies, Naipaul himself addressed the problem of "regional
barrier." In "London" (1958), written after the publication
of The Suffrage of Elvira, he ridiculed the patronizing
attitude of some of his early English reviewers:

> The social comedies I write can be fully
> appreciated only by someone who knows the region I
> write about. Without that knowledge it is easy for
> my books to be dismissed as farces and my
> characters as eccentrics. There can also be

>misuderstanding: the critic of the <u>Observer</u> thinks
>I get my dialect from Ronald Firbank. And there
>can be simple exasperation: the critic of the
><u>Yorkshire Post</u> says she is just fed up with
>Trinidad and Trinidad dialect. . . .[66]

Specifically referring to one comment that his "whole
purpose is to show how funny Trinidad Indians are" and to
another that he looks down "a long Oxford nose" at the land
of his birth, Naipaul stated that these remarks would not
have been made about Evelyn Waugh or any other writer from a
more developed culture. He complained about British critics
who have concerned themselves with making "political rather
than literary judgments," because, he surmised, they
represented the attitude of the public.[67] Francis Wyndham
has speculated that in the 1950's it "was considered rather
bad form, in literary circles, to approach an 'underdeveloped country' in a spirit of sophisticated humour," and
he attributed the early partronizing reviews of Naipaul's
works to the critics' unfamiliarity of the West Indian
background and to "attitudes of neo-colonialist
embarrassment." According to Wyndham, the early reviewers
would have preferred a "simple study in compassion where a
clear distinction is made between the oppressors and the
oppressed, or a 'charming' exercise in the <u>faux-naif</u>, or a
steamily incoherent drama of miscegenation and primitive
brutality."[68] However, in spite of the few disappointing
early reviews Naipaul has had, as he admitted, generally
good ratings from his Western audience.[69]

In the Caribbean, where there is, of course, no problem
with regional barrier, Naipaul has had to face a more stormy
reaction. As early as 1960, that is, just after the
publication of the first three comedies, and even before the
appearance of the controversial <u>The Middle Passage</u>, George
Lamming in <u>The Pleasures of Exile</u> uttered the following
bitter denunciation of Naipaul's early works:

>His books can't move beyond a castrated satire; and
>although satire may be a useful element in fiction,
>no important work, comparable to Selvon's can rest
>safely on satire alone. When such a writer is a
>colonial, ashamed of his cultural background and
>striving like mad to prove himself through
>promotion to the peaks of a 'superior' culture
>whose values are gravely in doubt, then satire,
>like the charge of philistinism, is for me nothing
>more than a refuge. And it is too small a refuge
>for a writer who wishes to be taken seriously.[70]

This appraisal directly followed Lamming's sharp dismissal
of Naipaul's intelligence as "limited to answering
examination questions." Bill Carr, who has lived in the
West Indies for over twenty years, defended Naipaul and
argued that while other writers of lesser merit are given

high ratings in Lamming's book, Naipaul is dismissed in a maliciously unfair manner by a critically irresponsible assessment based not on quality or achievement but on subject matter.[71] Australian critic Landeg White has also suggested that Lamming's outburst is "a very personal attack" which may have stemmed from professional pique.[72] For certain sections in The Pleasures of Exile reveal that the writer held personal reservations about Naipaul, who had not given a good review to Lamming's Of Age and Innocence.[73] Although White disagreed with Lamming's charge, he understood the core of the issue: "What is at stake here is a fundamental literary problem, faced by every writer, ex-colonial or not, who tries to apply the assumptions and resources of English literature to non-European societies."[74]

Indeed, Lamming's comment touches upon what is to be a frequently debated problem in Naipaul's works: the nature of the satire and the use of humor. Guyanese Victor Ramraj suggested that since Naipaul had not yet developed in his first three novels a consistent tone with which to confront the problems of his society, he shifted from "satirical laughter to the warm laughter of comedy and to the sheer fun of farce," the tendency of tolerance and understanding dominating.[75] Gordon Rohlehr, on the other hand, is ambivalent about Naipaul's early works. Using Lamming's comment as a basis for an essay, Rohlehr agreed that there is little "risible in a society whose history is one of underprivilege" and he concurred that the early Naipaul is at times an unsympathetic, irresponsible, insensitive, detached ironist. Rohlehr further argued:

> Satire is the sensitive measure of a society's departure from a norm inherent in itself. Since Naipaul starts with the conviction that such a norm is absent from his society, his task as satirist becomes doubly difficult. Not only must he recreate experience, but also simultaneously create the standards against which this experience is to be judged. This explains the mixture of farce and social consciousness which occurs in the two early novels [The Mystic Masseur and The Suffrage of Elvira]. . . .
>   The tone of these two books is almost the same . . . an absurd world is presented as real. . . . That Ganesh and Harbans are treated so genially conceals Naipaul's seriousness of purpose. . . . If the impulse behind Miguel Street is similar to that behind The Mystic Masseur, the whole tone is more serious. The farce has become a nightmare. Here one finds it difficult to accept Lamming's description of Naipaul's satire as a refuge and escape from experience. If satire is a means of running away, it is equally a means of fighting; an

act of bravery, not cowardice; the confrontation of
nightmare, not the seeking of a refuge.[76]

Rohlehr emphasized two other points: first, the use of
ironic distance enables Naipaul to analyze his society
without any sentimental self-indulgence; second, although
Naipaul does not make a conscious effort to aspire to the
standards of Europeans, he adopts too easily European
historians' views, which ignore positive aspects of West
Indian society, a society whose experience demands
sympathy.[77] Antiguan A. C. Derrick, using the popular
argument that Naipaul subjects his characters to alien
norms, also charged Naipaul with a lack of sympathy:

> In his satiric presentation of characters Naipaul
> rarely allows himself to show a humane
> understanding of their weaknesses. He tends to set
> his people at a distance and usually invites an
> analytically detached response from the reader. . .
> .
> That the standard against which the colonials
> are judged is brought to bear from the outside,
> underscores Naipaul's lack of sympathy. . . . It
> is this apparent lack of sympathy, coupled with the
> unbalanced, wholly destructive nature of his
> satire, that creates a sense of hollowness in the
> novels set in the West Indies.[78]

Criticisms such as those by Rohlehr and Derrick lend support
to White's statement that to West Indian critics, "novels
which set out to expose the inadequacies of a society whose
history is one of slavery and exploitation are acceptable if
the prevailing tone shows sympathy and understanding."[79]
   Naipaul's non-West Indian critics have generally argued
that, contrary to the feeling of many Caribbean readers,
Naipaul does not treat his characters with contempt or lack
of understanding. Referring to Lamming's statement, White
claimed: "It is hard to feel that Naipaul is really guilty
of the charges laid against him . . . his detachment is
always genial, verging towards irony and acceptance."[80]
Another Western critic, William Walsh, even contended that
in Naipaul's first three comedies there is, perhaps, "a
shade too much emphasis on charm."[81] And Robert Hamner,
taking both Lamming and Derrick to task, pointed out that it
is possible for an author to distance himself from his
material without being contemptuous:

> Naipaul is usually successful in maintaining
> distance from his material, but contrary to the
> objections of such men as George Lamming and A. C.
> Derrick, this does not necessarily mean that he is
> coldly detached or disdainful of that which he is
> depicting. Rather, his concerted effort to remove
> himself and his failure at times to keep his

personal feelings hidden are evidence of his deeply rooted attachment to the people he criticizes.[82]

This debate, starting from the early 1960's with Lamming's criticism, now extends to most of Naipaul's West Indian works.

From the foregoing discussion of the directions in Naipaul criticisms, it is clear that if he is not the victim of political judgment, he is at least subject to it as much as he is to literary judgment. Because of the widespread belief that the Caribbean has suffered enough and must now seek dignity and respect from the world, many West Indians expect that artists would at least project a favorable or positive image of the region and its people. Naipaul's apparent inability to empathize with nationalist trends--along with his residence overseas, non-involvement at home, and favorable Western press--accounts in large part for his hostile reception at home. As Landeg White suggested, "To many West Indians especially, reading his early novels at a time of nationalist fervour, at a time when the West Indian Federation was still in existence, this refusal to identify with local currents of strong feeling seemed like a betrayal."[83] Even though the Federation has been dissolved over two decades ago, and even though most Caribbean countries have long become independent, patriotic fervor still runs high. Meanwhile, Naipaul stands steadfast in his firm opposition to West Indians whom he has accused in The Middle Passage of having "an insecure wish to be heroically portrayed. Irony and satire, which might help more, are not acceptable" (pp. 68-9).

This chapter has shown, then, that from the beginning of his career as a novelist, Naipaul has been criticized by many West Indians dissatisfied with his portrayal of the Caribbean and its inhabitants. Although his talent has been generally recognized--sometimes though grudgingly --charges have been made about the inferior West Indian world presented, about the contemptuous and unsympathetic attitude expressed toward it and its people, about the lack of hope for regeneration and growth, about the adoption and acceptance of Western-oriented culture and standards, and about the negative portrayal of blacks in these apprenticeship novels. While some of these charges appear valid, others may well have been colored by Naipaul's non-fictional works on the West Indies, since, with the exception of Lamming's comment, most of the negative criticisms of the early books were registered after the publication of the provocative travelogue, The Middle Passage. What is noteworthy, however, is that the complaints made about the three early novels have been echoed in response to Naipaul's other West Indian books and have continued to dominate critical approach to the writer today. The only possible exception, to some extent, is reaction to A House for Mr Biswas, which will be examined in the next chapter.

Notes

[1] Ewart Rouse, "Naipaul: An Interview," *Trinidad Guardian*, 28 Nov. 1968, p. 9.

[2] "Is. V. S. Naipaul an Angry Young Man?" *Sunday Guardian Magazine* (Trinidad), 6 Aug. 1967, p. 9.

[3] "Prologue to an Autobiography," *Vanity Fair*, 46, No. 2 (April 1983), 55.

[4] *Miguel Street* (London: André Deutsch, 1959; rpt. New York: Penguin Books, 1981), p. 62. Subsequent references will be from this edition and will be indicated in the text.

[5] Seepersad Naipaul, *Gurudeva and Other Indian Tales* (Trinidad: Trinidad Publications, 1943), p. 32. See also Chapter II, p. 62 of this book.

[6] *V. S. Naipaul* (London: Macmillan Press, 1975), p. 49.

[7] "Prologue to an Autobiography," pp. 54–59.

[8] "Prologue to an Autobiography," p. 142.

[9] "Prologue to an Autobiography," p. 57.

[10] "Prologue to an Autobiography," p. 57.

[11] *The Middle Passage* (London: André Deutsch, 1962; rpt. New York: Vintage Books, 1981), p. 41. Subsequent references will be from this edition and will be indicated in the text.

[12] "Prologue to an Autobiography," p. 57.

[13] George McMichael, "A Gallery of Rogues Along Trinidad's Miguel Street," rev. of *Miguel Street*, *San Francisco Sunday Chronicle*, 22 May 1960, p. 26; Francis Wyndham, rev. of *Miguel Street*, *London Magazine*, 6, No. 9 (Sept. 1959), 81.

[14] White, p. 50. Robert D. Hamner, *V. S. Naipaul* (New York: Twayne Inc., 1973), pp. 84–85, also acknowledged the common existence of West Indian eccentrics.

[15] "Diminishing Satire," in *Awakened Conscience*, ed. C. D. Narasimhaiah (New Delhi: Sterling Publishers Pvt. Ltd., 1978), p. 269.

[16] "London," in The Overcrowded Barracoon (London: André Deutsch, 1972; rpt. New York: Penguin Books, 1981), p. 10.

[17] "London," pp. 14-15.

[18] Robert M. Malone, rev. of Miguel Street, Library Journal, 15 May 1960, p. 1938; Percy Wood, "Echoes of 'Cannery Row,' in a novel of Trinidad," rev. of Miguel Street, Chicago Sunday Tribune Magazine of Books, 15 May 1960, p. 6; John Coleman, rev. of Miguel Street, Spectator, 24 April 1959, p. 595; "Street Scene," rev. of Miguel Street, Times Literary Supplement, 24 April 1959, p. 237.

[19] Caribbean Writers (London: New Beacon Books, Ltd., 1968), p. 40.

[20] Robert Payne, "Caribbean Carnival," rev. of Miguel Street, Saturday Review, 2 July 1960, p. 18.

[21] "The Paradox of Freedom," Critique, 18, No. 1 (1976), 81. For a similar view, see Donald E. Herdeck, ed. Caribbean Writers (Washington, D.C.: Three Continents Press, Inc. 1979), p. 157.

[22] "The Ironic Approach," in The Islands in Between, ed. Louis James (London: Oxford University Press, 1968), p. 122.

[23] White, p. 50.

[24] "Prologue to an Autobiography," p. 142.

[25] "The Ironic Approach," p. 122.

[26] George Panton, "Let's Laugh at Ourselves," rev. of Miguel Street, Sunday Gleaner (Jamaica), 1 Nov. 1959, p. 14.

[27] "Diminishing Satire," p. 271; see also Frank Collymore, rev. of Miguel Street, Bim (Barbados), 8, No. 29 (June-Dec. 1959), 67.

[28] "Naipaul's Technique as a Novelist," Journal of Commonwealth Literature, 7 (July 1969), 33-34.

[29] V. S. Naipaul, The Mystic Masseur, introd. Paul Edwards and Kenneth Ramchand (London: André Deutsch, 1957; rpt. London: Heinemann Educational Books Ltd., 1978), p. 7. Subsequent references will be from this edition and will be indicated in the text.

143

30 "New Fiction," rev. of The Mystic Masseur, The
Times (London), 23 May 1957, p. 15; see also "Out of Joint,"
rev. of The Mystic Masseur, Times Literary Supplement, 31
May 1957, p. 333.

31 An Area of Darkness (London: André Deutsch, 1964;
rpt. New York: Vintage Books, 1981), 36-37. Subsequent
references will be from this edition and will be indicated
in the text.

32 Rev. of The Mystic Masseur, Library Journal, 1 May
1959, p. 1533.

33 Van Sertima, p. 39.

34 "Ganesh in the Years of Guilt," rev. of The Mystic
Masseur, Sunday Guardian (Trinidad), 16 June 1957, p. 23.

35 Rev. of The Mystic Masseur, Bim (Barbados), 7, No.
26 (Jan.-June 1958), 119.

36 Collymore, rev. of The Mystic Masseur, p. 119.

37 Derrick, p. 33.

38 "The Ironic Approach," p. 124.

39 The Pleasures of Exile (London: Michael Joseph,
1960), p. 225.

40 Kenneth Ramchand, "V. S. Naipaul and West Indian
Writers: Kenneth Ramchand Speaks with Selwyn Cudjoe,"
Antilia (University of West Indies), 1 (1983), 16.

41 "Diminishing Satire," p. 270.

42 Paul Edwards and Kenneth Ramchand, intro. The
Mystic Masseur, p. ix.

43 West Indian Societies (London: Oxford University
Press, 1972), p. 130.

44 V. S. Naipaul (Edinburgh: Oliver and Boyd, 1973),
pp. 7-8.

45 White, p. 66.

46 See, for example, White, p. 72; Martin Levin, "How
the Ball Bounces Down Trinidad Way," rev. of The Mystic
Masseur, New York Times Book Review, 12 April 1959, p. 5;
Gene Baro, "Ganesh's Beguiling Exploits," rev. of The Mystic
Masseur, New York Herald Tribune Book Review, 7 June 1959,
p. 6.

144

47 V. S. Naipaul, *The Suffrage of Elvira* (London: André Deutsch, 1958; rpt. New York: Penguin Books, 1981), p. 66. Subsequent references will be made from this edition and will be indicated in the text.

48 *V. S. Naipaul*, pp. 40-43.

49 "Beyond Trinidad," *South Atlantic Quarterly*, 73 (Summer 1974), 390-1. William Walsh, *V. S. Naipaul*, p. 10, does not see *The Suffrage* as a farce.

50 White, p. 82.

51 P. H. Newby, rev. of *The Suffrage of Elvira*, *London Magazine*, 5, No. 11 (Nov. 1958), 84.

52 White, p. 77.

53 "Tropical Heat," rev. of *The Suffrage of Elvira*, *Times Literary Supplement*, 2 May 1958, p. 237.

54 Derrick, p. 36.

55 Sylvia Wynter, "Strangers at the Gate," *Sunday Gleaner* (Jamaica), 18 Jan. 1959, p. 14; Van Sertima, p. 40.

56 George Panton, "Satire on Trinidad," rev. of *The Suffrage of Elvira*, *Sunday Gleaner* (Jamaica), 22 June 1958, p. 11.

57 *East Indians in Trinidad* (London: Oxford University Press, 1971), p. 89.

58 "Trinidad and Tobago General Election of 1961," in *The Aftermath of Sovereignty*, ed. David Lowenthal and Lambros Comitas (New York: Anchor Press, 1973), p. 138.

59 *The Growth of the Modern West Indies* (New York: Monthly Review Press, 1968), p. 210.

60 *V. S. Naipaul's Fiction* (Canada: York Press, 1983), pp. 30-34.

61 "Diminishing Satire," p. 271.

62 "The Ironic Approach," pp. 123-24.

63 *V. S. Naipaul*, p. 106.

64 Robert Boyers, "V. S. Naipaul," *The American Scholar*, 50 (Summer 1981), 360.

65 Rev. of A House for Mr Biswas, London Magazine, 1, No. 7 (Oct. 1961), 91.

66 "London," p. 11.

67 "London, pp. 11-13.

68 "V. S. Naipaul," Listener, 7 Oct. 1971, p. 461.

69 "London," p. 13; see also Bharati Mukherjee and Robert Boyers, "A Conversation with V. S. Naipaul," Salmagundi, 54 (Fall 1981), 9.

70 The Pleasures of Exile, p. 225.

71 W. I. [Bill] Carr, "Reflections on the Novel in the British Caribbean," Queen's Quarterly, 70, No. 4 (Winter 1963), 594.

72 White, p. 12.

73 The Pleasures of Exile, pp. 30, 224-25; V. S. Naipaul, rev. of Of Age and Innocence, by George Lamming, New Statesman, 6 Dec. 1958, pp. 826-27.

74 White, p. 12.

75 "Diminishing Satire," p. 269.

76 "The Ironic Approach," pp. 122-26.

77 "The Ironic Approach," pp. 124, 130 ff.

78 Derrick, pp. 32-33.

79 White, p. 12.

80 White, p. 12.

81 "V. S. Naipaul," in A Manifold Voice (New York: Barnes & Noble, 1970), p. 70.

82 V. S. Naipaul, p. 106.

83 White, p. 11.

Chapter IV

West Indian Response to Naipaul's
A House for Mr Biswas

With his first three apprenticeship works, Naipaul had
already launched his reputation--regionally and interna-
tionally--as a promising artist. Yet, as pointed out in
Chapter III, his books presented problems for his audience
at home and abroad. His apparent distance from his material
irked many West Indians, while the "regional barrier" alienated some Westerners. In spite of this misunderstanding
with his foreign audience, on whose patronage he depended,
Naipaul refused at this point to break the barrier by
writing about sex, race, or an English or American character
in a Caribbean setting. He expressed confidence in his
local material: "I feel I can never hope to know as much
about people here as I do about Trinidad Indians, people I
can place almost as soon as I see them."[1] Not
surprisingly, then, for material for his next novel, Naipaul
returned to Trinidad and to its East Indians he knows so
well. The result, A House for Mr Biswas (1961), firmly
established him as the author of what many critics consider
one of the greatest twentieth century novels in English.
Even in the Caribbean, where he was beginning to be regarded
as an unfaithful son, readers have generally made an
exception of this novel in their condemnation of his brand
of satire. This chapter will examine West Indian response
to A House and will show that in spite of some reservations,
this novel is ranked as Naipaul's best work.
        Symmetrically structured with a Prologue, two major
parts with six and seven chapters respectively, and an
Epilogue, A House is a mammoth epic of nearly six hundred
pages and with a multitudinous cast of well-delineated
characters. Naipaul relies mainly on the structure of the
traditional novel, chronologically tracing Mohan Biswas'
fortune from birth and simultaneously presenting a realistic
picture of the changing East Indian family life in colonial
Trinidad from about the beginning of the twentieth century
to the 1940's. The large frame, adroitly handled, is, as
Landeg White notes, among the features which clearly
distinguish this work from Naipaul's early novels:

>   One of the most remarkable things about A House for
>   Mr Biswas, compared to the earlier books, is its
>   solidity and comprehensiveness. Mr Biswas is only
>   forty-six when he dies, but by the end of the novel
>   a whole history has passed before our eyes.

148

Naipaul conveys the impression of decades elapsing.
. . . He chronicles the stages in the loss of
India, the shift from country to town, from Hindu
to English, from a preoccupation with Fate to a
preoccupation with ambition, so that as we move
from the world of Raghu [Biswas' father] to the
world of Anand [Biswas' son], we are dealing not
only with the life of a man but also with the
history of a culture. It is all done with a
marvellous attentiveness to the smallest details.[2]

In spite of its wide scope and large scale, the novel "has
none of the wordy clumsiness associated with those fat,
panoramic, pretentious volumes that form a part of a
trilogy, or a quartet, or a saga."[3] From the beginning to
the end, the focal point remains the determination of one
unimportant, ordinary man to own a house, to become
independent of his in-laws (the Tulsis), to live through his
son--in short, to strike out on his own and not to accept
Fate passively as his father did.

Although Naipaul uses an omniscient narrator, he
relates the story primarily from Mr. Biswas' point of view.
This technique is achieved, as Robert Hamner argues, "with
such unobtrusive ease that the reader's attention is seldom,
if ever, distracted from the evolving action."[4] Kenneth
Ramchand has pointed out--and Hamner agrees--that it is only
later in the novel when the Tulsis cease to be Mr. Biswas'
antagonists and when the authorial voice continues to
deflate them that the writer's "attitudes begin to show too
obtrusively as his own."[5] The story of Mr. Biswas is
generally told with what has been called "virtually filial
tenderness and understanding."[6] William Walsh, who has
often complained of a Brahminical aloofness in Naipaul,
calls attention to the author's sympathetic and compassionate attitude towards his hero:

A House for Mr. Biswas is free of both of the
butterfly-watching stance of the earliest work and
the despairing verdict on mankind which begins to
sound in the later . . . .
Sometimes in Naipaul's work the reader has the
sense of the cool eye of a well-bred stranger
analysing with superlative acuity some smothering,
medieval strangeness; one has the sense of a most
intelligent and gifted member of one species
probing and cataloguing the weaknesses of quite
another. But not in A House for Mr Biswas. The
relationship of author and subject . . . is one
which exists on a level, as between equals. Mr.
Biswas is felt and suffered with, not just seen and
suffered.[7]

Making a similar comparison, Dan Jacobson also notes that while there are initial "touches of affectation" in the novel, the "depth of the author's involvement with his characters becomes evident," since Naipaul no longer detaches himself from his material as he has done in previous novels.[8]

A House also shows a shift in the author's tone. While the book manages to retain the comic tone of the early novels, there are signs of Naipaul's growing somber note. As Michael Thorpe points out, in Naipaul's apprenticeship works, the characters' ambitions provide material for an "amusing sketch or aside," and "nothing . . . approaches the dark intensity of a 'mind in turmoil,'" as seen in A House.[9] As early as in the Prologue (which discloses how things will turn out for the hero), the seriousness of the theme is sounded when Naipaul presents a reflection of the life of Mr. Biswas, a sacked reporter, who at forty-six, is dying in his own house, "on his own half-lot of land, his own portion of the earth," on Sikkim Street, Port-of-Spain:

> How terrible it would have been, at this time, to be without it [a house]: to have died among the Tulsis, amid the squalor of that large, disintegrating and indifferent family; to have left Shama and the children among them, in one room; worse, to have lived without even attempting to lay claim to one's portion of the earth; to have lived and died as one had been born, unnecessary and unaccommodated.[10]

Yet, in spite of the many defeats that Mr. Biswas suffers during his quest, he remains an amused observer, making this serious novel an exceedingly funny one also. Sarel Eimerl rightly observes that "the tone mingles the grotesque, the absurd, and the comic," for although the quest for a house "symbolizes Everyman's aspiration toward independence, . . . Mr. Biswas, unlike most of us, is a gay warrior. . . . He can perceive the comic in poverty, humiliation, fear, and even death."[11] Undoubtedly, one of the chief strengths of the novel is the character of Mr. Biswas who shows rare good humor in his frantic and pathetic struggle for independence.

From the beginning Mr. Biswas is presented as an ordinary, typical person. But he is given epic stature by his inauspicious birth at a time assumed to be midnight. The attending pundit prophesies that the boy (born in the wrong way and with six fingers on one hand), will be a spendthrift, a lecher, and possibly a liar; the midwife predicts that he will be the cause of his parents' death. Mr. Biswas (given the title of Mr. from birth) is far from a majestic-looking hero, for malnutrition has given him eczema and sores, which leave permanent vaccination-like marks, and he develops swinging, "hammock-like" calves. With the drowning of his father (inadvertently caused by Mr. Biswas) and with the dissolution of the family unit, the boy is forced into the homes of the strangers. He receives a short, brutal education with intense drills of "ought oughts are oughts," which apparently echo Lear's warning that "Nothing will come out of nothing."[12] For, the hero's problem, as Anthony Boxill suggests, will be "to create himself and his world out of nothing."[13] Mr. Biswas is dismissed from his position as a live-in pundit apprentice when he accidentally defiles his guardian's oleander tree, and he begins his solitary odyssey through life: "The neighbours had heard, and came out to watch Mr Biswas as, in his dhoti, with his bundle slung on his shoulders, he walked through the village" (pp. 56-7). His service as an assistant at his aunt's rum-shop also comes to an abrupt end when he is physically abused by a dishonest manager. Mr. Biswas, then, a young East Indian Trinidadian, with a meager education, now finds himself in a predicament similar to that of Ganesh in The Mystic Masseur and many non-fictional Trinidadians, whose opportunities are limited on the undeveloped island. His one special gift of sign-painting, however, earns him a job with a powerful, conservative, land-owning family, the Tulsis.

Ensnared by this family, Mr. Biswas is inducted into the strange world of Tulsidom, henceforth both his bitter adversary and safe refuge. He awkwardly passes a love note to one of the Tulsi daughters, Shama, and, mainly because he is of the right caste (Brahmin), is quickly trapped into marriage when he is confronted and emotionally overpowered by Mrs. Tulsi, the ruling matriarch, and Seth, her equally shrewd brother-in-law. Because of his poverty, after his marriage Mr. Biswas moves to the Arwacas residence of the Tulsis, Hanuman House. Its description as "an alien white fortress . . . bulky, impregnable, and blank" suggests war, imprisonment, and decay.[14] Daily Mr. Biswas endures the sight of the "sleepers" everywhere in the crowded house ("floor space is bed space"); Shama's two "stern" brothers, groomed for scholarships, and, therefore, well fed and pampered; Hari, the constipated household pundit and noisy eater; and the competitive, ritualistic beatings of wives and children. He also notices a complicated system in which certain people mainly because of age, hold a privileged status, but others remain "lesser husbands"; sisters form alliances and discipline each other's children; the wife of the victorious husband is expected to placate the defeated husband after a family squabble; after a beating by her husband, a wife adopts an air of martyrdom and gains status; and Mrs. Tulsi's fainting spells trigger a complex ritual during which the Rose Room has to be prepared, with Seth's wife presiding and with each fawning daughter assigned a specific task to ease the old lady's discomfort. The most memorable, vivid, and comical part of the entire novel is this section--in fact, most of Part I--in which the Tulsis dominate. As Kenneth Ramchand points out, it is in this

unit that "Naipaul establishes the Tulsis in their
characteristic attitudes," and "each episode consolidates
our first impression of the crowded, noisy, ritualized life
and single-attribute people."[15]

Mr. Biswas' rebellious streak grows dangerously when he
realizes that he is expected to become an insignificant
Tulsi among the innumerable Tulsis. Hanuman House is a
place which provides sustenance, shelter, and protection,
but which demands in return subservience, conformity and
anonymity. Mr. Biswas may have been initially attracted to
the security of Hanuman House, but as Robert Hamner points
out, "he has simply exchanged one problem for another. He
has imprisoned himself; he is trapped."[16] At first he
takes the coward's way by fleeing; later he confronts the
problem by rebelling. One Christmas he buys a doll-house
for his daughter, Savi, although the Tulsis habitually give
the same gifts to all children in an apparent attempt to
discourage such symbols of independence. Boxill argues that
"Biswas's first real sense of himself arises out of his need
to oppose the Tulsis, who come to represent external chaos
and darkness, the void."[17] Deliberately courting trouble
by being a non-conformist, Mr. Biswas defies the family by
believing in the motto, "Paddle your own canoe," by speaking
in English when addressed in Hindi, and by associating with
the Aryans, who argue for the unimportance of caste, for the
abolition of idols and "cat-in-bag" marriages, and for education of women. He constantly ridicules and challenges the
family's conservatism, conventions, hierarchical system,
religious rituals, social practices and hypocrisy.

Mr. Biswas effectively combats the Tulsis by relying on
his engaging humor and wit. His wit, according to White, is
"the most creative thing in the book."[18] Mr. Biswas finds
relief in caricaturing his mother-in-law as "she-fox," and
"old queen," her sons, Shekhar and Owad, as "the gods," Seth
as "big boss" and Hari as the "holy ghost." To the Tulsis
he is nothing but a buffoon and trouble-maker, not to be
taken seriously. Eimerl notes that "Naipaul's triumph is
that he has assimilated the comedy and horror, the fun and
misery, into a coherent whole. Mr. Biswas is a clown and a
dreamer but he is also a little fearful man courageously
fighting a hostile world."[19] The Tulsis are no match for
him when he hurls invectives intended to provoke them. The
exchanges are conveyed in deftly handled dialogue, as the
following conversation (related in the Prologue and repeated
in the Epilogue) shows:

Suniti said to Shama, 'I hear that you come like a
big-shot, Aunt.' She didn't hide her amusement,
'Buying house and thing.'
'Yes, child,' Shama said, in her martyr's way.
The exchange took place on the back steps and
reached the ears of Mr Biswas. . . . 'Shama,' he
shouted, 'tell that girl to go back and help that

worthless husband of hers to look after their goats
at Pokima Halt.'
    The goats were an invention of Mr Biswas which
never fail to irritate Suniti. 'Goats!' she said
to the yard, and sucked her teeth. (pp. 11-12)

There is, in short, as Ramchand observes, constant "duelling
that takes place between Mr. Biswas and the Tulsi high com-
mand," and this "give and take . . . provides much of the
fun . . . and gives life to both contestants."[20] When
verbal battle turns to physical combat, and when it is
evident, especially after a fight with Shama's submissive
brother-in-law, Govind, that the defiant, independent-minded
Mr. Biswas does not--cannot--fit in the Tulsi household, he
is given his own canoe to paddle: the Tulsi shop at the
Chase Village. His own place or house, away from the
teeming enemies, becomes as Francis Wyndham notes, "a potent
symbol of personal independence and thus an affirmation of
human dignity."[21]
    However, by leaving the protection of the Indian
enclave for an unknown world, Mr. Biswas, in Mrs. Tulsi's
words, "jumps from the frying pan into the fire." The store
is a failure, and it is only now that he sees communal organization and order in the seemingly chaotic Hanuman House.
In addition, "The House was a world, more real than The
Chase, and less exposed; everything beyond its gates was
foreign and unimportant and could be ignored. He needed
such a sanctuary" (p. 188). He avoids reality by seeking
mental escape in reading Marcus Aurelius and Epictetus and
by painting "cool, ordered forest scenes." Naive, he is
cheated and legally outwitted by his customers and lawyer,
but he learns about how things work in colonial Trinidad
when Seth tells him of the strategy to "insuranburn" the
shop. His new job as a Tulsi "driver" or "sub-overseer" at
Green Vale (a misnomer) among sugar workers brings no hope
for better times, especially since his family spends
increasingly more time at the Tulsis. When after living in
a one-room laborer's barrack for a while, he manages to put
up a structure of his own; however, snake-like asphalt falls
from the roof. In a climactic storm scene, often compared
to the one in _King Lear_, the house is blown apart, and Mr.
Biswas stares blankly, even when myriads of winged ants
descend and bite Anand. Suffering from a mental breakdown,
he has to be "rescued" once more by what he sees as the
"warmth and reassurance" of Hanuman House. However, as
White points out, Green Vale represents a "false start, a
premature claim. But it is far from futile," for "its merit
is that for the first time he claims them [his children] as
his own."[22] Mr. Biswas demonstrates an extraordinary
amount of resilience as he makes another courageous decision
to resume his Sisyphean labor for independence: "He was
going out into the world, to test it for its power to

frighten. The past was counterfeit, a series of cheating accidents" (p. 305).

In Port-of-Spain, the setting of Part II, Mr. Biswas tests the Creole world but discovers that it is as frustrating as the rural, Indian one left behind. It has been suggested that Mr. Biswas' problem "is not just to live, but first of all to make for himself a world to live in," for the colonial society has not been fully formed.[23] It is a society with "no rules and patterns, . . . for no party had a programme, though all had the same objective: to make everyone in the colony rich and equal" (p. 510). Thus, White argues, "Mr. Biswas's journey from the old world to the new . . . becomes a journey from darkness to darkness, from a world where he is a creature of fate to a world in which he becomes a victim of circumstances, from an order which seems irrelevant to a disorder in which he is non-entity."[24] When, through his flair for the bizarre, he achieves some success as a writer for the Trinidad Sentinel, he earns the respect of the Tulsis and is able to reclaim his family. However, even with an independent livelihood, Mr. Biswas, as Boxill notes, is repeatedly "seduced by the false sense of security the Tulsis seem to offer . . . [and] is lulled into giving up the fight against the enemy until the outrages of the void become insupportable."[25] He settles to live at the crowded Port-of-Spain quarters of the Tulsis, and, after a rough period with a "new regime" at the Sentinel, he tells Anand: "I don't depend on them for a job. You know that. We could go back anytime to Hanuman House. All of us." (p. 380). Throughout his struggle for independence, Mr. Biswas repeatedly makes the mistake of leaning on the Tulsis when he feels insecure or pressured in the Creole world.

In fact, when the Tulsis become victims of creolization and urbanization, they recede as Mr. Biswas' enemy. Francis Wyndham contends that "the dominant characters are never static; they alter in fact, and also they seem to change with the shifting standpoint from which Mr. Biswas sees them."[26] Several changes collectively ruin the tenuously united Hanuman House. As the Tulsis are forced to come in increasing contact with the Creole world and with Western language and lifestyle, their traditional family clan structure becomes outmoded. Shekhar's Presbyterian-educated wife flaunts her modernity by using her English name, by wearing short dresses, and by talking of holidays, a luxury alien to the Tulsi women, who venture out only to attend weddings, funerals and house-blessings. The family itself is scattered and Mrs. Tulsi's firm control declines, while Seth falls from grace and moves away. The Tulsis are thrown into further disarray when they are forced to move to a French Creole estate, Shorthills, northeast of Port-of-Spain. Thinking of individual ownership and success, families conduct secret ravages on the estate and find themselves amid the competitive struggle for education of their

children. The Port-of-Spain base is used as a boarding
house for children ready to attend the city school. There
are cries of "Read! Learn! Learn! Read!" as this frantic
struggle intensifies. "There was no longer a Hanuman House
to protect them: everyone had to fight for himself in a new
world, the world Owad and Shekhar had entered where
education was the only protection" (p. 436). It is a new
world in which status is determined by education rather than
seniority. Mr. Biswas himself battles to adjust to this
world and takes a tender interest in the education of his
children, especially his son, Anand, to whom he now
transfers his ambitions. Subjected to such strains caused
by social and cultural disintegration and syncretism, the
Tulsis now appear more as protagonists than antagonists.

Instead of totally surrendering his link with the crumbling Tulsidom, Mr. Biswas dangles between the collapsing
enclave and the outside world. Hamner argues that Mr.
Biswas' "animosity toward the Tulsis remains alive, but
since their outmoded authoritarian structure soon begins to
disintegrate from within, there is little need for him to
instigate active rebellion."[27] Thus, when the Tulsis move
to Shorthills, Mr. Biswas is induced to vacate his Port-of-
Spain place and follow them, his rationale being that the
move is an insurance against his possibly being sacked at
the Sentinel. Pressures from Chinta (Shama's sister) and a
brother-in-law (a reader of W. C. Tuttle and henceforth
known as "W. C. Tuttle") drive him to build a house--his
second. However, when the house is accidentally burned, Mr.
Biswas feels again that he has no choice but to join some of
the Tulsis in Port-of-Spain. The rest of the extended
family soon follow, and old patterns of bickering occur.
Mr. Biswas endures the Tuttle's gramophone noise, the
children's buzzing sound, and Govind's whining of Ramayana
(although the monotony is frequently broken by the welcome
"series of grunts, thumps, cracks and crashes" as Chinta is
beaten). Expressions of jealousy, the invasion of the
capricious Mrs. Tulsi, and the taxing visits of Shekhar also
remind the hero of the limitations of his life as long as he
lives under a Tulsi roof. However, Mr. Biswas' determination
to be free from the Tulsis undoubtedly wanes, for he has
achieved some measure of success, and, therefore, has--but
does not use--the means to be on his own. He even has a new
job as Community Welfare Officer and resigns from his
uncertain position as administrator of the Deserving
Destitutes Fund at the Sentinel. Yet when he is asked to
make room for the return of Owad (now a pretentious doctor
idolized by the family), he accepts the limited space of
just one room.

When Mr. Biswas does find the mental strength to cut
his umbilical cord from Tulsidom, his victory is Pyrrhic.
He becomes vulnerable enough to be duped into purchasing a
makeshift, rickety house. The mortgage is high, and Mr.
Biswas is unaware of the dangerous staircase, rotten wooden

pillars, absence of a backdoor, and stuck windows. The important point to him, however, is that having lived a humiliated, dependent man most of his life, he now has a home, a monumental symbol of his achievement of personal identity and security. Mr. Biswas, in the words of the reviewer for the Spectator, emerges as "the classic 'little man' who retains his sense of dignity and purpose through every humiliation."[28] He has a taste of triumph when the Tuttles' scrutinizing visit goes smoothly, with all flaws of the house well concealed. The Epilogue reveals that Mr. Biswas returns to the Sentinel after the Community Welfare Department becomes defunct; that he is heavily burdened with debt; that after his failing health and hospitalization the Sentinel first puts him on half pay, then sacks him; that Savi returns home from abroad to support the family but Anand shows little interest; and, finally, that Mr. Biswas dies of a heart attack. Yet, such tragic events do not overshadow the hero's accomplishment of independence and of owning a home, to which his family can return in peace after his funeral.

This epic novel, with its giant sweep covering three generations, accurate attention to the minutest details, and universal applicability, distinguishes itself from Naipaul's first three social comedies. By no means provincial in the way the others can be considered to be, A House chronicles the obsessive aspiration of not just one man at one time but of all men in any age. Physically weak and ugly, Mr. Biswas is a representative of the ordinary man. But morally strong and determined, he assumes heroic proportions. He repeatedly bounces from the imprisoning, decaying Hindu enclave to the uncaring, disordered Creole world. But--unlike the old men under the Tulsi arcade who dream of returning to India and unlike the Govinds who weakly submit to Tulsidom--Mr. Biswas knows that his future must be made in Trinidad and by himself. He refuses to yield to despair. The society Mr. Biswas challenges is the same encountered in Naipaul's earlier novels--it is restrictive (Mr. Biswas is trapped by elements other than Tulsidom); imitative, incapable of generating its own values (the Sentinel copies London newspapers, and a black woman is angered when she asks for flesh-colored stockings and receives black ones); confused (the Tulsis, defenders of orthodox Hinduism flirt with Roman Catholicism); and corrupt (Seth "fixes" court cases, and property and cars "insuranburn"). Yet, clearly the emphasis is not on the satirical. In the earlier comedies Naipaul has been charged with being clinically detached and seeing his characters from the outside, but in A House the author is completely and sympathetically involved not only with Mr. Biswas' seemingly futile struggle for independence but also with the Tulsis' plight when they are confronted with a world for which they are unprepared. Despite signs of Naipaul's compassion and involvement with the characters, however, the novel never reaches the level of mawkishness, for the tone mingles seriousness with comedy.

With A House Naipaul may have broken his regional barrier sooner than he thought, even though the book was rejected by Knopf. Western reviewers hailed the work as a masterpiece and rated it as one of the few major post-war English novels.[29] Of course, some readers have complained about the need for historical data on East Indians, about the excessive length of the novel, about the implausibility of Mr. Biswas' employment as a reporter, and about the deus ex machina appearance of someone to buy the Shorthills house.[30] However, these critics still consider the novel a fine achievement. Even the "tagging" of characters (for example, "readers," "learners," and "the children") as a means of identification, a feature dismissed in Naipaul's earlier novels, is admired in A House.[31] The book has been specifically praised for its authentic picture ("dialect, customs, natural setting") of the West Indies, for its attention to and accuracy of minutest details, for its superb blend of comedy and pathos, for its compassionate handling of the hero, and for its excellent characterization.[32]

Of particular fascination is the character of Mr. Biswas. Some critics have examined him as a personification or an allegory of West Indian colonies seeking independence at whatever cost.[33] Others have seen a parallel between Mr. Biswas and such characters as Mr. Polly, Lear, and, most of all, Everyman.[34] The universality of theme and character has widely appealed to readers. Francis Wyndham praised Naipaul for creating "in depth, an original character whose extreme individuality illuminates the general experience of mankind," and Robert Hamner observed that the novel "transcends national boundaries and evokes universal human experiences" and that "Mr. Biswas' desire to own his own house is essentially a struggle to assert personal identity and to attain security--thoroughly human needs."[35] To the Times Literary Supplement reviewer Naipaul's hero is a "rather stupid little man, given to tummy aches and flippancy. . . . He is also cowardly and ugly, definitely not the stuff that heroes are made of. Yet, perversely, the author has made him perform labours that would have daunted Hercules and given him a degree of psychological penetration that might have baffled Socrates."[36] This contradiction is precisely what makes the protagonist a unique creation, for as Michael Thorpe argued, Mr. Biswas is "both ordinary and extraordinary--or he would not be interesting."[37] In their response to A House, Caribbean readers have generally pointed to the same merits recognized by Westerners.

Of all Naipaul's works, A House has drawn the most enthusiastic response from the West Indies. Derek Walcott likened the book to the great Russian novels; Gordon Rohlehr saw it as more "profound" than anything else Naipaul has written; and Edward Brathwaite rated it as "excellent by any

standards" and made a case for Naipaul's superiority to
fellow novelist, John Hearne.[38] Some reviewers greeted
the novel as a pioneering work in West Indian
literature--for example, the _Jamaican Gleaner_ welcomed
Naipaul's contribution as a breakthrough which will
challenge other artists: "Authors from the West Indies will
now have to find something to write about instead of jotting
down their descriptions of life"; and the Jamaican _Public
Opinion_, in an article reprinted in the Barbadian _Bim_,
hailed _A House_ as the first West Indian novel with a "total
Caribbean portrait, which, while still firmly rooted in its
island source, . . . soar[s] to universal meaning."[39]
Even most of Naipaul's bitter critics are compelled to
acknowledge the literary merit of this novel, widely
considered a West Indian epic.

West Indian readers often point out that Naipaul not
only shows that a great West Indian epic can be written
using the techniques of the traditional English novel but he
also places the spotlight on the silent, subdued East Indian
population of Trinidad, a people usually ignored in the
Caribbean and unknown in most of the world. In his non-
fiction, Naipaul has written of the surprise with which
foreigners greet East Indians from the West Indies. His
encounter with an Indian from India typifies the experience
of all overseas East Indian West Indian residents:

>   'You are coming from--?'
>   I had met enough Indians from India to know
> that this was less a serious inquiry than a
> greeting, in a distant land, from one Indian to
> another.
>   'Trinidad,' I said. 'In the West Indies. And
> you?'
>   He ignored my question. 'But you look Indian.'
>   'I am.'
>   'Red Indian?' He suppressed a nervous little
> giggle. . . . To be an Indian or East Indian from
> the West Indies is to be perpetual surprise to
> people outside the region. . . .
>   To be an Indian from Trinidad is to be
> unlikely. . . . and exotic.[40]

After reading _A House_, however, someone outside the
Caribbean gains an enormous amount of knowledge about the
Indian segment of the Trinidad population of the early part
of this century. George Moore, an English critic, writing
for _Black Orpheus_, observed that in the West Indies "the
despised 'coolie-man' has been silent for nearly a century,"
his values and culture unknown. But, Moore continued,
"Naipaul's advent makes us glad that the voice of the East
Indian is at last making itself heard in the Caribbean
West."[41] The novelty of the subject matter has appealed
to readers everywhere.

Black West Indians themselves have acknowledged the
educational value of Naipaul's epic. L. Edward Brathwaite
noted the tendency of most black West Indians to assume that
"West Indian" refers to someone of African descent only and
to forget the East Indian. "We meet for the first time . .
. that other, hitherto unremembered element in the West
Indian framework--the East Indian," wrote Brathwaite.
"Before Mr. Biswas the West Indian East Indian was without
form, features or voice. Now we know more about Hanuman
House then [sic] we do about Brandt's Pen [in John Hearne's
novels] or Village of Love [in Merrill Ferguson's
novel]."42 Trinidadian politician and writer C. L. R.
James lauded A House as the "finest study ever produced in
the West Indies . . . of a minority and the herculean
obstacles in the way of its achieving a room in the national
building," and he contended that after reading the novel,
"many of our people have a deeper understanding of the West
Indies than they did before."43 And Jamaican critic and
poet John Figueroa placed the work in the category of
"Re-creation" or "Innovation" since it is the first to
present the "sub-culture and family structure of 'East
Indian' West Indians."44 West Indian commentators not
only called attention to Naipaul's innovation in depicting
the social and cultural life of the local East Indian family
but they also noted the striking verisimilitude with which
this portrayal is done.

What Naipaul describes in A House corresponds
accurately to the historical facts about East Indians in the
Caribbean. In The Middle Passage Naipaul himself wrote of
the Trinidad East Indian world, a world that is a blueprint
for the one presented in his epic, that is "an enclosing
self-sufficient world absorbed with its quarrels and
jealousies, as difficult for the outsider to penetrate as
for one of its own members to escape. It protected and
imprisoned, a static world, awaiting decay."45 Not
surprisingly, therefore, West Indian critics have applauded
Naipaul's gift in presenting with deft accuracy the decaying
Indian enclave and the emerging Creole world in A House. R.
J. Owens' comment in the Caribbean Quarterly is typical of
West Indian sentiment: "The sights, sounds, and smells of
this environment are created by an almost incredible number
of detailed observations."46 This point is later echoed
by Gordon Rohlehr, who noted that "every sight, sound and
smell is recorded with fidelity and precision."47 And
Kenneth Ramchand, who compared the date of dissolution
(1941-45) of Naipaul's family life with that recorded in the
novel, emphasized the closeness of the novel's calendar to
the factual one.48

Naipaul himself acknowledged that a number of reviewers
admire A House because of its documentary aspect. But he
called attention to the fact that "an enormous amount" of
the book was written out of his imagination and that people
were consulted about little items of "inconsequential

information to lend vividness and verisimilitude to the
story." He mentioned, for example, that from London he
wrote his relatives in Trinidad to find out what time of
year the sugar crop took place.[49] In Trinidad he had
spent most of his time in the city of Port-of-Spain and,
thus, was not thoroughly familiar with all the minor details
of rural life; moreover, at the beginning of the novel, he
was recording events that had occurred before his birth, as
he himself explains:

> For me to write the story of a man like my father
> was, in the beginning at any rate, to attempt pure
> fiction, if only because I was writing of things
> before my time. The transplanted Hindu-Muslim
> rural culture of Trinidad into which my father was
> born early in the century was still a whole
> culture, close to India. When I was of an age to
> observe, that culture had begun to weaken; and the
> time of wholeness had seemed to me as far away as
> India itself, and, almost dateless. I knew little
> about the Trinidad Indian village way of life. . .
> . I had memories of my father's conversation; I
> also had his short stories. . . mainly about old
> rituals. . . . This was what my fantasy had to
> work on.
>   So the present novel begins with events twice
> removed, in an antique, "pastoral" time, and almost
> in a land of the imagination. . . . So the book is
> a work of imagination. It is obviously not "made
> up," created out of nothing. But it does not tell
> a literal truth.[50]

Naipaul nostalgically commented that of all his books, A
House "is the most personal, created out of what I saw and
felt as a child." Using memory and imagination, then, he
reconstructed a chronicle, which is, in his words,
"historically true of the people concerned."[51]
    The fortune of Naipaul's father, Seepersad Naipaul,
bears such a remarkable resemblance to that of Mr. Biswas
that the line between fact and fiction is almost invisible.
Both men, poor, being of high Hindu caste, were able to
marry into rich families who assisted them as they battled
for an independent livelihood; however, faced with life in
the atmosphere of the extended family, they became
rebellious and suffered nervous breakdowns. Examining the
parallels between the lives of the two men, Landeg White
noted: "The details of Naipaul's early years fit Anand's
almost exactly, even to the dates supplied in the text. . .
. The broad outlines of Mr. Biswas's career are taken from
life. The family did live in places corresponding to those
mentioned in the novel . . . the description is accurate in
every detail."[52] Naipaul's "Prologue to an Autobiography"
(1983) provides even further evidence that the life of Mr.

Biswas is roughly patterned after that of Seepersad Naipaul, who also worked as a sign-painter, shopkeeper, overseer, journalist, welfare officer, and journalist again:

> Our last two years in that house--our two years in the extended family--were very bad indeed. At the end of 1946, when I was fourteen, my father managed to buy his own house. . . . My father, when I got to know him, was full of rages against my mother's family. . . . Everyone in the family was expected to fall in line; and most people did . . . my father had always been on the other side. . . . He belonged, or was sympathetic, to the reforming movement known as Arya Samaj. . . . He lived in many places, many little towns, dependent now on my mother's family, now on the family of his wealthy uncle by marriage. For thirteen years he had no house of his own.[53]

Victor Ramraj, who compared these details to those in _A House_, concluded: "The parallels between the narratives and relationships, and the characters and their sensibilities in the autobiography and the novel are continuously evident."[54]

In _A House_ Naipaul used not only the basic framework of his father's life but also minor details which he remembered. There is, for example, the incident of the glass of milk which Mr. Biswas throws at Anand. (Naipaul still bears the scar of that parallel action.) Mr. Simbhoonath Capildeo, Naipaul's uncle, must have recognized the reality of the incidents and characters in the novel, for he remarked, "You know, I was the 'Big God' and my brother was the 'Little God'!"[55] In a _Trinidad Guardian_ article, "The House of Mr. Biswas," Therese Mills reported on her visit to the famous Capildeo house in Chaguanas, where Naipaul's father lived with his in-laws, in an elaborate Indian structure erected by Naipaul's maternal grandfather. Detailing the specific similarities between this house and the fictional one, Mills concluded: "Once inside this old Capildeo house it is difficult separating fact from fiction, so well did Naipaul draw his canvas. . . ."[56] Of course, what is important to note, too, is that Naipaul also modified and omitted some of the details of his father's life to suit his purpose, and, as White argued, "from the facts has been distilled a philosophy which the rearranged facts are then used to express."[57] Nevertheless, the appeal of _A House_ lies partly in the authenticity of vivid description, in minute details, of the lifestyle of an extended East Indian family in the early part of this century.

However, occasionally West Indian critics fail to note the important fact that _A House_ really concerns the Trinidadian Indian of the past, not of the present, although

light traces of Tulsidom, mainly in terms of family structure, may still be found in some rural areas. This point is
taken by Kenneth Ramchand, who examined the following
statement from L. Edward Brathwaite:

> In the world of Hanuman House, we have the first
> novel [from the West Indies] whose basic theme is
> not rootlessness and the search for social
> identity; in A House for Mr. Biswas we have at last
> a novel whose central character is clearly defined
> and who is really trying to get in rather than get
> out.58

Disagreeing with this idea, Ramchand classified the work as
"the West Indian novel of rootlessness par excellence." He
saw Mr. Biswas as someone who, expecting the imminent dissolution of Tulsidom, wants to escape from it rather than
belong to it but finds that the colonial society is also in
disorder. In short, as Ramchand put it, "Mr. Biswas
struggles between the tepid chaos of a decaying culture and
the void of a colonial society."59 Maureen Warner-Lewis,
who analyzed the cultural upheaval and change during
Tulsidom, and Gordon Rohlehr, who discussed the different
levels of the interpretation of Mr. Biswas' rebellion,
arrive at the same conclusion: that is, the hero finds both
worlds--the secure and stifling Tulsidom and the new hypocritical Creole world--equally unpalatable.60 This
reading is supported by Naipaul's non-fictional pieces on
the shortcomings of Trinidad society.

Although A House focuses primarily on the East Indian
community, West Indian readers generally see the novel as
encompassing universal themes, with the character of Mr.
Biswas representing anything from a rebellious slave to an
archetypal figure of Everyman. The most popular approach,
one also taken by Western critics, has been to examine the
hero as a parallel for the West Indian society as a
whole.61 For example, Gordon Rohlehr equated Tulsidom
with a slave society from which Mr. Biswas is seeking independence from Mrs. Tulsi and from Seth, both shrewd
colonizers remaking their crumbling empire through the aid
of different families brought together. Rohlehr further
suggested that it is possible to view Mr. Biswas' rebellion
as a

> paradigm of the perennial West Indian struggle for
> a more truly democratic society. . . .
>   No one can deny the danger of regarding Biswas
> as a figure representative of the Caribbean
> predicament. . . . Yet, . . . he is representative
> enough of our local predicament: a man without a
> past, an orphan wavering between equally dubious
> cultural alternatives; winning a sort of indepen-
> dence and returning in humiliation to the people he
> is still forced to fight. . . .62

In another essay the same critic stressed that the novel
transcends any simple preoccupation with race and the Hindu
world and describes instead a classic struggle for
personality and reveals that true independence does not
immediately follow rebellion.[63] Not particularly bothered
by Naipaul's decision to focus primarily on East Indian
communities, David Omerod, like Rohlehr, emphasized Mr.
Biswas' parallelism with Naipaul's homeless, nomadic
migrants and recalled that the black slave and the
indentured Indians experienced almost common backgrounds and
that the hero "is living a situation which is the
cornerstone of the predicament of a whole society,
irrespective of the racial origins of its individual
members."[64]
     Indeed, many West Indians have registered their
comments on the universality of the theme in A House. Wayne
Brown, who elsewhere vehemently denounced Naipaul for
attacking the West Indies, praised the wide application of
the novel: "Though intensely located in Trinidad's East
Indian community, [A House] transcends place and time to
become a lovingly executed metaphor for the condition of
'downpressed' man everywhere."[65] Referring to all of
Naipaul's early works, including A House, Arthur Drayton
admired the Trinidadianness of the characters (a quality, he
claimed, that overrides ethnic origin), and Derek Walcott
noted that Mr. Biswas is "symbolic of all West Indian
races."[66] John Figueroa also praised the universal theme
of A House, as did L. Edward Brathwaite, who observed that
Mr. Biswas becomes "a kind of timeless figure--a sort of
Everyman."[67] Thus, to these critics, the predominantly
East Indian cast does not weaken the stature of the novel.
     Not all West Indian readers, however, are convinced of
the heroism and universality of Mr. Biswas. Ivan Van
Sertima stated that "in spite of its challenging breadth of
life," this massively documented novel is "unable to strike
the deeper resonances that could lift it from its regional
context, throwing up no figure . . . that can grow and
expand into universal myth. . . ." Van Sertima, rejecting
any interpretation which reads the work as the rebellion of
an individual against "a totalitarian monster-state,"
claimed that

> both Naipaul as creator, and Mohan Biswas, his
> creation, lack the dynamic that is demanded to give
> memorable significance to such a grave creative
> rebellion. . . . The scarecrow figure of Biswas is
> not invested with that dimension of depth which
> alone could have redeemed it of its grotesque and
> absurd appearance . . . the effort to lift him
> through many levels . . . to the stature of a
> tragic hero ends in failure. . . . And Naipaul
> himself, stretched to the top of his power in this
> work, exposes his talent as one of fundamental
> mediocrity.[68]

Contrary to Van Sertima's opinion, however, it is precisely
the ordinariness of the "scarecrow figure" of Mr. Biswas--a
physically weak, feeble, unattractive, unskilled man--that
universalizes and heightens the theme of the novel. Van
Sertima in general has strong misgivings about the author's
attitude. Reviewing Naipaul's first four novels he wrote:
"His brilliancy of wit I do not deny but, in my opinion, he
has been overrated by English critics, whose sensibilities
he insidiously flatters by his stock-in-trade: self-
contempt."[69]

Nor is Van Sertima alone in his demeaning reference to
Mr. Biswas and to Naipaul's talent. Contending that
Naipaul's novelistic skills and prose manner are "disappointing" and suited to his vision of mediocrity," Lloyd
King criticized the hero's "sadomasochistic relationship" to
himself and others and "feelings of self-contempt and contempt for others."[70] Mr. Biswas' attitude, however, can
be explained by the fact that the hero battles to maintain
his self-respect and dignity by rebelling against the
Tulsis' shallow hypocritical world and against his demeaning
status as a live-in, dependent son-in-law. His position is
extremely humiliating, for Indian marriages are generally
virilocal, unless (as in this case) a poor son-in-law is
forced to live in the home of his wife's parents. Such a
groom, disparagingly called a ghardamda, is often subject to
ridicule.[71] Thus, Mr. Biswas rebels against this humiliation by venting his anger and frustration on others and on
himself. Referring to Mr. Biswas' humiliation in the "ritualistic role of the newly married Hindu girl," Gordon
Rohlehr admired the way in which the rebellion is handled:
"Initially Biswas enjoys it. It exhilarates him. But it
soon becomes a vicious and bitter struggle. . . . Indeed,
Biswas is at times petty, cowardly and contemptible, and
part of the book's triumph is that Naipaul has been able to
present a hero in all his littleness, and still preserve a
sense of the man's inner dignity."[72]

That Mr. Biswas is indeed a little man who rises to
heroic proportions is a point apparently missed by Guyanese
writer Wilson Harris in his essay "Tradition and the West
Indian Novel" (1964). Referring specifically to A House,
Harris contended that "the inner and outer poverty of
Naipaul's characters . . . never erupts into a revolutionary
or alien question of spirit":

> It is this 'common picture of humanity' so-called
> on which Naipaul's work rests. The novel for him,
> as for many contemporary readers and writers,
> restricts the open and original ground of choice,
> the vision and stress of transplantation in the
> person out of one world into another, the necessity
> for epic beyond its present framework, or tragedy
> within its present framework, since the assumption
> remains to the end a contemporary and limited one

of burial and classification, a persuasion of
singular and pathetic enlightenment rather than a
tragic centrality or a capacity for plural forms of
profound identity.[73]

Gerald Guinness, a non-West Indian critic, challenged
Harris: "Not only, in my opinion, is this a bad piece of
writing but it is also basically misguided. Surely it is
rather the author of A House . . . who displays a 'tragic
centrality' than [Harris]. . . ."[74] And Robert Hamner,
also disagreeing with Harris that Mr. Biswas' life never
emerges into a question of spirit, argued: "Naipaul deals
with insignificant men, but under his hand they assume
importance. Their field of action is life, and he infuses
their struggle with vision."[75] Harris' criticism of
Naipaul has received little, if any, attention from fellow
West Indians.
      Several Caribbean readers have also criticized the
early Naipaul for ignoring Trinidad's non-Indian groups or
for dealing with exclusively East Indian communities, even
though such communities exist. In fact, he has often been
compared to Samuel Selvon, a Trinidadian East Indian, who
confronts the issue of "color" in his works, whereas
Naipaul, according to Guyanese novelist O. R. Dawthorne,
portrays a "slightly less authentic version of a closed
racial world."[76] Some observers think that it is
necessary to eliminate exclusiveness in order to develop
West Indian nationalism. Thus, Guyanese poet and critic A.
J. Seymour implied that the type of Indian community in A
House, which never loses its grip on Indian cultural
heritage and which isolates itself from the Creole world,
encourages political and racial turmoil:

            We have the material for political clash such as we
            have deplored in Guyana and hope to avoid in
            Trinidad--a seeming exclusiveness of community ways
            of living which has and may create a wound in
            society. House for Mr. Biswas depicts a reality
            which we have all seen on the British Caribbean
            scene, and this is the material which politicians
            have been known to utilize.[77]

There appears to be some doubt in Seymour's mind about
Naipaul's decision to portray this "seeming exclusiveness of
community ways of living."
      George Lamming, who incidentally, spoke of Naipaul's
"impressive accuracy" in the characterizations in A House,
was more direct in his criticisms of Naipaul's Indian communities. Sensitive readers may object to Lamming's dispa-
raging reference, however frank, to the accomplishment of
East Indians in their move from Indian poverty to
Trinidadian prosperity: "This achievement, originating with
Mr. Biswas, symbolizes the journey which a whole generation

of his people have made from the squalid cells of their birth among flies, lice and animal excrement to the recent summits of office in their island."[78] The unpleasant or unhygienic life in India is not the focus of A House; in fact, the story picks up with the birth of Mr. Biswas in Trinidad. More importantly, though, is Lamming's charge that the novel fails to reflect the cosmopolitan quality of the islands:

> [A House] raises one crucial doubt about the range of Mr. Naipaul's interpretation. Trinidad is the most cosmopolitan of the islands. Chinese, Indians, Negroes, Portuguese--all native to this soil--are involved in a constant interplay of local forces. But Mr. Naipaul's world leaves us with the impression of one race surviving in isolation; insulated, as it were, within an unfamiliar landscape. One feels that he is particularly careful to avoid that total encounter which is the experience of any Trinidadian, whatever his race may be. Indeed, it is the fundamental West Indian experience.[79]

Lamming's criticism has received a surprising amount of notice, partly because of Naipaul's direct response to it in An Area of Darkness. Naipaul agreed with Lamming that the confrontation of races is the fundamental West Indian experience. "But," the novelist continued, "to see the attenuation of the culture of my childhood as the result of a dramatic confrontation of opposed worlds would be to distort the reality. To me the worlds were juxtaposed and mutually exclusive. . . . I can speak only out of my own experience."[80] Furthermore, in The Middle Passage Naipaul asserted that the subject of confrontation of racial groups has been abused in West Indian literature and that West Indian writers have "reflected and flattered the prejudices of their race or colour groups"; therefore, even if his experiences were not as he has claimed, he still may have avoided racial issues so that he could create a literature which is universal.[81]

In other ways, West Indian critics of Naipaul's predominantly East Indian cast in A House have shifted from serious literary analyses. Edward Brathwaite praised the novel as one which shows that the technique of "The Great Tradition" of the English novel can be applied to a West Indian work; however, he argued that without the "structure and cultural awareness" or without the "specific and self-conscious social framework" of the East Indian community, a novel of "this nature and magnitude" could hardly have been attempted.[82] Kenneth Ramchand rejected Brathwaite's implication that "the African in the West Indies doesn't have a community or a structured world and therefore he cannot have well-structured novels."[83] Ramchand disagreed not only with this idea but also with Brathwaite's interpretation of the novel:

> Brathwaite is so obsessed with his sentimental thesis about African deprivation in contrast to Indian solidity that he misreads the novel. . . . I found the whole discussion distasteful because there was in [sic] implication that the Africans in the society are looking for African novelists and the Indians are looking for Indian novelists. Or ought to be. . . .
>
> His main sorrow was that the Africans would not get a novel like A House . . . until they had a social world as equally ordered as the one upon which the fictional Biswas' world was drawn from. How can you say a thing like that when A House. . . is a chronicle of a disintegrating world. . .? I think that Brathwaite's socio-political and cultural obsessions led him to invent and re-invent A House . . . as evidence of the plural society, and as a chastising model to encourage Black creativity. [But] . . . novels like Biswas and In the Castle of My Skin [by Lamming] belong to all of us . . . A House . . . is about the dissolution of the Indian enclave . . . and [Biswas] tries to come to terms with the New World, not making a political decision but acting virtually out of instinct.[84]

Ramchand also took issue with Rohlehr who had argued that the novel does not involve the Creole world. According to Ramchand Mr. Biswas is "quite essentially Trinidadian" in his search for a different life, and the structure of the novel suggests a drifting towards the Creole world.[85] Thus, critical focus on Naipaul sometimes shifts to socio-political ideas.

Indian involvement with the Creole world leads to creolization, and this, a recurring social and political theme in all Naipaul's East Indian novels, is one often debated. West Indian nationalists strongly encourage the shedding of Indian cultural patterns and the adoption of Creole ones. Gordon Rohlehr has charged that Naipaul writes of creolization of East Indians with "bitterness, despair and regret."[86] And George Moore, asserting that Naipaul laments creolization as a loss, chided: "Naipaul does not seem to recognize that people like these [Indians] will soon need to define a West Indian existence, call it nationalism or what you will, quite as urgently as their Creole compatriots."[87] Ramchand, however, directly challenged both Moore and Rohlehr, noting that Naipaul does not regret the decay of East Indian cultural forms in the West Indies; rather, he laments it "as a growth into mimicry," an imitation of black imitation in "treading the weary road to whiteness."[88] Ramchand's reading is supported by one of

Naipaul's short stories, "A Christmas Story," in which the
author gives full expression to the specific theme of
creolization. Published in A Flag on the Island (1967), the
story was written in 1962, that is, shortly after the
publication of A House. The following brief examination of
this story will illuminate Naipaul's position on cultural
conflicts, often at the center of critical response to A
House.

Narrated by a Presbyterian convert who becomes a
teacher, "A Christmas Story" is an accurate document
reflecting the writer's view on creolization or the phasing
out of the Hindu culture. In praising the superficial
changes in his new-found life, in deriding Indian culture,
and in contemptuously referring to Indians as "these
people," the narrator unwittingly reveals his own
questionable values. His reason for conversion goes beyond
his rejection of the principles of Hinduism:

> It did not, after all, require much intelligence to
> see that Hinduism with its animistic rites, its
> idolatry, its emphasis on mango leaf, banana leaf
> and--the truth is the truth--cowdung, was a
> religion little fitted for the modern world. I had
> only to contrast the position of the Hindus with
> that of the Christians. I had only to consider the
> differing standards of dress, houses, food. Such
> differences have today more or less disappeared. .
> . . I did not have to be 'converted' by the
> Presbyterians of the Canadian Mission. I had only
> to look at the work they were doing among the
> backward Hindus and Moslems of my district. . . .
>
> My Presbyterianism . . . was a distinct
> advantage. It gave me a grace in the eyes of my
> superiors.[89]

He expresses his pleasure in hearing himself addressed by
his baptized name "Randolph" rather than by his Hindu name
"Choonilal"; he mentions his "shameful experiments" with the
"proper implements" of knife and fork and spoon as he gives
up eating with his fingers; he admits shame at witnessing a
traditional Hindu wedding tent and ceremonies; he speaks of
the filthiness of the cow which Hindus admire; he decribes
his joy in dressing in the "most spotless of garments" to
attend church, where the "most respectable and respected"
gather, and he comments on the admiration of the unconverted
"gaping crowd" that stares as he passes; he compares the
churchgoers' "trousers and jackets of white drill" to the
Hindus' "leg-revealing" dhotis; and he praises the hats and
short dresses worn by the converted women. In short, the
narrator himself proudly boasts of success at accurately
mimicking Western styles. In spite of this pride, Randolph
allows a supressed admiration to surface briefly when he
describes Indian culture--for example, the "good," "rich"

food and the "charm" of the wedding tent. Thus, while he
tries to convince himself that Western culture and Creole
standards are superior, he unconsciously harbors strong
doubts.

Clearly, then, Naipaul questions slavish mimicry such
as that exposed in "A Christmas Story"; however, this
objection does not mean that he endorses the preservation of
Indian cultural patterns. In fact, in A House, the author's
prejudice against the East Indianness of the Tulsis is so
evident that Kenneth Ramchand called attention to a "one-
sided" compassion in the early parts of the novel and
expressed concern that Naipaul engages the reader's sympathy
at the expense of the Tulsis, who are "just as deprived,
depressed, and in need of articulation as Mr. Biswas."[90]
Victor Ramraj suggested that Naipaul holds an ambivalent
view of the Indian community, as seen not only in his
non-fictional pieces but also specifically in A House and "A
Christmas Story."[91] And pointing to the portrayal of
Tulsidom, Maureen Warner-Lewis made a similar argument:

> [Naipaul] lets Mr. Biswas not only rile against a
> system which tends to destroy the individual
> personality, but . . . he also records Mr. Biswas'
> appreciation of the positive benefits of that
> system--the sense of security it gave its members
> and the psychological and financial support it
> afforded in times of illness and distress.[92]

It could be argued that Naipaul has no specific answers to
the dilemma facing East Indians, who are torn between
honoring outmoded Indian traditions and imitating Creole
culture. Warner-Lewis contended that in A House Naipaul
"hovers between condemnation of both the old and the new
systems," between the Indian enclave and the Creole
society.[93] What is important is that he never chooses one
world over another, and he adamantly rejects any pressures
to do so.

Some readers, perhaps because of national pride, are
uncomfortable with the type of Creole world Naipaul offers
Mr. Biswas as an alternative to Tulsidom. A. C. Derrick
argued that Naipaul presents a "shoddy and limiting world"
and that the "recurring images of darkness, decay and death,
make . . . failure appear throughout as the inevitable
outcome to the process of Biswas' struggle."[94] However,
refuting Derrick, Anthony Boxill pointed out that these
images, instead, challenge Mr. Biswas to bring "order and
light to the void," and that "those who are concerned that
after all he has been through Biswas is not allowed more
unqualified success, have clearly missed the point of the
novel."[95] But the following comment from Sylvia Wynter,
who dismissed Naipaul's talent in a subordinate clause and
emphasized the author's outlook on the West Indies, demonstrates how Naipaul's novelistic skill is overshadowed by

his views on his homeland: "A House . . . whilst it
celebrates the talent of its author, and awards him a
recognized place among the elite world, is nevertheless a
profound indictment of a deprived world in which, to realize
his being, Biswas must alienate himself from an impossible
community."[96]   To another West Indian reviewer, George
Panton, A House, threatened by its criticisms of Trinidad,
is salvaged because of the narrative: "At the beginning one
may be put off by Mr. Naipaul's trait of seeming to laugh at
the short-comings of his fellow Trinidadians--very noticeable in his earlier books--but in a short while this is
forgotten in the sincerity of the narrative."[97]
     Of course, the majority of West Indian critics feel
that Mr. Biswas eventually gains victory, even if it is a
Pyrrhic one. For example, Lamming asserted that Mr. Biswas'
dignity is retrieved by the purchase of a house, and
Ramchand noted that the acquisition of a house confirms the
possibility of order.[98]   Rohlehr also saw Mr. Biswas's
rebellion as "worthwhile"; however, he criticized Naipaul's
view of the West Indies:

> Biswas has no escape from society. . . . It is a
> terrible comment either on West Indian society or
> on Naipaul, that the alternatives which it offers
> him are escape or frustration. Naipaul is afraid
> of something vital but crude in Trinidad society as
> he shows in Miguel Street or more openly in The
> Middle Passage.[99]

Reviewing one of Rohlehr's later essays, which also linked
Naipaul's statements in The Middle Passage to the fictional
portrayal of Trinidad, Kenneth Ramchand argued: "The essay
is . . . of interest as an attempt (always hazardous) to
relate the author's real life attitudes to his fictional
stances, and as a classic illustration of the West Indian
ambivalence to the English reputation of the writer.
Rohlehr likes A House . . . but has doubts about Mr.
Naipaul."[100]
     In spite of reservations expressed, however, West
Indians generally recognize A House as a valuable epic
written by a talented novelist. First, they sense Naipaul's
involvement, compassion, and sympathy, which, they contend,
are generally missing in the earlier works.[101]   A. C.
Derrick is perhaps the only West Indian critic to argue that
the novel shows Naipaul's "lack of compassion and how
completely destructive his mode of satire can be."[102]
Second, Naipaul has created, in Walcott's words, "The most
real and most memorable character in West Indian
fiction."[103]   Because Biswas is richly symbolic of all
races and of many concepts, the novel invites different
levels of interpretation and, thus, has a wide appeal.
Finally, perhaps the most important reason for the
acceptability of A House is that West Indian readers see the

work as a valuable, detailed documentary of the East Indian community, which is in the process of change, change which they see as much needed. For instance, even Van Sertima, who has belittled Naipaul's talent, praised the book as one "filled with an insight into the depravity and meanness, the incestuous stifling clannishness of the East Indian family in the Caribbean" and lauded Naipaul's gift for vividly capturing the "intimate and unquestionable knowledge" of his material.[104] Yet, as many West Indians have pointed out, Naipaul, in writing the history of this specific community, metaphorically writes the history of the entire island, of all races.

To the majority of Caribbean readers, then, <u>A House for Mr Biswas</u> undoubtedly represents Naipaul at his best. No other single work of his has elicited as many favorable reviews from his fellow West Indians. In spite of this high rating, the novel has been criticized for restricting itself to the East Indian community and for not offering Mr. Biswas the Creole world as a viable alternative to Tulsidom. What has always infuriated West Indians is Naipaul's negative portrayal of West Indian Creole society, a view acidly articulated in his non-fiction. This body of writing, on which his notoriety as a writer is established, will be examined in the next chapter.

Notes

[1] "London," in <u>The Overcrowded Barracoon</u> (London: André Deutsch, 1972 rpt. New York: Penguin Books, 1976), p. 15.

[2] <u>V. S. Naipaul</u> (London: Macmillan Press, 1975), pp. 88-89.

[3] Rev. of <u>A House for Mr Biswas</u>, <u>London Magazine</u>, 1, No. 7 (Oct. 1961), 91.

[4] <u>V. S. Naipaul</u> (New York: Twayne Publishers Inc., 1973), p. 50.

[5] <u>The West Indian Novel and Its Background</u> (New York: Barnes and Noble Inc., 1970), p. 199.

[6] Morris Gilbert, "Hapless Defiance," rev. of <u>A House for Mr Biswas</u>, <u>New York Times Book Review</u>, 24 June 1962, p. 30.

[7] <u>V. S. Naipaul</u> (Edinburgh: Oliver Boyd, 1973), p. 43.

[8] "Self-Help in Hot Places, rev. of <u>A House for Mr Biswas</u>, <u>New Statesman</u>, 29 Sept. 1961, p. 441.

[9] <u>V. S. Naipaul</u> (London: The British Council/Longman Group Ltd., 1976), p. 16.

[10] <u>A House for Mr Biswas</u> (London: André Deutsch, 1961; rpt. New York: Penguin Books, 1981), pp. 13-14. Subsequent references will be from this edition and will be indicated in the text.

[11] "A Trinidadian Dickens," rev. of <u>A House</u>, <u>Reporter</u>, 19 July 1962, p. 56.

[12] See, for example, R. H. Lee, "The Novels of V. S. Naipaul," in <u>Critical Perspectives on V. S. Naipaul</u>, ed. Robert Hamner (Washington, D.C.: Three Continents Press, 1977), p. 76.

[13] <u>V. S. Naipaul's Fiction</u> (Canada: York Press, 1983), p. 37.

[14] Ramchand, <u>The West Indian Novel and Its Background</u>, pp. 194-95, examines the highly suggestive imagery used to describe Hanuman House.

[15] <u>The West Indian Novel and Its Background</u>, pp. 196-97.

16 _V. S. Naipaul_, p. 90.

17 _V. S. Naipaul's Fiction_, p. 40.

18 White, p. 112.

19 Eimerl, p. 57.

20 _The West Indian Novel and Its Background_, pp. 198-99.

21 Rev. of _A House for Mr Biswas_, p. 91.

22 White, p. 117.

23 Bernard Krikler, "V. S. Naipaul's 'A House for Mr Biswas,'" rev. of _A House for Mr Biswas, Listener_, 13 Feb. 1964, p. 270.

24 White, p. 106.

25 _V. S. Naipaul's Fiction_, p. 40.

26 Rev. of _A House for Mr Biswas_, p. 92.

27 _V. S. Naipaul_, p. 92.

28 Julian Mitchell, "Everyman's Island," rev. of _A House for Mr Biswas, Spectator_, 6 Oct. 1961, p. 472.

29 See, for example, Krikler, rev. of _A House for Mr Biswas_, pp. 270-71.

30 Jacobson, p. 441; Eimerl, p. 57; "High Jinks in Trinidad," rev. of _A House for Mr Biswas, Times Literary Supplement_, 29 Sept. 1961, p. 641.

31 Louis Chapin, rev. of _A House for Mr Biswas, Christian Science Monitor_, 19 July 1962, p. 11. See also Hamner, _V. S. Naipaul_, p. 94.

32 Hamner, _V. S. Naipaul_, pp. 48 and 89; Charles Mann, rev. of _A House for Mr Biswas, Library Journal_, 15 May 1962, p. 1917; "New Fiction," rev. of _A House for Mr Biswas, Times_ (London), 5 Oct. 1961, p. 16; Whitney Balliet, rev. of _A House for Mr Biswas, New Yorker_, 4 Aug. 1962, p. 70; Krikler, rev. of _A House for Mr Biswas_, p. 271; Eimerl, p. 57.

33 George Woodcock, "Two Great Commonwealth Novelists," _Sewanee Review_, 87 (1979), 26; John Thieme, "V. S. Naipaul's Third World," _Journal of Commonwealth Literature_, 10, No. 1 (August 1975), 13; Krikler, rev. of _A House for Mr Biswas_, pp. 270-71.

34 Margaret Shenfield, "Mr. Biswas and Mr. Polly," English, 23, No. 117 (Autumn 1974), 95-100; Gilbert, p. 30; Michael Thorpe, V. S. Naipaul, p. 16; Eimerl, p. 56.

35 Hamner, V. S. Naipaul, p. 48; Wyndham, rev. of A House, p. 90.

36 "High Jinks in Trinidad," p. 641.

37 Thorpe, p. 16.

38 Derek Walcott, "The Achievement of V. S. Naipaul," Sunday Guardian (Trinidad), 12 April 1964, p. 15; Gordon Rohlehr, "The Ironic Approach," in The Islands in Between, ed. Louis James (London: Oxford Univ. Press, 1968), p. 132; L. Edward Brathwaite, "Roots," Bim (Barbados), 10, No. 37 (July-Dec. 1963), 18-19.

39 Colin MacInnes, rev. of A House for Mr Biswas, Bim (Barbados), 9, No. 35 (July-Dec. 1962), 221; George Panton, "West Indian Writing Comes of Age," Sunday Gleaner (Jamaica), 3 Dec. 1961, p. 1.

40 "East Indian," in The Overcrowded Barracoon, pp. 32-38.

41 "East Indians and West," Black Orpheus, 7 (June 1960), 11-15.

42 "Roots," pp. 16-17.

43 "Introduction to 'Tradition and the West Indian Novel,'" in Tradition, the Writer and Society (London: New Beacon Publications, 1967), p. 74, and as quoted by Ramchand, The West Indian Novel and Its Background, p. 192.

44 "Some Provisional Comments on West Indian Novels," in Commonwealth Literature, ed. John Press (London: Heinemann, 1965), p. 96.

45 The Middle Passage (London: André Deutsch, 1962; rpt. New York: Vintage Books, 1981), pp. 81-82.

46 Rev. of A House for Mr Biswas, Caribbean Quarterly, 7, No. 4 (April 1962), 217.

47 "The Ironic Approach," p. 138.

48 The West Indian Novel and Its Background, p. 191.

49 "Speaking of Writing," The Times (London), 2 Jan. 1964, p. 11.

174

50 "Writing 'A House for Mr. Biswas,'" _New York Review_, 24 Nov. 1983, p. 22.

51 "Writing 'A House for Mr. Biswas,'" p. 22.

52 White, pp. 92-93.

53 "Prologue to an Autobiography," _Vanity Fair_, 46, No. 2 (April 1983), 142, 154-56.

54 "V. S. Naipaul's Identity in Fact and Fiction," Paper given at the European Association for Commonwealth Literature and Language Studies Conference, Barcelona, Spain, April 1984.

55 Therese Mills, "The House of Mr. Biswas," _Sunday Guardian_ (Trinidad), 28 Jan. 1973, p. 11.

56 Mills, p. 11.

57 White, p. 96.

58 "Roots," p. 17.

59 _The West Indian Novel and Its Background_, pp. 191-92.

60 Maureen Warner-Lewis, "Cultural Confrontation, Disintegration and Syncretism in _A House for Mr Biswas_," _Caribbean Quarterly_, 16, No. 4 (December 1970), 70 ff; Rohlehr, "The Ironic Approach," p. 133.

61 See, for example, Gerald Guinness, "Naipaul's Four Early Trinidad Novels," _Revista/Review Interamericana_, 6, No. 4 (Winter 1976-77), 570.

62 "Character and Rebellion in _A House for Mr. Biswas_," in _Critical Perspectives on V. S. Naipaul_, ed. Robert Hamner, pp. 91-3. William Walsh, "Necessary and Accommodated," _Lugano Review_, 1, Nos. 3-4 (1965), 169-81, also examined the theme of slavery in Naipaul's first novels.

63 "The Ironic Approach," pp. 134-36.

64 "In a Derelict Land: The Novels of V. S. Naipaul," in _Critical Perspectives on V. S. Naipaul_, ed. Robert Hamner, pp. 167-72.

65 "The First Generation of West Indian Novelists," _Sunday Guardian_ (Trinidad), 7 June 1970, p. 6; see also Colin MacInnes, p. 221.

⁶⁶ Arthur Drayton, "West Indian Fiction and West Indian Society," Kenyon Review, 25, No. 1 (Winter 1963), 131; Derek Walcott, "The Achievement of V. S. Naipaul," Sunday Guardian (Trinidad) 12 April 1964, p. 15.

⁶⁷ Figueroa, "Some Provisional Comments," pp. 95-96; Brathwaite, "Roots," p. 20.

⁶⁸ Van Sertima, pp. 40-41.

⁶⁹ Van Sertima, p. 6.

⁷⁰ "The Trauma of Naipauland," Trinidad Guardian, 24 Sept. 1967, p. 16.

⁷¹ Morton Klass, East Indians in Trinidad (New York: Columbia University Press, 1961), p. 112.

⁷² "The Ironic Approach," p. 135.

⁷³ "Tradition and the West Indian Novel," in Tradition, the Writer and Society, p. 40.

⁷⁴ Guinness, p. 572.

⁷⁵ V. S. Naipaul, p. 122.

⁷⁶ Ed. Caribbean Narrative (London: Heinemann, 1966), p. 9.

⁷⁷ "The Novel in the British Caribbean," Bim (Barbados), 12, No. 44 (Jan.-June 1967), 240.

⁷⁸ "A Trinidad Experience," Time and Tide, 5 Oct. 1961, p. 1657.

⁷⁹ "A Trinidad Experience," p. 1657.

⁸⁰ An Area of Darkness (London: André Deutsch, 1964, rpt. New York: Vintage Books, 1981), p. 37.

⁸¹ The Middle Passage, pp. 68-70.

⁸² "West Indian Prose Fiction in the Sixties," "Critical Survey, 3, No. 3 (Winter 1967), 170.

⁸³ "V. S. Naipaul and West Indian Writers," p. 13.

⁸⁴ "V. S. Naipaul and West Indian Writers," p. 13.

⁸⁵ "V. S. Naipaul and West Indian Writers," pp. 13-14.

⁸⁶ "The Ironic Approach," p. 124.

87 The Chosen Tongue (London: Longmans, Green & Co. Ltd., 1969), p. 7. The British critic Michael Thorpe, p. 34, argued that Naipaul is "too 'Indian' at bottom" to accept creolization.

88 "Concern for Criticism," Literary Half-Yearly, 12, No. 2 (July 1970), 156. See also Paul Edwards and Kenneth Ramchand, intro., The Mystic Masseur, pp. viii-ix.

89 A Flag on the Island (Middlesex: Penguin Books, 1967; rpt. New York: Penguin Books, 1982). pp. 24-25.

90 "V. S. Naipaul and West Indian Writers," pp. 11-12.

91 "Sly Compassion," Commonwealth, 6, No. 1 (Autumn 1983), 61-70.

92 Warner-Lewis, p. 79.

93 Warner-Lewis, p. 79.

94 "Naipaul's Technique as a Novelist," Journal of Commonwealth Literature, 7 (July 1969), 32-39.

95 V. S. Naipaul's Fiction, pp. 38-39.

96 "Novel and History, Plot and Plantation," Savacou (Jamaica), 5 (June 1971), 97.

97 "West Indian Writing Comes of Age," p. 14.

98 Lamming, "A Trinidad Experience," p. 1657; Ramchand, The West Indian Novel and Its Background, p. 204.

99 "Predestination, Frustration and Symbolic Darkness in Naipaul's A House for Mr. Biswas, Caribbean Quarterly, 10, No. 1 (March 1964), 10.

100 "In Between," rev. of The Islands in Between, ed. Louis James, Journal of Commonwealth Literature, 9 (July 1970), 126-27.

101 See, for example, Wayne Brown, "The First Generation of West Indian Novelists," Sunday Guardian (Trinidad), 7 June 1970, p. 6; Victor Ramraj, "Diminishing Satire," in Awakened Conscience, ed. C. D. Narasimhaiah (New Delhi: Sterling Pub. Pvt. 1978), pp. 271-72.

102 "Naipaul's Technique as a Novelist," p. 44.

103 Walcott, "The Achievement of V. S. Naipaul," p. 15.

104 Van Sertima, p. 41.

Chapter V

West Indian Response to Naipaul's
West Indian Non-fiction

With the completion of <u>A House for Mr Biswas</u> (1961), V. S. Naipaul ended the first phase of his development as a writer. No longer concerned with the comic depiction of rural Trinidadian East Indian communities, he enlarged his canvas and shifted his main focus to the dark portrayal of fictional multiracial Caribbean islands and other Third World societies and displaced individuals in alien lands. More importantly, he now divided his world-wide interest-- and specifically his West Indian concerns--almost evenly between fiction and non-fiction. Bridging the early novels, set in pre-independent Trinidad, and the later ones, placed in post-independent West Indies, is <u>The Middle Passage</u> (1962), which, significantly, examines non-fictionally the author's impression of five newly independent Caribbean societies. It is with the publication of <u>The Middle Passage</u> that Naipaul launched his new career as an international journalist/traveler. Thereafter he increased his West Indian non-fictional output with <u>The Loss of El Dorado</u> (1969), several Caribbean articles, most of which have been reprinted in <u>The Overcrowded Barracoon</u> (1972), and a lengthy work of reportage on the black power murders in Trinidad, "The Killings in Trinidad" (1973). This chapter will focus on West Indian reaction to these journalistic works on which Naipaul's notoriety in the region is primarily based.

The reasons for the hostile West Indian response to Naipaul's Caribbean non-fiction are complex. But the primary factors that have contributed largely to the hostility are Naipaul's own tendency to gamble in high-lighting the flaws and ignoring the positive aspects in West Indian societies, in registering little or no hope for the region, in taking unpopular positions, and in employing inflammatory, provocative language. With the help of a peevish and supercilious persona (discussed in Chapter II), Naipaul deals with highly sensitive issues--such as Black Power--in a way which he knows will irritate and provoke his Caribbean readers and place them on the defensive. What is even more disconcerting to West Indians is that as a person and writer, he is not troubled by their outrage; rather, he appears to court it. He himself has claimed that his intention or strategy is to effect some change in the region by producing the "most brutal sort of analysis," which he thinks will spur people into thinking and acting.[1] How successful he has been will be seen from the specific responses his books have elicited.

Naipaul's works of non-fiction appear to defy any clear-cut classification. One reviewer has argued that the shorter non-fiction is "different in kind from nearly everything else that passes for journalism: it can perhaps best be thought of as personal or familiar essay, though at all times he [Naipaul] remains a reporter on assignment intent on getting the 'story' as exactly as he can."[2] Perhaps Naipaul's brand of journalism can best be described as a hybrid of the familiar essay, the travelogue, and serious social analysis--all of this coming from a novelist's pen. Although he is writing primarily for a foreign audience, Naipaul does not follow the pattern of his predecessors by paying much attention to natural sceneries, landscapes, architectural structures, exotic customs and people. Rather, his concern is with institutions and attitudes--the psychology behind the historical transformation of these "half-made" "slave societies" into bogus, parasitic "countries," run (or run down) by protest leaders or mimic men obsessed with metropolitan values, from color preferences to jargons. In an informal and intimately conversational manner, Naipaul generally augments his theme by quoting from past thinkers and tourists, by reproducing conversations or interviews with contemporary politicians and laymen, and by citing newspaper and radio items. His precise narrative and descriptive skill misses nothing in the process, and everything, even the apparently trivial, soon assumes importance as Naipaul builds his case. It has been said that he is a "masterly reporter" with a "novelist's eye" and a "moralist's vision" and that his essays are like "marvelous conversations with a perceptive traveler . . . like good conversation they flow easily."[3] In fact, one critic has noted, "You don't read Naipaul--you listen to him."[4]

Although his journalistic impulse, inherited from his father, might have eventually surfaced anyway, Naipaul became a traveling reporter almost by chance. In 1959 he contributed to Vogue a short article, "Caribbean Medley," in which he presented the West Indies as "indeed a medley," a place that now labors to live up to that created image of travel brochures--"people lounging on crowded private beaches, or dancing and beating drums under coconut trees," in the "island in the sun."[5] But he was really lured to this new genre in 1960 when he accepted from the Trinidad government a "refresher" fellowship, a newly implemented program whereby recognized artists, who have established their reputation overseas, could return home, tour the region and "refresh" themselves with their soil.[6] Apart from a three-month visit to the island during the 1956 general elections, Naipaul had been abroad for ten years. The terms of the award carried no commitment to produce anything, but the then Premier, Dr. Eric Williams, suggested that Naipaul write a non-fictional book about the Caribbean. The novelist, aware of the difference between his job and that of a social analyst, was initially cautious:

The novelist works towards conclusions of which he
is often unaware; and it is better that he
should. To analyse and decide before writing
would rob the writer of the excitement which
supports him during his solitude, and would be the
opposite of my method as a novelist. I also felt
it as a danger that, having factually analyzed the
society as far as I was able, I would be unable
afterwards to think of it in terms of fiction and
that in anything I might write I would be
concerned only to prove a point.[7]

Naipaul, however, yielded to what he has called the "risk,"
thus commencing a new career with The Middle Passage, his
report of over six months of observation in the Caribbean.
The Middle Passage, whose title refers to the slave
trade journey from Africa to the New World, adds uniquely to
the list of travel books written about the West Indies. The
place has captured the imagination and interest of many
foreigners, such as Alexander Barclay, Sir Walter Raleigh,
James Anthony Froude, Anthony Trollope, Charles Kingsley,
Daniel Defoe, Ronald Firbanks, James Pope-Hennessy, and
Patrick Leigh Fermor. But what makes Naipaul's contribution
significant is that the report is done with remarkable
candor--however distasteful the result may be to nation-
alists--by an insider familiar with the area and its
people. Discussing the problems of writing a travel book,
D. J. Enright has noted that an author becomes "dependent on
the confrontation of his personality with the small minority
of facts which happen to come his way."[8] Fortunately,
Naipaul, who lived in the region for eighteen years prior to
this visit, faces no such problem, and thus had a clear edge
over his predecessors. Throughout his report he quotes
copiously from and agrees with various nineteenth-century
writers, the most notable and controversial being Froude,
whose observation that "There are no people there in the
true sense of the word, with a character and purpose of
their own" (p. 10), hints at Naipaul's own conclusions.
    A general introduction and a chapter on each of the
five Caribbean societies--Trinidad, British ·Guiana (now
Guyana), Surinam, Martinique, and Jamaica--form the
structure of the travelogue. In the Introduction Naipaul
recounts his amusing and unpleasant experiences with some
immigrant West Indians as he journeys from England to the
Caribbean on board the immigrant ship, Francisco Bobadilla.
He sets the tone from the opening sentence: "There was such
a crowd of immigrant-type West Indians on the boat-train
platform at Waterloo that I was glad I was traveling first
class to the West Indies. . . . 'You wouldn't want to
travel with all of them West Indians,' the man at the travel
agency had said. 'Even the dockers are sick when they come
off those ships'" (pp. 10-14). Naipaul is writing a

travelogue, but using his sharp novelist's eye, ear, and humor. He notices a man "with a Nat King Cole hairstyle . . . dandling a fat bonneted baby that was gift-wrapped in ribbons and frills, with a rubber nipple stuck like a gag and a final flourish in its drooping, dripping mouth." There are vivid character-like sketches of a "very tall and ill-made Negro" with a "ruined face" and a "much smaller Negro" with "big blank eyes as lack-lustre as boiled eggs." Perhaps most memorable is the description of Mr. Correia, who suffers an uneviable plight:

> 'You ain't have a lil Eno's or Andrews with you? Stomach giving me hell, boy. Went three times already this morning. Not one blasted thing. Is this damn manana food. First and last Spanish ship you catch me on.'
> And all that morning he padded up and down outside the lavatories, smoking, head bowed as if in meditation, tie slackened, spectacles half-way down his nose, hands in pockets. Whenever I went down he gave me a progress report.
> 'It coming, it coming. I feel it coming.'
> (p. 17)

Conversation subjects range from frivolous to serious, Naipaul in each case highlighting the sensibility and attitude of a people he is about to examine.

It is also in this introductory section that the major theme of race and color is introduced. Blacks trade vivid stories of racial discrimination in England, and East Indians emotionally condemn miscegenation and black racism in Trinidad. Discussions on race quickly remind Naipaul that in the West Indies "Black had a precise meaning" and people "had a nice eye for shades of black." West Indians easily form and accept generalizations ("only Jamaicans were beaten up in race riots, and deservedly, for they were uneducated and ungrateful and provoked the English people"). As immigrants from St Kitts board the ship, one passenger remarks, "The wild cows are coming on board," a statement which throws Naipaul into serious reflection about the attitude of the West Indian middle class:

> He spoke in earnest. And what was he, this tourist? A petty official perhaps, an elementary school teacher. The wild cows are coming on board. No attitude in the West Indies is new. Two hundred years before, when he would have been a slave, the tourist would have said the same. 'The creole slaves,' says a writer of 1805, 'looked upon the newly imported Africans with scorn, and sustained in their turn that of the mulattoes, whose complexions were browner; while

all were kept at a distance from the intercourse
of the whites.' On this ship only the Portuguese
and the Indians were alien elements. Mr Mackay
and his black fellers, the tourist and the wild
cows: these relationships had been fixed
centuries before.

(pp. 26-27)

Looking at the task ahead of him, Naipaul muses: "How can
the history of this West Indian futility be written? What
tone shall the historian adopt? . . . The history of the
islands can never be satisfactorily told. Brutality is not
the only difficulty. History is built around achievement
and creation; and nothing was created in the West Indies"
(pp. 28-9). This provocative observation, along with his
conclusions after visiting each of the five societies, leads
Naipaul to lament on the last page of the book in response
to another famous novelist turned traveler-writer: "'If we
could,' wrote Trollope, 'we would fain forget Jamaica altogether.' The West Indies, he might have said" (p. 231).

The chapter on Trinidad, the first society to be examined, is, perhaps, the most arresting in the book, since the
analysis is unusually thorough, and attention is given to
the entire West Indies in general. In addition, it is here
that Naipaul launches his most severe attacks on the region.
In an essay "London" (1958), written before The Middle
Passage, he had described Trinidad as a "simple colonial
philistine society," a description which Barbadian writer
George Lamming bitterly denounced:

> One can't say philistine and leave it at that.
> This would be to describe their present, and in
> doing so by the absolute judgment of philistine,
> condemn them permanently to a future which you
> have already chosen. I reject this attitude; and
> when it comes from a colonial who is nervous both
> in and away from his native country, I interpret
> it as simple confession of the man's inadequacy--
> inadequacy which must be rationalised since the
> man himself has come to accept it.[9]

This early exchange predicts the form and level of West
Indian reaction to Naipaul's assessment of the Caribbean.

As Naipaul now passes through the city of
Port-of-Spain, he notices the steel bands and recalls: "The
steel band used to be regarded as a high manifestation of
West Indian Culture, and it was a sound I detested" (p.
41). He reflects on an inexplicable phobia he has had about
Trinidad, a place he knew to be "unimportant, uncreative,
cynical":

> I had never wanted to stay in Trinidad. When I
> was in the fourth form I wrote a vow on the

182

endpaper of my Kennedy's <u>Revised Latin Primer</u> to leave within five years. I left after six; and for many years afterwards in England, falling asleep in bedsitters with the electric fire on, I had been awakened by the nightmare that I was back in tropical Trinidad.
I had never examined this fear of Trinidad.
(p. 41)

After a few general observations on the absence of heroes (except cricketers as hero figures), on the lack of nationalist feeling, and on the individualism of Trinidadians whose main interest is far off countries instead of their own island, Naipaul goes on to criticize and cite several humorous examples of Trinidad's obsession with modernity or with American (not British) things. Trinidadians, for instance, prefer Maxwell House, Nescafe, and other more expensive coffees to their rich, local ones, an attitude which both Trollope and Kingsley had lamented. Briefly scanning the island's history, Naipaul observes:

Trinidad was and remains a materialist immigrant society, continually growing and changing, never settling into any pattern, always retaining the atmosphere of the camp; unique in the West Indies in the absence of a history of enduring brutality . . . not an expanding society but a colonial society. . . . All this has combined to give it its special character, its ebullience and irresponsibility . . . an indifference to virtue as well as vice. (p. 54)

Naipaul then calls attention to the influence of radio, the film industry, and newspapers, which depend largely on "space-filling syndicated American and English columns, comic strips, the film gossip of Louella Parsons and beauty hints about the preservation of peaches-and-cream complexions" (p. 58). He concludes that Trinidad is a colonial society which does not value efficiency or quality; in this society "with no standards of its own, subjected for years to the second-rate in newspapers, radio and cinema, minds are rigidly closed; and Trinidadians of all races and classes are remaking themselves in the image of the Hollywood B-man. This is the full meaning of modernity in Trinidad" (p. 61).
Addressing more directly the condition of blacks, Naipaul condemns their past reluctance to examine and accept their history. He finds absurd the country's embarrassment at promoting "blackface" advertisements. He charges that "The Negro in the New World was, until recently, unwilling to look at his past. . . . Twenty million Africans made the middle passage, and scarcely an African name remains in the New World. Until the other day African tribesmen on the

screen excited derisive West Indian laughter. . . . Black
will be made white" (pp. 65-7). Quoting Trollope on the
emaciation of black language and culture during slavery,
Naipaul believes that the greatest damage was that blacks
accepted self-contempt. He argues that West Indian writers,
concerned with flattering the prejudices of their race or
color groups, have failed and that only in the calypso do
Trinidadians touch reality. With no native culture or
nationalism, the West Indian individualistic attitude
creates a picaroon society, which relishes trickery and
accepts violence and brutality. In Trinidad, where the race
problem refers to the Indian/black rivalry, there is a
deep-rooted division of labor: "whites in business, Indians
in business and the professions, Negroes in the professions
and the civil service." Naipaul then quotes the following
prediction from one of Sparrow's prophetic calypsos:

> Well, the way how things shaping up,
> All this nigger business going to stop.
> And soon in the West Indies
> It will be 'Please, Mr Nigger, please.'
> (p. 78)

Naipaul likewise castigates Trinidadian East Indians
and their "deplorable" leadership. East Indians, he claims,
have degenerated into

> A peasant-minded, money-minded community, spirit-
> ually static because cut off from its roots, its
> religion reduced to rites without philosophy, set
> in a materialist colonial society: a combination
> of historical accidents and national temperament
> has turned the Trinidad Indian into the complete
> colonial, even more philistine than the white. (p.
> 82)

Although Indians comprise more than one-third of Trinidad's
population, no effort is made by blacks to understand Indian
culture or even pronounce Indian names, "partly because of
the attitude that nothing which is not white is worth
bothering about." Agreeing with Froude's words that Indians
and blacks are "more absolutely apart than the white and
black," Naipaul carelessly gambles on a highly offensive and
provocative simile to describe the attitudes of the two
major races: "Like monkeys pleading for evolution, each
claiming to be whiter than the other, Indians and Negroes
appeal to the unacknowledged white audience to see how much
they despise one another" (p. 80). With such strong
antipathies between the two groups, he predicts racial war
on the island.
The theme of racial division between Indians and blacks
is also central in the next chapter on Guyana, although the
section is more narrative and descriptive than reflective.

Naipaul vividly describes his trip to Guyana's vast interior and the Brazilian border and relates his encounter with the native Ameridinians, whom, he had great difficulty understanding. He gives his overall impression of Guyana:

> Slavery, the land, the latifundia, Bookers [merchants and planters], indenture, the colonial system, malaria: all these have helped to make a society that is at once revolutionary and intensely reactionary, and have made the Guianese what he is: slow, sullen, independent though deceptively yielding, proud of his particular corner of Guiana, and sensitive to any criticism he does not utter himself. (p. 119)

But most of the chapter focuses on Naipaul's experience with the government leaders: Dr. Cheddi Jagan, the East Indian head of the People's Progressive Party, and his wife, Janet Jagan, a white American and Minister of Labor, Health and Housing. Hardly anyone--anywhere--passes Naipaul's scrutinizing eyes, but the Jagans do. In fact, Naipaul does not conceal his admiration and respect for the pair, who, in addition to contending with foreign enemies, have lost the friendship of their black friend, Mr. Burnham, now their serious political foe:

> I had read and heard so many malicious accounts of Mrs Jagan that I was prejudiced in her favour. Although she has suffered much from visiting writers, she received me kindly. . . . Race had . . . now become a major issue in British Guiana. She spoke of this with genuine regret . . . there was regret for the camaraderie and the friendships of 1953. She remembered what certain people, now enemies, ate, how they talked, what her children had said to them. . . .
> The side door of the office opened, and Cheddi Jagan himself came in. . . . He had just come in to say that he was off to the bank to sign the agreement for the loan to buy over the Georgetown Electric Company.
> It was an oddly domestic scene, and I felt an intruder. (pp. 93-94)

The more Naipaul follows the Jagans on their campaign trail, the more impressed he becomes with their organization, simplicity, accessibility and honesty ("it is true that after his election victory in 1957 Dr Jagan sought a reconciliation with Mr Burnham"). To Naipaul, Burnham is an entertaining orator but with little substance, as one of his campaign speeches illustrates:

Unfortunately, Mr Burnham had little to say. He indicated a general disapproval of what was going on, without documenting his case effectively. He spoke of the need for education, and promised to establish an economic planning unit when he came to power . . . he played indirectly . . . on the racial issue. 'I warn the Indians . . . Jagan has said he wants to gain control of the commanding heights of the economy. The commanding heights. Let me translate for you: your businesses, your land, your shops.' To the Negroes in the audience the message was clear. (pp. 131-32)

It is with glee, however, that Naipaul reports Jagan's patience and deftness in reasoning:

Questioners were being invited to speak from the stage, and over and over again Dr Jagan explained to people who had applied unsuccessfully for land that applications had been carefully considered and preference given to the neediest. . . .

DR JAGAN: How much land you have?
THE QUESTIONER mumbles. Whispers in the audience of 'You see him? You see him? You see how quiet he playing now?'
DR JAGAN: You have a hundred acres? Gasps from the audience, of astonishment, genuine and simulated. . . .
DR JAGAN: And how much of this hundred acres you planting?
THE QUESTIONER mumbles.
DR JAGAN: Twelve acres. . . . But I alone, man, with a cutlass could do better than that. (Dr Jagan's tone now changes from the conversational to the oratorical.) This is the curse of this country. So many people without land. And so much good land . . . just going to waste. . . .
THE AUDIENCE hums with approval. . . .
DR JAGAN: . . . We know you work hard. But tell me. Who rice-land your cows does mash down? And where you does pump your water out? In the next man land, not so? So what about him?
The roar is one of approval for DR JAGAN'S cleverness in demolishing an argument which had at first seemed fair and unassailable. (pp. 137-38)

Such enthusiasm, alien in Naipaul, is a credit to Jagan, who appears to epitomize the best kind of replacement for colo-nialism. But the electorate is still immature, and Naipaul's expression of disappointment with the people's political attitude is reminiscent of the campaign in fictional Elvira: "Wherever ministers go they are met with trivial complaints. . . . That the government is elected does not matter; the people require it to be as paternalistic as before. . . . 'The people' have learned their power" (p. 120). Before concluding the section, Naipaul takes a gibe at white Christian missionaries, who "condition" the colonials by teaching them self-contempt. Christianity, he claims, has "confirmed the colonial in his role as imitator, the traveler who never arrives" (p. 157).

In the former Dutch colony of Surinam, the next society described, no major race problem exists. Naipaul observes that the Dutch show a greater tolerance than do the British to alien culture; thus, different peoples--East Indians, Javanese, Dutch, and Creoles--reside together, while the "bush-Negroes," who live in the forest, have recreated and preserved their African culture. However, black nationalists view the existence of other cultures as a threat to nationalism and hope to make "negerengels" or "Negro English" the national language. Analyzing the problem, Naipaul doubts that the movement can avoid black racism:

> One Nationalist even suggested that the existence of Javanese and Indian culture in Surinam was a barrier to the development of a national culture! . . . The cultural problem in Surinam is mainly a problem for the Negro; it is only he who has rejected his past. . . . And it is hard to see how racial feeling can be avoided. . . . Their [nationalists'] view of Christianity is historical: they see it as much a part of European culture as the Dutch language.
> But how can Christianity . . . be replaced? . . . Religions cannot be replaced by decree any more than languages can. Negro English is no substitute for a developed language. The bush-Negroes are interesting and in some respects admirable, but between these forest-dwellers and the sophisticated Continental Surinamer there can be no deep sympathy. It would appear then either that the solution to this problem has to be violent and extreme, or that there is no solution at all. . . . And perhaps . . . all that is required is a profound awareness that countries and cultures exist beyond the white mother country. . . .
> Whether the Nationalists can create this awareness in Surinam without slipping into a futile black racism is problematical. . . . (pp. 170-79)

It is in this chapter that Naipaul describes his encounter with the only Indian who has settled among the Coronie blacks, reputed as the idlest people in Surinam. The Indian appears to be a "derelict man in a derelict land; a man

discovering himself, with surprise and resignation, lost in
a landscape which had never ceased to be unreal . . . an
enforced and always temporary residence" (p. 190). This
image has become popular since it is often cited as a
recurring motif in Naipaul's works.[10]

Journeying to Martinique, Naipaul reflects on his
depression during Trinidadian Carnival and on the
"unavoidable degradation" of tourism in whose name the West
Indian islands are "selling themselves into a new slavery"
(p. 191). The short chapter on this former French colony
focuses on two societal traits. First, the helplessness of
the country is encouraged by a total dependence on the
mother country, France. Second, "shade distinctions" are
more important here than in Trinidad:

> One of the futile skills unconsciously acquired by
> anyone who has grown up in the West Indies is the
> ability to distinguish persons of Negro ancestry.
> I thought I possessed this skill to a reasonable
> degree until I went to Martinique. Time and time
> again I was told that a white-skinned, light-eyed,
> straight-haired person I had just met really was
> 'coloured'. (p. 196)

Naipaul also learns about the existence and the culture of
Martinique Indians, whose forefathers, like other Caribbean
East Indians, were indentured from India. Tired of the
"French colonial monkey-game," Naipaul leaves the island,
briefly stopping over the Antigua, where his taxi driver
whines: "'I am not a native of this place, you know. I
know these Antiguans well, man. Is only when you live here
as long as me you know the sort of animal it is.'" (p. 211).

In Jamaica, the subject of the final chapter, unemployment, overpopulation, and frustration generate "self-
destructive rage." The disorganized Ras Tafarians (Rastas),
living in slums, believe that the "white man and his brown
ally have held the black man in slavery" (p. 215). Relying
on information from a pamphlet published under the auspices
of the University of the West Indies, Naipaul describes the
Rastas, who have developed their "psychology of survival":

> They reply to rejection with rejection. They will
> not cut their hair or wash. . . . Many will not
> work . . . and many console themselves with
> marijuana, which God himself smokes. They will
> vote for no party, because Jamaica is not their
> country and the Jamaican Government not one they
> recognize. Their country is Ethiopia, and they
> worship Ras Tafari, the Emperor Haile Selassie.
> They no longer wish to be part of that world which
> has no place for them--Babylon, the world of the
> white and brown and even yellow man . . . they
> want only to be repatriated to Africa and Ethiopia

> . . . the black race is his [God's] chosen race,
> the true Israelites: the Jews have been punished
> by Hitler for their imposture . . . . Photographs
> of the Emperor went up in thousands of Negro homes
> throughout the West Indies. (pp. 216-17)

Naipaul observes that the Rastas articulate the racial attitudes of the majority of Jamaican blacks, who are envious of
and hostile to the Chinese and Syrian businesses. Quoting
an anonymous letter printed in the Jamaican Gleaner, he
shows that the black intelligentsia, in its racial
attitudes, has moved closer to Ras Tafarianism, even
ignoring Marcus Garvey's powerful metaphor of the harmony of
white and black piano keys. Naipaul completes the chapter
by describing his stay at Frenchman's Cove, a luxurious
holiday resort. (With minor variations, this section, under
the title of "Living Like a Millionaire," had been published
in 1961 in Vogue.[11]) His general impression of Jamaica is
far from flattering:

> Race--in the sense of black against brown, yellow
> and white, in that order--is the most important
> issue in Jamaica today. . . . Everyday I saw the
> same things--unemployment, ugliness, over-
> population, race. . . . The young intellectuals .
> . . were looking for an enemy, and there was none.
> . . . They were the accumulated pressures of the
> slave society, the colonial society, the
> under-developed, overpopulated agricultural
> country. (pp. 219-24)

So it is in the entire Caribbean, Naipaul claims: "I had
seen how deep in nearly every West Indian, high and low,
were the prejudices of race; how often these prejudices were
rooted in self-contempt" (p. 230).
    British and American reviews of The Middle Passage are
mixed but with the scale tilting heavily in Naipaul's
favor. The most damaging criticism has come from the
Library Journal: "While the reviewer recommends this often
dull book to the humanist and historian interested in the
spirit of the times, he feels that many readers will prefer
something more factual and descriptive."[12] Some commentators, even those who have praised Naipaul's literary
skill, have voiced suspicions about his exaggeration of
facts, about his partiality to Cheddi Jagan, and about his
objectivity to Trinidad.[13] These judgments, however, are
by no means representative of Western response. Praised as
a "gifted" and an "impressive" writer, Naipaul has been
rated by one critic as "one of the most sensitive and
musical handlers of the English language to-day."[14] Many
readers have argued that it is the narrative detail or the
novelist's touch that distinguishes The Middle Passage from
the dozens of other travel books on the West Indies.[15] In

addition, Naipaul's position as an "insider looking on familiar scenes as if he were on the outside," or, as the Times Literary Supplement reviewer noted, the writer's "multiple personalities" has been seen as a remarkable asset.[16] Testimonies of Naipaul's acute perception have come from those who know the territories. Noni Jabavu, a black Southern African, who reviewed The Middle Passage for the New York Times Book Review, has claimed that the book suggests why she felt a "peculiar malaise" during her stay in the West Indies.[17] Another traveler, Norman T. di Giovanni, attested to the same: "My admiration for Naipaul's achievements . . . comes from something other than his vivid accounts of pure travel. Having recently returned from the Caribbean after nearly three years in Puerto Rico, I was stopped on page after page of this book by the incisive summaries of social problems and situations. It was the shock of recognition. . . ." Observing that Naipaul "knows Caribbean history thoroughly and is a clear and sympathetic observer of men," di Giovanni has rated The Middle Passage higher than George Lamming's The Pleasures of Exile and Edgar Mittelholzer's With a Carib Eye.[18]

In the Caribbean, however, opinions are different. West Indian critics generally do acknowledge Naipaul's literary talent in the work but vociferously complain that the work is maliciously unfair and Naipaul strangely contemptuous of his people and origin. George Panton in a Jamaican Gleaner article, for example, recognized the quality of writing and the "extraordinarily vivid" scenes of the introductory section but was clearly disappointed with the tone and content:

> Mr. Naipaul is a first-class writer and his style in this book puts him head and shoulders above nearly every other writer from this part of the world. He has a keen sense of observation and the right sense of picking out the vivid scene as well as frequent use of the telling phrase. The pity is that with these virtues is [sic] allied a biting tongue and a most unhappy outlook on life.[19]

Similarly, while both St Lucian poet and playwright Derek Walcott and Jamaican novelist John Hearne admired the brilliance of the book, they criticized its content--the former observed that Naipaul wore "Victorian spectacles" on the tour, and the latter classified the book as a "lively Upper Second essay," "deeply disappointing."[20] It is a work which nationalists, nervous about a good overseas image, would like to forget or ignore, but cannot. For Naipaul commands an international audience which pays keen attention to what he writes, regardless of subjectivity.

Seeking to discredit The Middle Passage, a number of West Indian critics have doubted Naipaul's objectivity and his qualification as a professional examiner of societies. Gordon Rohlehr used Naipaul's statement about his early fear of Trinidad to show that it is difficult to distinguish between the writer's "sensitive examination of history and his honest expression of hysteria"; likewise, Arthur Drayton suggested that Naipaul's fear is "too morbid and pathological to permit accurate analysis."[21] In the same vein Wayne Brown, clearly outraged by Naipaul's pessimism, dismissed the book as "sadly disguised as objective analysis."[22] Finally, Robert A. Chee Mooke argued that Naipaul is not a social analyst but a novelist who should not have taken the "risk" of examining societies nonfictionally, especially since he has confessed his uneasiness and apprehensions:

> Naipaul sees and experiences many things but does not know their significance. This latter fact is alright [sic] but he claims to try to explain them, and he does not even come close. . . . It takes little deciphering to understand what is at stake: from a good writer of prose fiction an unwarranted inference is made that as a result of this alone, he is a good writer of non-fictional prose, specifically social analysis. At best this is a grand non-sequitur.
> It is clear that the two roles are not identical. The world the literary creator projects is the invention or the creation of an object which is his own in the sense that he is not guided by social scientific theoretical considerations. . . . [Naipaul] is primarily an artist--a good one--no one can deny that, but . . . his social utterances have to be taken with a grain of salt. Naipaul's "Middle Passage" [sic] his passage to the world of social analysis, is a passage to nowhere.[23]

It should be pointed out, however, that Naipaul does not assume the posture of a social analyst, a point that European-born Bill Carr has made: "It's pretty plain that he doesn't offer himself out as professional inspector of societies, and I have no doubt at all that he is at times oblivious of the evidence which the professional is bound to require."[24] Naipaul specifically cautioned that his book, merely his own "impressions" (a word used in the subtitle), is by no means "official."

West Indians have also questioned Naipaul's detachment and seemingly prejudicial selection of quotations from past writers. One critic, for example, has written:

> [Naipaul] selects those aspects of the past that make his case about the destitution of the society. He quotes Trollope and Froude, but not

J. J. Thomas who refuted Froude. . . . Anybody
who was going to approach West Indian history
attempting to show the continuities between the
19th and 20th centuries, has absolutely no excuse
for choosing only Trollope and Froude.[25]

Australian critic Landeg White argued that by adopting the
tone of nineteenth-century travelers and by detaching
himself, Naipaul "falls into the very trap Lamming dug for
him."[26] White's reference here is to the fact that in
1960 Lamming had charged Naipaul with "being ashamed of his
cultural background and striving like mad to prove himself
through promotion to the peaks of a 'superior' culture."[27]
Referring to Naipaul as a "West Indian scholarship winner
bitterly ashamed of his origins," John Hearne saw in The
Middle Passage an effort by the writer to "detach himself
clinically from . . . a society of which . . . he is a
part."[28] However, it may be precisely because of this
detachment and his own sense of rootlessness that Naipaul is
able to be critical, given the advantage of being an insider
who has become an outsider.

A few West Indians have conceded that The Middle
Passage records truth, however unpalatable, but they
apparently believe, nonetheless, that it is the writer's
obligation to point out positive aspects of the society.
Recommending the book to everyone, including members of the
Tourist Board, George Panton observed that the West Indian
usually "delights in running down his native land" and that
Naipaul has appeared as a "champion denigrator": "He finds
almost nothing to commend in the Caribbean. . . . Nothing
he says is untrue, although the emphasis may be misplaced. .
. . There are innumerable passages worth quoting--even if
they drive you to anger."[29] Politician and writer C. L.
R. James cited the following examples of Naipaul's specific
omissions:

What Vidia said about the West Indies in Middle
Passage [sic] was very true and very important.
But what he left out was twice as true and four
times as important.

In his portrayal of the West Indian people
Vidia wrote not a line about Captain Cipriani and
the great movement he founded and led. He said
not a word about strikes of 1937-38 which have
made us what we are. It was the strikes,
political strikes, that bought the Moyne
Commission.

In his book Vidia said not a word about the
public enthusiasm which surrounded the formation
of the PNM, about the reserves of political energy
and aspirations which were unfolded by all West
Indians in the struggle over Chaguaramas. . . .

> I read Middle Passage and was sorry for what
> I did not see.[30]

Notwithstanding, it was not Naipaul's intention to write about the political history of Trinidad. In fact, despite his family's close involvement with Trinidad's politics, Naipaul has remained somewhat quiet about specific details of local affairs. His family, incidentally, was opposed to both Cipriani (who allegedly tried to prevent Trinidad's East Indians from voting) and the ruling PNM (which was in direct conflict with the opposition headed by Naipaul's uncle, Dr. Capildeo).[31] Yet Naipaul's omission of any positive element in West Indian history understandably raises the question of the fairness of his report and damages his credibility.

Other West Indian readers have been even less generous than was C. L. R. James in their evaluation. For example, John Hearne claimed that the book is made up of a "tissue of half-portraits, facile, publisher's party observations and weekend review epigrams." About the specific chapters Hearne charged:

> His [Naipaul's] virtuoso piece on Trinidad--a society of which I know something, but not enough--taught me nothing I had not learned for myself in a fortnight.
> His discussion of the British Guiana coast carefully skirts every problem that bedevils that sad, meaningful strip; while his section on Jamaica is plain fraud--no reader, I mean, should be asked to pay money for a paraphrase of the University's report on Ras Tafari and a confession about a masochistic holiday spent at one of the more improbably luxurious North Coast resorts.[32]

Hearne's evaluation of the chapter on Trinidad is questionable, especially when compared with Derek Walcott's statement that the "best part of the book" is this section which draws Naipaul "nearer to us."[33] Implicit in Hearne's comments on Trinidad is the admission that Naipaul is accurate in his report, a fact which many West Indians are embarrassed and reluctant to admit. Hearne does not comment on the chapters on Surinam and Martinique. And although he suggested that the section on Guyana is weak, he does not supply the specific omissions. Indeed, the main problem of race politics, which Naipaul discusses in this section, is responsible today for the collapse of every Guyanese institution in that racially divided country. Finally, in the section on Jamaica, the University report on Rastafarianism provides vital information on this popular cult of the 1960's, and the description of the Frenchman Cove is presented as a deliberate contrast to the depressing reality of the Jamaican background. The loaded language of Hearne's

emotional response, especially on Jamaica, demonstrates that
the issue is not whether Naipaul is accurate or inaccurate
in his statements but whether West Indian shortcomings
should be exposed. For, in spite of all his complaints,
Hearne has admitted that Naipaul's "unsentimental journey .
. . contains whole pages of acutest observation, the most
entertaining description, the nicest impalement of West
Indian attitudes."[34]
    Hearne is not the only Caribbean critic to express his
dissatisfaction with the chapter on Jamaica. Wayne Brown
has claimed that the book "collapses into mutterings by the
time Jamaica is reached."[35] And George Panton, also
disappointed about Naipaul's treatment of Jamaica, reduced
his evaluation to a mere counting of pages devoted to that
island:

> [Naipaul] reserves his most scathing comment for
> Jamaica, the comment being that of dismissing us
> with contempt, devoting only 18 pages to this
> island, eight of them dealing exclusively with the
> life of a tourist (Mr. Naipaul himself) at
> Frenchman's Cove, two being a reprint from a
> letter to the Gleaner and the remaining eight
> largely a summary of the University's report on
> the Ras Tafari movement.[36]

It is possible that much of this discontent stems from
Naipaul's severe criticisms of the Ras Tafaris, who were
generally seen as underprivileged and were romanticized by
West Indians.
    Naipaul's own comments about the reception of The
Middle Passage have confirmed the suggestion that Caribbean
readers find his pronouncements on Ras Tafarianism
particularly offensive. In a 1979 interview, Naipaul,
referring to the book as one he continues to "like a great
deal," gave the following reason for his fellow West
Indians' attack against him:

> In the 1960's people were shouting for certain
> political movements in those places I visited, so
> when I stepped in to say that this is stupid, that
> this is just routine, nothing more than public
> affairs, those who were shouting did not approve.
> By now of course I think they've given up. The
> particular holy man [Selassie] they were pushing
> at the time in those places has been abandoned. .
> . . You read it now and I think you see that it's
> fair--it's fair. Or is it not fair? But
> obviously it offended people who had their own
> prejudices, who thought that shouting racist
> slogans in 1960 was wonderful. . . . You must
> read the book and tell me that the chapter on
> Jamaica is not marvelously prescient,

194

> pre-visionary of what has happened lately. If you
> can tell me that, <u>then</u> attack me. Don't tell me
> otherwise that I shouldn't have said what I say
> about the illiterate black man shouting for racial
> redemption and found to get nowhere.[37]

The Rastafarian Movement, along with public interest in the
cult, has somewhat declined since the 1960's.

Naipaul's impressions of the West Indies can be
compared to those of Bill Carr, who has brought to his
analysis distance and insight. He is an outsider who,
having lived in the region since the 1950's, has become an
insider--the reversal of Naipaul's status. Carr stated that
he has never felt superior to the societies under
examination, and he modestly confessed that his experience
has been confined mainly to Jamaica. However, he declared
that Naipaul's conclusions on the West Indies have confirmed
his own observations. Although Carr conceded that the
chapter on Jamaica is weak (no writer can satisfactorily
cover a region which is well-known to his readers), he
defended Naipaul's use of the ironic and satiric mode:

> The West Indian doesn't naturally welcome an
> intelligence which finds its fullest expression in
> irony, and irony is among Mr. Naipaul's most
> generous gifts. . . . A society which never
> required efficiency and, therefore, never got it,
> he says. Well, the only business in Kingston that
> I have found to be efficient are [sic] the liquor
> business--which surely tells one something. In
> Kingston itself one has a haunting sense of the
> ramshackle and the temporary. . . . Mr. Naipaul's
> view is that time is not on the side of the West
> Indies--and he may be right. . . . The attitude
> isn't one of expatriate insolence. . . . Mr.
> Naipaul's impulse is not one of 'It serves you all
> right, and thank God I am not involved in it.'
> Nor is his tone one of ignorant patronage. . . .
> He feels that the West Indies is worth so much
> more than it has had and is likely to get.
> The satire isn't spiteful, and his feeling that
> satire is the necessary probing tool seems to me
> just.[38]

Naipaul himself has asserted in <u>The Middle Passage</u> that West
Indians have the "insecure wish to be heroically portrayed.
Irony and satire which might help more are not acceptable;
and no writer wishes to let down his group" (p. 69). Like
Carr, Jamaican-born Edward Lucie-Smith also testified to
Naipaul's honesty:

> The real reason why I found the book uncomfortable
> (though very often admirable) is that Mr. Naipaul

> tackles from the inside the problem which most
> writers of West Indian travel books have been glad
> to ignore or glide over--the intricate, strangling
> relationship between three things: class, race,
> and colonialism. . . . I am a white Jamaican.
> The mere fact that this has to be said proves, I
> think, many of Naipaul's points.[39]

It becomes increasingly clear why Naipaul's refusal to
flatter the Caribbean and to suppress his vision of the
truth is met with bitter rejection.

The extent to which West Indians are sensitive to
Naipaul's criticisms, justified as these criticisms are, can
be seen from the petty items to which John Hearne objected
and from the personal sort of attack which inevitably
accompanies such objections:

> Mr. Naipaul is too intelligent not to recognize
> how many of these limitations he shares with
> fellow West Indians.
> He is, for instance, never so parochial, and
> never so typical, as in his use of the parenthe-
> tical "(sic)". From time to time in the course of
> his narrative, he interpolates quotation from the
> newspapers of the area. Almost every quotation is
> punctuated by a "(sic)" as Mr. Naipaul's
> infallible eye picks up some syntactical or
> grammatical error.
> That, in most cases, these errors are plainly
> the work of poorly educated type setters, or the
> result of badly understaffed sub-editorial desks
> is never indicated. He relishes them with all the
> morbid self-contempt of which only a West Indian
> snob is capable.[40]

Derek Walcott raised a similar objection in noting that the
society columns of the newspapers are "cunningly
ridiculed."[41] But Naipaul's goal was not to ridicule the
newspapers; rather, it was to use them to illustrate
specific points. At any rate, the editorial "sic" appeared
less frequently than Hearne has suggested. Calling
attention to Naipaul's portrayal of the "worst aspects of
our 'Americanisation,' the belligerence of our humour, Negro
churlishness, East Indian apathy, canned coffee, tourists,
stray dogs and noise, including folk art and steelbands,"
Walcott also caustically charged that Naipaul "must prefer
things as they are, since they are rich resources for the
satirist."[42]

There are, however, more serious objections to the tone
and content of The Middle Passage. Derek Walcott, in
another essay "Is Naipaul an Angry Young Man?", speculated
on the reasons why West Indians have taken offense at the
writer's tone:

> He seems cynical, pessimistic, without trust in
> those characteristics in which we take pride: the
> peaceful integration of races, our material
> development, our supposedly irresistible gaiety.
> Where we boast that "all o' we" is one,
> Naipaul finds uncertain and suspicious division,
> our industrial programmes, our tourist boom
> depress him, and that supreme, strenuous effort at
> mass happiness, Carnival, seems to him a shout of
> hollow desperation.[43]

Undoubtedly, readers are uncomfortable with the kind of
image that Naipaul projects of the West Indies. Good race
relations, successful industrial programs, nationwide joy at
Carnival--these enviable characteristics, publicized, would
do a lot for the image of Trinidad. Naipaul, the artist and
journalist, is expected to serve as a goodwill ambassador.

Walcott's boasts that "all o' we is one," the motto of
the ruling People's National Movement, remains wishful
thinking. Trevor Sudama, one of the few West Indian critics
to come to Naipaul's defense and one who also knows the
Trinidadian society, has directly refuted Walcott's idea of
unity of races:

> Anyone who has taken more than a superficial
> interest in our heterogeneity could see more
> clearly the lines of demarcation in our society.
> In some cases the lines are consciously drawn, in
> other cases unconsciously and unwittingly but
> demarcations nevertheless. The outward cracks
> have been papered over. . . . The official
> conspiracy of silence is complete.
> The whole structure of so-called harmony is
> based on an apathy, acquiescence and fear
> characteristic of a people without courage,
> character or enlightenment.[44]

Making a similar observation about politicians' denial of
the existence of racial antagonism between blacks and East
Indians, Winston Hackett, in the Trinidadian journal _Moko_,
called for a confrontation of the problem:

> If 'antagonism' is too gaudy a word to use, let us at
> least be prepared to admit that a certain degree of
> mutual distrust, enough to thwart effective
> collaboration between the two racial groups, does
> exist. To deny this is to shut one's eyes to reality.
> . . . The old boast that 'all of we is one' is simply
> a national untruth. Even on Carnival day the
> differences show up. Unity can never be imposed.[45]

Since the East Indians lack political power, they tend,
through (in Sudama's words) "apathy, acquiescence, and

fear," to accept the drive of blacks to project an image of
an all black Caribbean and a consciousness of Africa. The
appearance of Indian-black assimilation is, therefore,
misleading. As explained in Chapter I, both races openly
refuse to admit to each other and to outsiders that there is
a collision--the black because he is satisfied with his
position of dominance, and the East Indian because he is
afraid to challenge it. Hence, Naipaul's acknowledgment
that "antipathy exists" and that "Negroes' animosity that
might have been directed against the whites has been
channelled off against the Indians" (pp. 79-80) is met with
firm denial.

Walcott's next point about readers' dissatisfaction
with The Middle Passage touched upon Naipaul's lack of pride
in Trinidad's material development. This criticism, while
understandable, suggests that a travelogue writer is obliged
to promote his country by accentuating its positive
elements. Sudama expressed his disagreement with this
demand:

> To take pride in industrial development is not the
> stuff of art nor does it reflect on one's
> patriotism. Even travel books make scant
> reference to it. . . .
> That a betterment in material conditions may
> have both favourable and adverse effects on the
> personality is undoubted. . . . If Naipaul does
> not concern himself with the building of roads and
> factories, the human condition in an increasingly
> industrial environment, if worthy of mention,
> would certainly not escape his attention.[46]

A reasonable argument may be made that The Middle Passage is
not "art" as is a novel, for example, and that Naipaul,
instead of assuming an attitude of total contempt, could
have at least mentioned some of the strengths and potential
of these undeveloped countries. But Jamaican poet and
critic John Figueroa argued that "Naipaul is basically a
satirist, and therefore he tends to deal with the
incongruous and to show up the bogus--but does one bother to
'expose' weaknesses unless one cares about them?"[47] West
Indians, however, sensitive about criticisms of their
society, generally do not see The Middle Passage as an
indication of care and concern but as an expression of
rejection and ridicule.

Walcott's other charge on the list of grievances
against Naipaul is that the writer regards tourism in the
Caribbean as demeaning to the natives. But many West
Indians share Naipaul's view that the industry is a form of
"new slavery." In his sociological study of the West Indian
societies, David Lowenthal has described this common
reaction to tourism by quoting from a Jamaican who observed
that West Indians treat the average tourist as a "rich man

to be robbed" or as a "god to be propitiated": "We beg for alms, we demand tips, we tell him how much we need him, and we try our best to show him what happy dancing souls the 'natives' are."[48] Refuting the specific charge of Naipaul's depression with the tourist boom, Sudama makes a similar point:

> A tourist influx may bring us into contact with people of a number of other countries who may leave behind with us a quantity of their money and thereby enable us to be better off. But what is the average American, Canadian or even English tourist looking for? He is looking for an environment geared to his pleasure. . . . He expects a whole society to wait on him; to adopt a posture of servility. The experience of wholly tourist-oriented societies serves as a warning. He invokes the worst features of a taste-deadening commercialism. Frankly, the prospect of a beggar tourist boom can be nothing short of depressing.[49]

This criticism supports the strong views of nationalists, who insist on relying on the nation's natural resources rather than depending on the tourist industry. Naipaul is more or less in agreement with a number of West Indians on this point.

Walcott's final complaint focused on Naipaul's attitude toward Trinidad's "supposedly irresistible gaiety" at Carnival, a popular Trinidadian celebration originally marking the beginning of Lent. By using "supposedly" Walcott, of course, has unwittingly supported Naipaul, who in The Middle Passage had registered his depression at Carnival: "I have never cared for dressing up or 'jumping up' in the street, and Carnival in Trinidad has always depressed me. This year, too, the 'military' bands were not so funny: they vividly recalled the photographs of the tragic absurdities in the Congo" (p. 191). Naipaul also admitted detesting the sound of the steel band, which is an integral part of Carnival. Robert A. Chee Mooke voiced an emotional objection: "For whom does Naipaul speak . . . it is Naipaul's prerogative to detest what he likes. But what Naipaul detests, is one of the most remarkable musical phenomena that has enchanted millions of people around the world. . . . So I say to Vidia, he may detest all he may, the Steelband marches on!"[50] It is not surprising that Naipaul's indifference to Carnival and the steel band sets him at odds with West Indians. This is a good example of how Naipaul can be deliberately provocative. Knowing that Carnival is an event cherished by a large number of West Indians, he must have anticipated such outbursts from his readers. Yet, he took a chance, for his personality is such that he will not allow his subject matter to be dictated by public opinion.

However, the charge is sometimes made that in expressing his dislike for the steel band and Carnival, Naipaul exposes himself as anti-nationalist. The flaw in this argument can be seen if the cultural context of Carnival and the steel band is understood. These forms of cultural expression are essentially elements of black West Indian culture. The steel band, like the calypso (which Naipaul admires), was invented and developed by Trinidadian blacks and is seldom used by East Indians. However, as pointed out in Chapter I, nationalists generally promote Carnival and the steel band as expressions of national culture, rather than specifically of black culture. Thus, Lloyd King angrily scolded Naipaul for being indifferent: "For Trinidadians the Carnival spirit is one of the sustaining values of the national environment. Therefore, the kind of national who is not sparked by the Carnival spirit is out-of-tune, is a non-entity."[51] And Guyanese Gordon Rohlehr, who noted that Naipaul treats the West Indies as a "rubbish heap," interpreted the writer's rejection of the "steel band and Carnival as a rejection of the single common ground where Trinidadians of all races meet on the basis of equality." Rohlehr saw Carnival as a sign of racial unity:

> It is apparently beyond Naipaul to be able to understand why there is music in spite of the rubbishheap. . . . Carnival in Trinidad, dominated by steel band, calypso and costume, is more than a time of general merry-making. One can, without naively propounding a West Indian version of the myth of the happy Negro, recognize Carnival as one of the few symbols, however tenuous, of a oneness in the Trinidadian people. Naipaul can show us how both Indians and Negroes despise each other in a monkey-like struggle to ape standards of pseudowhiteness. But he rejects as crude, noisy and unsophisticated the sole symbol of their miscibility, the one sign that the people themselves are reconstructing something to take the place of the personality which history destroyed.[52]

In West Indian Societies David Lowenthal used Rohlehr's criticism of Naipaul to show that "middle class creoles laud the national scene as cosmopolitan but demand cultural homogeneity and social integration on their own terms."[53] The point to be noted here is that Naipaul's rejection of the steel band is not necessarily a rejection of any group, idea, or symbol; rather, it is an expression of personal taste.

Familiarity with the history of Carnival reveals that
the occasion has not been a symbol of oneness of West
Indians. In an article published in the <u>Caribbean Quarterly</u>
in 1956, Barbara Powrie discussed the issue of ethnic
participation during Carnival festivities:

> In a true sense, Carnival "belongs" to the black,
> lower class. It is they who, through most of its
> history, have been the outstanding participants. .
> . . A common remark to be heard with regard to
> the attraction of Carnival is that 'everyone joins
> in, it breaks down all social barriers.' In fact,
> this is but a comforting myth. For example, it is
> a rare sight to come upon East Indian revellers,
> and except as part of the audience at the Carnival
> contests, the whites take no part in the public
> merrymaking.[54]

Admittedly, within recent years Carnival has attracted more
East Indians and other minorities, but still on a limited
scale. This growing tendency has been enthusiastically
received and encouraged by people hoping to see unity in the
Caribbean. The fact that Naipaul repudiated the Carnival
celebration does not mean that he rejects any symbol of
unity (which Carnival is <u>not</u>); in fact, he believes in
"racial coexistence" (p. 23) and regrets that the black/
Indian "rivalry threatens to destroy the Land of the
Calypso" (p. 83).
Commenting on Walcott's statement that Naipaul views
Carnival, the "supreme, strenuous effort at mass happiness,"
as a "shout of hollow desperation," Sudama claimed that the
event is futile and meaningless and that it is, instead, a
"supreme, strenuous effort of mass mimicry--the admission of
a society that it can only express itself through
mimicry."[55] Sudama raised an important issue--the
tendency of West Indians to indulge in mimicry, the root of
which goes back to the days of slavery and continues to
pervade all aspects of the social, cultural and political
life in the formless Caribbean societies. In fact, in an
article "Power?" published in the <u>New York Review of Books</u>
in 1970 and reprinted in <u>The Overcrowded Barracoon</u>, Naipaul
himself noted that the current Carnival celebration and
masquerade is a carry-over from the mimicking rites in which
slaves used to indulge. He explained: "The bands, flags
and costumes have little to do with Lent, and much to do
with slavery. . . . The people who were slaves by day saw
themselves as kings, queens, dauphins, princesses. There
were pretty uniforms, flags and painted wooden swords. . .
. At night the Negroes played at being people, mimicking
the rites of the upper world . . . the fantasies
remained."[56] Clearly, then, Naipaul's strong denunciation
of Carnival is a denunciation of West Indian mimicry, a

latent characteristic dominant in other West Indian
attitudes, for example, the Black Power Movement.
    The impression has been created, however, that Naipaul
is prejudiced against blacks and the form of their cultural
expressions. For example, in his thesis at the University
of Leeds, Antiguan A. C. Derrick examined the images of
black in The Middle Passage and concluded that they are all
negative. Referring to this thesis Selwyn R. Cudjoe, in his
interview with Kenneth Ramchand, asked whether Naipaul could
be called a racist. Cudjoe explained the reason for the
question, which Ramchand ventured to answer:

S.R.C.:   You will discover that V. S. Naipaul never
          presents an African character that is whole and
          sensitive. They are always grotesque, ill-formed
          and negative. . . . It is from this kind of
          evidence that one can deduce that a writer is or
          may be a racist.

K.R.:   . . . There is no doubt that he knows people of
          Indian origin a lot better. . . . A writer writes
          about what he knows. I don't know if we can make
          the jump from that to say that he's a racist. I
          see a racist as a man who is both negative and
          hostile against other races and very positive
          towards his own. His works may reveal fear,
          prejudice, and a lack of intimacy and maybe even
          unexamined feelings about Africans, but I wouldn't
          say that these things mean simply that he's a
          racist. We have a great problem in this society
          about how Indians and Africans see and fail to see
          one another. There's a great deal of fear and
          ignorance on both sides.[57]

This question is an important one since the charge of racial
prejudice repeatedly arises in West Indian reaction to
Naipaul's other non-fiction and fiction.
    Press exchanges in West Indian newspapers about
Naipaul's alleged prejudice against blacks show that this
issue has caused grave concern among readers. John Hearne,
for example, levels his broadside bluntly:

          "The Middle Passage" is not the record of a real
          country, but some black fairyland of the mind,
          inhabited by hobgoblins who must be made
          manageable by caricature.
          . . . The book's recurrent fear symbol is . . .
          that of a grotesque, garish and misshapen Negro.
          . . .
              To him [Naipaul], the Negro is hardly a man
          capable of some sort of reciprocal encounter, but
          rather a portent, an image from the dark caves of
          the psyche, all the more terrible because, in the
          Caribbean, he is not anchored to an older civili-

202

zation--as is the European, the East Indian and the Chinese. "Malevolent" "exotic" "alien", these terms are all Mr. Naipaul's and they are all applied to Negroes.[58]

Having made such a charge, Hearne (anticipating an attack) tried to deny that he was accusing Naipaul of racial prejudice. Yet he maintained that faced with blacks, Naipaul experiences "deep convulsions of his soul" and that "it cannot be denied that his obsession with the Negro as a portent, an image and an incomprehensible life form is the hole through which the book as [sic] shallow."[59] Similarly, Derek Walcott complained of feeling "uncomfortable when a people or a race are a source of infinite amusement of benign tolerance to a writer," and, in another article, he referred to "Naipaul's refusal to be gracious, a Brahmin mask," which gives a "nasty edge" to many of the observations in The Middle Passage.[60] The Jamaican Gleaner reviewer, George Panton, also asserted that "Naipaul is a Hindu, not a Negro, but his remarks about the Negro could equally apply to himself."[61]

It must be conceded that Naipaul is often crude in his portrayal of the people he met during his West Indian tour. Descriptions of passengers aboard the Francisco Bobadilla are typical examples (cited earlier). What must be guarded against, however, is the assumption that Naipaul applies these negative descriptions to the individuals because they are black. Since the book records his visit to predominantly black territories, most of the people described are black. But careful readers of Naipaul will attest to the fact that he is equally brutal in his description of people of other races. As the Appendix of this book shows, Indian critics complain that during his one year stay in India, Naipaul never met a good, wholesome character; instead, he kept running into "obtuse, unsympathetic Indians, bland, silly. . . . Most . . . were grotesques, contemptible or pathetic creatures. . . ."[62] In The Middle Passage Mr. Correia, a Portuguese, is a toothless, "small, bald man," who had a "booming voice" and a "sharp hooked nose" (p. 15); Mr. Rahimtoolah, a Guyanese East Indian, is a "big man with fat quivering thighs . . . and a blotched face and a turtle-like neck" (p. 89); a Martinician Indian is "course-featured," another has a "bulbous nose," and still another appears "worn away by undernourishment and underprivilege," and his head "rocked like a bird's on his stick-like neck" as he "continually scratched one muddy foot with his big toe of the other" (pp. 206-07). Negative images of blacks can also be contrasted against positive ones, such as those of the "tall handsome Negro" (p. 19) and "a Negro woman of energy, charm and sensibility" (p. 128). Picking out such images--positive and negative images of all races--in Naipaul's fiction and non-fiction will perhaps show that the writer employs negative images more often than he does

positive ones (an unfortunate quirk) but that he applies
them to black and non-black characters in a non-discrimina-
tory way, sometimes offensive to all. Mere suspicion of
bias should not be the basis on which to impute all
criticisms to prejudice. For such an attitude will encourage a tacit understanding that only blacks can criticize
blacks, only Chamars can criticize Chamars, and only Moslems
can criticize Moslems, and so forth. (Naipaul's Among the
Believers drew bitter reviews which accused the writer of
religious bias.) What can be said, then, is that there is
indeed a fastidious nature in Naipaul; however, there is no
conclusive proof that he is prejudiced against any racial or
religious group.

Hearne's interpretation of Naipaul's portrayal of
blacks has been challenged as totally misleading and
inaccurate. In an article entitled "Was John Hearne
Inspired by Professional Jealousy?" a writer, who signed
himself merely as G. R. J., conceded that The Middle Passage
is "blatantly one-sided," but he strongly rejected Hearne's
allegations:

> Hearne's review is as one-sided as the book
> itself. He seizes upon a couple of descriptive
> passages in the book in order to lay against
> Naipaul the blanket charge that he has serious
> problems with the Negro presence and personality.
> . . . But apart from indicating Hearne's own
> pre-occupation with the Negro presence and person-
> ality, it shows clearly also that this is how
> Hearne believes the average Indian in Trinidad
> regards his Negro fellow national. For Hearne
> holds fast to his argument in spite of other
> passages in "The Middle Passage" which contradict
> effectively this theory and would tend to show
> that the reviewer misunderstood deliberately (or
> accidentally to give him the benefit of the
> doubt) what Naipaul was trying to say.[63]

Claiming that The Middle Passage recorded things that ought
to be said, G. R. J. maintained that this "valuable" and
"brilliantly" written book "will be read and quoted from
West Indians who are not afraid to take a sweeping look at
themselves." G. R. J. took issue not only with Hearne but
also with Lamming: "Lamming . . . reveals the point of
view, held by many West Indians, that unless a West Indian
writer is able to wrestle with the angels and devils of his
society . . . he is totally without significance. If Hearne
and Lamming want to shield us from our absurdities. . . let
them go ahead. . . . But there is room for the Naipaul
brand of writing also."[64] To G. R. J., then, the real
issue behind The Middle Passage is not race but acceptance
of truth.

Few West Indians, however, are willing to argue that
Naipaul evokes hostile response not because he is wrong in
his assessment of the West Indies but because he is right.
Speculating on all possible reasons--admitted and
concealed--why readers find the travelogue repugnant, Bill
Carr suggested that perhaps the suspicion is that Naipaul is
correct:

> Those who are repelled by the book need to be
> strictly honest in their account to themselves of
> what they find repelling.
>   Is it really the naivete of Mr. Naipaul's
> social analysis which offends his admitted
> idiosyncracy of perception? Is it the snobbery,
> the East Indian Englishness, so frequently and
> easily alleged against him? Is it distaste for
> the ironic revulsion with which he contemplates
> certain people and scenes? Is it a smothered
> regret advertising itself as something else, at
> not having got out along with him? Is it jealousy
> at the competence and firmness of his prose, a
> prose which so sharply registers what he sees? Or
> are these all variants of the lurking feeling that
> he might be in some measure right, that his vision
> is one which experience entitles him to hold?[65]

Occasionally some of these questions arise when Naipaul's
reputation is discussed. In another essay, written two
years later, Carr reiterated his main theme:

> The irritation his book [Middle Passage] aroused
> in the area when it first appeared (and the
> hostility or suspicion the mention of his name
> invariably produces) are a curious guarantee of
> his accuracy as an analyst. . . . The present
> writer is frequently informed, for example, that
> Naipaul's sociology is "all wrong" that he
> "doesn't know the society." . . . Many West Indian
> intellectuals and artists . . . manufacture a
> known and more or less comfortable world.[66]

Jamaican critic John Figueroa also contended that Naipaul is
not "out of touch": he is "so much in touch that he
hurts."[67] However, the dominant image of Naipaul is, in
Walcott's words, that of a "kind of treacherous gossip, an
intellect that should be above giggling at the skeletons it
likes to pull out of cupboards."[68]
    The greatest test of the worth of any book, however, is
time. Confident that The Middle Passage has passed the
test, Naipaul in a 1979 interview challenged his readers to
prove that the book is untrue today: "A writer's book has
to stand even after the events have changed. . . . If The
Middle Passage is found untrue today, 18 years later, then I

will debate what seems untrue. If it remains true, if you
cannot bring yourself to say, 'You were wrong here, and
here, or here,' then there is no sense asking how I came to
arrive at these things."[69] Today, more than two decades
after the publication of the travelogue, the prophetic
nature of its observations is evident. In the same
interview, Naipaul expressed his deep concern and
disappointment at conditions in the West Indies in general
and Jamaica in particular:

> I say they've taken several large steps back to
> the bush. And it's surprised me. I never thought
> that after 300 years of the new world an African
> people could return to the bush. That is very
> sad. . . . I'm being very provocative, but I'm
> also speaking with a lot of bitterness. And much
> unhappiness. Because it is not pleasant to see
> the place where you were born destroyed. . . .
> There are no institutions, nothing to refer to any
> longer. You cannot refer to any idea of law, or
> honesty about public money or the rights of all
> men, because racialist politics in a way rejects
> all these values. And I wish that people would
> see that in fact one is really bitter because of
> the collapse of human values. I'm not fighting a
> racial war; the people who ban me over there are
> fighting a racial war. And that is a sign of the
> collapse of civilization, of the possibility of
> movement forward.[70]

Of course, implicit in Naipaul's statement is the
contentious assumption that there is no value system in the
Old World. And while his observations on the breakdown of
institutions in the Caribbean are not grossly exaggerated,
his diction, as he himself admits, is indeed provocative.
His frequent references to the word "bush" (that is, lack of
order) to describe the West Indian condition have incensed
sensitive readers and will be discussed below. However, his
statement confirms what only a few West Indians will
accept: Naipaul's censure of the region stems not from
bitter contempt growing from a rejection of his origin, as
is usually alleged, but from deep concern.

Most Caribbean readers believe that Naipaul's supposed
rejection of his origin is linked to his endorsement of a
Euro-centered concept of history. His provocative assertion
in The Middle Passage that "nothing was created in the West
Indies" and his concern about the problems involved in
writing the brutal "history of West Indian futility" (p. 29)
are usually cited as examples of his subscription to the
"brilliant myth of Europe" and of his idolization of the
Western world.[71] Arthur Drayton argued that Naipaul
"measures achievement by the grand and the spectacular,"
that he is a "casualty of the European complex," and that he

reveals this attitude early in the travelogue in his treatment of the passengers and immigrants aboard the ship,
<u>Francisco Bobadilla</u>.[72] Naipaul's statement, as Anthony
Boxill pointed out, has also inspired some West Indian poets
to reflect on the achievement of the islanders.[73] For
example, Edward Brathwaite in <u>The Arrivants</u> took the comment
as a direct challenge:

> for we who have achieved nothing
> work
> who have not built
> dream
> who have forgotten all
> dance
> and dare to remember.

So did Derek Walcott in "Another Life": "they will absolve
us, perhaps, if we begin again,/ from what we have always
known, nothing." Echoes of Naipaul's words also ring
through Walcott's "The Almond Trees":

> There's nothing here
> this early;
> cold sand
> cold churning ocean, the Atlantic,
> no visible history.

Walcott, fond of using a Robinson Crusoe figure as a
parallel to suggest the beginning of a new order, envisioned
an island on which all races will join to create something
from a place of nothing. Examining the dismay caused by
Naipaul's statement, Boxill argued that the writer did not
indict blacks and East Indians, for how can they "be held
responsible for not creating when they lacked power over
even themselves?" Instead, Boxill suggested that in <u>The
Loss of El Dorado</u> (1969), Naipaul throws the blame at the
feet of the colonialists, the Europeans, who, obsessed with
materialism rather than noble ideals, failed to create a new
society in the West Indies.[74] West Indian commentators,
however, have generally read <u>The Loss</u> as a sequel to <u>The
Middle Passage</u> and as an attempt to prove the point that the
history of Trinidad is a "chronicle of failure and lost
ideals."[75]

In <u>The Loss</u>, Naipaul apparently settled for himself the
issue of the historian's difficulty in writing about "West
Indian futility." In addition, he made a late discovery, as
he has confessed: "I thought the place had no history. I
thought I would swiftly look at the records and produce
something, and then I discovered this appalling history that
hadn't been ignored but had just somehow dropped out because
the place itself had ceased to be important."[76]
Structured from neglected personal papers, printed sources,
and archival materials, most of which Naipaul translated for

himself, <u>The Loss</u> offers an imaginative treatment of
Trinidad's history.[77] Especially striking is Naipaul's
personal analysis of figures and events throughout as he
resuscitates dry records. The text itself gives no precise
references, but the depth of the scholarship can be seen not
only in the meticulous details and exact dialogue reproduced
but also in the maps and the Postcript, which gives an
annotated list of sources consulted. The Foreword, in which
Naipaul reflects on the history of his birthplace,
Chaguanas, Trinidad, promises to record "two moments when
Trinidad was touched by history." The Prologue provides a
short but rich outline of the "two forgotten stories" on
which the book will be based. The first tale is woven
around the end of the search of El Dorado, "an essentially
Spanish delusion," fiercely pursued by a seventy-five year
old Spanish conquistador, whose base Sir Walter Ralegh
(Naipaul chose the spelling <u>Ralegh</u>) successfully raided. It
is an enchanted Indian tale that lured and infected one
adventurer after another:

> There had been a golden man, <u>el dorado</u>, the gilded
> one, in what is now Colombia: a chief who once a
> year rolled in turpentine, was covered with gold
> dust and then dived into a lake. But the tribe of
> the golden man had been conquered a generation
> before Columbus came to the New World. It was an
> Indian memory that the Spaniards pursued; and the
> memory was confused with the legend, among jungle
> Indians, of the Peru the Spaniards already
> conquered.
> Always the Indians told of a rich and
> civilized people just a few days' march away.
> Sometimes there were pieces of gold, finely
> worked; once a temple of the sun was found in the
> jungle; once a crazed explorer returned with a
> tale of an enormous city of long straight streets,
> its temples full of golden idols. (pp. 18-19)

The second story, which takes place about two hundred years
later, centers on a British-sponsored attempt to establish
Trinidad as the base of a revolution designed to open
Spanish America to British commercial interests. The
venture failed since complications arose with the
simultaneous setting up of the island as a British slave
colony and with the sensationalism created by the torture of
a young Spanish Mulatto girl, Luisa Calderon. "The history
of Port of Spain," writes Naipaul, "is contained in these
stories."
    Part One, entitled "The Third Marquisate," opens with
the identification of the Spanish conquistador as Antonio de
Berrio, who crossed the Atlantic in 1580 at the age of sixty
pursuing the mythical kingdom of El Dorado. At seventy he
undertook the last of his three journeys along the Orinoco.

Berrio repeatedly referred to this last "great" expedition
because "half-way across he performed a deed which linked
him in his own mind with the heroes of antiquity": after
traveling a year under difficult conditions he ordered all
his remaining horses killed in order to prevent further
desertions and temptations of turning back. Hollowing out
canoes from tree trunks, Berrio ended up in Trinidad and
used Port-of-Spain as a stage from which he could launch his
search for El Dorado. He argued that "all the island needed
to become 'the richest commercial centre of the Indies' were
merchants of probity and some tax-free Negroes, perhaps five
hundred pieces" (p. 36). He was excited by the romantic
story of Albujar, a survivor of a forgotten El Dorado
expedition, who once found himself in the "great Manoa city
of the golden man" and who reportedly left with some gold he
had hidden. Berrio was assisted in his quest by a Spaniard,
Domingo de Vera, but suffered a series of setbacks partly
caused by personal jealousies and by difficulties with
Indians. While Vera was en route to Spain to seek assistance on behalf of Berrio, Sir Walter Ralegh had already
heard the news. This British adventurer arrived on the
scene with ships and guns and sacked Port-of-Spain and
dispossessed Berrio. Questioned by Ralegh, Berrio, who did
not initially understand that he had been dispossessed, told
everything he knew. As his reward, Berrio, along with a few
of his followers, was marooned on an island in the Orinoco
river. Assistance from Vera was intercepted at Caracas, and
Berrio, after a cold, indifferent meeting with Vera, died
eight months later in solitude and lunacy.

Unlike Berrio, Ralegh did not think of personal glory
only. His ideas were grandiose and sophisticated:

> He [Ralegh] was planning more than the plunder of
> St Joseph and the El Dorado quest. He was
> planning an empire of Guiana in which Indian
> numbers and English skill would destroy the power
> of Spain at its source, in the Indies. The quest
> he could share with Berrio; but he went beyond
> Berrio. Berrio, if at this stage he could have
> explained his purpose, might have said that he
> wanted gold and the third marquisate; and he might
> have represented this as a service to his King. .
> . . It would have stopped there, a personal
> achievement . . . Ralegh could merge personal
> ambition into a greater cause. He had an idea of
> society and association which Berrio, for all his
> old soldier's diplomacy with disaffected natives .
> . . didn't begin to have. (pp. 42-43)

Ralegh, insecure about the small number of men and limited
supplies, postponed the request of Indians to march on El
Dorado. Instead, he returned to England but promised to
come back again. Still dreaming about mines and a crystal

mountain, Ralegh, at the age of sixty-four in 1616, was released from the Tower of London on the condition that he would find the Spanish mine without disturbing the Spaniards, the penalty for failure being death. His difficulties were almost the same as Berrio's--his men quarrelled, some died from disease, his own health declined, and his spirit sank. His friend, Laurence Keymis, who supposedly knew the location of the mine, took five ships, 400 men, and Ralegh's son. But the expedition failed ("like every Indian guide to El Dorado, Keymis knew nothing") and Ralegh's son was killed. In addition, Ralegh's credit with the king had been destroyed and his fortune wasted. Keymis committed suicide and Ralegh's life, too, ended tragically in the Tower of London.

Thus, the first of the twin tales portrays the complexity of early imperialist ventures, with minute details about explorations, fights, sufferings, treacheries, and confrontations with indigenous people. Naipaul concluded by equating the end of the expedition with the end of the New World as medieval adventure:

> It was the end of the quest. It had begun as a dream as large as the New World itself; it had ended in this search for a mine no one had seen, in an action of amateurs, in which all the great ones, and few of the lesser, perished. . . . These men, Keymis and Ralegh, saw themselves as actors in great events, classical figures, even as Vera saw Antonio Berrio and himself. And the quest was heroic. But their world was as small as the classical world, and the world was changing by their own efforts. The Indians had changed. . . .
> The ships from Europe came and went. The plantations grew. The brazil-wood, felled by slaves in the New World was rasped by criminals in the rasp-houses of Amsterdam. The New World as medieval adventure had ended. . . . (pp. 106-08)

To the explorers Trinidad was nothing more than a passageway to be used, a base for an assault on El Dorado, the mythical city of gold. Naipaul sees Ralegh's book, The Discovery of Guiana, as catching "part of the New World at that moment between the unseeing brutality of the discovery and conquest and the later brutality of colonization."

The short section of Part Two, called "The Spanish Capitulation," is a resting point between the two stories. In the two centuries since Ralegh's expedition, Trinidad, still under Spanish control, had become a liability, a "Ghost Province," for which it was even difficult to find a governor. Naipaul puts it bluntly: "Trinidad had dropped out of history. Nobody came to raid or to trade. The Spaniards lived like shipwrecked people, close to nature, concerned only with survival" (p. 117). An Indian rising, a roofless church, a cacao blight, a smallpox epidemic--any such concern, small or grave, took years to be noticed by the Spanish bureaucracy. "Exempt from history," the people, Naipaul noted, "might have gone on scratching for food." However, Spain, needing Trinidad as a strategic point, suddenly took an interest:

> It [Trinidad] could guard provinces as tempting now as El Dorado had been . . . against the movements of fleets and armies. It was to be populated and fortified; it was to be another arsenal of the Empire . . . it was to be a centre of South American trade. But to be all this Trinidad would have to cease to be Spanish. Spain didn't have the men. She would have to get foreign immigrants. (p. 126)

Thus, to strengthen the island against Britain's might in the West Indies, the last Spanish governor, Chacon, offered sanctuary to Irish and French settlers from neighboring slave islands. By 1792, three years after the French revolution and the passage of the Trinidad Negro Code (which "represented fairly the Spanish mildness"), the island had become a refuge for Haitians, Frenchmen, Martinicians, and San Domingo white and mulatto planters, who, driven by sparks of French revolution and republican control, brought their loyal slaves with them. These groups were quickly joined by fleeing French republicans, whose islands were captured by the British. Thus, a dangerous amalgam was created: "Whites, mulattoes, Negroes, royalist, and republican: within three years--after all the discussion about terms for settlers--a composite French colony had been assembled in Trinidad, and it was a colony in a state of insurrection and anarchy" (p. 135). It was this explosive situation the British inherited in 1797, when Admiral Harvey and General Abercromby took Trinidad without any resistance. The conquerors planned to use the island as an outpost from which to export a Latin American revolution and thus to open Spanish America to British commercial interests. However, like the El Dorado quest, this grandiose dream, with Trinidad as a pawn, did not materialize.

Part Three, "The Torture of Luisa Calderon," the longest and most arresting section in the book, focuses on Naipaul's second story and explains why Trinidad failed to become that "great British trading point for an independent South America." The British found themselves with a slave colony, in which the legal code for protection of slaves was based on the original Spanish system of law. The laws were usually ignored and the small number of émigré slave owners were able to control several thousand blacks by clinging to their old practice of the most brutal and savage system of punishment for everything, especially poisonings. Whippings, nose splittings, ear slashings, brandings, hangings, quarterings, burnings, head spikings were commonly accepted. A peculiarly barbarous method to extract confession or information was the use of a torture apparatus, whereby the victim was suspended by the left wrist, while the ball of the right foot rested on a half-inch point of wooden stake and carried the full weight of the body. In 1801, Thomas Picton, a professional soldier and English governor of Trinidad, signed an order for such a torture to be used on a fourteen-year-old Spanish mulatto girl, Luisa Calderon (whose jealous protector falsely accused her of helping another man rob him). This wicked deed, along with its subsequent sensationalism and Picton's trial, forms the bulk of Naipaul's second story.

Picton's ignominious reign as military governor vividly dramatized the cruelty and brutality which had always reigned on the island. Naipaul observed that Picton, the "victim of people's conscience," would be tried not just for ordering the torture of Luisa Calderon but simply for being governor of Trinidad at the end of the eighteenth century. Along with the main line of the Picton story, Naipaul simulataneously weaves several other adventures, a nest of subplots, with small villains and heroes. The most significant of these narratives is the one involving Francisco Miranda, who, in his glamorous role of a South American exile and traveler ("sometimes disguised by a wig and green spectacles"), continually planned and lobbied in vain for a joint British and American invasion of a South America. But the main focus remains on Picton, who, after four and a half years in office, had transformed himself into a defender of slavery, a colonial, a planter, no longer interested in revolutionaries and the Spaniards. A savage and brutal slaver owner, allegedly "bred among goats," Picton believed in severe punishment and allied himself with the French aristocrats for whom he even rewrote the Negro Code and legally instituted a reign of terror against slaves. His mulatto mistress, Rosette Smith, with whom he was deeply infatuated, treated her slaves with a severity matching Picton's and showed the same streaks of ruthlessness and greed. In fresh and telling details Naipaul exposes the administration of cruel "justice" under this governor, aided by his chief magistrate St Hilaire Begorrat, by a French jailer, Vallot (who often complained of unpaid fees earned from punishing slaves), and by six alguazils or policemen. There were occasional murmurs of complaints stemming from the news of Picton's excesses, which Naipaul sums up as follows:

> This was the gossip of English outrage: an exclusion [of incoming Englishmen] from Government House, a widow [resented by Rosette Smith] insulted by black soldiers, a soldier [Picton's rival for the favors of a prostitute] unfairly

hanged. The Negroes in Vallot's jail, the dirt-eating Negroes dying from mal d' estomac: that appeared to exist elsewhere. (p. 194)

Even amid such cruelties, however, there is to be found a place for humor and fantasy. Naipaul offers a brilliant description of the underground life, the make-believe world, which evolved in the slave colony. The planters were lords and kings by day, but it was the slaves' turn at nights when many blacks secretly mimicked their rulers by presiding over kingdoms, by assuming their owner's roles (clothes, titles), by fting and by singing. The chorus of a favorite song was, interestingly enough, "Bread is white man flesh; wine is white man blood. We going to drink white man blood." In his later writings, Naipaul will return to the subject of mimicry and the fantasy of black domination, but for the moment the main interest is on cruelty. Picton had gone too far when he signed the warrant for the torture of Luisa Calderon. Eight months later Calderon was released, her wrists marked for life, and complaints to England were eventually answered by the assignment in 1803 of the First Commissioner, Colonel William Fullarton, to investigate the governor's brutality.

Almost immediately Fullarton developed a personal vendetta against Picton, and the two men constantly tried to out-maneuver each other. With his experiences as a member of Parliament for Ayrshire and as a colonel in the East India Company, Fullarton worked vigorously and collected evidence of Picton's atrocities from witnesses and victims and from visits to the Port-of-Spain jail, whose condition was horrifying. Naipaul contends that logic should have taken Fullarton to the side of the abolitionists, but the First Commissioner became "entangled" as did Picton, and never articulated his cause well, since his obsessive hatred for the governor made him forget the real reason for his investigation. Fullarton's supporters were the English opposition and a Scottish pamphleteer, P. E. McCallum. Commodore Samuel Hood, the Third Commissioner, who sided with Picton, interrogated McCallum:

'Pray, sir,' Hood pressed, 'where was you born?'
'I really cannot exactly say, though I was present at the time. It was somewhere in the island of Great Britain.'
'Where was you baptized?'
'I must have been present at the time the ceremony was performed, yet I do not recollect it.' . . .
'What school was you educated at?'
'Have you perceived that my education has been neglected?' (pp. 255-56)

It is in this atmosphere of spirited exchanges and tension
that Picton, having served six and a half years as governor,
was summoned to London to answer for his cruelties.
      The sensationalism created eventually dissipated.
Picton's arrest, the appearances in London of witnesses,
especially Luisa Calderon ("suddenly an exotic . . . of 'an
interesting countenance' and 'genteel appearance'; 'slender
and graceful,' with a muslin turban") created a stir, at
least for a while. Only two charges could have held: the
torture of Calderon and Begorrat's "poisoning commission"
with its rituals of live burnings. Describing the fine
legal points colorfully and reproducing the dramatic court
room dialogue, Naipaul captures the flavor or the trial,
which ironically shifted focus from the cruelty of the
torture to Calderon's torturable age. Spanish law forbade
the torture of anyone below fourteen. (Naipaul had read
about this trial in the Newgate Calendar and then labori-
ously unearthed the background details.) By the time the
lengthy legal process was completed--for five years Calderon
extended her scarred wrists and told her story--the public
had lost interest. Fullarton, alone, had died in a London
hotel, and Picton, by now a major-general, was finally
acquitted and met a hero's death at Waterloo under
Wellington, who described him as a "rough foul-mouth devil
as ever lived." Back in Trinidad, in that "simple" society
in which only money and race mattered, George Smith,
commissioned to set the complicated Trinidadian laws right,
carried on the usual squabbles and power struggles with
Governor Hislop.
      Trinidad, then, lured but never satisfied its dreamers.
With the Spanish empire declining and with Britain shifting
its own interest to the East, the island was not to be the
base for a South American revolution, and Miranda, the "man
of action who had always had bad luck and had always bungled
action," ended up in prison, a setting, Naipaul thinks, he,
"like Ralegh, subconsciously required." From Berrio to
Ralegh, from Picton to Fullarton, and from Smith to
Hislop, the lesson is that there is a difference between
dream and reality, between imperial goals and colonial
achievement. In the Epilogue Naipaul suggests that there is
a pattern of brutality in the history of Trinidad, an island
destined to be unimportant, "no more than an outpost, a
backwater . . . it was an error and a failure." He contends
that Trinidad would never again witness another time of
intellectual liveliness such as that of Fullarton, Hislop
and Smith, men who knew that something was amiss in the
colony. Visiting writers, such as Trollope, Kingsley, and
Froude were concerned only with the maintenance of a productive estate. To Naipaul the importation of indentured labor
for this purpose of productivity was a "new dereliction, in
the pattern of what had gone before." Reflecting on the
lessons of history he had received as a schoolboy in the

1930's and 1940's, he finds that the inheritors of the
island have searched for myths too:

> Port of Spain was a place where things had
> happened and nothing showed. Only people
> remained, and their past had dropped out of all
> the history books. Picton was the name of a
> street; no one knew more. History was a fairytale
> about Columbus and a fairytale about the strange
> customs of the aboriginal Caribs and Arawaks. . .
> . History was also a fairytale not so much about
> slavery as about its abolition, the good defeating
> the bad. It was the only way the tale could be
> told. Any other version would have ended in
> ambiguity and alarm. The slave was never real.
> (p. 375)

The writer of The Loss, however, has obviously chosen the
route of "ambiguity and alarm."

While British and American reviewers have debated the
classification of The Loss, the consensus is that the work
is a brilliant achievement by one of the finest writers of
English prose. According to J. H. Elliott, the book,
"neither exactly a novel nor exactly history," defies
classification.[78] One reviewer noted that the manner of
presentation may irritate the professional historian, and
another cautioned that the work is not be regarded as a
serious authority, but they both recognized Naipaul's
scholarship and gave high commendations.[79] The Loss may
not meet the rigorous standards of the professional
historian, but its superiority to anything in the historical
category has been fully honored by J. H. Plumb:

> This is a remarkable book. It is history by a
> sensitive and highly intelligent novelist and as
> remote from professional history as one can
> imagine. Yet it often presents truths about
> society that are both more profound and more
> moving. . . . What a story and a what a writer!
> Not only are the personalities vivid, but also
> they are realized in all their complexity--their
> dreams made as moving as their brutalities are
> horrifying. . . . Narrative, description, sudden
> stabs of analysis are handled with enviable
> dexterity. From the point of view of professional
> history, this book could be faulted here and
> there, largely through what it omits, not so much
> for what it contains. At times the documentary
> evidence almost submerges the novelist and
> occasionally there is a sense of anachronism.
> Nevertheless, professional historians should read
> it, ponder on its skills and techniques and ask
> themselves as candidly as they can whether or not

the truth about men and societies in time is not
more forcibly, more convincingly conveyed than in
the limited and rigid techniques which now
dominate the writing of history.[80]

Generally, seen as a hybrid between a novel and history, The
Loss has been praised as "personalised history that makes
intentional use of the novelist's technique to colour and
elaborate," or "an imaginative history . . . by a novelist
who puts professionals to shame," or "history as literature,
meticulously researched and masterfully written, as in the
manner of Thucydides," or even "history as a fine art rather
than history as an academic discipline."[81] Of course,
complaints have been registered about Naipaul's bewildering
cast of characters, who are "yanked on and off the stage
with scarcely the courtesy of an introduction," about the
weightiness of details, and about the dullness of dryness of
the narrative, making "dense and demanding reading."[82]
However, these concerns are all overshadowed by a recognition of the book as "valuable simply as annals, as an
enhancement of the record," a most brilliant [study] of the
grassroots of imperialism."[83] And Naipaul's tone, which
has been described as "low-keyed, matter-of-fact, passion-
less even," has been defended by several readers.[84]
Derwent May, for example, contended that Naipaul guards his
voice against echoing any "sound of outrage," for his purpose is not to "excite his readers' anger, all these years
later"; similarly, Karl Miller suggested that Naipaul's
apparent "dandyish asperity" or "dispassionateness" is
merely a way of saying that all history is a history of
cruelty.[85] To these reviewers Naipaul is not merciless.
In fact, admiring Naipaul's human sympathy and gift of
compassion, Elliott noted that the "sense of what it was to
be a slave, the human suffering that slavery imposed, has
nowhere been more sharply evoked than in The Loss of El
Dorado."[86] West Indian readers will strongly challenge
this reading.
   The Times Literary Supplement reviewer predicted
(correctly as it has turned out) that West Indian nationalists will not be able to draw much consolation from The
Loss.[87] Indeed, attempts have been made to discredit the
book as a serious history and to minimize the one salient
feature praised by many Western reviewers: the novelist's
brilliant insight into characters and situations. J. A.
Carnegie, for example, questioned the accuracy of the
subtitle, A History: "One must challenge one of the basic
premises of Loss of El Dorado right away, the one that it is
'History.' . . . Naipaul is not concerned . . . anywhere . .
. with the social history of any of the West Indian peoples,
but he somehow gives us the tragedy of men like Ralegh . . .
and Berrio."[88] Jesse Noel, in an equally caustic tone,
consigned the work to the category of fiction:

> No one will seriously recommend it [The Loss] as a
> prescribed text in any history course at univer-
> sity level. . . . The sweeping generalization,
> the highly subjective innuendo, the deliberate
> characterization, do not readily lend themselves
> to scientific social studies. . . . Naipaul's
> presentation is always neatly, even delicately
> contrived in accordance with his novelistic
> craft. Thus characterization appears to have the
> charming ring of fiction and little attempt is
> made to look fully at the circumstances in which
> characters like Walter Ralegh or Antonio de Berrio
> operated.[89]

Regardless of the question about the genre, the book
generally falls short of West Indian wishes.

Complaints from Caribbean readers range from dryness of
detail to structural problems in the book. In an article in
the Trinidad Guardian, James H. Paterson stated that the
subject is not gripping or moving, a problem compounded by
the scholarly manner in which the material is handled. He
contended that there is no detail or dialogue which could
not be gathered and recorded from available contemporary
sources and that the undeveloped portraits fall too easily
into categories of Maddy (Berrio), Baddy (Picton), and Goody
(Fullarton and Calderon). Paterson suggested that Naipaul
should have devoted more time to exploring the El Dorado
legend itself.[90] Both Clyde Hosein (who recommended the
book) and J. A. Carnegie also argued that the work offers
nothing new, the former regretting the two-hundred-year gap
in the history presented in the book, and the latter criticizing the aimlessness of the early section.[91] It
appears, however, that The Loss has disappointed reviewers
primarily because it fails to glamorize the history of the
island.

In fact, Naipaul has been seen as maliciously capitalizing on the historical events and ignoring significant data
in order to show a cyclical pattern of failure and to prove
his long-held view recorded in The Middle Passage that in
the West Indies "there were only plantation, decline and
neglect."[92] C. Alan Wade, who interpreted Naipaul as
implying that "any possible Negro development in this world
is destroyed by the cruelty of the colonial experience,"
characterized the purpose of the book as follows:

> [The Loss] is an attempt . . . to trace the
> brutality, sterility and materialism which, in his
> [Naipaul's] view, have solely characterized West
> Indian history. . . . Naipaul attempts, it seems,
> to provide a line of continuity between the
> derelict society which his novels portray and the
> savage world of history which shaped this
> community. . . . The emphasis [is] as usual on

brutality and treachery, loss, failure and
nothingness seen by Naipaul as the sole
ingredients of our heritage.[93]

Wade also complained of the lack of treatment of blacks and
Amerindians, the two largest groups in the West Indies at
that time, but he attributed the omission, or what he called
the "one-sideness," to the reliance on the records of the
colonizers.[94] Again, as with the novels, one implied
criterion for judging this historical work is complete
identification with contemporary West Indies.

West Indian readers have also charged Naipaul with
lacking sympathy and optimism. In his review Carnegie
speculated that the Loss fails because it is devoid of
understanding and because, like An Area of Darkness and The
Middle Passage, the book offers nothing to replace what is
being criticized.[95] This raises the question as to
whether the obligation of the historian is to produce an
alternative or simply to chronicle accurately past events.
Naipaul has been unfavorably compared with Wilson Harris,
who, according to Wade, does not accept brutality as the end
of West Indian history but, rather, insists on the more
positive aspects and "a way of finding new possibilities for
the future."[96] Carnegie offered an interesting, though
not uncommon, theory of Naipaul's pessimism:

> Naipaul has obviously had tortuous personal
> problems of intellect and identity, but it is not
> a glib comment to state that part of the problem
> of Caribbean society is perfectly reflected by the
> fact that such a man is the most famous,
> critically accepted, and financially successful
> artistic figure that these islands have
> produced.[97]

Carnegie also contended that Naipaul is "casually Euro-
centered" and that The Loss "does not read very much like
the work of a West Indian," thus suggesting that a West
Indian writing the history of his region is expected to
adopt a tone different from that of an outsider.[98] Such
charges have also have been leveled against Naipaul's
magazine articles and casual statements about the condition
and future of West Indies.

During the period between the publication of The Middle
Passage (1962) and The Loss of El Dorado (1969), Naipaul
interspersed fiction (Mr Stone and the Knights Companion,
The Mimic Men, and A Flag on the Island) with non-fiction
(Area of Darkness and several short essays on his predi-
cament as a West Indian artist, on famous personalities, and
on places, especially India). Included among the essays are
three articles on the Caribbean: "Trinidad" (1964) in
Mademoiselle, "East Indian" (1965) in the The Reporter, and
"West Indian Culture?" (1965) in The Illustrated Weekly of

218

<u>India</u>. These articles are important mainly because they
show that Naipaul has kept his journalistic interest in the
Caribbean alive, even when he was engaged in other projects.
Written for the foreigner, "Trinidad" presents a short
sketch of that unexotic, immigrant, ebullient society--its
English tradition, its cosmopolitanism, its emphasis on
tourist-oriented pleasures ("calypso, carnival and the
steelbands have been cultivated into 'culture'"), and its
delicious local foods, including East Indian cuisine.[99]
Reprinted in <u>The Overcrowded Barracoon</u> (1972), which
contains a selection of twenty-one of Naipaul's articles
published between 1958 and 1972, "East Indian" is also
informative reading for the outsider unaware of the existence of the East Indians in Trinidad, a place usually
associated with calypso, Carnival, and sun. Explaining the
various appellations intially applied to the immigrants,
Naipaul discusses the complete recreation in Trinidad of a
miniature India, which steadily shrank after World War II.
The newly emerging attitude is exemplified in his meeting
with another Trinidadian Indian in a Delhi club:

> 'Tell me. I think we are way ahead of this
> bunch, don't you think?'
> 'But there's no question,' I said.
> He brightened; he looked relieved. He
> smiled; he laughed.
> 'I'm <u>so</u> glad you think so. It's what I
> <u>always</u> tell them. Come, have a drink.'
> We drank. We became loud, colonials
> together.[100]

In "A West Indian Culture?" Naipaul covers a more
political subject. Apart from his controversial assertion
that the move to attach Trinidad to Grenada was based on
racial politics designed to give blacks a majority in a
Unitary State, he adds nothing new to what he had already
addressed in <u>The Middle Passage</u>. What he emphasizes in this
essay, however, is that "slavery, exploitation, followed by
neglect" may not be as important as Trinidad's smallness,
which has forced the island into the "voluntary"
"subjection" of tourism. Rejecting the politician's
favorite parallel between Trinidad and Greece, Naipaul
stresses the island's dependence:

> To be born in a Greek city was to be at the centre
> of everything. To be born in Trinidad was to be
> aware from the first of one's unimportance.
> Everything we used, every film we saw, every book
> we read came from remote cities that were truly
> famous. . . . To know ourselves, to get a
> necessary self-esteem, we did not need writers.
> We required tourists. . . . Self-discovery went
> hand in hand with that other discovery . . . of

> the West Indies as that crazy resort place. We
> became exotic even to ourselves. . . . "Massa day
> done" sums up the mood. Yet the larger dependence
> always remains. Is there a West Indian culture?
> Yes; and the tourist sees the truth.[101]

This problem--smallness and dependence--which Naipaul sees
as the twin curse of the islands is one to which he
frequently refers.

Returning to the issue of the Caribbean political
attitudes, Naipaul published during the 1969 and 1970 a few
more magazine articles, most of them in the New York Review
of Books. Reprinted in The Overcrowded Barracoon, these
essays examine the problems of the Caribbean trouble spots,
former colonies--for example, Anguilla, St Kitts and the
other islands in general. Anguilla, seventeen miles long
and two miles wide, with a population of six thousand,
seceded, with little difficulty, from St Kitts and became
the world's smallest republic, with its five-man police
force. "For more than 200 years . . . no one had really
wanted Anguilla or had known what to do with it. The place
was a mistake" (p. 256). Thus, it was a confused London
which the "shipwrecked and isolated" island lobbied for
support. Naipaul, bored with one Anguillan's harangue on
the pride and dignity of small countries, delivers a grim
analysis, which typifies his view on all small former
colonies:

> Independence, as a smooth administration: that
> worked. Independence as the preserver of an old
> community: that made sense. Independence as
> 'development' and quick tourist money: that . . .
> defeats itself. Anguilla was going to disappoint
> more of its supporters. Independence had only
> just come; and Anguilla already required
> pacification. . . . The Anguilla problem
> remains: the problem of a tiny colony set adrift,
> part of the jetsam of an empire, a near-primitive
> people suddenly returned to a free state, their
> renewed or continuing exploitation. (pp. 264-65)

In St Kitts, an island of 153 square miles and a population
of 57,000 (made even smaller by the secession of Anguilla),
the eccentric legendary folk leader and Premier, Robert
Bradshaw, or "Papa," suppresses his dangerous opposition in
order to remain in power. In his usual contentious manner,
Naipaul writes: "The opposition union is called WAM, the
opposition party PAM. WAM and PAM: it is part of the
deadly comic strip humour of Negro politics" (p. 239). Its
mulatto founder, William Herbert, succeeded as leader of
"literate protest" and became a celebrated Caribbean figure
when, after the Anguillan secession, he was jailed, tried
and acquitted. Bradshaw, isolated, "appeared to be on the

way out," but his newly recruited Public Relations Officer
saved him by accidentally discovering the usefulness of
Black Power politics:

> He [Bradshaw] is no longer the established leader
> on the defensive, attracting fresh agitation. He
> has become once again the leader of protest. It
> is in protest that he now competes with Herbert. .
> . . The cause is Black Power. . . . Both parties
> are parties of protest, in the vacuum of
> independence; . . . for both parties the cause of
> protest is that past, of slavery. . . . The
> difficult message of Black Power--identity,
> economic involvement, solidarity, as the PRO
> defines it--has become mangled in transmission.
> It can now be heard that Bradshaw, for all the
> English aspirations of his past, is a full-blooded
> Ashanti. Herbert is visibly mulatto. (pp. 248-49)

The PRO's car has a sticker "cut from a petrol
advertisement: Join the Power Set." Naipaul sees this type
of politics, which he also encounters in Belize and
Mauritius, as most dangerous in the Caribbean.
    The application of the Black Power Movement in the
Caribbean islands is the subject of Naipaul's most
controversial essay "Power?" (1970). While the other West
Indian articles have generally passed unchallenged, "Power?"
has drawn more bitter reviews from local critics than has
anything else written by Naipaul. Tracing the root of the
Black Power Movement to Carnival and to the slaves' fantasy
or the make-believe world so eloquently described in The
Loss, Naipaul interprets Carnival as the "original dream of
black power." He notes: "After the [1970] Carnival there
were Black Power disturbances. After the masquerade and the
music, anger and terror. . . . Carnival and Black Power are
not as opposed as they appear" (pp. 267-68). What he
strongly objects to is the importation of the jargon of the
overseas Black Power Movement to a society in which it has
no relevance, since blacks already enjoy full political
participation and total domination of other races:

> These islanders are disturbed. They already have
> black government and black power . . . they await
> crusades and messiahs. Now they have Black
> Power. It isn't the Black Power of the United
> States. That is the protest of a disadvantaged
> minority. . . .
>   In the islands the intellectual equivocations
> of Black Power are part of its strength. After
> the sharp analysis of black degradation, the
> spokesmen for Black Power usually become mystical,
> vague, and threatening. . . .

> Black Power as rage, drama and style, as revolutionary jargon, offers something to everybody. . . . It also means clearing the Chinese and the Jews and the tourists out of Jamaica. It is identity and it is also miscegenation. (pp. 269-70)

(Naipaul's reference to miscegenation in this context appears to echo Fantz Fanon's famous chapter "The Man of Color and the White Woman" in Black Skin, White Masks, a popular book in the Caribbean; however, the entire spirit of the Black Power Movement rejects the necessity of conquering the white woman as a symbol of conquering "white civilization." In fact, Trinidadian Black Power activist Michael Abdul Malik was charged under the Race Relations Act because of his public statement that a white man should be killed immediately if he is seen with a black woman.)[102]

One of Naipaul's main contentions in "Power?" is that West Indians are confused about the identification of the enemy in their society. He again assails the Jamaican Rastafarians (who believe that Haile Selassie is God) for demonstrating for Black Power against a black government; "Papa" Bradshaw for using Black Power to defeat his opposition; and radicals in "half black" Belize for undermining the multiracial government and opposition. In his interviews, too, Naipaul has repeatedly expressed concern about the creation of "absurd" myths (citing, for example, Eric Williams' hope of political redemption or the Black Power Movement's offer of salvation), and he has suggested that, instead of mimicking the Black Power "bogus sort of television revolution," those interested in the condition of blacks should champion the cause of black West Indians in London.[103] Believing that Black Power in the islands is merely protest without an enemy, and that racial minorities, "elites" and "white niggers" (mulattoes) are "phantom enemies," he diagnoses what he perceives as the real problem: "The enemy is the past, of slavery and colonial neglect and a society uneducated from top to bottom; the enemy is the smallness of the islands and the absence of resources" (p. 271).

The first problem, slavery, established, according to Naipaul, an "inferior" society. In an interview with Israel Shenker, he has asserted that the society has a double inferiority in that it is a "slave society, which created nothing, which depended for everything on the master society--and the Asiatic. . . . The people I saw were little people who were mimicking upper-class respectability. They had been slaves."[104] The second point Naipaul makes is that the society is at a further disadvantage because of the lack of an adequate educational system which could provide skills for the development of the people. During colonialism, the white administrators sent their children "home" (England) to be educated, and,

222

therefore, neglected the educational needs of the local
population. Naipaul's argument in "Power?" is that West
Indians are condemned to "an inferiority of skill and
achievement" (p. 274). Asked in an interview whether
individuals who happen to have intelligence, skill and wit
would also be condemned to a state of hopelessness, Naipaul
contended:

> I will say that I don't think they have much
> chance . . . not only is the democratic process in
> a fairly uneducated society against them, I also
> think that a lot of borrowed jargon is against
> them, and they can be wiped out for 'noble' causes
> at any time. This terrible word, 'elite'--which
> is something which Europe has shipped out to
> uncivilised, backward countries with damaging
> effect. It's a word that can completely get rid
> of your people. . . .
> Very soon, anyone who wants to live with a nice
> garden and not on a hillside with dirt all around
> him will also belong to an elite. And we'll all
> be told that we should all be living in dirt
> yards, in bits of land that we just seized and
> massacred and vandalised. . . . It's odd that
> these people should be ruined by these words which
> are really borrowed from abroad. . . . The
> borrowed jargon. The very pretty, Harlem words
> that are used for the things which everyone knows
> to be utterly vile. Like stealing and begging
> called, hustling. It's all very dramatic and
> romantic but they're just good, old fashioned
> words for it. They're just damn beggars! They
> should be sent to the YODI [Reform School] and
> taught not to beg.
> These very, very pretty words. And this absurd
> word of the 'ghetto'. . . . These people should
> realise . . . that they're living in their own
> country. . . . They're not colonials any
> longer.[105]

According to Naipaul, West Indian societies are in "so many
ways close to gangsterism that someone who is a gangster has
a kind of natural camouflage," and with this current
"attitude of plunder," "these half-dead little territories"
cannot be rebuilt.[106] In his view, the colonial mentality
can be eliminated not by "slogans" or rage but by "real
achievement and real work and real men."[107]
The final problem, the size of the islands and the
absence of resources, Naipaul sees as a major disadvantage
to the development of skills or self-sufficiency. He
delivers a blistering prognosis for the islands:

> The small islands of the Caribbean will remain
> islands, impoverished and unskilled . . . their
> people not needed anywhere. . . . The island
> blacks will continue to be dependent on the books,
> films and goods of others; in this important way
> they will continue to be half-made societies of a
> dependent people, the Third World's third world.
> They will forever consume; they will never create.
> . . . Again and again the protest leader will
> appear and the millennium will seem about to come.
> . . . The islands will always be subject to an
> external police. The United States helicopters
> will be there, to take away United States
> citizens, tourists. . . . These islands, black
> and poor, are dangerous only to themselves. (pp.
> 271-75)

As an escape from this insularity and dependency, Naipaul
recommends a Latin American identity for some of the smaller
countries, including Guyana and Trinidad, countries which,
though independent, are "manufactured societies," created by
colonialism, and totally and habitually dependent on large
powers.

British and American reviewers have had lukewarm praise
for the quality of writing in The Overcrowded Barracoon, and
beyond offering a scanty description, have had little to say
about the content of the West Indian articles.[108] To the
reviewer for the New York Times, Naipaul "displays an
affection for colonialism that might even be called
sentimentality."[109] However, for whatever reason, critics
have generally avoided committing themselves to any position
on such controversial articles as "Power?" and the other
Caribbean pieces. According to one critic, "the section on
life in the West Indies provides much information on a part
of the world about which we know little and care less. . . .
Although the author writes about contemporary persons and
events, the reader . . . may well feel the same remoteness
from the present world that he feels when rereading Addison
and Steele."[110] This is certainly not the case in the
West Indies, for Naipaul's observations in "Power?", which
soon became the subject of lively press exchanges in
Trinidad, have incensed many black West Indians, who
interpret the statements as an indication of ignorance of
the goals of the movement, as an exploitation of sensational
material, or simply as contempt for blacks.

In an article "Challenging CLR and the Naipauls,"
written from London but printed in the Trinidad Guardian,
John Patterson castigated Trinidadian politician and
historian C. L. R. James, Naipaul, and his brother, Shiva,
for the distortion of history and for the lack of
understanding of the island's Black Power Movement and
demonstrations.[111] Ironically, while Patterson himself
wrote from London, he criticized the authors for writing "so

authoritatively" about a society which they have abandoned. Quoting copiously from Naipaul's "Power?" Patterson catalogued the statements which he found intolerably offensive. Significantly, on the specific issue of Black Power he did not explain the goal of the movement or the cause of the demonstrations in Trinidad, an omission which Trevor Sudama pointed out in a subsequent rebuttal article, "Defending CLR and the Naipauls."[112] Patterson, instead, merely accused Naipaul of showing "complete ignorance of present political developments when he limited Black Power in the Caribbean to the Negro and his fantasy."[113] This statement implies that the East Indians and other minorities in the Caribbean have been a part of the Black Power drive. It is true that many well-intentioned politicians, embarrassed and confused about the Black Power Movement in countries already ruled by black governments, have tried to explain that "black" encompasses all "non-whites" (a usage prevalent, for example, in England). In America this reasoning could work and could attract other disadvantaged "non-whites." However, as noted in Chapter I, in the Caribbean, where the major races, East Indians and blacks, distinctly separate themselves, the movement has had a disastrous effect on race relations. This division became evident especially after Trinidadian-born Stokely Carmichael, one of the spokesmen for the movement, took the firm position that the protest is primarily a black cause.

However, Caribbean Black Power Movement proponents have often overlooked or minimized the damaging race relations and have insisted that objections to the movement stem from ignorance. Accusing Naipaul of not understanding the international nature of Black Power, Trinidadian novelist Earl Lovelace, writing for the _Trinidad Express_, outlined the objectives of the movement:

> Black Power is not limited to protest. It cannot be. Black Power in these islands means what it says: Power to black people to change the brutality to which we are subject and to which we subject each other, to remove the waste of human and material resources from our society, to encourage and upkeep human values by which we can live.
> In it's [sic] largest sense, Black Power is a revolutionary philosophy whose objective is to create human beings and a human society for black people and all others who would uphold human dignity and freedom.
> Naipaul misses the point completely when he suggests that we already have Black Power.[114]

Naipaul would probably argue that this general objective proves his point that spokesmen for the movement in the West Indies become "mystical" and "vague" and that the problems

and concerns of the movement are a matter for local
politics. Certainly, Lovelace does not explain why the
controversial racist content inherent in the term "<u>black</u>
power" is necessary if the issue is merely one of
revolutionary philosophy.

Supporters of the Black Power Movement also accuse
Naipaul of pandering to whites to collect royalties on his
books. Rejecting "Power?" Rudolph Lord in <u>Moko</u> asserted
that Naipaul either "displays his ignorance" about the "new
West Indian Consciousness" or "prostitutes his talents."
Lord vehemently argued for the latter, claiming that Naipaul
caters to the taste of the "enemies" of black power:
"Naipaul's aim is to ridicule the movement for the benefit
of his white patrons. We must remember that the people who
buy the majority of Naipaul's books are white." Lord,
obviously disturbed by Naipaul's denunciation of the
islanders, accentuated the race theme and rejected what he
saw as an echo of the "bigoted prejudiced view of those in
the metropolitan countries." To Naipaul's comment that
Black Power will not effect any change; that the region will
remain impoverished, dependent, and unskilled; and that its
people will not be needed anywhere, Lord retorted:

> Here Naipaul exposes himself. He says anywhere,
> but what he really means, is anywhere in the white
> western world. What Naipaul failed to take into
> consideration is the fact that like him too many
> of us only look to the North Atlantic when we
> think about emigration. But if only the skilled
> and professional men who have gone to Europe and
> the U.S. had gone to Tanzania, Zambia, and Guinea
> they would have been accorded the dignity and
> identity. . . . How long have we been left to
> ourselves to show what we can do. It is only now
> that we are beginning to see our potential. Has
> Naipaul forgotten the steelband? How it came into
> being? . . . Unfortunately things like music
> fails [sic] to impress those whose only criterion
> of success is material acquisition.[115]

Similarly, angered by Naipaul's comments on the island's
size, lack of resources, and creativity, Earl Lovelace
questioned the writer's point of view: "Naipaul has been
getting away with a lot of negative nonsense. . . . What
frame of reference does he use when he comes to judge this
Caribbean society? What store of values does he have in
mind when he makes his bombastic criticisms? The higher the
values of the Western world?"[116] Trinidadian poet Eric
Roach's comment that Naipaul writes "glib facile half truths
intended seemingly to please the ear of the tourist and the
outlander"[117] is representative of West Indian sentiment.

West Indian commentators have frequently referred to
Naipaul's seeming bias in favor of whites, and have used

this charge to full advantage in their criticisms of his
works. Undeniably, Naipaul has by intent or inadvertence,
made himself vulnerable in this regard. Before concluding
"Power?" Naipaul, in examining the attitudes of young West
Indians, quotes responses from the Rubin and Zavalloni
report on surveys of high school students, who were asked to
write about their "expectations, plans, and hopes for the
future." He interprets the surveys, conducted in 1957 and
1961, that is, at the time of, what he calls, "messianic
optimism": "Without the calm of white responses, the
society might appear remote, fantastic and backward" (pp.
272-3). Patterson challenged Naipaul: "The Black and East
Indian students' answers are idealistic and ambitious; the
Whites' answers mundane and unimaginative." Patterson then
eventually yielded to the temptation of a racial attack:
"Ironically, one of the East Indian students . . . wanted to
become a great writer--like Shakespeare, though,"[118] thus
subtly implying that it is Shakespeare's race, not talent,
which is desirable. Commenting on the same section on the
results of the survey, Rudolph Lord made a similar charge,
and, surprisingly, chided Naipaul for separating East
Indians and blacks:

> Speaking about Trinidad, he describes our citizens
> as Black, East Indian, and White. Here we are
> hearing the same Naipaul who is obsessed with his
> Aryan forebears in his novel 'mimic men' [sic].
> And here at last is Naipaul fully exposed. . . .
> He . . . harps back to the fact that the East
> Indian is Different [sic]. He has Aryan
> forebears. Not quite white but almost. Seen in
> this light Naipaul needs more sympathy than the
> people whose aspirations he so cruelly
> castigates. Again, "there is a black and East
> Indian fantasy." He is always careful to separate
> the black people into two distinct groups
> throughout his analyses.[119]

Somewhat related to this issue is Guyanese poet and critic
A. J. Seymour's conclusion that Naipaul has "opted for
Anglisation," a tendency which is a "normal development of
Anglo-Indian sensibilities."[120]
To many black West Indian critics, Naipaul carries an
East Indian bias and, therefore, does not understand blacks.
For example, calling attention to Naipaul's inclusion of
miscegenation as one of the many issues that the Black Power
Movement covers, Lord acrimoniously retorted: "But Black
Power, in its essence, rejects miscegenation, even more
forcefully than the whites do. What exactly does he think
we are talking about when we say Black is beautiful?"[121]
Eric Roach, having quoted certain sections of "Power?"
offensive to him, lashed out with a racial slur against
Naipaul: "The writer does not know; does not understand.

He has been prodigal too long. He is not of the blacks on
whom he has always looked down his fine Brahmin nose."[122]
Similarly, John Patterson also accused Naipaul of racial
prejudice and succumbed to finger pointing: "Throughout his
article . . . Naipaul makes ruthless references to the
Negro slave past, but no mention of the East Indians'
indentured past." As evidence of Naipaul's ethnic bias,
Patterson quoted the following description in "Power?" of
the Ras Tafarians' reaction to their idol, the Ethiopian
Emperor, Haile Selassie: "Recently the Emperor visited
Jamaica. The Ras Tafarian were expecting a black-lion of a
man; they saw someone like a Hindu, mild-featured, brown and
small. The disappointment was great; but somehow the sect
survives" (p. 269). From this statement Patterson concluded
that Naipaul "exults" in Selassie's appearance and that his
"ethnic identification--and prejudice--is revealed in one
moment of weakness."[123] However, Trevor Sudama,
disagreeing with Patterson's inferences, claimed that
"Naipaul would not be human if he did not bear some traces
of his early up-bringing which was Hindu, but this merely
gives him a larger perspective than a strictly Western
up-bringing would have given and, in view of many subsequent
residences and travels, it would be malicious to say that
his affinity has hardened into prejudice."[124] What
appears clear is that Naipaul is obviously disturbed about
the attitudes of West Indians, a disturbance mistaken for
racial prejudice.

Aspersions against him notwithstanding--that is, his
alleged ignorance of the protest movement, his exploitative
misuse of his talent for profit, and his racial prejudice--
Naipaul found himself in dire straits when he condemned the
region of a state of hopelessness and described the pursuit
of black identity as a "dead end" and a "sentimental trap."
Labeling the search for black identity as "red herring in
the urgent quest for economic well-being," and as a
"readymade vehicle on which the politicians can jump and
deny their own impotence," Sudama claimed that he preferred
Naipaul's cynicism to any "spurious sentimental nationalism
which is the bane of the apologist."[125] Yet readers
appear to look for encouragement and solutions, and even
Sudama admitted that, unlike Naipaul, he has seen a ray of
hope. Lovelace warned against the trap of the "Naipaulian
attitude of despair" or the "trap to use our gifts to
inspire hopelessness," and Lord defiantly protested: "No,
No, No, Mr. Naipaul. No. If you feel that we are
hopelessly lost and can reconcile yourself to living within
the belly of the monster, at least spare us your pity. You
need it more than we do. All power to the people."[126]
Reaction to "Power?" is often buried in the language of
propaganda releases on the vision of Trinidad's future. In
his article, significantly called "Naipaul's Death Wish is
not Our Bag," Eric Roach argued:

> We are inching our way out of the Caribbean dark
> ages to join the mainstreams of Western
> Civilisation, and our slow painful movement
> forward, beset with mistakes, confusions,
> tragedies and comedies, is the Caribbean drama,
> our history.
>   This forward movement is most difficult for
> the Africans. . . .
>   How strange that a man of Naipaul's acute
> perception cannot understand or recognize this
> forward drive and human growth in the
> Caribbean.[127]

To West Indians who remain in the region and make it their
home, frustration, cynicism and despair will never—perhaps
can never—be accepted.
    West Indian critics have reacted to Naipaul's prophecy
concerning the "Third World's third world" by associating
his pessimism with his personality, that is, his own sense
of frustration with, or superiorty to, the society which he
so fiercely attacks. Raoul Pantin, who recommended The
Overcrowded Barracoon, made such a connection:

> There is in this almost savage put down, a
> contradiction that Naipaul, a Trinidadian of
> humble origins who has become one of the leading
> literary figures of our time, represents. Perhaps
> the failure here is that Naipaul can speak only of
> his own time, of his own frustration and despair
> about Trinidad and the Caribbean when he had to
> get out in order to achieve.[128]

However, Pantin ignored the fact that today, more than in
the past, many people obviously feel, as the high emigration
figures show, that leaving the region is the only way to
better themselves, whether creatively or materially. The
crux of the matter, as Pantin himself contradictorily wrote,
may be that "in this current phase of our evolution, in the
new groping about for an identity, or a way out, we have not
often been able to be generous enough to admit that Naipaul
is what he is acclaimed to be outside of the region: a
magnificent writer and an intensely honest person."[129]
Other Caribbean writers, believing that the problem is
Naipaul and not the West Indies, have taken a more
controversial approach, insisting on a personal indictment.
For example, Earl Lovelace rationalized Naipaul's plight in
this way:

> Naipaul's stance with regard to the Caribbean has
> less to do with the facts of the Caribbean reality
> and the Black Power movement here than it has to
> do with Naipaul's own predicament.
>   Naipaul's judgment on Black Power and the

> Caribbean is the discouraging song of a
> discontented and alienated individual desperately
> attempting to justify his alienation. . . .
> That Naipaul has given us not one single
> positive option is the clearest indication of the
> extreme degree of his own hopeless
> discouragement.[130]

Eric Roach, who also equated Naipaul's pessimism with
personality problems, offered two reasons for the writer's
"peculiar disability": first, Naipaul is a prodigy in the
Western world; second, he inwardly resents his origin and
laments his uprooting from India.[131]
Naipaul's concern over West Indian imitation of the
overseas Black Power Movement led to his interest in the
sensational story of the notorious Michael Abdul Malik, a
Trinidad black power activist who was tried and hanged for
the gruesome murders of Trinidadian Joseph Skerritt and
Englishwoman Gale Benson. In an interview conducted in 1973
while researching the case in Trinidad, Naipaul attributed
Malik's popularity to white liberals' manipulation of an
uneducated man and to Malik's skill at mimicking a
society.[132] In his report, published in the London Sunday
Times Magazine and later with two other travel pieces and an
essay on Conrad in The Return of Eva Peron (1980), Naipaul's
sentiments on the West Indian Black Power Movement, a
"revolution without a program," have remained the same as in
his controversial "Power?":

> Black Power in the United States was the protest
> of an ill-equipped minority. In Trinidad, with
> its 55 percent black population, with the Asian
> and other minorities already excluded from
> government, Black Power became something else,
> added something very old to rational protest: a
> mystical sense of race, a millenarian expectation
> of imminent redemption. . . .
> Malik's career proves how much of Black
> Power--away from its United States source--is
> jargon, how much a sentimental hoax. In a place
> like Trinidad, racial redemption is as irrelevant
> for the Negro as for everybody else. (pp. 41 and
> 74)

Naipaul's study of Malik's case thus supports his earlier
statements about the irrelevance of the movement in the
Caribbean.
The essay begins dramatically and ominously with the
purchase of a "corner file," used in the West Indies for
sharpening a cutlass, an item popular as an agricultural
tool for cutting cane--and as a brutal weapon for "chopping"
people. Making frequent chronological shifts, Naipaul
pieces together from newspaper clippings, personal papers,

interviews, and court records the fashioning of the career
of an illiterate half-black, half-Portuguese Trinidadianborn
seaman, Michael de Freitas. Assuming the Moslem name
Michael Abdul Malik or Michael X after a spiritual
conversion from a life as a Notting Hill drug dealer and
pimp, he became a Carnival figure, an entertainer,
"performing" as a black man for a foreign audience. With
his hustler's knack for fraud, he mimicked the jargon of the
Black Power Movement, borrowing "every attitude, every
statement," and "his very absence of originality, his
plasticity, his ability to give people the kind of Negro
they wanted, made him acceptable to journalists" (p. 25).
Indeed, it was the establishment press and particularly the
white middle-class liberals who "made" Malik. It was they
who offered the image, the finance, the endorsement
necessary to convert him into an overnight "writer" and
"leader," with plans for a messianic redemption and for the
implementation of Black Power ideology in an island already
ruled by a black government. He knew what was expected and
he accommodated himself and his patrons with an appropriate
system of values, a system which Naipaul has always blamed
for the lack of achievement in the West Indies:

> In Malik's system, the Negro who had not dropped
> out, who was educated, had a skill or a
> profession, was not quite a Negro. . . . The real
> Negro . . . lived in a place called "the ghetto,"
> which was awful but had its enviable gaieties; and
> in the ghetto the Negro lived close to crime. He
> was a ponce or a drug peddler; he begged and
> stole; he was that attractive Negro thing, a
> "hustler." . . . The real Negro, as it turned
> out, was someone like Malik; and only Malik could
> be his spokesman. (p. 35)

At the pinnacle of his press fame in 1967, Malik was jailed
for one year under the Race Relations Act for an anti-white
speech. He published his ghosted autobiography, became a
"minister without Portfolio" for the Black Eagles ("Malcolm
X, Michael X, Black Panthers, Black Eagles"), traveled, and
found himself to be a hero. To him and his white patrons
"Negroes existed now only that Malik might lead them." But
with the failure of a black "urban village" project, funded
by one of his wealthy sponsors, and with more trouble on the
horizon, Malik, after fourteen years in London, fled to
Trinidad in 1971.

In Trinidad Malik capitalized on his London fame and
expressed an interest in the "politics of revolution," not
"elections and stuff like that." Naipaul interprets this
thinking: "Revolution, change, system: London words,
London abstraction, capable of supporting any meaning Malik
. . . chose to give them" (p. 23). Malik flaunted money and
showed style. Assisted by Steve Yeates, he rented an

agricultural commune and planned a People's Store, which existed on letterheads only. He was later joined by an American Black Power activist, Hakim Jamal, and his mistress, Gale Benson (who served as the white audience Malik needed). Malik worked on a novel, while Jamal churned out commune literature, portraying Malik in American terms as a "triumphant 'nigger'." John Lennon visited. "Malik claimed that he was the best-known black man in the world, and Jamal appeared to agree. Jamal's own claim was that he himself was God. And Gale Benson outdid them both: she believed that Jamal was God" (pp. 5-6). Benson assumed the name Hale Kimga, an anagram for Gale and Hakim, and she wore African style clothes. A "fake among fakes," she was, as Naipaul describes her, "as shallow and vain and parasitic as many middle-class dropouts of her time; she became as corrupt as her master; she was part of the corruption by which she was destroyed" (p. 75). She seemed to deserve her fate, when after about a year in the commune, Malik turned against her and another of his followers, Joseph Skerritt and arranged their murders. Naipaul intimates that the society may yet produce another Malik and a duplicate of this drama, as long as the dream of racial redemption is alive. For, "the streets . . . are still full of Joe Skerritts. The walls are still scrawled with easy threats and easy promises of Black Power. The street are still full of 'hustlers' and 'scrunters,' words that glamorize and seem to give dispensation to those who beg and steal" (p. 74).

Malik had found that Trinidad was not England; there were no rich patrons and white audiences to feed his ego. On December 31, 1971, he reportedly drank the blood of a calf killed for a party festivities. Two days later, Benson was taken to a grave and Malik's friend, Stanley Abbott, and a few henchmen chopped her several times with a cutlass. She struggled, for "at that moment all the lunacy and play fell from her; she knew who she was then, and wanted to live." Her belongings were burned by the seashore while the men cleansed themselves in the river. In his fragmented novel, which reads like a "pattern book, a guide" foreshadowing the real events, Malik vented his rage at the English middle class. Benson became his victim in, what Naipaul calls, a "literary murder":

> This was a literary murder, if ever there was one. . . . Blood in the morning, fire in the afternoon. . . . Like an episode in a dense novel, it served many purposes and had many meanings. . . . Such plotting, such symbolism! The blood of the calf at Christmas time, the blood of Gale Benson in the new year. And then, at the end of the sacrificial day, the cleansing in the river. (pp. 78-93)

On February 7, 1971, assisted by Abbott, Malik decapitated Skerritt, who had literally helped to dig his own grave. It was not until February 22 that the body was discovered, and two days later Benson's. In jail, still role-playing and relishing a prediction of a local fortune-teller that would be "ruler of the Negroes of the United States," Malik pleaded insane only after all other legal channels were exhausted. He was hanged in May 1975. And in April 1979, after six years in prison, Stanley Abbott was hanged--nobody's cause then, for "that caravan had gone by."

For his efforts in The Return of Eva Peron, in which "The Killings" have been published, Naipaul has again been dubbed with such superlatives as "unarguably the most brilliant interpreter in English (perhaps in any language) of the maelstrom of the Third World" or as "indisputably one of the greatest practitioners of English writing today."[133] There are critics who have argued that Naipaul portrays Michael de Freitas through "deeply condescending and offended Western eyes," that he ignores Trinidad's cultural flowering, or that he records inaccuracies; however, these same reviewers and others have also praised his prescient, perceptive analysis, enhanced by both an insider's view and a philosophical detachment.[134] It has also been said that Naipaul, in his status as "one of them," secures a type of ethnic privilege and license to see and get away with saying certain things in a way that whites cannot.[135] Nothing is further from the truth, however. Given the strong antipathy between Caribbean blacks and Indians, Naipaul, in criticizing a black movement, places himself again in a precarious position, open to the charge of racial prejudice.

Nowhere is the misunderstanding of Naipaul's racial attitude more evident than in Gordon Rohlehr's reading of a passage in "The Killings in Trinidad." The section, which refers to the spread of the Black Power Movement, contains the word "infected": "There were daily anti-government marches in Port of Spain; revolutionary pamphlets appeared everywhere, even in schools; sections of the regiment declared for the marchers. Even the Asian countryside began to be infected. A spontaneous, anarchic outburst . . ." (p. 43). In an interview, Rohlehr, discussing Naipaul's identification with East Indians in the Caribbean, misrepresented Naipaul's one-line reference to East Indians:

> In that brief section he [Naipaul] devoted to the 1970 march to Caroni . . . he used words to the effect that the Black Power marchers almost contaminated the Asiatic countryside. I found it a strange interpretation of what seemed to be a romantic but genuine gesture; namely that the march was a violation of something that that [sic] was pure and whole.

> It was a notion, very current in 1970, that
> the movement consisted of lazy, unemployed or
> unemployable blacks. . . . The idea that these
> marchers were going to Caroni to <u>contaminate</u>
> Asiatics if twisted or intensified somewhat, is
> not so different from the idea that "they coming
> to rape we women" which is where a slightly
> hysterical mind, beginning from the point of
> contamination, can end up.[136]

The point which Naipaul made, however, is that the movement
spread like a contagious disease. There is no
overprotective attitude towards the Asian countryside, a
place which Naipaul singled out here because of its history
of being isolated from currents that sweep the cities.
"Infection" is a word that he has frequently used to
describe the growth of the movement anywhere, not just
Indian countrysides. For example, "Power?" contains a
reference to a twenty-one-year-old student as "the carrier
of the infection" from America to Belize (p. 270). Many
West Indians, however, raise the issue of race and also
challenge Naipaul's "one-sided" journalism.[137]

Throughout the years Naipaul's assessment of the
Caribbean has remained consistent, as seen in his most
recent article on Grenada, a place supposedly "freed" by an
American invasion. For it appears to Naipaul that what
operated in that small island was the same type of politics
he had described in St Kitts and the identical assurances of
racial redemption offered by the Black Power Movement and by
Eric Williams. In the "black-Hansel-and-Gretel world" of
Grenada, both Eric Gairy, who grew into an "eccentric Negro
shepherd-king," and Maurice Bishop, who later imposed
"manners" (silence) on the opposition, offered the same
vision: "sudden racial redemption." This vision, combined
with "socialist mimicry" and the necessary "imported
apparatus" and fancy slogans, could only have led to failure
and disaster. In his writings, Naipaul has suggested that
this recurring pattern of destruction in the Caribbean will
continue unless people stop permitting themselves to be
deceived by movements which "promise Jerusalem."[139]

Naipaul's constant salvos on the West Indies, as
recorded in his various interviews, have added to his tense
reception in the region. For example, there was quite a
furor in the Trinidadian press when Naipaul injudiciously
selected the words "bush," "primitive," and "backward" to
describe the islands. West Indian reaction will be better
understood if the context of Naipaul's remarks is kept in
mind. In addition to his 1979 statement (quoted earlier)
that West Indians have gone back to the bush because
racialist politics have led to the collapse of institutions
and human values,[140] Naipaul, in an interview with
Elizabeth Hardwick the same year, spoke of seeing the "bush
creeping back, entangling, choking all those places 'going

forward.'" In the Congo he saw "a rich town, abandoned by the Belgians. Street lamps rusty, sand everywhere, collapsed verandahs. . . . Here again in Africa one was back in the 5th [sic] century. Native people camping in the ruins of civilization. You could see the bush creeping back as you stood there." He specifically defined the "bush" in downtown Trinidad: "It is the breakdown of institutions, of the contract between man and man. It is theft, corruption, racist incitement. . . . The Indians are one-third of the population, what is called a large minority. They have no say about anything, of course."[141] Again in a 1981 interview when Naipaul was asked about his cultural affinity, he took the occasion to complain of Trinidad's simplicity, retrogression, and philistine attitude:

> I come from a primitive island which achieved
> independence a quarter of a century ago and has
> gone back to the bush. . . . Today every little
> corner of bush that achieves independence thinks
> it has to have a national anthem and a flag. And
> what happens? This little piece of bush goes to
> Seattle, buys a Boeing, dresses the local girls up
> as stewardesses in native costumes and thinks it's
> got a national culture. It's what I call Bongo
> Airlines. . . . Some countries don't believe in
> intellectual life, particularly the backward
> countries.[142]

This denunciatory statement, not the earlier ones in which the key word "bush" is defined, was reprinted in the Trinidadian newspapers and drew a series of emotional letters to the editors.

The responses have shown that popular opinion of Naipaul is no different from the literary one. Suggesting that Naipaul takes a vain and snobbish stance either because he feels that it is fashionable to sneer at his roots or because he thinks that it is economically profitable to take a provocative approach, one reader concluded that had Naipaul been born in a "so-called more sophisticated and cultured country and society," he might not have developed and succeeded as an author.[143] It is noteworthy to mention that this speculation is quite contrary to Naipaul's own intuition about his development, as revealed in a 1973 interview: "I've often thought that if I'd started in another country I would have started from a higher base."[144] In an angry, emotional letter printed in both the _Guardian_ and _Express_, another reader, "M.B.," wondering "what Trinidad or indeed the entire region had done to Mr. Naipaul to deserve the contempt he shows for them," dismissed the statement about Bongo Airlines as the "meaningless ramblings of a disturbed individual" and advised the writer to remember that "his 'British Empire' was built upon slave labor." M.B.'s conclusion, deleted from the _Express_ version, reiterated much of what has been said in intellectual circles:

> I firmly believe that Naipaul is afflicted with all of the following which provides an explanation for his attitude towards the West Indies:
> 1. He is a snob.
> 2. He believes that white is good and black bad.
> 3. He has an inferiority complex.
> 4. He wants to be white.
>
> Naipaul, you can overcome the first three problems, but I am sorry, no matter how much you try, you can never be white.[145]

Negating each of these charges against Naipaul and accusing "M. B." of being myopic and of misrepresenting and misunderstanding Naipaul, Dr. Mahabir Maharajh, in an equally emotional response, offered his interpretation of Naipaul's use of "bush":

> The sensitive reader will notice that "bush" has become a symbol, a symbol opposite to "tapia". . . . The first big "bush" is that majority of Trinidadians want to be white. Go into any home and in eight out of ten one will find hair straighteners, hair dyes, rollers, bleaching creams and other cosmetics intended to assist the individual to become white. . . .
> If we had no inferiority complex, we would go on our way, the way of nature. . . . We would not go to extremes to inter-marry, to change our skin and hair. . . .
> Our steel mill and American planes . . . are "bush", because we can't fill up pot-holes, can't make proper sidewalks, cannot cope with the transportation problem. . . . Our education system and what we call professionalism and intellectualism are also bush. . . .
> Vidia Naipaul cannot be pigeon-holed. The man has risen above the common man. . . . Our Carnival mentality has stupefied us, except in cricket.[146]

Mac Donald C. Taylor urged a more careful examination of Naipaul's honesty and represented a more balanced view on both sides of the spectrum: "One does not usually accept in totality a writer's position in an interview, or even from a lecture. It is his broader works, such as the compilation of a book . . . that would give more explanatory exposition of his doctrine."[147] Petty squabbles over isolated statements in interviews merely deflect effort from a serious critical assessment and cement the popular perception of

Naipaul as a provocative Euro-centered snob.

From the foregoing discussion, it is obvious that
Naipaul has incurred the wrath of fervent Caribbean nationalists, be they serious critics or casual readers. In a
1976 interview he attributed their misunderstanding of him
to their tendency to make quick generalizations: "People
have a myth about me, which is very damaging to me--that I'm
reactionary, totally out sympathy with progressive
movements, that I'm hard-hearted and cruel--none of which is
true. People make divisions very quickly on the world.
Because you are not left-wing, they automatically say that
you're right-wing." This myth, he claimed, grew from the
position he took with certain Caribbean issues: "I wasn't
applauding all the various movements of liberation here [in
the West Indies]. . . . Many of them turned out to have
seeds of corruption."[148] Naipaul himself has contributed to this misunderstanding--in fact, even courted it--by
attacking black mass movements at the peak of their popularity and by making the Third World, or specifically the
Caribbean, the main butt of his incisive criticism, while
apparently sparing the developed nations. There is every
indication, however, as will be seen in Chapter VI, that had
he directed his attention to the developed world, the
indictment would have been just as serious. Contrary to
popular West Indian perception, Naipaul carries no party or
group affiliation and espouses no ideological line, for he
condemns not only the colonials but also the colonialists,
not only the mimics but also the masters. What is
irritating to West Indians is that Naipaul belittles the
region, making his contentious statements in a provocative
and seemingly arrogant manner. His works, published at the
height of nationalism, appear to many readers to epitomize a
denial of their self-esteem and pride.

West Indians will be surprised to learn that Naipaul
claims that he looks for hopeful signs in the societies he
condemns. In response to the question of whether he is an
optimist he asserts: "I am not sure. I think I do look for
the seeds of regeneration in a situation; I long to find
what is good and hopeful and really do hope that by the most
brutal sort of analysis one is possibly opening up the
situation to some sort of action; an action which is not
based on self-deception."[149] If he has indeed looked for
signs of regenerative growth, there is hardly any evidence
from his books that he has found any. Naipaul's strategy is
that his brand of honest (though brutal) analysis will serve
as a prerequisite to a breakthrough and will eventually lead
to change in attitude. To some extent this strategy has
worked. He has angered readers--deliberately, one feels--
but in doing so, he has inspired a number of West Indians to
reflect deeply on their condition, on the concept of
mimicry, for example. Undoubtedly, Naipaul would not have
attracted as much attention, stirred such controversy, and

stimulated healthy discussions about West Indian attitudes
had his tone and style been different.

This chapter has shown, then, that in his West Indian
non-fiction Naipaul recognizes the irreparable damages of
colonialism, and he laments the conditions of the poor,
newly-independent islands, imprisoned by freedom, obsessed
with messianic redemption, and shipwrecked with borrowed
culture, ideas and jargon. Because of his provocative
language and his lack of sensitivity, he draws hostile
response from his readers who see him as being hypercritical
and contemptuous of West Indian propensities, one-sided and
Anglophile in his approach, cynical and pessimistic in his
vision of West Indian life and politics, and insensitive to
and prejudiced against blacks. Although these complaints
have been echoed in reactions to his early fiction, it is
primarily from his unequivocal utterances in his non-fiction
that Naipaul has been perceived as a defender of neo-
colonialism and imperialism. His later fictional works set
in the Caribbean echo the main themes of his West Indian
journalism and will be examined in the next chapter.

Notes

1 Adrian Rowe-Evans, "The Writer as Colonial"
(Interview), Quest, 78 (Sept.-Oct. 1972), 51.

2 Dorothy Parker, rev. of The Overcrowded Barracoon,
Christian Science Monitor, 14 March 1973, p. 13.

3 Jane Kramer, "From the Third World," rev. of The
Return of Eva Peron, New York Times Book Review, 13 April
1980, p. 30; Frederic Hunter, "V. S. Naipaul Wanders the
Post-colonial World," rev. of The Return of Eva Peron,
Christian Science Monitor, 10 March 1980, p. B2.

4 Rev. of The Overcrowded Barracoon, Kirkus Reviews,
1 Feb. 1973, p. 171.

5 "Caribbean Medley," Vogue, 15 Nov. 1959, pp. 90,
92-93.

6 "An Exile Returns," Trinidad Guardian, 25 Sept.
1960, p. 7.

7 V. S. Naipaul, "Foreword," The Middle Passage
(London: André Deutsch, 1962), p. 5. Subsequent references
will be made to the Vintage Books, 1981 edition, and page
numbers will be indicated in the text.

8 "Who is India?" Rev. of An Area of Darkness,
Encounter, 23 (Dec. 1964), 59.

9 "London," in The Overcrowded Barracoon (London:
André Deutsch, 1972; rpt. New York: Penguin Books, 1976),
p. 9. References to articles reprinted in this collection
will be to this edition, and page numbers will be indicated
in the text. George Lamming, The Pleasures of Exile
(London: Michael Joseph, 1960), p. 30.

10 See, for example, David Omerod, "In a Derelict
Land," in Critical Perspectives on V. S. Naipaul, ed. Robert
Hamner (Washington, D.C.: Three Continents Press, 1977), p.
161.

11 "Living Like a Millionaire," Vogue, 15 Oct. 1961,
pp. 92-93, 144, 147.

12 Harrison B. Malan, rev. of The Middle Passage,
Library Journal, 15 Oct. 1963, p. 3843.

13 Charles Poore, "A Native's Return to the Caribbean
World," rev. of The Middle Passage, New York Times, 7 Sept.
1963, p. 17; Walter Allen, "Fear of Trinidad," rev. of The

240

Middle Passage, New Statesman, 3 Aug. 1962, p. 150; Bertram
B. Johansson, "Caribbean Counterpoint," rev. of The Middle
Passage, Christian Science Monitor, 30 Oct. 1963, p. 9.

14 Rev. of The Middle Passage, The New Yorker, 12
Oct. 1963, p. 213; rev. of The Middle Passage, Encounter, 19
Sept. 1962, p. 84; Geoffrey Nicholson, "A Passage to the
Indies," rev. of The Middle Passage, Manchester Guardian
Weekly, 9 Aug. 1962, p. 10.

15 Allen, "Fear of Trinidad," p. 149; Poore, "A
Native's Return," p. 17; Norman T. di Giovanni, "Return of a
West Indian," rev. of The Middle Passage, Nation, 26 Oct.
1963, p. 262.

16 Noni Jabavu, "Return of an Insider," rev. of The
Middle Passage, New York Times Book Review, 22 Sept. 1963,
p. 14; "The Re-Engagement of Mr. Naipaul," rev. of The
Middle Passage, Times Literary Supplement, 10 Aug. 1962, p.
578.

17 Jabavu, p. 14.

18 di Giovanni, pp. 262-63.

19 "Slavery's Greatest Damage," Sunday Gleaner
(Jamaica), 9 Sept. 1962, p. 14.

20 Derek Walcott, "History and Picong," Sunday
Guardian (Trinidad), 30 Sept. 1962, p. 9; John Hearne,
"Unsentimental Journey with V. S. Naipaul," Sunday Guardian
(Trinidad), 3 Feb. 1963, p. 4.

21 Gordon Rohlehr, "The Ironic Approach," in The
Islands in Between, ed. Louis James (London: Oxford
University Press, 1968), p. 127; Arthur Drayton, "The
European Factor in West Indian Literature," The Literary
Half-Yearly (Mysore), 11, No. 1 (July 1970), 81.

22 "On Exile and the Dialect of the Tribe," Sunday
Guardian (Trinidad), 8 Nov. 1970, p. 19.

23 "The Middle Passage of Naipaul," Sunday Express
(Trinidad), 16 March 1982, p. 6.

24 "The Irony of W. I. Society," Sunday Gleaner
(Jamaica), 27 Jan. 1963, p. 14.

25 Lennox Grant, "Naipaul Joins the Chorus: An
Interview with Gordon Rohlehr," Tapia, 6 July 1975, p. 6.

26 V. S. Naipaul (London: MacMillan Press, 1975), p.
21.

241

27 The Pleasures of Exile, p. 225.

28 Hearne, "Unsentimental Journey," pp. 3-4.

29 "Slavery's Greatest Damage," p. 14.

30 "The Disorder of Vidia Naipaul, " Trinidad Guardian Magazine (Trinidad), 21 Feb. 1965, p. 6.

31 Yogendra Malik, East Indians in Trinidad (London: Oxford University Press, 1971), p. 75; V. S. Naipaul, "Prologue to an Autobiography," Vanity Fair, 46, No. 2 (April 1983), 154.

32 Hearne, "Unsentimental Journey," p. 4.

33 Walcott, "History and Picong," p. 9

34 Hearne, "Unsentimental Journey," p. 3.

35 "The First Generation of West Indian Novelists," Sunday Guardian (Trinidad), 7 June 1970, p. 6.

36 "Slavery's Greatest Damage," p. 14.

37 Bharati Mukherjee and Robert Boyers, "A Conversation with V. S. Naipaul," Salmagundi, 54 (Fall 1981), 12-13.

38 "The Irony of W. I. Society," p. 14.

39 Rev. of The Middle Passage, Listener, 16 Aug. 1962, p. 254.

40 Hearne, "Unsentimental Journey," pp. 3-4.

41 Walcott, "History and Picong," p. 9.

42 Walcott, "History and Picong," p. 9.

43 "Is Naipaul an Angry Young Man?" Sunday Guardian Magazine (Trinidad), 6 Aug. 1967, p. 9.

44 "Walcott-Naipaul," Trinidad Guardian, 20 Aug. 1967, p. 9.

45 "The Writer and Society," Moko (Trinidad), 13 Dec. 1968, p. 4.

46 "Walcott-Naipaul," p. 9.

47 "Introduction--V. S. Naipaul: A Panel Discussion," Revista/Review Interamericana, 6 (1976-77), 561.

242

48 <u>West Indian Societies</u> (London: Oxford University Press, 1972,) p. 247.

49 "Walcott-Naipaul," p. 9.

50 Mooke, p. 6.

51 "The Trauma of Naipauland," <u>Trinidad Guardian</u>, 24 Sept. 1967, p. 19.

52 "The Ironic Approach," pp. 130-31.

53 <u>West Indian Societies</u>, p. 175.

54 "The Changing Attitude of the Coloured Middle Class Towards Carnival," <u>Caribbean Quarterly</u>, 4, No. 3 (1956), 227.

55 "Walcott-Naipaul," p. 9.

56 "Power?" in <u>The Overcrowded Barracoon</u>, pp. 267-68. All further references to this work appear in the text.

57 "V. S. Naipaul and West Indian Writers," <u>Antilia</u> (University of the West Indies), 1 (1983), 16-17.

58 "Unsentimental Journey," p. 3.

59 "Unsentimental Journey," p. 3.

60 "History and Picong" p. 9 and "The Achievement of V. S. Naipaul," <u>Sunday Guardian</u> (Trinidad), 12 April 1964, p. 15.
61 "Slavery's Greatest Damage," p. 14.

62 Nissim Ezikiel, "Naipaul's India and Mine," in <u>New Writing in India</u>, ed. Adil Jussawalla (Baltimore, MD: Penguin, 1974), p. 75.

63 "Was John Hearne Inspired by Professional Jealousy?" <u>Sunday Guardian</u> (Trinidad), 17 Feb. 1963, p. 3

64 "Was John Hearne Inspired by Professional Jealousy?" p. 3.

65 "The Irony of W. I. Society," p. 14.

66 "The West Indian Novelist," <u>Caribbean Quarterly</u>, 11, Nos. 1 & 2 (March-June 1965), 73-74.

67 Figueroa, "Introduction--V. S. Naipaul," p. 560.

68 "Is V. S. Naipaul an Angry Young Man?" p. 9.

69 Mukherjee and Boyers, p. 12.

70 Mukherjee and Boyers, p. 13. Naipaul has not been officially banned in any of the Caribbean territories.

71 Sylvia Wynter, "Reflections on West Indian Writing and Criticism," Jamaica Journal, 2, No. 4 (Dec. 1969), 28; Gerald Moore, The Chosen Tongue (London: Longmans, Green and Co. Ltd., 1969), p. 7.

72 "The European Factor in West Indian Literature," p. 82.

73 V. S. Naipaul's Fiction (Canada: York Press, 1983), pp. 35-36. The poetry quotations below are taken from Boxill.

74 V. S. Naipaul's Fiction, p. 35.

75 Jesse Noel, "Historicity and Homelessness in Naipaul," Caribbean Studies, 11, No. 3 (Oct. 1971), 83.

76 "The Novelist V. S. Naipaul Talks about his Work to Ronald Bryden," Listener, 22 March 1973, p. 368.

77 The Loss of El Dorado (London: André Deutsch, 1962; rpt. New York: Vintage Books, 1978). References will be to this edition, and page numbers will be indicated in the text.

78 "Triste Trinidad," rev. of The Loss of El Dorado, New York Review of Books, 21 May 1970, p. 26.

79 Peter Marshall, rev. of The Loss of El Dorado, American Historical Review, 76, No. 3 (June 1971), 848; "The Failings of an Empire," rev. of The Loss of El Dorado, Times Literary Supplement, 25 Dec. 1969, p. 1471. See also J. A. Borome, rev. of The Loss of El Dorado, Library Journal, 1 April 1970, p. 1367.

80 "A Nightmare World of Fantasy and Murder," rev. of The Loss of El Dorado, Book World (Washington Post) 19 April 1970, pp. 1 and 3.

81 Hammond Innes, "For God and Profit," rev. of The Loss of El Dorado, Spectator, 8 Nov. 1969, p. 647; rev. of The Loss of El Dorado, Book World (Washington Post), 6 Dec. 1970, p. 22; Gregory Rabassa, "The Dark, Obverse Side of the Shining Myth," rev. of The Loss of El Dorado, New York Times Book Review, 24 May 1970, p. 7; Neil Millar, "Slavery's High Cost," rev. of The Loss of El Dorado, Christian Science Monitor, 28 May 1970, p. 13.

244

82 Ronald Bryden, "Between the Epics," rev. of The Loss of El Dorado, New Statesman, 7 Nov. 1969, p. 662; Derwent May, "A Black Tale," rev. of The Loss of El Dorado, The Times (London), 1 Nov. 1969, p. V; rev. of The Loss of El Dorado, Kirkus Reviews, 15 Feb. 1970, p. 224.

83 Karl Miller, "Power, Glory and Imposture," rev. of The Loss of El Dorado, Listener, 13 Nov. 1969, p. 674; Bryden, "Between the Epics," p. 661.

84 "The Failings of an Empire," p. 1471.

85 May, "A Black Tale," p. V; Karl Miller, "Power, Glory and Imposture," p. 674.

86 "Triste Trinidad," p. 26.

87 "The Failings of an Empire," p. 1471.

88 "Rediscovery from Outside," rev. of The Loss of El Dorado, Savacou (Jamaica), 5 (June 1971), 126-27.

89 Noel, p. 84.

90 "Hot Little Offshore Island," Sunday Guardian (Trinidad), 16 Nov. 1969, p. 5.

91 Clyde Hosein, "Naipaul's Latest Called a Novel about History," Trinidad Guardian, 14 Dec. 1969, p. 20; Carnegie, pp. 126-27.

92 Noel, p. 83; C. Alan Wade, "The Novelist as Historian," The Literary Half-Yearly (Mysore), 11, No. 2 (1970), 179.

93 Wade, pp. 179-80; see also Noel, pp. 83-85.

94 Wade. pp. 180-83.

95 Carnegie, p. 128.

96 Wade, p. 184.

97 Carnegie, p. 128.

98 Carnegie, pp. 126-27.

99 "Trinidad," Mademoiselle, 59 (May 1964), 187-88.

100 "East Indian," in The Overcrowded Barracoon, p. 41.

101 "West Indian Culture?" <u>The Illustrated Weekly of India</u>, 30 May 1965, p. 23. In a 1971 interview Naipaul labeled as absurd the idea that "People saw that primitive society [Trinidad] as Athens"--see Ian Hamilton, "Without a Place" in <u>Critical Perspectives on V. S. Naipaul</u>, ed. Robert Hamner (Washington, D.C.: Three Continents Press, 1977), p. 40.

102 Frantz Fanon, <u>Black Skin, White Masks</u>, trans. Charles Lam Markmann (New York: Grove Press, Inc., 1967), pp. 63 ff. <u>The Return of Eva Peron with the Killings in Trinidad</u> (New York: Alfred Knopf, 1980; rpt. New York: Vintage Books, 1981), p. 37. All subsequent references will be to this edition, and page numbers will be indicated in the text.

103 Rowe-Evans, p. 51; Hamilton, "Without a Place," pp. 40-41.

104 "V. S. Naipaul: Man Without Society," in <u>Critical Perspectives on V. S. Naipaul</u>, ed. Robert Hamner, p. 49.

105 Raoul Pantin, "Portrait of an Artist," <u>Caribbean Contact</u>, 1, No. 6 (May 1973), 18.

106 Pantin, "Portrait of an Artist," p. 18; Hamilton, "Without a Place," p. 40.

107 Pantin, "Portrait of an Artist," p. 18.

108 See, for example, rev. of <u>The Overcrowded Barracoon</u>, <u>Kirkus Reviews</u>, 1 Feb. 1973, p. 171; "Editor's Column," rev. of <u>The Overcrowded Barracoon</u>, <u>Queen's Quarterly</u>, 80, No. 3 (Autumn 1973), 496-97.

109 Rev. of <u>The Overcrowded Barracoon</u>, <u>New York Times Book Review</u>, 16 Sept. 1973, p. 18.

110 Rev. of <u>The Overcrowded Barracoon</u>, <u>Choice</u>, June 1973, p. 610.

111 "Challenging CLR and the Naipauls," <u>Sunday Guardian</u> (Trinidad), 18 Oct. 1970, pp. 7 and 10.

112 "Defending CLR and the Naipauls," <u>Sunday Guardian</u> (Trinidad), 1 Nov. 1970, p. 5.

113 "Challenging CLR and the Naipauls," p. 7.

114 "Poor Naipaul: He Has Become His Biggest Joke," <u>Express</u> (Trinidad), 26 Oct. 1970, p. 10.

115 "Naipaul's Article on Black Power Criticised," Moko (Trinidad), 23 Oct. 1970. p. 3.

116 Lovelace, p. 10.

117 "Naipaul's Death Wish is not Our Bag," Trinidad Guardian, 1 Feb. 1973, p. 4.

118 "Challenging CLR and the Naipauls," p. 10.

119 Lord, p. 3.

120 A. J. Seymour, "The Novel in the British Caribbean," Bim (Barbados), 12, No. 44 (Jan.-June 1967), 240.

121 Lord, p. 3.

122 "Naipaul's Death Wish is not Our Bag," p. 4.

123 "Challenging CLR and the Naipauls," p. 7.

124 "Defending CLR and the Naipauls," p. 5.

125 "Defending CLR and the Naipauls," p. 5. See also John Figueroa, rev. of The Overcrowded Barracoon, by V. S. Naipaul, Caribbean Studies, 13, No. 4 (Jan. 1974), 135-40.

126 Lovelace, p. 10; Lord, p. 3.

127 "Naipaul's Death Wish is not Our Bag," p. 4.

128 "The Ultimate Transient," Caribbean Contact, 2, No. 2 (Jan 1973), p. 4.

129 "The Ultimate Transient," p. 4.

130 Lovelace, p. 10.

131 "Naipaul's Death Wish is not Our Bag," p. 4.

132 Pantin, "Portrait of an Artist," pp. 15 and 18-19.

133 Rev. of The Return of Eva Peron, New Yorker, 19 May 1980, p. 158; Elaine Windrich, rev. of The Return of Eva Peron, Library Journal, 1 March 1980, p. 615; Phillis Rose, "Of Moral Bonds and Men," rev. of The Return of Eva Peron, Yale Review, 70, No. 1 (Oct. 1980), 156.

134 Edward W. Said, "Bitter Dispatches from the Third World," rev. of The Return of Eva Peron, Nation, 3 May 1980, p. 524; Selden Rodman, "The Bush Moves Closer," rev. of The Return of Eva Peron, National Review, 14 Nov. 1980, p. 1406; Patrick Breslin, "Naipaul and the Empire of Discontent,"

rev. of <u>The Return of Eva Peron</u>, <u>Book World</u> (<u>Washington Post</u>), 30 March 1980, p. 6; Frederic Hunter," V. S. Naipaul Wanders the Post-colonial World," p. B2; Jack Beatty, rev. of <u>The Return of Eva Peron</u>, <u>New Republic</u>, 12 April 1980, p. 39.

135 Jane Kramer, "From the Third World," p. 1.

136 Lennox Grant, "For Naipaul There is a Challenge of Faith," <u>Tapia</u> (Trinidad), 13 July 1975, p. 7.

137 See, for example, Roger McTair, "Critical Response to Naipaul," rev. of <u>The Return of Eva Peron</u>, <u>Caribbean Contact</u>, 8 No. 6, (Oct. 1980), 3.

138 "An Island Betrayed," <u>Harper's</u>, March 1984, pp. 63-68.

139 See, for example, Adrian Rowe-Evans, p. 51.

140 See page 335 of this chapter.

141 Elizabeth Hardwick, "Meeting V. S. Naipaul," <u>New York Times Book Review</u>, 13 May 1979, p. 36.

142 "V. S. Naipaul in Paris," <u>Manchester Guardian</u>, 26 July 1981, p. 13. Excerpts of this interview have been reprinted in Mac Donald C. Taylor, Letter, "Naipaul: 'T'dad his Gone Back to the Bush," <u>Express</u> (Trinidad), 10 Dec. 1981, p. 5.

143 M. Gary, Letter, "Naipaul--Snob, Provocative Artist, or What?" <u>Express</u> (Trinidad), 28 Dec. 1981, p. 5.

144 "The Novelist V.S. Naipaul Talks about his Work to Ronald Bryden," <u>Listener</u>, 22 March 1973, p. 370.

145 Letter, "An Explanation for Naipaul's Attitude," <u>Trinidad Guardian</u>, 18 Dec. 1981, p. 8.

146 Letter, "The Deeper Meaning of Naipaul's 'bush,': <u>Trinidad Guardian</u>, 13 Jan. 1982, p. 8.

147 Letter, "A Little Scrutiny of Naipaul's Honesty," <u>Trinidad Guardian</u>, 12 Jan. 1982, p. 8. For a similar view, see Anthony Milne, "In Defense of V. S. Naipaul, <u>Express</u> (Trinidad), 4 Jan. 1982, p. 21.

148 Mel Gussow, "Writer Without Roots," <u>New York Times Magazine</u>, 26 Dec. 1976, p. 19.

149 Adrian Rowe-Evans, p. 51.

Chapter VI

West Indian Response to Naipaul's
Later West Indian Fiction

Although Naipaul shifted his attention to journalism after
the completion of <u>A House for Mr Biswas</u> (1961), he
nevertheless continued writing fiction. Apart from his one
"English" novel, <u>Mr Stone and the Knights Companion</u> (1963),
he has, in his later fiction, remained within the boundaries
of the Third World or placed Third World characters in alien
settings. Thus, <u>In a Free State</u> (1971), which contains
three stories, depicts alien characters in England, America,
and Africa, while <u>A Bend in the River</u> (1979) alternates its
setting between Africa and London and uses an Indian as its
main protagonist-narrator. For the remaining later novels
written to date--<u>The Mimic Men</u> (1967), <u>A Flag on the Island</u>
(1967), and <u>Guerrillas</u> (1975)--Naipaul returned to the
Caribbean for setting, themes and characters. Some changes
are apparent in these later works. Whereas in his early
West Indian novels he limited the setting to Trinidad and
portrayed that island's East Indian characters, in these
later novels, the geography and characters are less
restrictive. Written after he had been away from the West
Indies for over seventeen years, the works also betray the
author as, in the words of one critic, "the dépaysé cosmopolitan who sees Trinidad through a veil woven by absence."[1]
Most significant, though, is an apparent shift in tone,
which seems to complement the grim declaration in his
Caribbean non-fiction and which has widened his alienation
from fellow West Indians. Their response to these three
later West Indian novels reflects this alienation and will
be discussed in this chapter.

So apparent is the change in Naipaul's style and vision
that his early novels have been seen as "discontinuous" from
his later works.[2] The light, amused tone of the first
three comedies and the blending of pathos and humor in <u>A
House</u> have gradually yielded to deep rage, depression, and
despair. Irving Howe has referred to this growing somber
note as a "dark vision," and Richard Freedman has pinpointed
<u>The Mimic Men</u> as the book that "shows a darkening of this
tone, which has culminated in the ferocity of
<u>Guerrillas</u>."[3] In a 1971 interview, Naipaul himself
admitted that he had changed, but he attributed the change
to his eventual recognition that the world is not as simple
as he has hitherto thought. To him such a realization has
made him more sympathetic: "The world is so complex. As you
get older and understand more, you no longer have the flat

view of the world--flat and sometimes cruel. As you grow
older you understand people a lot more; you have greater
sympathy with people; you enter into them much more."[4]   In
another interview conducted the same year, he claimed to
have developed a more analytical approach to his craft:

> In writing my first four or five books . . . I was
> simply recording my reactions to the world; I
> hadn't come to any conclusion about it. . . . But
> since then, through my writing, through the effort
> honestly to respond, I I [sic] have begun to have
> ideas about the world. I have begun to analyze.
> First of all, the deficiencies of the society from
> which I came, and then, through that, what goes to
> make this much more complex society in which I have
> worked so long.[5]

Interestingly enough, Naipaul has categorically denied that
he has a "dark vision": "If the vision were really dark then
it would be very hard to put pen to paper. One would be . .
. distressed. There'd be no point."[6]   However, this
denial not only contradicts the themes in his later fiction
but also his own statements in other interviews and in his
non-fiction.   And in spite of his claims of better
understanding and of conscious analysis, an atmosphere of
gloom and pessimism over the post-independent Caribbean
societies pervades the later West Indian novels and disturbs
Naipaul's Caribbean readers.
     When Naipaul was debating the "risk" of attempting The
Middle Passage (1962), he expressed some apprehension that
his new role as a social analyst could later conflict with
his job as a novelist and possibly interfere with his
"conclusions." Whether his journalistic works were responsible for his grim conclusions about the Caribbean in his
later novels is difficult to establish.   But it is clear
that this first four novels--while they do not carry the
somber note of the later ones--had already registered a deep
concern about the condition of the colonial man or ex-
colonial man. Chronologically reshuffled, these early works
depict the transition of Trinidad's middle-class East
Indians during the early part of the twentieth century and
up to the eve of political independence, as they move from a
decadent Hindu subculture to a multiracial urban society.
Forced to exorcise from their minds the fantasy of returning
to India, and pressured into shedding their traditional
cultural patterns, they have ended up maladjusted in the
adopted world.   In addition, corrupt political machinery,
the insularity of island life, colonial dependence, and
limited opportunities have conspired to push them to a route
of mimicry or escape to the metropolis, thus condemning them
to a state of placelessness.   Trinidadian Selwyn Cudjoe
argued that Naipaul's first four novels raise one central

question: "How does an East Indian person, one generation removed from indentureship, entangled in certain feudal practices and governed by an Eastern philosophical view of the world become a Trinidadian person governed, as it were, by capitalist relations and a Western vision of the world?"[7] In The Mystic Masseur, Ganesh Ramsumair tries to wrestle with this problem and is propelled by circumstances into becoming an Anglicized "mimic man" and an opportunistic politician. It is in The Mimic Men that Naipaul elaborates on the theme of colonial displacement and political exploitation and then branches off in subsequent novels into a wider examination of the universal problems of cultural identity, afflicting not only West Indians but also all mankind.

The Mimic Men is a study of the fortunes of an East Indian West Indian and of the plight of a newly independent country.[8] In a modest suburban London rooming-house, the narrator, forty-year-old Ralph Singh (ne Ranjit Kripalsingh), a displaced, disillusioned, former cabinet minister from the multiracial West Indian island of Isabella, reflects on and reevaluates his life. It has been his hope to arrive at an understanding of himself and events by writing a "more than autobiographical work, the exposition of the malaise of our times pointed and illuminated by personal experience" (p. 8). In an interview Naipaul explained his search for a suitable setting and structure for the writer, Singh, whose situation parallels his creator's:

> I was trying to do the simply thing of beginning at
> the beginning, but it didn't work: the nature of
> the book, which is about placelessness, soon made
> it too diffuse.
>   Then I realized I needed a physical centre--and
> this would be the place where the man was writing
> his memoirs. Now it appears to begin in the
> middle--but it couldn't be written in any other
> way. . . . A man writing his first book sits down
> and pretends he's writing a book; that element is
> still with me . . . You have to pretend to be
> writing a book until you discover who you are.[9]

Forgoing dialogue and depending heavily instead on narrative done in flashback and flashforward, The Mimic Men has turned out to be an expository, socio-political novel in serious diary-style writing. Everything is recalled, sorted, and analyzed through the point of view of Singh, Naipaul's most detached, contemplative, and intellectual first-person narrator.

The thesis, implicit in the title of this confessional novel, can be summed up in Singh's own words: "We had been

abandoned and forgotten. We pretended to be real . . . we
mimic men of the New World, one unknown corner of it" (p.
146). The different people, deserted on the alien shores of
Isabella, mimic their former British masters and clumsily
model their lives, culture and politics on those of the
mother country. Thus, Singh repudiates his cultural identity (although he relishes his Aryan ancestry, he Anglicizes
his name) and superficially apes the behavioral mannerisms
of the colonialists. This is apparently the natural direction of things on Isabella and, therefore, not specifically
an indictment of Singh, who emerges as a typical product and
victim of the society. In fact, in introducing his story,
he himself takes a cynical view of colonial politics:

> The career of the colonial politician is short and
> ends brutally. We lack order. Above all, we lack
> power, and we do not understand that we lack power
> . . . We mistake words and the acclamation of
> words for power; as soon as our bluff is called we
> are lost. . . . For those who lose, and nearly
> everyone in the end loses, there is only one
> course: flight. Flight to the greater disorder,
> the final emptiness: London and the home
> countries. (p. 8)

Many colonial politicians, once "manipulators" and "power
seekers," fawned over by the obsequious, end up in
self-exile in home countries without recognition and in more
disorder. Home is nowhere--not the West Indies, not
England, and, although Singh does not realize this yet, not
India. As he begins reconstructing a hopscotch tour of his
life in an effort to treat this complex theme of colonial
mimicry, politics, and displacement, the chronology and
setting constantly shift, covering his life as a child in
Isabella, a college student in London, a land developer and
politician back on Isabella, and finally an exile in London.
     Singh tries to account for his current condition by
taking a nostalgic trip back in time, recalling his occasionally humorous childhood and adolescence in colonial
Isabella during and after World War II. But it is a period,
as he succinctly puts it, of "incompetence, bewilderment,
solitude, and shameful fantasies." He spends much of his
time with this mother's wealthy family, owners of Bella
Bella Bottling Works, a franchise of Cola-Cola. However, it
is his eccentric father who makes an indelible imprint on
his mind. The elder Singh abandons his family and
schoolmastership, dons the yellow robes of a sanyani, takes
to the hills, changes his name to "Gurudeva," and becomes a
rebel leader of a short-lived revolutionary religious
movement, a mere "gesture of mass protest, a statement of
despair, without a philosophy or cause." Singh has other
significant memories. The elaborate and delightful descrip-

tions of his seaside adventures (and misadventures) with his
whimsical, rich young uncle, Cecil, are rivaled by those of
the social, academic, and recreational climate at Isabella
Imperial College. There each boy carries the weight of his
own secret and nurtures a fantasy of another world. Hok,
part Chinese, secretly reads up on China and is humiliated
when his classmates discover his black ancestry. Singh, who
has to cope with his new prestige--and irritation--caused by
his father's growing reputation, fancies himself a needed
leader of Aryans and plods through The Aryan People and
their Migrations. Browne, whose home is decorated with
pictures of blacks, such as Haile Selassie, reveals to Singh
his secret findings that some of the tropical plants of
Isabella are not indigenous, the seeds of some trees having
been brought to the island in "the intestines of the
slaves." With each boy privately obsessed with his own
ethnic group, Naipaul seems to be suggesting that emotional
security and nationalism are not possible when different
peoples, shipped from other continents, are castaways on an
island left to "complete our own little bastard world."
   Singh believes that he has a formula for happiness, one
shared perhaps by most of Isabella's residents. Remembering
the saying of a Greek that a requisite for happiness was to
be born in a famous city, and, realizing that "to be born on
an island like Isabella, an obscure New World transplant-
ation, second-hand and barbarous, was to be born to
disorder," Singh decides to leave the "shipwrecked island"
(a recurring image) and to seek his chieftainship in the
outside world. He accepts a scholarship to London as a
deliverance from the insularity of the island. To him
England offers "Escape! To bigger fears, to bigger men, to
bigger lands, to continents. . . . Good-bye to this
encircling, tainted sea!" (p. 179).[10] However,
Deschampsneufs, a French Creole aristocrat, argues emotionally but convincingly that the solution is not that simple:

> Oh, yes, we all want to get away and so on. But
> where you are born is a funny thing. My great-
> grandfather and even my grandfather, they always
> talked about going back for good. They went. But
> they came back. You know, you are born in a place
> and you grow up there. You get to know the trees
> and the plants. You will never know any other
> trees and plants like that. You grow up watching a
> guava tree, say. You know that browny-green bark
> peeling like old paint. . . . You go away. You
> ask, "What is that tree?" Somebody will tell you,
> "An elm." You see another tree. Somebody will
> tell you, "That is an oak," Good; you know them.
> But it isn't the same . . . . Where you born, man,
> you born. (pp. 171-72)

Indeed, wherever Singh lives, in Isabella or London, his
sense of displacement tortures him. The transplanted
colonial has no real home.

As a student in London, where he poses as a wealthy
dandy, Singh, aloof, arrogant, and indifferent, is consumed
by restlessness. He once thought that he could have found
relief from his condition by doing historical writing:

> It was my hope to give expression to the
> restlessness, the deep disorder, which the great
> exploations, the overthrow in three continents of
> established social organizations, the unnatural
> bringing together of people who could achieve
> fulfilment [sic] only within the security of their
> own societies and the landscapes hymned by their
> ancestors, it was my hope to give practical
> expression to the restlessness which this great
> upheaval has brought about. . . . But this work
> will not now be written by me; I am too much a
> victim of that restlessness which was to have been
> my subject. (p. 32)

Singh's recollections of his London days also include his
sexual escapades--all clinical and aimless--and his court-
ship of an English fellow student, Sandra, whom he marries
against family traditions. With his wife, he returns to
Isabella, runs a successful community project, Kripalville
(aptly corrupted to Crippleville), and builds a luxurious
imitation Roman Villa. But happiness continues to elude
Singh as he experiences the "textbook case of an ill-advised
mixed marriage" and as he returns to his old addiction to
sexual adventures, most of them still disgusting and
unsatisfying. It is an insecure and restless Singh who
increasingly leans on his fantasy of being a Central Asian
horseman, a chieftain, riding on mountainous, snowy plains
to the end of an empty world--a vision he had nurtured as a
child.

The political fortunes of Singh after his estrangement
from Sandra, along with the economic and political problems
of the colony, constitute the briefest but most serious
section of the novel. Singh is drawn into politics as he
assists his old friend, Browne, with the publication of the
Socialist, espousing an anti-colonial ideology. Naipaul's
earlier novels have expressed cynicism towards self-
government and politicians, and his interviews are replete
with comments about his own rejection of political activity
because of the "silliness of political life."[11] But
nowhere in his writings are colonial politicians--the mimic
men, who depend on "borrowed phrases" and relish pomp and
ceremony of the imperialist masters--more ludicrous than in
this novel:

Their names and photographs appeared frequently in
the newspapers, but they were slightly ridiculous
figures; stories about their illiteracy or
crookedness constantly circulated. . . . We could
see them in their new suits even on the hottest
days . . . shirt-sleeved--their coats prominent on
hangers--as they were driven in government cars
marked with the letter M, on which they had
insisted, to proclaim their status as Ministers. .
. . At sports meetings they went to the very front
row of the stands, and over the months we could see
the flesh swelling on the back of their necks, from
the good living and the lack of exercise. And
always about them, policemen in growing numbers.
(pp. 190-91)

Critical of these mimic men and (by association) of himself,
Singh describes their movement as socialist, but "left-wing,
right-wing: did it matter?" The party men "zestfully
abolished an order" and never defined their purpose, but
they were never short of grand visions: "They promised to
abolish poverty in twelve months. They promised to abolish
bicycle licenses. They promised to discipline the police.
They promised intermarriage. They promised farmers higher
prices. . . . They promised . . . to nationalize every
foreign-owned estate. They promised to kick the whites into
the sea and send the Asiatics back to Asia. They promised;
they promised. . . ." (pp. 198-99). In a general election,
Browne, in the role of messianic redeemer of his people,
becomes Prime Minister of a now independent state, while
Singh reaches the peak of his success when he negotiates a
bauxite contract. However, Naipaul does not give specific
details (about the election, for example), and his generalizations about the political situation seem to suggest that
precise information is unimportant since what is happening
in Isabella has "all happened in twenty countries, islands,
colonies, territories."

Isabella's political independence, however, appears to
be merely ceremonial and nominal and generates more
problems. The mimic men may play-act and rave, but their
small island, by extension any small island, lacks the
resources to be self-sufficient and lapses into a debased,
tourist-oriented society. Industrialization "seems to be a
process of filling imported tubes and tins with various
imported substances," and the imported products turn out to
be cheaper than locally produced ones. Matters on Isabella
are complicated by a sugar crisis and by the eruption of
racial riots, which the politicians are ill-equipped to
handle. Told of the horrors committed against Asiatic women
and children, Singh retreats to his favorite reverie and
hopes that the victimized could join him in his mental ride
to the end of the world. When he is sent to England on the

difficult mission of negotiating the nationalization of
private estates, he is shunned and humiliated abroad and
distrusted and undermined at home. He knows too well the
value of the philosophy, "Hate oppression, fear the
oppressed," for the oppressed eventually become the
oppressors. Like many failed colonial politicians, he seeks
refuge in the metropolis, where, burdened with a feeling of
homelessness but relieved by the end of political life, he
becomes pensive and mellow. As John Thieme argued, in The
Mimic Men "escape has become a way of life and displacement
a perennial condition. For the dispossessed colonial,
political independence solves no problems. A kind of cyclic
determinism makes it impossible for him to find a home.
Neither colony nor 'mother country' provide a matrix.
Dependence and displacement are his ultimates."[12]
     Reviewers everywhere appear to be haunted by the need
to identify Isabella. Bill Carr theorized that the island
is a composite of Guyana, Trinidad, and Jamaica.[13]
However, suggestions have also been made that the book is
specifically a veiled attack on Trinidad. The popular
Barbados journal Bim made that assertion, and the Trinidad
Guardian claimed that the pseudonym "Isabella" is only a
"necessary legal pretence" and that "Trinidadians unfortunately know this fleeting, vanishing dandy [Singh] only
too well," a subtle reference to R. Capildeo.[14] Both
Capildeo and Guyanese Cheddi Jagan, with the strong support
of the East Indian population in their respective countries,
took, like Singh, a downward plunge in their political
careers immediately after independence talks in London--
Capildeo was pushed into self-imposed exile and Jagan was
deposed by the CIA. Thus, an equally strong case can be
made that Isabella is Guyana, with references to a messianic
black leader (Burnham), an orator, who exploits the
"distress of his race," and a perceived "radical" East
Indian politician (Jagan), whose stronghold is primarily in
the rural areas. There are also the "organized violence"
and racial disturbances affecting Asiatics, bauxite
contracts, agitation for independence, promotion of
nationalism, and a delegation to London. The anonymous
reviewer for the Times Literary Supplement suggested a
parallel to Guyana but noted that there is no mention of the
CIA which might link Singh to Jagan.[15] Karl Miller,
however, is convinced that Naipaul was using his experiences
of his campaign tour with the Jagans in Guyana, even though
unlike The Middle Passage, The Mimic Men does not make
mention of the "positive nationalism" which the Jagans
promoted.[16] In the final analysis, it seems that the
identification of Isabella hardly matters, since the island
apparently represents any of the newly independent Caribbean
countries with a mixed population.

A more important issue, raised by reviewers of all nationalities, has to do with point of view in The Mimic Men, that is, whether Singh is an alter ego of Naipaul the rootless wanderer. Immediately after the book was published, Naipaul seemed to encourage identification of himself with writer Singh:

> Writing is always a lonely occupation: you have no models, what do you do? That is why I'm particularly pleased with 'The Mimic Men': it deals with my own problems, the disassociation of a man from the simplicity around him. . . .
> There's an image in it: the horseman riding to the end of the flat world. It's a very private image, not at all political. Just a sense of loss and rootlessness and despair--a very consoling image for these things.[17]

However, in a 1979 interview with Naipaul, when Robert Boyers cited a specific line from the novel and asked whether the narrator was speaking for the author, Naipaul asserted that he, in fact, held a view opposite to the one quoted.[18] The question of the distinction between the author and the narrator is an important one, since the allegation has been made that Naipaul uses his fiction merely to continue his onslaught against the West Indies. American critic Robert Hamner saw some validity in this charge but regretted that too many readers have permitted Naipaul's "explicit statements to distract them from the primary texts."[19] Guyanese Victor Ramraj also criticized the practice of connecting narrator and author, a danger which, he claimed, has "contributed largely to a misunderstanding of Naipaul's perception of and attitude to the experiences of individuals, particularly those associated with the third world."[20] However, many of Naipaul's political and sociological findings in The Middle Passage, are incorporated in The Mimic Men, and a number of Singh's statement on colonial politics and restlessness coincide--sometimes verbatim--with Naipaul's pronouncements in his non-fiction and interviews. Not surprisingly, then, many readers, while aware of the danger of equating a writer with his fictional creation, have contended that Singh represents Naipaul.[21]

In his full-length study of Naipaul, Michael Thorpe called attention to the similarities between Singh and Naipaul:

> A clear pattern of ideas soon becomes apparent to the reader familiar with Naipaul's work, who sees that many of Singh's attitudes and perceptions parallel his creator's. They share a sense of formlessness of their society, a deep scepticism

about its capacity to found a vital culture, a
desire for order and form; at many points Singh
obviously speaks for the author. . . .[22]

Thorpe is not the only Naipaul critic to suggest such an
identification. Arguing that Naipaul intentionally makes no
effort to detach himself from Singh or to portray him
ironically, Landeg White also noted: "For those who have
followed Naipaul's work from the beginning, the task of
distinguishing the author from his creation in all but
matters of obvious fact is virtually hopeless." White went
into elaborate details to prove that much of Singh's account
of life at Isabella Imperial College is based on Naipaul's
own school experiences at Queen's Royal College and that
Singh is the same "patrician, fastidious, hyper-sensitive
spectator" as Naipaul is, disillusioned with London as a
center.[23] Other readers have also recognized the over-
lapping personality traits in Singh and Naipaul. Sara
Blackburn, for example, saw Singh clearly as "an extension
of V. S. Naipaul's own Indian/Trinidadian background," and
Karl Miller observed that "Ralph's patrician (or
Brahminical) outlook tallies at certain points with the
author's as displayed in the travel books."[24] Calling
attention to the similarity between Singh's vision of being
an Asian chieftain on snowy mountains and Naipaul's own
fantasy (recorded in An Area of Darkness) of the Himalayas
as his secret land, Keith Garebian made what, perhaps, is
the safest conclusion: "Ralph is not Naipaul but his
problems with embarrassment and identity are of personal
relevance to Naipaul, who, in his travel books, treats the
same issues with documentary evidence."[25] For, while the
author disengages himself from Singh, he puts in the mind of
his character many of the issues confronting colonial life
and politics that preoccupy Naipaul himself.

British and American reviewers have generally lauded
The Mimic Men for its richness of subject matter and of
details, but some readers have expressed deep reservation
about the advantage of the point of view used. Richard
Boston pointed out that this "complex novel . . . contains
enough themes, ideas and perceptions for a dozen of the
run-of-the-mill novels that come out every week," and
R. G. G. Price noted that Naipaul dealt with the "black-
brown relations when most novelists . . . were seeing only
white and coloured."[26] Sara Blackburn, who admitted that
the book is beautifully written, stood almost alone in her
contention that the concerns of the novel are "curiously out
of touch with any tangible kind of reality."[27] Naipaul's
portrayal of character and presentation of vivid details
have been widely praised, most critics singling out the
description of Singh's boyhood and adolescence as the best
segment in the entire novel.[28] At the same time, however,
some of these same reviewers have argued that the point of

view, or the use of Singh as the first-person narrator, has
marred (though not entirely ruined) the novel. V. S.
Pritchett, for example, charged that Singh is "too sweeping,
too apt to be essayish and generalized, to be quite
accountable all the time," and John Wain observed that the
"tendency to summarize, to see everything unremittingly
through the narrator's memory . . . makes all the characters
seem as if they had been through some refrigerating process."[29] It is essentially Singh's expository recapitu-
lation of events that is at the center of most criticisms,
including those having to do with the political theme.

Western reviewers appear to be divided about Naipaul's
handling of the political material, which occupied the last
section of The Mimic Men. V. S. Pritchett noted that the
section on Singh's political career is "over-generalized in
its tone," but he praised this final unit as
"brilliant."[30] Richard Boston argued that Naipaul presents
an "extremely perceptive account of the political and
cultural situation of a colonial country and of an
individual who is produced by that situation."[31] And
Bruce King declared that the "narrator's despairing analysis
of the problems of the Third World is probably more accurate
than most liberals would admit."[32] Other critics,
however, show reservations about the presentation of the
political theme. Patrick Parrinder suggested that the novel
failed as a political work because of Naipaul's reliance on
an atypical character to tell the story.[33] But Karl
Miller, who read the novel as a document on the problems of
an emergent nation, thought that the flaw, failure of
persuasion, may have to do not only with the glossing over
of political descriptions in favor of "excellent studies of
childhood and adolescence" but also with the blurring of the
narrator and the writer.[34] In another article Miller
predicted that Caribbean readers will be "inclined to treat
the novel as Naipaul's political testament and to scan it
for traces of disaffection, for racist or reactionary
tendencies." Noting that critics will point to the
resemblances between the opinions of Ralph Singh and those
of the author in The Middle Passage, Miller urged that a
distinction be drawn between Naipaul and his "supercilious
hero, a narcissist and dandy."[35] To M. M. Mahood the
political material becomes blurred because Isabella ceases
to resemble Trinidad and Eric Williams' PNM as Naipaul
shifts his interest to the collapse of the Guyanese
Indian-black alliance under Burnham and Jagan and to the
condition of Indians in East Africa. Mahood also argued
that the author uses Singh as his mouthpiece and becomes
vulnerable to the "charge of 'colonial-mindedness' so often
levelled at him by West Indian critics."[36] The allusions
which Miller and Mahood made to reaction in the Caribbean to
Naipaul suggest that there is a distinction between West
Indian and non-West Indian approaches to Naipaul.

Caribbean readers echo some of the criticisms of Western reviewers but predictably demonstrate a more personal concern about Naipaul's ruthless judgments about their society. Bill Carr, who regarded the schooldays section as the best and the political section as the worst, noted that the novel lacks the vivid details and acute observations found in A House for Mr Biswas. To Carr the problem with the book is that it focuses on attitudes rather than on things and people, and "the narrator wants you to keep on looking at him as he performs in a gallery of mirrors, and so his meditations upon his experience are never transformed into something that all of us can possess." Yet Carr maintained that the book undoubtedly has a mark of distinction, "even though the distinction is often the consequence of a demonstration of skill."[37] A. C. Derrick also complained about the expository and narrative technique, which, he suggested, stifles the growth of the characters. His main argument is that the book "fails to go beyond mere verbal statement, for though the narrative asserts that Isabella is a second-hand colony of uncreative men and untalented clerks, where society is fragmented and inorganic, exhausted, fraudulent, and cruel, there is hardly enough concrete demonstration of such qualities." Apparently what bothered Derrick is Naipaul's continuing expression of pessimism in this novel as well as in the earlier ones. In fact, he exasperatedly complained: "Again and again one finds the narrator stating motifs demonstrated in the earlier novels: the ultimate necessity of flight, the 'pointlessness and hopelessness' of the situation, the absurdity of the colonial experience."[38]

To many West Indians the problem with The Mimic Men is not that Naipaul is too nebulous or general but that he is too vivid and insensitive in repeatedly pointing out the shortcomings of the new West Indies. In his review of the novel for Bim Gerald Moore admitted that "no reader of Naipaul will need to be assured that he documents this indictment with deadly irony and an unfailing eye for the absurd." However, Moore took offense at Naipaul's depiction of the island and its black inhabitants:

> Isabella is "the slave island," a place irre-trievably farcical and absurd. . . . He [Naipaul] sees an element of clownishness in the Negro majority--"squat men with bright eyes and dull faces". He speaks of someone sucking a pipe "in ole-time Negro style" and laments the politician's exposure to "the smell of Negro sweat". He would be shocked to learn that all sweat smells alike.[39]

Such examples do show the narrator's use of stereotyped image of blacks. But is Singh's view necessarily Naipaul's? Singh, who echoes Naipaul on a number of ideas, seems to speak for his creator often--for example, when he admits that he was "accused of arrogance and aloofness," or when he states that he no longer tries to find beauty in the lives of the poor. But unless Singh is assumed to be a spokesman for Naipaul at all times, the argument cannot be made that Singh's perception of blacks reflects Naipaul's or that Naipaul, under the guise of fiction, registers his own prejudice against blacks. Lloyd King argued that "both racial groups [blacks and Indians] stand in an inferior position before a certain ideal of 'dignity and culture' which is associated with British colonial power."[40]

The expression of despair in The Mimic Men has stirred some controversy in the West Indies. In her literary analysis of the novel Marjorie Thorpe argued that the book records the "horror inherent in the unnatural yoking together of races physically, mentally and spiritually at variance."[41] On Naipaul's solution to this problem, she wrote, "It is, perhaps, indicative of Naipaul's much bruited pessimism, that he continues to deny the tenability of a satisfactory and positive solution. . . . Mimicry or evasion--these are the only alternatives he will allow. . . ."[42] Novelist John Hearne's response is not as non-committal as Thorpe's. Ranking The Mimic Men as the most pessimistic novel in English, Hearne noted that Naipaul "has hammered out from God knows what personal wounds, disappointments and betrayals, an authentic work of art without a shred of hope."[43] And Eric Roach, who praised Naipaul's "impeccable" prose in the novel as "strong, supple and lucid," chided the writer and injected a personal political lesson about not yielding to despair:

> He [Naipaul] praised the order, the discipline of the metropolitan community, while he swipes at the disorder across the Atlantic. . . .
> We, the Caribbean "mob" cannot take flight like Kripalsingh and if we cannot fly we cannot abandon hope in our generation, and must of necessity nourish its seeds in our children.
> We dare not accept Naipaul's negation. He is a cold and sneering prophet of gloom. . . .
> We cannot accept satire and disdain and speak sneeringly as Naipaul does of our generations of failure and incompetence. We must talk of hope and seek ways and means of imposing order on the chaos.
> We cannot forever be the mimic men. And even now we must think of spurning the sneering title.[44]

While the proclivity to mimic has always been embedded in West Indian attitudes, Naipaul has done much to arouse self-consciousness of this trait. Perhaps this self-consciousness must be gained before the mimicry can be rejected or transcended.

West Indians themselves have different views about the concept of "mimic men" and about where the responsibility falls in Naipaul's novel. Rex Nettleford, an artist and sociologist, tried to discount the importance of the title of Naipaul's book by asserting that the expression could be widely extended since "all people play roles."[45] However, in From Columbus to Castro (1970), Dr. Eric Williams, the late Premier of Trinidad and Tobago, stated that Naipaul's "description of West Indians as mimic men is harsh but true . . . psychological dependence strongly reinforces other forms of dependence."[46] Gordon Rohlehr, while chiding Williams, also agreed with Naipaul's observation: "For Williams simply to acquiesce in Naipaul's definition of West Indians as mimic men is, first of all, to fail to see that Naipaul was in that book talking particularly about West Indian politicians. As usual, Dr. Williams does not apply the lesson to himself, but . . . the statement does apply to him as much as it does to any part of the society."[47] Selwyn Cudjoe, reviewing The Mimic Men, saw a more relevant literary question raised in the novel: "How . . . does the colonial person rid her/him of a tendency to imitate (mimic) the colonial master as one goes from colonialism to independence?"[48] Many West Indians--educators and literary critics--blame an outmoded British-inherited educational system for creating mimic men and for not responding more to the needs of the local population.

Caribbean critics have not responded with unanimity in analyzing the "copycat" factor Naipaul so forcefully reveals in The Mimic Men. Bill Carr found confusion in the themes of condemnation and despair:

> Are we meant to register, in the experience of the narrator, a private tragedy? Or is defeat simply the point at which Naipaul can focus his sense of a lost and defeated society? The society is never, in so many words, "blamed". . . . I am not certain in The Mimic Men where the primary stress is supposed to fall. . . . The defeat of the narrator mirrors the limitations of the world he inhabits. Or so it would seem. I am not always able to see what is reflecting what.[49]

However, several Caribbean readers have definitely concluded that the indictment is of history and society rather than of individuals. Marjorie Thorpe admitted that the politicians are severely censured but that "one feels the author's sense of compassion for would-be revolutionaries condemned by their country's economic insufficiency. . . ."[50] Victor Ramraj argued that the novel is not merely a political one

focusing on an emerging independent nation (a reading
suggested by many reviewers); instead, he saw the book as
one enabling the narrator to muse discursively on the
"nature of the mimic man in all phases of his experience,"
for example, on isolation and displacement, on racial conflicts and identity, on the colonial educational systems, on
mixed marriage, and on foreign students in the metropolis.
Ramraj contended that "for Naipaul, both Ralph and Browne
are mimic men and he is sympathetically aware of the situation in which they find themselves. . . . Ralph apportions
blame to no one in particular in this therapeutic autobiography: the personages are all seen as victims of forces
beyond their control."[51] Anthony Boxill, discussing The
Mimic Men and A Flag on the Island simultaneously, offered a
similar reading: that is, West Indian mimics are a product
of their environment and society at large.[52]

Indeed, the same general theme of an insufficient,
dependent, mimic society runs through Naipaul's title story
from the collection A Flag on the Island, written since 1965
but published in 1967.[53] According to the author's note,
the story, subtitled "A Fantasy for a Small Screen," was
commissioned by a film company which demanded that the piece
be "'musical' and comic and set in the Caribbean; it was to
have a leading American character and many subsidiary
characters; it was to have much sex and much dialogue; it
was to explicit" (p. 4). In other words, Naipaul now
undertook to do the same things, which, in 1958, he had
refused to do even though they could have helped him break
his "regional barrier."[54] In this lead story, a middle-
aged American, Frank, along with 500 tourists aboard a
Moore-McCormack liner, is diverted by a hurricane to anchor
on a tiny, unnamed Caribbean island, where he was once
stationed as a wartime soldier. With a feeling of uneasiness, caused by vague, guilty memories of his former
influence on the place, Frank reluctantly disembarks. What
he encounters during his visit is the essence of the film
script. As Robert Hamner noted, the "basic structure hinges
upon the personality of a limited narrator. Readers see
through his eyes and feel through his emotions. The
narrator's voice is so consistently in control that in this
story the author's hand never appears . . . the fictional
veil is not disturbed."[55] Frank's sensations and
reactions to the dreadful changes on this once paradisaic
island are conveyed primarily through a kind of first person
stream-of-consciousness, dream-like narrative, which Karl
Miller has called a "rather jagged and hallucinatory
style."[56]

As Frank surveys the place, visiting familiar places
and renewing old acquaintances, he sees a newly
"independent" island which has degenerated into an
artificial, tourist-oriented society. Plastic flowers are

preferred to fresh, local ones, and open spaces are
converted into parking lots. Confronted everywhere by the
popular, trite slogan "Pride, Toil, Culture," Frank also
notices the new flag, the purpose of which is to confirm the
island's existence and to encourage national identity. In a
typical Naipaulian way, the taxi driver remarks: "To tell
the truth I prefer the Union Jack. . . . It look like a
real flag. This look like something they make. You know,
like foreign money?" (p. 132). Equally disappointing are
Frank's eccentric friends (there are no East Indian
characters), all transformed into role players. Henry, once
his companion and mentor, is now an unhappy hen-pecked
nightclub owner; Priest, a former preacher and an insurance
agent, has become a television personality under the assumed
name of Gary Priestland; J. J. Blackwhite, an aspiring
writer, now aptly using the name H. J. B. White, is obsessed
with promoting negritude and the native dialect as the
national language; finally, Selma, the mistress Frank had
left behind, is cohabiting with Priest. In explaining why
he has been reluctant to use local material in his novels,
Blackwhite echoes the theme of <u>The Mimic Men</u>: "These people
don't exist, you know. This place . . . doesn't exist.
People are just born here. They all want to go away, and
for you it is only a holiday" (p. 164). Frank, disgusted by
the inauthencity and artificiality of the place, is
comforted by the thought that an approaching hurricane may
annihilate and, therefore, purge the island:

> The world was ending and the cries that greeted
> this end were cries of joy. We all began to dance.
> . . . No picking of cotton, no cutting of cane; no
> carrying of water, no orchestrated wails. We
> danced with earnestness. . . . Benediction never
> came. . . . We gave up the hurricane. (pp. 211-12)

Frank departs from the island, with the names of big
companies, "Hilton" and "Moore McCormack," symbols of
foreign dominance and dependence, ringing in his ears.

Of all Naipaul's fiction, the title story of <u>A Flag on
the Island</u> has received the least critical acclaim from
readers everywhere. A few Western reviewers have maintained
that the story ranks in the collection as the "most remarkable," that the theme, though common, "bears retelling a
thousand different times if it is as well done as this," and
that Naipaul has an "acute perception" and "writes vividly
and forcefully with telling pictures of human weaknesses and
conceits."[57] However, most readers, citing different
reasons, have seen the work as a failure and have claimed to
understand why it was never filmed.[58] R. G. G. Price
threw the blame on the "old-fashioned, stream-of-fantastic-
events technique"; Richard Plant suggested that the outline
"wavers as giddily through the landscape as its alcoholic

chronicler [Frank]"; and the Publishers' Weekly reviewer
described the novelette as "chaotic" and "rambling."[59]
Other critics, such as the Kirkus reviewer and John Wain
(who, incidentally, did note the potentially of rich ideas
of the piece), classified the work as a sketch, a fragment,
or a groundwork for something more expansive.[60] Probably
the most legitimate complaint is that, as Wain asserted,
most parts of the book "fail to come to life; key characters
are so faintly drawn that we simply cannot see them.[61]
Landeg White, usually a strong admirer of Naipaul, also
complained of the lack of freshness and spontaneity:

> One wonders how much after fifteen years of
> learning about England Naipaul really knows about
> the new Caribbean. He writes about independence. .
> . . But the details used to place it in this
> island with a flag lack the spontaneity of the
> earlier novels. . . . The problem remains of
> creating a credible American. . . . Naipaul's
> meticulous eye, his greatest asset in reproducing
> the unfamiliar, is useless because he has chosen to
> see the island through Frank's spectacles. . . .
> What we are left with is . . . the irresistible
> impression that the narrator is Naipaul himself in
> an ill-fitting disguise.[62]

Perhaps the criteria used to judge literary works should not
be applied to a screen script meant to be seen and not
read. As a published novelette, A Flag stands as one of
Naipaul's few failures.
"A Flag" has fared even worse with West Indian
readers. The Jamaican Gleaner's brief judgment is that the
lead story is a "disappointment" and that the satire "does
not come off."[63] Anthony Boxill is the only West Indian
critic thus far to discuss this tale at length. Analyzing
both The Mimic Men and "A Flag," Boxill took an unpopular
stance with Third World readers: that is, Naipaul is "too
rigorous a thinker to allow himself to glamorize and thus
ascribe virtue to slavery or colonialism."[64] Boxill saw
"A Flag" as somewhat more pessimistic than The Mimic Men and
read in both books an implied element of concern for the
West Indian condition:

> In these two works Naipaul seems to be asking
> himself how can a society which is profoundly mimic
> produce anything which is not itself mimic; how can
> a man who is not sure what he is produce anything
> which is genuinely his own. . . . Naipaul suggests
> that unreal worlds are usually inhabited by unreal
> people, and that meaningful relationships are never
> possible between mimic men. Many readers, espe-
> cially West Indian readers, of Naipaul, find this

kind of statement about the West Indies depressing
and hopeless. In fact, throughout both these
novels there is great sympathy and understanding
for the predicament of the modern West Indies. . .
. In both works Naipaul's sadness at the plight of
the small and insignificant is moving indeed. . . .
The reader understands clearly the plight of the
politician who finds himself condemned by circumstance to play a role which can only perpetuate the
bastard status of his little world. . . . A Flag
on the Island offers no real solutions. . . .
Annihilation is the only hope offered.[65]

For whatever reason, "A Flag" is rarely mentioned by
Caribbean readers. In fact, Kenneth Ramchand's review of
Naipaul's later fiction contains no reference at all to the
entire collection.[66]
        Included with the title tale in A Flag on the Island
are ten other, shorter stories, the earliest dated 1954, and
some published previously in such periodicals as Vogue and
the London Evening Standard. Most of the tales, which vary
in tone and mood, are related by a first-person narrator,
but with different personas, ranging from an East Indian
child, student, and teacher to a black semi-literate
businessman and desk clerk. The narrator's religious-
schizophrenic aunt, Gold Teeth, in "My Aunt Gold Teeth"
invites comparison with Naipaul's non-fictional portrait of
Gold Teeth Nanee (grandmother) in An Area of Darkness.[67]
The use of another first-person narrator named Vidiadhar
Naipaul at Queen's Royal College in "The Raffle" has
prompted Naipaul to issue a prefatory caution that "the
autobiographical detail is deliberately misleading."
Undoubtedly, he drew materials from his reservoir of
Trinidadian memories, but it is dangerous to yield to the
temptation to comb some of the stories for autobiographical
elements. Resembling the sketches in Miguel Street, a few
of these comic yarns are set in London but most are placed
in Trinidad, with West Indians of all ethnic and religious
groups represented. One reader argued that the stories show
"a slight taste of condescension in their amusement over the
limitations of West Indians and the British working-class,
but it is all good-humored . . . and many historical and
sociological points of interest are made."[68] Indeed, many
of the sketches--"A Christmas Story," for example--explore
the social and cultural dislocation of the various ethnic
groups in a colonial setting.[69]
        Two of these humorous tales merit passing attention:
"The Night Watchman's Occurrence Book" and "The Baker's
Story." The former is written in the form of a log-book
exchange between a nagging hotel manager, Inskip, and his
semi-literate watchman, Hillyard, who frantically tries to

keep up with the peculiar, nocturnal activities of the white patrons and guests. The story is appealing not only because it illuminates the gap between the white elite and native workers but also because it does so through the use of humor at the expense of the fretful manager. Inskip, for example, blames Hillyard for the frequent disturbances and queries the vague log entry "Nothing Unusual." The watchman brilliantly justifies his position and complains: "Sir, nothing unusual means everything usual . . . since when people have to start getting Cambridge certificate to get night watchman job. . . . I don't know when the people in this place does sleep . . . I dont [sic] have four hands and six eyes" (pp. 57–59). "The Baker's Story," also using a first-person semi-literate narrator, is a monologue account of how a black Grenadian became a successful businessman in Trinidad by circumventing the island's traditional racial/occupational code, a code Naipaul mentioned in The Middle Passage. The baker's business does not flourish until he realizes that things are different in Trinidad:

> Every race have to do special things. . . . Who ever see a Indian carpenter? . . . You ever see anybody buying their bread off a black man?
> I ask Percy [a black friend] why he didn't like black people meddling with his food in public places. The question throw him a little. He stop and think and say. 'It don't look nice.' (p. 122)

Since baking is understood to be for Chinese, the black baker employs a half-Chinese to face customers, names his bakery "Yung Man," keeps out of the public eye, and prospers.
Western reviewers have generally expressed preference for these shorter stories to "A Flag" and have registered their greatest applause for "The Night Watchman's Occurrence Book," which is mentioned by almost every critic as the funniest and the most appealing.[70] Its popularity is rivaled by that of "The Baker's Story," the full implications of which, David Omerod stated, "are not apparent to a reader who is uninformed on the subtleties of economic and racial stratification in Trinidad."[71] However, the story can be appreciated by all if the baker's account is treated not as an exaggeration but as a commentary on the island's occupational specification. Richard Plant of the Saturday Review noted that the stories have "enough in them to insult everybody, with special machine-gun bursts reserved for preachers of the Black Power gospel."[72] Except for sparse, passing reference to one or two stories, and except for the Jamaican Gleaner's recommendation of them, especially "The Night Watchman's

Occurrence Book," Caribbean readers have not paid attention to these tales.[73]

It was not until 1975--eight years after the publication of The Mimic Men and A Flag on the Island--that Naipaul issued his next, and thus far his last, Caribbean fiction, Guerrillas.[74] During the interim he had published two non-fictional works, The Loss of El Dorado (1969) and The Overcrowded Barracoon (1972), and one collection of novellas, In a Free State (1971), set in Washington, D. C., London, and Africa. In addition, he had written several journalistic pieces for newspapers, mainly about Third World politics. But as he himself noted, "from the end of 1970 to the end of 1973 no novel offered itself" to him.[75] Yet, the period was not altogether sterile, for the research he conducted in the 1970's for "The Killings" and "A New King for the Congo" provided the nucleus for his later fiction, Guerrillas and A Bend in the River (1979). Jane Kramer observed that "Naipaul's journalism is always a cartoon for the finished canvas of his fiction, a drafting of outlines and impressions that will eventually reappear, transformed but faithful in detail, in a novel or story. He wastes nothing."[76] From the actual story of Michael de Freitas, then, comes the fictional world of Jimmy Ahmed in Guerrillas, with plot, character and theme all duplicated. It has been said that Naipaul's "chill prophecies" in "Power?" are also fulfilled here with "angry compassion."[77] It is a work in which Naipaul explores further the same subjects he had rejected in 1958: violence, race, sex, and a white character in a Caribbean setting.

For his fictional setting Naipaul uses an unnamed Caribbean island, resembling Jamaica and Trinidad, with a mixed but predominantly black population. Peter Roche, a white South African liberal, and his mistress, Jane, an Englishwoman, become involved with the work of a self-styled Moslem black power leader, "Haji" Jimmy Ahmed, ne Jimmy Leung. The novel has an ominous beginning as Jane and Roche drive out to the decaying and desolate suburbs to visit Jimmy's agricultural commune, which is called Thrushcross Grange (favorite names from Victorian fiction abound). Distracting slogans, such as Basic Black, Don't Vote, Birth Control Is a Plot Against the Negro Race, line the roadway. But most memorable is the description of the actual parched scenic background, a hazy rubbish dump and morass which Jane and Roche pass. The scene conveys a feeling of repugnance and suggests, according to one reader, "a final judgment and perdition," and to another a tone of "impermanence, violence and change"[78]:

> The sea smelled of swamp . . . and the heat
> seemed trapped below the pink haze of bauxite dust
> from the bauxite loading station. . . . After the
> market . . . after the rubbish dump burning in the
> remnant of mangrove swamp, with black carrion
> corbeaux squatting hunched on fence posts . . .
> after the naked children playing in the red dust .
> . . the land cleared a little. . . . The openness
> didn't last for long. . . .
> The hills smoked . . . thin lines of white smoke
> that become the color of dust and blended with
> haze. Above the settlements lower down which
> showed ocher, drought had browned the hills; and
> through this brown the bush fires had cut irregular
> dark red patches. The asphalt road was wet-black,
> distorted in the distance by heat waves. The grass
> verges had been blackened by fire, and in some
> places still burned. (pp. 1-2)

This description is seen through Jane's and Roche's eyes.
In fact, most of the landscape and events are not delivered
through an omniscient narrator. Rather, they are conveyed
through the point of view of the characters, who, according
to one critic, are almost like a "ventriloquist's dummies,
enabling Naipaul to assume "a petty omnipotence as author
vis-a-vis his characters."[79] The narrative covers the
tension of a few critical days, during which the principal
figures--Jane, Roche, and Jimmy--reveal through their viewpoint their internal confusion of purpose. In fact, as
Victor Ramraj pointed out, the novel is "primarily a series
of character sketches," offering "detailed portraits of
several major and minor characters, the majority of whom are
only peripherally involved in politics."[80]

The sinister atmosphere of the island and Thruchcross
seems to be an appropriate setting for the central characters, each of whom is marked by "self-disgust, mutual
irritation, idle curiosity and misdirected impulse."[81] A
Hakwai (half-Chinese, half-black), Jimmy, a former notorious
criminal had enjoyed good press coverage in England, where
he was sponsored as a black "leader" and blindly idolized by
confused white liberals. When he fell from his zenith and
was charged with rape, he, like Malik de Freitas, escaped to
his island of birth and ran a sham, eerie commune. Covered
with wild vines and inhabited by frightened youths
controlled by Jimmy, the commune professes to offer an
alternative to the derelicts of the island. However, this
bisexual, narcissistic "leader" craves self-aggrandizement
and needs both the following of the helpless poor and the
endorsement of the gullible rich in his chimerical quest to
be hero of a black power revolution. The details of the
movement are never explored in the novel, although there are
references to protests against unemployment and against

continued foreign domination of the island's economy. Betraying a deranged mind, Jimmy writes letters (again as did de Freitas), using the persona of a white woman fascinated by him and he puts out communiques which read like "a fairy story, a school composition, ungrammatical and confused" (p. 11). However, the commune is slowly crumbling. This disintegration is evident from the disappearance of one member and from the erratic behavior of the frightened Bryant, Jimmy's young "lieutenant" and lover, who sneaks off to see a Sydney Poitier double feature: "Watching the film, he [Bryant] began to grieve for what was denied him; that future in which he became what he truly was, not a man with a gun, a big profession, or big talk, but himself, and as himself was loved and readmitted to the house and to the people in the house. He began to sob" (p. 35). Yet Jimmy manages to convey the impression--at least temporarily--that he is a force to be reckoned with.

Jimmy and Roche have a symbiotic relationship. Johannes Riis has identified Roche as "by far the most interesting character" and "the standard representative of the liberal idealistic, individual fighter against injustice and oppression."[82] Jane was attracted to him because she saw him as a "doer" with an enviable history of political martyrdom. For, Roche has championed the cause of the down-trodden blacks, earned himself a glamorous record of torture in South African prison, and written a book, though disjointed, about these experiences. He is now employed as a public relations officer for a local, old imperialist firm, Sablich, which is refurbishing its image and is financing Jimmy's project. But as well-intentioned as Roche is, he has a misconceived notion of politics in this tropical island. He begins to learn more about local affairs when the death of a commune boy precipitates an angry explosion between the establishment and the guerrillas (who never actually surface in the novel). A vibrant Jimmy "organizes" mass demonstrations and violence, and buildings burn. During this tense period Roche and Jane remain confined in their home on the hill of the Ridge, a distant place of peace and refuge from the inferno below. The revolt is swiftly quelled by the local police patrols and American helicopters, and order is restored.

In a tense, brilliantly done radio interview, conducted by a local black politician, Meredith, an uncomfortable Roche is grilled about his life and motives. Roche's attempt to justify his employment at Sablich and to explain his support for the commune exposes not only his misjudgment and shallowness but also the failure and the irrelevance of a "movement" such as Jimmy's. Meredith comes close to being a mouthpiece for his creator when he belittles Roche and gives him a lesson in Third World politics and the motives of liberals:

We're a dependent people, Peter. We need other
people's approval. And when people come to us with
reputations made abroad we tend to look up to them
. . . . You know the difficulties, the campaigns
of hate. Yet some of us get taken up by certain
people and are made famous. Then we are sent back
here as leaders. . . . You're a stranger, you
don't feel involved. You're involved with an
agricultural commune which you consider anti-
historical and which you don't think can succeed.
But for you it's an opportunity for creative work.
The human need, as you say. For you work is
important. You aren't too concerned about
results. (pp. 237-45)

Recognizing the "fragility" of the world and realizing that
Jimmy has merely been "acting out a role" in the "hoax" (a
word Naipaul has used to describe the de Freitas' movement),
Roche decides to leave the island.

Roche is an ambiguously drawn character, but on Jane
Naipaul pours his venom. He has stated that she is a "study
in vanity."[83] An adulterated version of Gale Benson in
"The Killings," she is an empty, misguided, disenchanted
member of the white elite. "She was without memory. . . .
She was without consistency or even coherence. She knew
only what she was and what she had been born to" (p. 20).
Mesmerized by Jimmy's charisma--and confessedly ignorant of
the goals of the movement--she inevitably becomes his
mistress. Their first casual, sexual encounter is conveyed
in the most revolting manner, and Jimmy possesses the acumen
to read her character: "The starved woman had had many
lovers, nevertheless; she was as inexperienced as a girl,
yet she was spoiled; and without knowing it she had
developed the bad temper, and the manners, of a prostitute .
. . . He was full of hate of her" (p. 88). Her fascination
for adventure quickly changes to disillusionment and boredom:
"They were dull people, she decided, sheep being led to
slaughter; they deserved their future" (p. 109). However,
when she pays a farewell visit to the commune, she is
sexually assaulted by Jimmy and brutally murdered by him and
his programmed follower, Bryant. This hideous scene,
covering several pages of difficult reading, has been called
one of the "harshest scenes of sexual violation in modern
literature."[84] Naipaul has admitted that he hated writing
it, but he explained its importance:

The novel . . . hangs between two sexual scenes.
The first explains the second. I was very nervous
before I wrote the first one. And I was appalled
by the second. . . . I know it's offended a lot of
people. . . . But you see, the terror of that book
is inevitable. It's a book about lies and

> self-deception and people inhabiting different
> worlds or cultures . . . the fact that it shocks
> you is part of its success.[85]

The disturbing element about the conclusion of Guerrillas is
that nothing is resolved, for Roche, who has guessed Jane's
fate, has decided to cover up the crime by remaining silent
and by making an implicit agreement with Jimmy.
  Guerrillas has, with good reason, been called Naipaul's
"bleakest, most disillusioned novel" to 1979.[86] Asked
about the cruelty of the story and about his increasingly
pessimistic tone, Naipaul justified his position:

> It's frightening but it's true. It's a mature
> work: as you get older you learn things. A heap
> of lies has been spread about the awakening of the
> bush peoples and a number of catastrophes have
> resulted from these lies. Many countries have
> achieved independence and become tyrannies. Both
> colonial dependence and independence have been
> distorted and perverted by the liberal falsehoods
> of the big nations. . . .
>   I want to show why things went so wrong with
> the revolutions. . . . I would like people to take
> a closer look. . . . Many of these peoples are
> defenceless even though they have their govern-
> ment. Liberals think that these countries are
> independent now, but it happens that they're
> governed by real tyrants--and liberals keep their
> mouths shut.[87]

To Naipaul, then, the most dangerous enemy of the Third
World is liberalism and the glamorization of countries in
which the oppressed have become the oppressors. Guerrillas
may invite comparison to Joseph Conrad's Nostromo. Set in
the mythical, exotic Latin American republic of Costaguana
from which the province Sulaco secedes, Conrad's novel also
touches on foreign interests in local exploits, race
relations (Blanc aristocrats and blacks), the ideals and
ulterior motives of the characters, most of whom are
Europeans, and, above all, Nostromo's vanity and passion for
the attention and endorsement of others. Although Naipaul
confessed that he had found Nostromo impenetrable, with "a
confusion of characters and themes," which he "couldn't get
through at all,"[88] his vision in Guerrillas seems to be
the same as that which he saw in Conrad's novel: "a vision
of the world's half-made societies as places which continuously made and unmade themselves, where there was no
goal."[89] The epigraph to Guerrillas, uttered by Jimmy
himself, captures the theme: "When everybody wants to fight
there's nothing to fight for. Everybody wants to fight his
own little war, everybody is a guerrilla."

Western reviewers have given Naipaul the highest rating
for <u>Guerrillas,</u> but they are divided about matters of character interpretation and point of view. To the anonymous
writer in the <u>Yale Review</u> and to Kerry McSweeney, the major
characters--Roche, Jane and Jimmy--are depicted as hollow,
limited and belittled, whereas Mededith appears to have some
substance and authorial sanction.[90] The consensus among
critics is that Jane is the most repulsive character in all
of Naipaul, and although a few readers have seen in Jimmy
the author's touch of tenderness and an attempt to explain
his behavior, they have agreed that he is a pretentious,
"pathetic pervert."[91] Such concurrence cannot be reached
on Roche's character. Peter Ackroyd and Benjamin DeMott
interpreted Roche as one who lacks an inner core, profound
insight, and selfless motivation, but Michael Thorpe and
Patrick Parrinder identified him as a character whose ideas
tally most with the author's.[92] Striking a compromise
between the two disparate readings, Johannes Riis contended
that Roche started out with good intentions but soon found
himself enmeshed in a dangerous game from which he could not
be extricated.[93] Not much different from this view is
Francis Wyndham's argument that Roche remains a "shadowy
figure" with his motives obscured until the interview, when
he is forced into admitting that his involvement with Jimmy
derived from some type of physical shame.[94] It has been
suggested that the heterogeneous readings of <u>Guerrillas</u> are
due primarily to Naipaul's use of a "'polyphonic' narrative
technique: the point of view changes constantly among the
main characters."[95] Indeed, some readers have complained
about the shift in point of view and about authorial
pressure, which denies the characters the autonomy to choose
their own destinies.[96]

Apart from these differences of opinions and minor
reservations, however, <u>Guerrillas</u> gained Naipaul a much
coveted American readership.[97] Noting that the use of
hitherto taboo elements--violence, race, sex, and white
characters--may have given <u>Guerrillas</u> a boost, Elaine
Campbell suggested that the novel attracted American readers
primarily because it is read, or rather misread, as a
document denouncing guerrilla warfare in the Caribbean.[98]
Many readers attributed the particular distinction to the
excellent dramatic study of the psychological motivations of
the characters.[99] Robert Hamner asserted that the book
"reinforces Naipaul's reputation as one of the finest
novelists now writing in English," and Paul Gray claimed
that the writer again "proves himself the laureate of the
West Indies."[100] Several critics noted that Naipaul is
aptly qualified to handle the West Indian Black Power
Movement and race tension, about which he writes <u>without</u>
"condescension," "contempt," "irresponsibility," or
"bitterness"--and with "accuracy."[101]

274

In the West Indies, however, where reaction ranges from indifference to condemnation, there is a debate about Naipaul's perception of the social and political status of the region. Many readers are convinced that, apart from the obvious parallelism between Michael de Freitas and Jimmy Ahmed, the novel draws heavily from the Trinidadian Black Power Movement, from its followers who were dubbed "guerrillas," and from the aborted mutiny of the army in the 1970's.[102] Because West Indian readers have lived through this experience it is natural that they would be more inclined to pay closer attention and make judgments about Naipaul's politics. The Trinidad Guardian hailed the novel as "compelling, vivid, full of suspense"; so does the Jamaican Gleaner: "Naipaul accurately, vividly and bitingly holds up to us many of our foibles both Caribbean and world widely human."[103] However, George R. John, a persistent defender of Naipaul, made a passing reference to Guerrillas as "Naipaul's worst book," a view shared by Selwyn R. Cudjoe.[104] And Elizabeth Nunez-Harrell pointed to the novel as evidence of Naipaul's "lack of concern for telling the whole truth [which] has alienated West Indian audiences who look to the artist for a mirror, image, perhaps a utopian one of their society."[105] Asked specifically if he agreed with readers who felt that the novel lacked truth because it was written from a distance, Wayne Brown replied:

> The nationalist lash has always struck me as a brutish, a boorish response to Naipaul's work. But yet, there comes a time when it must be permissible when it may be necessary to throw up your hands and say 'But it is not like that!'
> Every writer has the right to exorcise his demons, to write his nightmare out of existence. But to present a subjective terror as an objective and representative truth--that is something else.[106]

Brown noted that it is dangerous for exile artists who have been abroad for a long period to write about contemporary events at home. He complained: "I don't like the results, where I see them . . . I didn't like 'Guerrillas' at all."[107]

Some West Indians who admit that Guerrillas does contain elements of truth still reiterate the familiar charges made against Naipaul's other Caribbean books. Raoul Pantin, the reviewer for the popular regional monthly, The Caribbean Contact, noted that the novel contains "flashes of truth of Trinidad," but he read the work as indicative of the "deepening sense of personal distress, of private desolation, that Naipaul feels." Referring to the "now predictable Naipaul view of these islands," Pantin also faulted Naipaul's repetition of themes from previous works:

> Readers who come to the novel expecting to learn
> something, to get some insight into those scattered
> young Trinidadians who two years ago the Press
> named "guerrillas," and most of whom have since
> been massacred in "shootouts" with the police, will
> be disappointed. . . . In the sense that Naipaul
> repeats. . . [his] savage attacks on the society
> that weaned him (and obviously the physical and
> moral deterioration of the society pains him), the
> novel contains nothing new. What "Guerrillas" does
> contain is a private desolation, an emptiness that
> produces insane action and almost irretrievable
> despair. . . . Naipaul tries very hard to say
> almost everything. But everything is clouded.[108]

Admittedly, _Guerrillas_ is a fictionalized treatment of the
subject matter already handled in "Power?" and "The
Killings." However, as the British critic Michael Thorpe
observed, while the novel develops common Naipaulian themes,
"our apprehension of them is deepened by the multiplicity of
viewpoints and lives presented."[109] The non-fictional
accounts are skeletal forms with no allowances for character
exploration. In addition, even though the subject is no
longer current (another criticism of the book), Naipaul, by
broadening and universalizing the theme, intimates that the
potential of a repetition of the explosion of the 1970's is
still there as long as people are swept up by self-
deception. Pantin predicted that West Indian readers will
accuse Naipaul of oversimplification of the Black Power
Movement and of deliberately distorting the "reality of life
in these lands to pander to the prejudices of his largely
foreign, white audience."[110]

Guerrillas has indeed brought the race issue once more
to the forefront. Maureen Warner-Lewis, who, incidentally,
mentioned Naipaul's "accuracy and sureness of detail,"
objected to the portrayal of blacks:

> Naipaul continues to lose no opportunity to refer
> to or describe blacks in the most repulsive of
> terms. It strikes me as one among several matters
> over which Naipaul shows a perversity of
> character. Like so many of this own fictional
> characters, he insists on speaking of certain
> things in a way which he knows to be irritating.
> In his characters, he depicts the satisfaction of
> hurting as a negative compensation for the pain of
> being misunderstood and the longing for sympathy.
> The vicious circle is created by the hostility of
> those who find themselves persecuted and maligned,
> by an apparently arrogant individual. It seems to
> me that Naipaul may very well resemble these
> perversely arrogant characters he creates so well.

> Certainly some aspects of <u>The Guerrillas</u> [sic] will
> perpetuate his uneasy relationship with his West
> Indian audience.[111]

Anthony Boxill, referring to Warner-Lewis's criticism,
acknowledged that it is "possible that black critics have a
point when they claim that black characters are made to
appear uglier, smellier, and more stupid than people of
other races in his books," and that it is "even possible
that Naipaul does not like black people." However, Boxill
went on to wonder whether the negative portrayal of blacks
may be intended to "shock them out of the complacency of
their mimic lives." What Boxill emphasized is that many of
Naipaul's portraits of whites and Indians are also "far from
flattering" and that although all his characters are physically and morally unattractive and although their actions are
"mimic and depraved," they are presented as human beings,
capable of good, and worthy of respect and dignity as they
struggle to survive in a "difficult and bewildering
world."[112] Warner-Lewis did not elaborate on Naipaul's
attitude towards the white characters, Jane and Roche, whose
intellectual weakness is heightened by Naipaul's use of
uncomfortable and unpleasant images to describe them. Roche
is unattractive with his ugly molars, "widely spaced,
blackened at the roots, the gums high: like a glimpse of a
skull." Jane, unquestionably far more repulsive than Jimmy,
is revoltingly described in both sex scenes: her "red, aged
skin below her neck" looks "like a rash," her blouses are
always wet with odorous perspiration (Jimmy finds himself
uncomfortably trapped under her wet arm), her posture and
manners are "masculine," and her unnatural response when
Jimmy spits in her mouth is to say "'that was lovely.'" The
only conclusion that can be safely made, then, is that
Naipaul's characters--of all shades--are far from perfect
and are wracked with some type of personal disturbance.
Certainly, the indictment in <u>Guerrillas</u> is specifically
against white liberals who "made" Jimmy into the type of
person he has become, and the novel ends, as Kenneth
Ramchand noted, with a "reaffirmation in more sinister terms
of the pact between White Liberal and Black leader."[113]

West Indian response to <u>Guerrillas</u> is by no means
confined to mere complaints about Naipaul's socio-political
perception and the depiction of blacks. Kenneth Ramchand
contended that Naipaul "stumbled" in the novel because he
attempted a kind of fiction too akin to journalism and
because he reversed his stance expressed in the Foreword in
<u>The Middle Passage</u>, that is, that the "novelist works
towards conclusions of which he is often unaware." To
Ramchand the characters lack "development and spontaneity":
"they are established and fixed from their first entry
because what they exemplify is more to the author's point
than what they may be. . . . <u>Guerrillas</u> is strictly

designed to express ideas about society and human possibilities that Naipaul has worked out beforehand."[114] Anthony Boxill, on the other hand, expressed no such concern as he examined the interior monologues of Jane and Roche, and the fantasies of Jimmy for clues about the psychological problems with cause misunderstanding among the principal characters.[115] Victor Ramraj in his article subtitled "The Irrelevance of Nationalism," also argued that Naipaul is mainly occupied with the psychological exploration of his characters. Ramraj contended that although the writer captures the political mood of the Caribbean and depicts politicians, he "never hobbles himself with issues of Nationalism" or addresses politics as such:

> [Naipaul] does not concern himself with the virtues or limitations of political creeds. . . he does not reduce his characters to mouthpieces for particular ideologies. . . he does not focus on the corridors or intrigues of power. . . . What he provides is a profoundly insightful and understanding study of Jimmy Ahmed . . . . In accounting for Jimmy Adhmed's behaviour. . . Naipaul takes pains to show the influence of factors other than politics. . . the novel is a profound study of a confused and troubled individual and not a political commentary. . . . There is no authorial conception of Jimmy simply as a political creature who is adjudged politically . . . . Jane and Jimmy are not reduced to political or national mouthpieces or symbols; they remain complex human individuals.[116]

Repeating an assertion he had made earlier that Naipaul's non-fiction has had much to do with his reputation as a political writer who makes "unremittingly harsh comments on the Third World," Ramraj recommended that readers maintain a clear distinction between Naipaul the novelist and Naipaul the journalist. Such a distinction has been difficult for readers to make, especially since--as Ramraj himself acknowledged--"novelists' non-fiction pieces do often complement and illuminate their fictional efforts."[117]

This chapter has shown that the unpopular and provocative ideas in Naipaul's later Caribbean fiction has also tantalizingly invited hostility from West Indian readers. In these works Naipaul continued the same somber note of his non-fiction, mirroring the theme of colonial rootlessness; the psyche of the colonial mimic man and politician; the predicament of small, emergent nations; the insignificance of political independence for the colonies and their continued dependence on the West; and the absurdity and futility of messianic and imported protest movements.

Notes

¹ Gerald Guinness, "Naipaul's Four Early Trinidadian Novels," Revista/Review Interamerica, 6, No. 4 (Winter 1976-77), 564.

² John Rothfork, "V. S. Naipaul and the Third World," Research Studies, 49, No. 3 (Sept. 1981), 183.

³ Irving Howe, "A Dark Vision," rev. of A Bend in the River, New York Times Book Review, 13 May 1979, p. 1; Richard Freedman, "Three by Naipaul," Book World (Washington Post), 10 Oct. 1976, p. E5.

⁴ Israel Shenker, "V. S. Naipaul" (Interview), in Critical Perspectives on V. S. Naipaul, ed. Robert D. Hamner (Washington, D.C.: Three Continents Press, 1977), p. 53.

⁵ Adrian Rowe-Evans, "The Writer as Colonial" (Interview), Quest, 78 (Sept.-Oct. 1972), 48.

⁶ Cathleen Medwick, "Life, Literature and Politics: An Interview with V. S. Naipaul," Vogue, 171 (Aug. 1981), 130.

⁷ Selwyn Cudjoe, "Trying to Understand Naipaul," Sunday Express (Trinidad), 30 May 1982, p. 41.

⁸ The Mimic Men (London; André Deutsch, 1967; rpt. New York Penguin Books, 1981). All references to this work will be from this edition and will be indicated in the text.

⁹ Francis Wyndham, "Writing is Magic," (Interview), Trinidad Guardian, 15 Nov. 1968, p. 12.

¹⁰ Patrick Parrinder, "V. S. Naipaul and the Uses of Literacy," Critical Quarterly, 21, No. 2 (Summer 1979), 6, noted that Singh's exaltation was also probably shared by many of Naipaul's contemporaries.

¹¹ Ian Hamilton, "Without a Place" (Interview with V. S. Naipaul), in Critical Perspectives, ed. Robert D. Hamner, p. 40; Raoul Pantin, "Portrait of an Artist," Caribbean Contact, 1, No. 6 (May 1973), 18.

¹² "Naipaul's Third World," Journal of Commonwealth Literature, 10 (Aug. 1975), 16.

¹³ "Excess of Skill," rev. of The Mimic Men, New World Quarterly, 1, No. 1 (1969), 35.

280

Gerald Moore, rev. of <u>The Mimic Men</u>, <u>Bim</u> (Barbados), 12, No. 46 (Jan.-June 1968), 134; Eric Roach, "As Naipaul Sees Us," rev. of <u>The Mimic Men</u>, <u>Trinidad Guardian</u>, 15 May 1967, p. 7.

¹⁵ "Suburbia in the Sun," rev. of <u>The Mimic Men</u>, <u>Times Literary Supplement</u>, 27 April 1967, p. 349.

¹⁶ "V. S. Naipaul and the New Order," rev. of <u>The Mimic Men</u>, <u>Kenyon Review</u>, 29 (Nov. 1967), 690.

¹⁷ Wyndham, "Writing is Magic," p. 12.

¹⁸ Bharati Mukherjee and Robert Boyers, "Conversation with V. S. Naipaul," <u>Salmagundi</u>, 54 (Fall 1981), 21.

¹⁹ <u>V. S. Naipaul</u> (New York: Twayne Inc., 1973), p. 98.

²⁰ "Voice in V. S. Naipaul's Fiction," Item 117, MLA Convention, New York, 28 Dec. 1983.

²¹ See, for example, S. Waiyaki, "V. S. Naipaul and the West Indian Situation," <u>Busara</u>, 5, No. 1 (1973), 74.

²² <u>V. S. Naipaul</u> (London: The British Council/ Longmans, 1976), p. 27.

²³ <u>V. S. Naipaul</u> (London: MacMillan Press, 1975), pp. 157-59.

²⁴ Sara Blackburn, "Book Marks," rev. of <u>The Mimic Men</u>, <u>Nation</u>, 9 Oct. 1967, p. 348; Karl Miller, "Naipaul's Emergent Country," rev. of <u>A Flag on the Island</u>, <u>Listener</u>, 28 Sept. 1967, p. 402.

²⁵ "V. S. Naipaul's Negative Sense of Place," <u>Journal of Commonwealth Literature</u>, 10, No. 1 (Aug. 1975), 26.

²⁶ Richard Boston, "Caribbean and Aegean," rev. of <u>The Mimic Men</u>, <u>The Times</u> (London), 27 April 1967, p. 16; R. G. G. Price, rev. of <u>The Mimic Men</u>, <u>Punch</u>, 10 May 1967, p. 696.

²⁷ Blackburn, pp. 347-48.

²⁸ See, for example, V. S. Pritchett, "Crack-Up," rev. of <u>The Mimic Men</u>, <u>New York Review of Books</u>, 11 April 1968, p. 10; Martin Seymour-Smith, "Exile's Story," rev. of <u>The Mimic Men</u>, <u>Spectator</u>, 5 May 1967, p. 528; Richard Plant, "Caribbean Seesaw," rev. of <u>The Mimic Men</u>, <u>Saturday Review</u>, 23 Dec. 1967, p. 32; and Robert K. Morris, <u>Paradoxes of Order</u> (Columbia, Missouri: University of Missouri Press, 1975), p. 60.

29 V. S. Pritchett, "Crack-Up," pp. 13-14; Wain, "Trouble in the Family," p. 34. See also Boston, p. 16 and Saul Maloff, rev. of The Mimic Men, 15 Oct. 1967, p. 55.

30 "Crack-Up," p. 13.

31 Boston, p. 16.

32 Bruce King, The New English Literatures (New York: St. Martin's Press, 1980), p. 105.

33 Parrinder, p. 10.

34 "Naipaul's Emergent Country," p. 402. See also Agnus Wilson, "Between Two Islands," rev. of The Mimic Men, London Sunday Observer, 30 April 1967, p. 27.

35 Miller, "V. S. Naipaul and the New Order," p. 690.

36 M. M. Mahood, The Colonial Encounter (New Jersey: Rowman and Littlefield, 1977), pp. 159-60.

37 "Excess of Skill," pp. 34-38.

38 "Naipaul's Technique as a Novelist," Journal of Commonwealth Literature, 7 (July 1969), 43. Carr, "Excess of Skill," p. 36, quoted some of Naipaul's cynical statements in The Middle Passage and An Area of Darkness to show continuity of the same thinking in The Mimic Men.

39 Rev. of The Mimic Men, p. 134.

40 "The Trauma of Naipauland," Trinidad Guardian, 24 Sept. 1967, p. 16.

41 "'The Mimic Men,'" New World Quarterly, 4, No. 4 (1968), 55.

42 "'The Mimic Men,'" p. 57.

43 "The Snow Virgin," Caribbean Quarterly, 23, Nos. 2 & 3 (Jan.-June 1977), 31.

44 "As Naipaul Sees Us," rev. of The Mimic Men, Trinidad Guardian, 17 May 1967, p. 9.

45 Ulric Mentus, "Is There Something Called Black Art?" Caribbean Contact, 3, No. 11 (Feb. 1976), 7.

46 As quoted by Gordon Rohlehr, "History as Absurdity," in Is Massa Day Dead?" ed. Orde Coombs (New York: Anchor Press, 1974), p. 101.

Rohlehr, "History as Absurdity," p. 103.

Cudjoe, p. 51.

"Excess of Skill," p. 37.

Marjorie Thorpe, p. 58.

"The All-Embracing Christlike Vision," in _Critical Perspectives_, ed. Robert Hamner, pp. 134-35.

"The Little Bastard Worlds of V. S. Naipaul's _The Mimic Men_ and _A Flag on the Island_," _International Fiction Review_, 3, No. 1 (Jan. 1976), 129-41.

A Flag on the Island (Harmondsworth: Penguin Books, 1967; rpt. New York: Penguin Books, 1982). All references to this work will be from this edition and will be indicated in the text.

"London," in _The Overcrowded Barraccoon_ (London: André Deutsch, 1972; rpt. New York: Penguin Books, 1976), pp. 12-13.

V. S. Naipaul, p. 63.

"Naipaul's Emergent Country," p. 403.

"Movietone," rev. of _A Flag on the Island_, _Times Literary Supplement_, 14 Sept. 1967, p. 813; Desmond Mac Namara, rev. of _A Flag_, _New Statesman_, 15 Sept. 1967, p. 325; Raymond G. McInnis, rev. of _A Flag_, _Library Journal_, 1 March 1969, p. 1021. For similar words of praise, see also Hamner, _V. S. Naipaul_, p. 64 and Pamela Marsh, "Fiction Concentrate," rev. of _A Flag_, _Christian Science Monitor_, 29 March 1968, p. 13.

See, for example, Karl Miller, "Naipaul's Emergent Country," p. 403; Paul Barker, rev. of _A Flag_, _The Times_ (London), 14 Sept. 1967, p. 11.

R. G. G. Price, rev. of _A Flag_, _Punch_, 27 Sept. 1967, p. 484; Richard Plant, "Potpourri of the Antilles," rev. of _A Flag_, _Saturday Review_, 8 June 1968, p. 52; rev. of _A Flag_, _Publishers' Weekly_, 15 Jan. 1968, p. 83.

Rev. of _A Flag_, _Kirkus_, 1 Jan. 1968, p. 25; John Wain, "Characters in the Sun," rev. of _A Flag_, _New York Times Book Review_, 7 April 1968, p. 4.

Wain, "Characters in the Sun," p. 4.

White, pp. 140-41.

63 George Panton, "West Indian Satirist," rev. of A Flag, Sunday Gleaner (Jamaica), 3 Dec. 1967, p. 4.

64 Boxill, "The Little Bastard Worlds," p. 15.

65 Boxill, "The Little Bastard Worlds," pp. 13-15.

66 "Partial Truths," Unpublished Manuscript, n.d.

67 An Area of Darkness (London: André Deutsch, 1964; rpt. New York: Vintage Books, 1981), pp. 29-30.

68 R. G. G. Price, rev. of A Flag, p. 484.

69 "A Christmas Story" is discussed in Chapter IV.

70 Marsh, "Fiction Concentrate," p. 13; "Movietone," p. 813; John Wain, "Characters in the Sun," p. 4; Raymond McInnis, rev. of A Flag, p. 1021; Paul Barker, rev. of A Flag, p. 11; Desmond MacNamara, rev. of A Flag, p. 325; rev. of A Flag, Publishers' Weekly, 15 Jan. 1968, p. 83.

71 Omerod, "In a Derelict Land," in Critical Perspectives, ed. Robert Hamner, p. 169.

72 "Potpourri of the Antilles," Saturday Review, 8 June 1968, p. 52.

73 George Panton, "West Indian Satirist," p. 4.

74 Guerrillas (London: Andre Deutsch, 1975; rpt. New York: Vintage Books, 1980). All references to this work will be from this edition and will be indicated in the text.

75 Author's Note to The Return of Eva Peron with The Killings in Trinidad (New York: Alfred Knopf, 1980; rpt. New York: Vintage Books, 1981).

76 "From the Third World," rev. of The Return of Eva Peron, New York Times Book Review, 13 April, 1980, p. 1.

77 Peter Murray, "Guerrillas: A Prefatory Note," Journal of Commonwealth Literature, 14, No. 1 (Aug. 1979), 88.

78 Rev. of Guerrillas, The Yale Review, 65 (Spring 1976), XV; Peter Ackroyd, "On Heat," rev. of Guerrillas, Spectator, 13 Sept. 1975, p. 350. See also John Spurling, "The Novelist as Dictator," rev. of Guerrillas, Encounter, Dec. 1975, p. 74; Michael Thorpe, "Naipaul Again," rev. of Guerrillas, The Literary Half-Yearly, 17, No. 1 (Jan. 1976), 124; Paul Theroux, "An Intelligence from the Third World," rev. of Guerrillas, New York Times Book Review, 16 Nov. 1975, p. 1.

79 Rev. of <u>Guerrillas</u>, <u>Yale Review</u>, pp. XIV-V.

80 "V. S. Naipaul: The Irrelevance of Nationalism," <u>World Literature Written in English</u>, 23, No. 1 (1984), 192.

81 Francis Wyndham, "Services Rendered," rev. of <u>Guerrillas</u>, <u>New Statesman</u>, 19 Sept. 1975, p. 339.

82 "Naipaul's Woodlanders," <u>Journal of Commonwealth Literature</u>, 14, No. 1 (Aug. 1979), 111.

83 Mukherjee and Boyers, p. 16.

84 Michael Thorpe, rev. of <u>Guerrillas</u>, p. 126.

85 Mukherjee and Boyers, p. 16. See also Mel Gussow, "Writer Without Roots," <u>New York Times Magazine</u>, 26 Dec. 1976, p. 22.

86 Riis, p. 110.

87 "V. S. Naipaul in Paris," <u>Manchester Guardian</u>, 26 July 1981, p. 13.

88 "Conrad's Darkness," in <u>The Return of Eva Peron</u>, p. 229.

89 "Conrad's Darkness," p. 233.

90 Rev. of <u>Guerrillas</u>, <u>Yale Review</u>, pp. XIV-V; McSweeney, p. 76; Riis, p. 114.

91 Rev. of <u>Guerrillas</u>, <u>Yale Review</u>, pp. XIV-V; D. A. N. Jones, "Little Warriors in Search of War," rev. of <u>Guerrillas</u>, <u>Times Literary Supplement</u>, 12 Sept. 1975, p. 1013; Wyndham, "Services Rendered," p. 339.

92 Peter Ackroyd, "On Heat," p. 350; Benjamin DeMott, "Lost Words, Lost Heroes," rev. of <u>Guerrillas</u>, <u>Saturday Review</u>, 15 Nov. 1975, p. 24; Michael Thorpe, "Naipaul Again," p. 125; Parrinder, p. 12.

93 Riis, p. 112.

94 Wyndham, "Services Rendered," p. 339.

95 Riis, p. 110.

96 McSweeney, p. 78; Robert Boyers, "V. S. Naipaul," <u>The American Scholar</u>, 50 (Summer 1981), 363. Spurling, p. 76; Anatole Broyard, "The Author vs. His Characters," rev. of <u>Guerrillas</u>, <u>New York Times</u>, 25 Nov. 1975, p. 39.

[97] Mel Gussow, "Writer Without Roots," p. 19. Naipaul has claimed that _Guerrillas_ lost him half his following in England, see Mukherjee and Boyers, p. 16.

[98] "A Refinement of Rage," _World Literature Written in English_, 18, No. 2 (Nov. 1979), 394-95. See also, John L. Brown, "V. S. Naipaul," _World Literature Today_, 57, No. 2 (Spring 1983), 226.

[99] Robert D. Hamner, rev. of _Guerrillas_, _Library Journal_, 1 Oct. 1975, p. 1846.

[100] Hamner, rev. of _Guerrillas_, p. 1846; Paul Gray, "Burnt-Out Cases," rev. of _Guerrillas_, _Time_, 1 Dec. 1975, p. 84.

[101] DeMott, "Lost Words," p. 23; Michael Thorpe, "Naipaul Again," p. 125; Gray, "Burnt-Out Cases," p. 86; Joseph Epstein, "Nowhere Men," rev. of _Guerrillas_, _Book World_ (_Washington Post_), 16 Nov. 1975, p. Ell; rev. of _Guerrillas_, _New Yorker_, 22 Dec. 1975, p. 95.

[102] Ramchand, "Partial Truths," p. 16; Raoul Pantin, "The Wasteland of Naipaul," rev. of _Guerrillas_, _Caribbean Contact_, 3, No. 8 (Nov. 1975), 3. Pantin even identified the opening landscape in _Guerrillas_ as Trinidad's Beetham Highway.

[103] Vishnu R. Gosine, "Shades of Abdul Malik in Naipaul's _Guerrillas_," rev. of _Guerrillas_, _Trinidad Guardian_, 3 Oct. 1975, p. 4; "West Indian Guerrillas," rev. of _Guerrillas_, _Sunday Gleaner_ (Jamaica), 23 Nov. 1975, p. 23.

[104] George R. John, "In Defense of Naipaul," _Trinidad Guardian_, 22 Aug. 1982, p. 8; Selwyn R. Cudjoe, "Revolutionary Struggle and the Novel," _Caribbean Quarterly_, 24, No. 4 (Dec. 1979), 9.

[105] "Lamming and Naipaul," _Contemporary Literature_, 19, No. 1 (1978), 33.

[106] "Why Wayne Brown Chose Edna Manley," _Trinidad Guardian_, 11 Jan. 1976, p. 10.

[107] "Why Wayne Brown Chose Edna Manley," p. 10.

[108] "The Wasteland of Naipaul," pp. 3, 8; see also Cudjoe, "Revolutionary Struggle and the Novel," pp. 9-11.

[109] Thorpe, rev. of _Guerrillas_, p. 126.

[110] "The Wasteland of Naipaul," p. 3.

111 Rev. of _Guerrillas_, _Caribbean Quarterly_, 23, Nos. 2 & 3 (June-Sept. 1977), 105. The same charge has been made in connection with Naipaul's story "One Out of Many" in _In a Free State_. Eric Roach, "Merciless in Aim for Perfection," _Trinidad Guardian_, 30 Dec. 1971, p. 7, charged that Naipaul's "fastidious Brahmin nose sniffs everywhere; the 'hushbi' [blacks] smell. They are their surroundings are squalid and odorous in Africa as in America."

112 _V. S. Naipaul's Fiction_ (Canada: York Press, 1983), pp. 82-83.

113 "Partial Truths," p. 17.

114 "Partial Truths," pp. 21-24.

115 _V. S. Naipaul's Fiction_, pp. 66-71.

116 "The Irrelevance of Nationalism," pp. 190-95.

117 "The Irrelevance of Nationalism," pp. 191-92; Ramraj, "Diminishing Satire," in _Awakened Conscience_, ed. C. D. Narasimhaiah (New Delhi: Sterling Publishers Pvt. Ltd., 1978), p. 262.

Conclusion

Much of Naipaul's notoriety is a matter of gossip rather than informed opinion; some people have hastily and emotionally formed their opinion despite their confession that their knowledge of his works is limited or that his books are "difficult."[1] George R. John reported two interesting incidents involving this type of response:

> I remember some 10 years ago, the late Prime Minister, Dr. Eric Williams, telling me that Naipaul had done considerable harm to the relations between India and this country [Trinidad]. He had been talking about "Area of Darkness". . . . But he provided no supporting evidence for his claim.
>
> Two or three years ago, an Indian diplomat resident in Port-of-Spain launched into a vitriolic attack against Naipaul. He followed it up by asking me to lend him "Area of Darkness" (clearly he had not yet read it) and returned it to me sometime after without comment.[2]

John, quoting from one of Ivan Van Sertima's public lectures denouncing Naipaul, advised that the "professor like the Indian diplomat, needs to read Naipaul before he speaks again about him."[3] Popular opinion aside, however, Naipaul has been challenged by serious readers, qualified and competent critics, conversant with his works and familiar with the Caribbean.

All responses cannot be attributed entirely to, in John's words, "pen-envy," nor can they be oversimplified on the issue of racial prejudice against an East Indian writer.[4] And they cannot even be explained by Naipaul's captious judgments (other critics—C. L. R. James, for example—have not met so much hostility) or by his choice of exile (other emigrés—Lamming, for instance—are well received). What is it, then, that causes Naipaul's detractors, many West Indians, to tag him at one time or another as a snob, a racist, a "brown sahib," an anti-nationalist, a neo-colonial apologist with a "mercenary instinct," an Anglophile, a "Quintessential mimic man," and, above all the _gunga din_, wild beast, of Caribbean literature?[5]

One of the most frequently uttered allegations is that Naipaul is selective in his attacks; that is, he is quick to call attention to the shortcomings in undeveloped countries but not in developed ones. In an interview with Robert Boyers and Bharati Mukherjee, Naipaul, after having referred to Indians as "stupid," is directly confronted on this issue. His response may surprise some of his Caribbean readers who have charged that he is an Anglophile:

> BM: But why haven't you applied this kind of soul-searching and possible breakthrough of insight to British society, too? You haven't really dealt with England except in the early novel [Mr Stone], have you?
> VSN: That's right.
> BM: And if you were to turn your whole intellectual machinery on the English, would they also be likely to come up seeming incredibly stupid?
> VSN: They are in trouble. And it's the trouble that comes to every country that has really been tremendously successful. . . . Great vanity can set in when a people are so successful. They begin to believe in racial magic, and finally exalt the form rather than the substance . . . . A great success begins to breed a kind of corrupting vanity.[6]

Naipaul has also been credited with saying that England is a country of "second-rate people--bum politicians, scruffy writers and crooked aristocrats."[7] He has indicted the British for their attitude towards the period of slavery: "The British . . . reduce the history of slavery not to the horrors extending over a couple of hundred years, but to the few years of the fight to abolish it."[8] In America he sees a problem of vanity as well, and he has complained about the attitude of some elite American students: "The students I have met think that they, by being Americans and well-to-do, bring privilege to what they touch. This vanity is becoming an empty caste arrogance. Ignorant people in preppy clothes are more dangerous to America than oil embargoes."[9] Eugene Goodheart has observed that nothing pleases Naipaul:

> What is disturbing, but essential to an understanding of Naipaul's work, is that all the alternatives are negative. He is scornful of the inefficiency and sloppiness of Trinidad society (its backwardness), yet he is also contemptuous of its Americanization. . . . It is hard to imagine anything that would satisfy Naipaul.[10]

Apart from his argument that a writer is better off if he comes from an "ordered," "organized" society with a tradition, Naipaul promulgates no Euro-centered, pro-Western theory, and he has, as Michael Thorpe noticed, treated "white norms also with an even-handed scepticism."[11]

Much of the hostility that Naipaul has generated in the West Indies could, perhaps, be attributed simply to his

stringent standards and peevish manner. He not only doles
out cynicism and prophesies despair but he also does so in a
brusque way which offends readers. If, for example, West
Indians accept Naipaul's diagnosis, what are they to do to
remedy the situation? When pressed for answers, Naipaul has
spoken evasively of the value of education, an attitude
which has exasperated critics such as Gordon Rohlehr:

> What comes out of Naipaul most of the time is that
> it doesn't seem to be any point trying to solve the
> situation. It is only after a lot of questioning
> that one gets some statement from him about the
> necessity for education. And by education he
> clearly means the kind of thing which has happened
> to him. . . but the relevance of that kind of
> education to the West Indian situation he hasn't
> really demonstrated.[12]

Perhaps no clear-cut answers can be wrested from Naipaul
because he has none. Certainly, his attitude suggests that
readers should not demand any from him. He identifies
problems but does not solve them. While Caribbean readers
find his criticisms discomfiting and would like for him to
focus on the good aspects of their society too, they are
more irritated by, in the words of Trinidad's former
Minister of External Affairs, his "cruel disdain and
scorn."[13] Some readers are restrained and disciplined
enough to ignore Naipaul's attitude and concentrate on his
ideas; for example, Selwyn Cudjoe has written: "[Naipaul]
may even have become an unsalvageable intellectual snob who
looks down at his people with superciliousness, contempt and
callous indifference. But these limitations should not
detract us from giving serious consideration to what he has
had to say, for paradoxically as it may seem, it is the
duality of vision which inheres in his perception of our
reality that allows for both his strengths and weaknesses."[14]

Naipaul's admirers, mostly Western, generally appear not
to be troubled by his personality. To them, what he says is
far more important than how he says it. Kerry McSweeney,
who noted that Naipaul's fastidiousness is a mixed blessing,
recommended more emphasis on Naipaul's form and technique:
"If Naipaul is as distinguished a novelist as he is often
said to be, his work should be assessed by less provincial
and less content-oriented criteria than those invoked by
some Commonwealth literature critics, and by standards more
sophisticated and less impressionistic than the presence or
absence of warm human sympathy or the degree of political
commitment."[15] And Patrick Parrinder contended that
"accusations of misanthrophy are beside the point, since the
self-delusions and perversities that Naipaul describes
really exist."[16] To a number of readers outside the
Caribbean, he is "beyond partisanship"; he eschews the

"placebos of more optimistic commentators" and instead prefers "caustic appraisals," which could prove more "therapeutic"; he refuses to be coerced into "compromising his own aesthetic ideals out of homage to a revered, but dead, tradition"; he is not afraid to address the "inequality, the despotism, and the climate of cruelty" in poor countries, which liberals close their eyes to; and, above all, he writes not for whites, but for "everyone and nobody."[17]

Naipaul, too, has absolved himself of affiliation to any particular ideology. Whether he is honest with himself or not, he has stated that a good writer does not know what kind of vision he has, that he himself never had any ideas about Left or Right (a demarcation which results in a "distorted view of the world"), and that he does not try to fit what he sees into a pattern to suit any political dogma.[18] Asked whether he is not afraid of being called a reactionary, he replied, "I am used to that sort of criticism. I don't think about it anymore. In any case, nobody listens. That's what protects me."[19] And although Naipaul's readership in the United States is small compared to that in England--reasons often cited for this difference include lack of American interest in the West Indian scene, his exotic background, his seriousness and austerity[20] --his British reputation as one of the finest post-war writers in English is firmly established.[21]

To many West Indians this evaluation is grossly exaggerated. One critic, for example, reviewing Paul Theroux's appreciative book on Naipaul, charged: "Naipaul is perfect as far as the writer is concerned. . . . Theroux is a non-West Indian, unaware of us and perhaps unconcerned with our very existence, who looks at Naipaul from the point of view of the Western non-African world. That, of course, is the way in which most readers of Naipaul will look at his writings and the way, no doubt, that Naipaul would have it."[22] What is apparent from this review and from many other West Indian criticisms of Naipaul is that Caribbean readers expect a different scale of values to be applied to the region, which they view as an underdog. Irving Howe, responding to protests from Jamaican Michael Thelwell about his appreciative review of Naipaul's A Bend in the River, raises the following questions:

> Suppose . . . Naipaul were to seek "signs of sickness and rot," not in Third World countries, but in the Western countries? Would Professor Thelwell still be so passionate in his attack? I think not. I'm reasonably sure he would then be celebrating Naipaul as a caustic critic of a decadent, indeed "historically irrelevant" society. . . . Professor Thelwell seems . . . to feel that it's a betrayal for a writer born in Trinidad to find in the Third World countries an abundance of

the inhumanity, injustice and cupidity that is
abundantly present everywhere else. . . .
    If we look at the brutalities associated with
Third World dictatorships, whether mere old-style
military or bespangled with "leftist" ornament . . .
we have the right to ask why should not this
historical phenomenon be as open to scathing
criticism as anything that our writers have
attacked in the West?[23]

The same questions may be put to West Indians readers of
Naipaul. Since they are the subject of Naipaul's incisive
criticism, they are more apt than are their Western
counterparts to respond in a sensitive way to Naipaul's
portrayal of their society. Physically and emotionally tied
to the region, they lack the objectivity that distance gives
the Westerner.
    From the inception of his career as a regional writer
who restricted himself to the comic portrayal of Trinidad's
East Indians, Naipaul has generally been subject more to
political than to literary judgments in the Caribbean.[24]
His critical acclaim in the region was at its height in the
early 1960's just after the completion of his first four
novels.[25] His non-fiction, which he seriously pursued
thereafter, earned him the reputation of a waspish writer
who roams the world in search of despair.[26] When he
returned to fiction set in the West Indies, he continued to
convey this gloom and pessimism in what appears as a
derisive and disdainful manner. In the later Caribbean
novels, he has provoked a general outburst of rage that
manifested itself in the repetition of a barrage of old
charges against him. It is a reaction received with cries
of protest from a few Naipaul admirers, who rally to the
writer's defense, and from some serious critics, who insist
on a more purely literary and more objective evaluation. At
the moment the dominant perception of Naipaul as a
mischievous prophet of doom remains.

Notes

1 Several letters from the public to the daily newspapers prove this point. See, for example, M. B., "Naipaul Angers a Reader," Express (Trinidad), 21 Dec. 1981, p. 5.

2 George R. John, "In Defense of Naipaul," p. 8.

3 George R. John, "In Defense of Naipaul," p. 8.

4 George R. John, "In Defense of Naipaul," p. 8; Mahabir Maharajh, "Failure to Understand Naipaul," Trinidad Guardian, 30 Aug. 1982, p. 8.

5 The list of references is endless, but see, for example, H. B. Singh, "V. S. Naipaul: A Spokesman for Neo-Colonialism," Literature and Ideology, 2 (Summer 1969), 71-85; Andrew Johnson, "Gunga Din of Caribbean Literature," Express (Trinidad), 3 July 1982.

6 Mukherjee and Boyers, pp. 14-15.

7 As quoted by Gussow, "Writer Without Roots," p. 18.

8 Shenkar, "V. S. Naipaul (Interview), p. 50.

9 As quoted by Phillis Rose, "Of Moral Bonds and Men," rev. of The Return of Eva Peron, Yale Review, 70, No. (Oct. 1980), 150.

10 "Naipaul and the Voices of Negation," Salmagundi, 54 (Fall 1981), 47-51.

11 Michael Thorpe, V. S. Naipaul, p. 35.

12 Lennox Grant, "Naipaul Joins the Chorus" (Interview with Gordon Rohlehr), Tapia (Trinidad), 6 July 1975, pp. 6-7.

13 As quoted by George R. John, "In Defense of Naipaul," p. 8.

14 Cudjoe, p. 41.

15 McSweeney, pp. 74-75.

16 Parrinder, p. 12.

294

17 Gussow, "Writer Without Roots," p. 19; Campbell, p. 405; Garebian, p. 34; Jack Beatty, rev. of The Return of Eva Peron, New Republic, 12 April 1980, p. 36; Colin Mac Innes, "Not Just of Today but Long Tomorrows," rev. of The Overcrowded Barracoon, Sunday Guardian (Trinidad), 12 Nov. 1972, p. 6.

18 Keith Hamish, "The Ridiculous Panic Behind Vidia Naipaul" (Interview), Trinidad Guardian, 29 Nov. 1973, p. 9; "The Novelist V. S. Naipaul Talks about his Work to Ronald Bryden," Listener, 22 March 1973, p. 369.

19 "V. S. Naipaul in Paris," p. 13.

20 Freedman, p. E5; Boyers, "V. S. Naipaul," p. 359; Harriet Blodgett, "Beyond Trinidad," South Atlantic Quarterly, 73 (Summer 1974), 88.

21 Miller, "Naipaul's Emergent Country," p. 402; J. H. Elliott, "Triste Trinidad, rev. of The Loss of El Dorado, New York Review of Books, 21 May 1970, p. 26; Ronald Bryden, "Between the Epics," rev. of The Loss of El Dorado, New Statesman, 7 Nov. 1969, p. 661. However, Naipaul's rising popularity in the United Sttes can be seen from the increasing attention paid to him in American periodicals. In November 1981 Naipaul appeared on the cover of Newsweek, and in the fall of the same year Salmagundi ran a frontpiece photograph of him and carried several articles on him. In Autumn 1984 Modern Fiction Studies (Purdue University) devoted a special issue on Naipaul.

22 C[edric] L[indo], "All about Naipaul," rev. of The Overcrowded Barraccoon and rev. of V. S. Naipaul, by Paul Theroux, Sunday Gleaner (Jamaica), 5 Nov. 1972, p. 39.

23 "Irving Howe Replies," letter, New York Times Book Review, 24 June 1979, p. 45.

24 Johnstone, p. 140; White, p. 11.

25 George R. John, "In Defense of Naipaul," p. 8; George Panton, "V. S. Naipaul," Sunday Gleaner (Jamaica), 22 June 1975, p. 23.

26 Gordon Rohlehr, "History as Absurdity," in "Is Massa Day Dead?" p. 104.

Appendix

Indian Response to Naipaul's Indian Books

India had in a special way been the background of my
childhood. It was the country from which my
grandfather came, a country never physically described
and therefore never real, a country out in the void
beyond the dot of Trinidad; and from it our journey had
been final. . . . The India . . . which was the
background of my childhood was an area of the
imagination. It was not the real country I presently
began to read about. . . . I became a nationalist;
even a book like Beverley Nichols's Verdict on India
could anger me. But this came almost at the end. The
next year India became independent; and I found my
interest was failing.[1]

So wrote V. S. Naipaul about the ancestral land from which
his grandfather had emigrated in the nineteenth century to
settle as an indentured laborer in Trinidad. Naipaul's
grandfather eventually returned to India, but he left behind
with his family a legacy of Indian village culture and
tradition which he and others like him brought from the
Gangetic plain and implanted on the island. The established
"miniature India" gradually yielded to some Creole
influence, but many people and household items from the old
country surrounded Naipaul, who grew up in a Brahmin
household. Thus, although West Indian by birth, Naipaul is
Indian by upbringing. An examination of this writer's
critical reception in his place of origin would be
incomplete, therefore, without the inclusion of some
discussion of Indian reaction to Naipaul's two Indian
books: An Area of Darkness (1963) and India: A Wounded
Civilization (1977).
    It must be pointed out that Indian response to Naipaul
is by no means limited to his Indian books. While The
Middle Passage, The Overcrowded Barraccoon, and The Loss of
El Dorado have generally passed unnoticed, a number of
Indian studies have been devoted to Naipaul's fiction. The
typical Naipaulian displaced and rootless characters
drifting in the changing West Indian scene have been
analyzed by such critics as Shyam Asnani and K. I.
Madhusudana Rao.[2] Prema Nandakumar has argued that Ganesh
Ramsamuir of The Mystic Masseur and Mohun Biswas of A House
for Mr Biswas are not caricatures as often thought, but
"recognizable creatures," while Satendra Nandan has praised

Naipaul for treating the experience of the immigrant Indian
in the West Indies.[3] Indian critics have also found
Naipaul a fertile ground for comparative studies as
evidenced by M. K. Naik's article on Naipaul and Narayan; by
D. V. K. Raghavacharyulu's essay on the same; by C. S.
Srinath's examination of Naipaul and Arun Joshi; and by K.
S. Ramamurti's analysis of Achebe, Naipaul, Narayan and
Nagaragan.[4] Recognizing Naipaul's increasing popularity,
the Osmania Journal of English Studies in 1982 devoted a
special issue to the writer, with articles on A House for Mr
Biswas, Mr Stone and the Knights Companion, The Mimic Men,
and A Bend in the River.[5] There have been scattered
complaints about Naipaul's mode of writing--Raghavacharyulu
has found no "heartiness, gratitude, affection, concern, and
charity" in Naipaul who, according to him, "takes up a
position far away from the polluting touch of his own
characters," and Srinath has seen a limitation in Naipaul's
satire which demolishes but does not create.[6] Yet
Naipaul's fiction has generally met with favorable
reception. The same, however, cannot be said of his
journalistic works on India.
      In 1962, at the age of thirty and with twelve years of
residence in London, Naipaul visited India for the first
time, intending to find material for a novel; to escape from
the confines of London, which he realized was not the
"center" of his world after all; and to tease out his
childhood memories of India, memories which he would soon
discover are like "trapdoors to a bottomless past."[7]
Perhaps he inwardly hoped to claim his roots and to make a
connection between his memories of India and the real
India. Whatever his original desires, the traumatic
experiences of this visit produced not only a curious
love-hate relationship with that country but also a most
passionate and acrimonious assault, An Area of Darkness
(1963), which many of his Western critics nonetheless rate
as superior to his other travelogue, The Middle Passage.[8]
      Divided into eleven chapters with a prologue
"Traveller's Prelude" and an epilogue "Flight," An Area of
Darkness records Naipaul's personal impression of India
beginning with his childhood memories, then to his nervous
arrival and trail through the country (from Bombay to
Kashmir to Shiva's lingam in a Himalayan cave to Delhi,
South India, Calcutta), and on through his disappointing
visit to his ancestral village in Uttar Pradesh. In setting
the tone of the book, "Traveller's Prelude" minutely details
Naipaul's frustrating experience with the Indian bureaucracy
as he circles from one agency to another in an effort to
recover two opened bottles of liquor seized by customs upon
his arrival in hot Bombay. Surprised by a clerk's request
for a transport permit which no one had ever mentioned to
him, Naipaul is exasperated: "I was exhausted, sweating,

and when I opened my mouth to speak I found I was on the
verge of tears" (p. 20). At another office anger gains the
upper hand as he screams, startling everyone: "I rushed to
the head of the queue and began to shout at Mr Kulkarni,
waving my papers at him" (p. 25). (In the course of his
stay he developed a habit of shouting from the time he
enters an office.) The entire exercise presages his
opinions on Indian attitudes, for a male clerk in one of the
offices remains largely indifferent to Naipaul's request for
water to assist a woman who has fainted. Naipaul
understands when he sees that it is a messenger who brings
the water: "I should have known better. A clerk was a
clerk; a messenger was a messenger" (p. 24).

The first chapter, a rich one, offers flashes of
Naipaul's childhood memories of people born in India, of
Indian objects and of Indian culture. "Gold Teeth Nanee
[Grandmother]," known for her excessive greed for food,
"dwindled to a rustic oddity" as Naipaul moved from the
country to the city; Babu, a handyman and permanent guest in
the family's back room, remained an enigma and also belonged
to a world distant to Naipaul. "More than in people,"
Naipaul explains, "India lay about us in things." His
grandfather had "carried his village with him"; thus, there
were Indian imports ranging from a string bed to straw mats
to items used in Hindu religious services. Naipaul
describes the cumulative effect:

> To me as a child the India that had produced so
> many of the persons and things around me was
> featureless, and I thought of the time when the
> transference was made as a period of darkness,
> darkness which also extended to the land, as
> darkness surrounds a hut at evening, though for a
> little way around the hut there is still light.
> (p. 32)

Although he could not, like his grandfather, "deny" multiracial Trinidad, he was influenced by the family's Hindu
prejudice against Moslems, and he developed a "horror of the
unclean," finding himself repulsed by women sipping from pot
ladles, people using plates to put out food for animals, and
boys sharing the same popsicles.

Naipaul finds himself with an ambivalent attitude
towards religion. Reared in a Brahmin household populated
by pundits, he surprisingly remained unschooled in
Hinduism. In fact, he resented religious ceremonies and
refused to perform the initiation ceremony of "janaywa."
Yet, in spite of his lack of Hindi religious sympathies,
Naipaul confesses his pleasure when in school one of his
science classmates, noticing that he refused to suck from
the beaker used by other boys, whispered "Real Brahmin." In

London, he found himself wanting his friend Ramon to be
buried according to proper Hindu rites. And in Bombay he
was outraged when he discovered that Indians use for Divali
festival artificial lights instead of the old-fashioned
rustic clay lamps. He comments on this contradiction: "I
had been born an unbeliever. Yet the thought of the decay
of the old customs and reverences saddened me. . ."(p. 38).
Generally Naipaul remained separated from India--that area
of darkness--by the language; by the Indian "delight in
decay, agony and death" as seen in Hindi films; by the
astute Indian businessmen, such as the Guyaratis and
Sindhis, who, in Trinidad, secluded themselves; and most of
all by religion. This important autobiographical chapter
ends as Naipaul leaves the mythical India of his imagination
and steps into the real land. At once he is troubled by the
loss of his identity:

> For the first time in my life I was one of the
> crowd. There was nothing in my appearance or dress
> to distinguish me from the crowd eternally hurrying
> into Churchgate Station. . . . I entered a shop or
> a restaurant and awaited a special quality of
> response. And there was nothing. . . . Again and
> again I was caught. I was faceless. I might sink
> without a trace into that Indian crowd. I had been
> made by Trinidad and England; recognition of my
> difference was necessary to me. I felt the need to
> impose myself, and I didn't know how. (pp. 45-46)

After a few months in the country, he muses, "I was not
English or Indian; I was denied the victories of both" (p.
104).
     The Indian attitudes of "withdrawal, denial, confusion
of values" top the list of irritants in the first section of
An Area of Darkness, a book whose biting generalizations and
moralizings are preceded by personal encounters, character
sketches, and short anecdotal stories. It takes Naipaul
several months to conquer his hysteria at witnessing poverty
which Indians have managed to fit neatly into their scheme
of things:

> They tell the story of the Sikh who, returning to
> India after many years, sat down among his
> suitcases on the Bombay docks and wept. He had
> forgotten what Indian poverty was like. It is an
> Indian story, in its arrangement of figure and
> properties, its melodrama, its pathos. It is
> Indian above all in its attitude to poverty as
> something which, thought about from time to time in
> the midst of other preoccupations, releases the
> sweetest of emotions. This is poverty, our
> especial poverty, and how sad it is! Poverty not

as an urge to anger or improving action, but
poverty as an inexhaustible source of tears, an
exercise of the purest sensibility. (p. 47)

Naipaul reports that his eye was forced to make an
adjustment:

> Ten months later, I was to revisit Bombay and to
> wonder at my hysteria. . . . I had seen Indian
> villages: the narrow, broken lanes with green
> slime in the gutters, the choked back-to-back mud
> houses, the jumble of filth and food and animals
> and people, the baby in the dust, swollen-bellied
> with flies, but wearing its good-luck amulet. I
> had seen the starved child defecating at the
> roadside while the mangy dog waited to eat the
> excrement. I had seen the physique of the people
> of Andhra, which had suggested the possibility of
> an evolution downwards, wasted body to wasted body.
> . . . In India the easiest and most necessary
> thing to ignore was the most obvious. . . .
> But in the beginning the obvious was
> overwhelming. . . . (pp. 48-9)

It was necessary to adopt the Indian habit of withdrawal to
experience serenity. Naipaul realizes that however chaotic
the situation appears, degrees of degration are charted into
the system--"an English endeavor answering the Indian needs:
definition, distinction"--which confines individuals to
their assigned positions in life.

Naipaul presents small portraitures of individuals,
each incorporated into the rule of degree. The Gita's
dictum on degree is followed strictly to the letter: "And
do thy duty, even if it be humble, rather than another's,
even if it be great." (p. 51). Thus, Ramnauth, a stenographer, will not type his superior's letter dictated to him
because he is a stenographer, not a typist. Jivan, a poor
pavement boy, eventually finds a job and manages to purchase
a taxi which he rents out, but still, out of habit, sleeps
on the pavements. Vasant, another Bombay slum dweller, who
becomes a tycoon, continues to run his affairs from his
little "telegraph office" because "he could think nowhere
else." Few adventurous Indians reject degree but are in
turn rejected by society. For example, Malik, a 1,200
rupees a month engineer, complains of his failure to get a
job because he does not own a car; the European-styled
Maholtra, Ramnauth's 600 rupees a month superior officer,
cannot find a bride because he has rejected the "badges of
food and caste and dress." Social confusion, disorder of
castes or adventure, therefore, hardly exist, in spite of
the sickening mimicry of the English; in spite of the
Anglicized executives or "box-wallahs"; in spite of the army

300

officers swearing by out-dated English slang; in spite of
the leisurely Buntys and Andys whose well-clad wives sit
idly at home reading yellow-covered copies of the overseas
<u>Daily Mirror</u> and <u>Woman's Own</u>; and in spite of individuals
such as the hostess, Mrs. Mahindra, with her admitted "craze
for foreign," "just craze for foreign."

To the foreigner, equally troubling as the beggar, who
has his place in degree, is Indian public defecation.
Naipaul spares no detail:

> Shankaracharya Hill, overlooking the Dal lake, is
> one of the beauty spots of Srinagar . . . its lower
> slopes are used as latrines by Indian tourists. If
> you surprise a group of three women, companionably
> defecating, they will giggle: the shame is yours.
> . . .
> In Madras the bus station near the High Court is
> one of the more popular latrines. The traveller
> arrives; to pass the time he raises his dhoti,
> defecates in the gutter. The bus arrives; he
> boards it; the woman sweeper cleans up after him. .
> . .
> Indians defecate everywhere. They defecate,
> mostly, beside the railway tracks. But they also
> defecate on the beaches; they defecate on the
> hills; they defecate on the river banks; they
> defecate on the streets; they never look for cover.
> . . . The truth is that <u>Indians do not see these
> squatters</u> and might even, with complete sincerity,
> deny that they exist: a collective blindness
> arising out of the Indian fear of pollution and the
> resulting conviction that Indians are the cleanest
> people in the world. (pp. 73-75)

According to Naipaul, these problems--the beggars, poor
sanitation--and Indian blindness to them did not escape the
notice of Mohandas Gandhi. Yet the Mahatma failed to
communicate his clear vision, his "way of direct looking."
He was "reverenced for what he was; his message became
irrelevant" and lost because he was "absorbed into the
formless spirituality and decayed pragmatism of India."
Ghandi was typically Indian in that he, too, dealt in
symbols--latrine-cleaning, for example, became an occasional
symbolic ritual.

Indian action becomes merely symbolic, and what is the
obvious to the outsider is ignored by the native. Since
physical effort is considered degrading, the train traveler
would rather suffer and wait for the porter to take down the
bedding. To understand the society is to understand that
"sanitation was linked to caste, caste to callousness,
inefficiency and a hopelessly divided country, division to

weakness, weakness to foreign rule" (p. 78). Naipaul
illustrates the blindness of the effect of caste on
sanitation:

> Study these four men washing down the steps of this
> unpalatable Bombay hotel. The first pours water
> from a bucket, the second scratches the tiles with
> a twig broom, the third uses a rag to slop the
> dirty water down the steps into another bucket,
> which is held by the fourth. After they have
> passed, the steps are as dirty as before; but now
> above the blackened skirting-tiles the walls are
> freshly and dirtily splashed. . . . You cannot
> complain that the hotel is dirty. No Indian will
> agree with you. Four sweepers are in daily
> attendance, and it is enough in India that the
> sweepers attend. They are not required to <u>clean</u>.
> They must stoop when they sweep; cleaning the floor
> of the smart Delhi café, they will squat and move
> like crabs between the feet of the customers,
> careful to touch no one, never looking up, never
> rising. This is the degradation the society
> requires of them, and to this they willingly
> submit. They are dirt; they wish to appear as
> dirt. (p. 79)

Caste, approved by the Gita, frustrates any attempt at
improvement and encourages symbolic action.

The middle section of <u>An Area of Darkness</u> describes
Naipaul's sober stay at a lakeside hotel in cool Kashmir
where depressing sights and encounters are forgotten and
nerves repaired. The atmosphere is soothing: "When the
wind blew across the lake the young reeds swayed; on the
ripples water reflections were abolished; the magenta discs
of the lotus curled upwards; and all the craft on the lake
made for shelter" (p. 112). Here Naipaul becomes totally
involved with the operations of the hotel and with individuals, such as the eccentric hotel manager Butt, his
officious servant Aziz, the sensitive cook Ali Mohammed, and
other staff members, assisting them in managing day to day
affairs, in typing applications and letters, and in
installing the important "flush system." Naipaul is
enthusiastic:

> Our prices were reasonable, and soon we began to
> get guests. I had been full of plans for
> publicising the hotel. I had put some of these
> plans to Aziz and, through him, to Mr Butt. They
> smiled, grateful for my interest; but all they
> wanted me to do was to talk to those tourists in
> jacket and tie whom Ali brought back from the

> Reception Centre. . . . I was jealous. I wanted
> the hotel for myself. (p. 117)

Naipaul's plans are often matched by those of the staff:

> "Sahib, I request one thing. You write Touriasm
> Office, invite Mr Madan to tea."
> "But Aziz, he didn't come the last time."
> "Sahib, you write Touriasm."
> "No, Aziz. No more invitations to tea."
> "Sahib, I request one thing. You go see Mr
> Madan."
> Another plot had been hatched in the kitchen. . .
> . (p. 124)

Ali needs a season permit to enter the compound of the
Tourist Reception Center. Naipaul understands and takes up
the banner: "My lake hotel, unorthodox, unrecognized, was
being discriminated against." His success at securing the
permit prompts the painter to ask, "You typewrite give me
painting certificate, sahib?" (p. 128).

In this middle section, Naipaul manages to enjoy much
of the landscape, as he surveys Kashmir and learns about its
politics and religion. He muses: "In India I had so far
felt myself as a visitor. . . . The landscape was harsh and
wrong. I could not relate it to myself" (pp. 148-49).
However, his pilgrimage in the company of Aziz and the cook
to the Cave of Amarnath (made holy by a five-foot ice
lingam, Shiva's symbol, formed during the summer) makes up
for any disappointment, despite the disasters with the
ponies and despite the polluting habits of pilgrims:

> A special joy had been with me throughout the
> pilgrimage and during all my time in Kashmir. It
> was the joy of being among mountains; it was the
> special joy of being among the Himalayas. I felt
> linked to them; I liked speaking the name. India,
> the Himalayas: they went together. . . . They had
> become part of the India of my fantasy. (p. 176)

Discouraged by large crowds, Naipaul does not enter the
cave. When Aziz emerges and reports that there is no
lingam, a traveler scolds: "It's the spirit of the thing."
Naipaul is dazed by the logic: "A physical growth, because
it is extraordinary, was a spiritual symbol. The growth
failed; it becomes the symbol of a symbol."

His four-month interlude eventually up, Naipaul goes
through a tipping ceremony with the happy hotel personnel.
He has had a serene stay. The petty jealousies and conspi-
racies of the staff, along with Mr. Butt's attempt to
overcharge Naipaul for the Amarnath trip, are nothing in

comparison to the depressing sights on the outside. Even in
Kashmir, there are moments of concern whenever Naipaul
ventures out--the reminder of poverty as children chant for
"paisa" (money) and the intrusion of caste as people unquestionably permit themselves to be served food by unwashed
Brahmin hands. In fact, Naipaul's endurance is tested to
the end:

> In four months I had established among the lakeside
> tongas that I never paid more than one and a
> quarter rupees for the ride into town. But the
> circumstances were extraordinary. I offered two.
> The tonga-wallah refused to touch the notes. I
> offered no more. He threatened me with his whip;
> and I found, to my surprise--it must have been the
> earliness of the hour--that I had seized him by the
> throat. (p. 191)

Naipaul remains alert even when he bids the tearful Aziz
final farewell: "Even at that moment I could not be sure
that he had ever been mine." (p. 192)
    The third section of the book opens with reflections on
the difference between reminders of British presence in
India and Trinidad. In commenting on the loss of Indian
culture in Trinidad, Naipaul notes the effect of Indian
philosophy on him:

> We knew that something which was once whole had
> been washed away. What was whole was the idea of
> India.
>   To preserve this conception of India as a
> country still whole, historical facts had not been
> suppressed. They had been acknowledged and
> ignored; and it was only in India that I was able
> to see this as part of the Indian ability to
> retreat, the ability genuinely not to see what was
> obvious; with others a foundation of neurosis, but
> with Indians only part of a greater philosophy of
> despair, leading to passivity, detachment,
> acceptance. . . . I see how much this philosophy
> had also been mine. It has enabled me, through the
> stresses of a long residence in England, to
> withdraw completely from nationality and loyalties
> except to persons . . . it had convinced me that
> every man was an island, and taught me to shield
> all that I knew to be good and pure within myself
> from the corruption of causes. (p. 198)

He then continues, saying that in Trinidad people unquestionably accepted English rule, institutions, and language.
"Yet England and Englishness as displayed in India were
absent. And to me this remained the peculiar quality of the

Raj; this affectation of being very English, this sense of a
nation at play, acting out a fantasy" (p. 210). To substan-
tiate his thesis about the mimicking of Englishness, Naipaul
makes generous references to several British writers,
including Kipling who "left us Anglo-India; to people these
relics of the Raj we have only to read him. . . . The total
effect is that of a people at play" (p. 201). A visit to
Simla, the summer seat of the Raj, confirms this tendency to
mimic. Naipaul's general indictment is harsh:

> It is well that Indians are unable to look at their
> country directly, for the distress they would see
> would drive them mad. And it is well that they
> have no sense of history, for how then would they
> be able to continue to squat amid their ruins, and
> which Indian would be able to read the history of
> his country for the last thousand years without
> anger and pain? It is better to retreat into
> fantasy and fatalism. (p. 212)

India is now a country in ruins, which indicate waste and
failure--"somewhere something has snapped." It is a country
which, forced into nationalism (really mimicry), has turned
to spirituality and ancient culture. The Indo-British
encounter presented a dilemma for Indians: "Their new self-
awareness makes it impossible for Indians to go back; their
cherishing of Indianness makes it difficult for them to go
ahead. . . . Shiva has ceased to dance" (pp. 228-29).
     Whether reflective or narrative, details in An Area of
Darkness never fail to be provocative. Traveling by rail
(the sign on the platform, where dogs howl and people sleep,
reads Trains running late are likely to make up lost time),
Naipaul finds himself among a group of South Indians:

> South Indian languages, excessively vowelled,
> rattled about me. The South Indians were beginning
> to unwind; they were lapping up their liquidised
> foods. Food was a pleasure to their hands.
> Chewing, sighing with pleasure, they squelched
> curds and rice between their fingers. They
> squelched and squelched; then, in one swift
> circular action, as though they wished to take
> their food by surprise, they gathered some of the
> mixture into a ball, brought their dripping palms
> close to their mouths and--flick!--rice and curds
> were shot inside; and the squelching, chattering
> and sighing began again. (pp. 235-36)

This observation is interrupted by a Sikh, who had earlier
attracted Naipaul's attention by his appearance and his
defiance of posted rail rules:

> 'At last,' he said, as the train moved off. "I
> didn't want any other Sikhs to come in. Have a
> fag."
>   'But Sikhs don't smoke.'
>   'This one does.'
> The woman looked up from her <u>sambar</u>. The
> squelchers paused, looked at us and looked away
> quickly as if in horror.
>   'Punks,' the Sikh said. His expression
> changed. 'You see how these monkeys stare at
> you?' He leaned forward. 'You know my trouble?'
>   'Tell me.'
>   'I am colour-prejudiced.' . . .
> Many of his stories were overtly humorous, but
> often, as in his references to the Sikh religious
> leaders, I saw humour where none was intended. Our
> relationship had begun in mutual misunderstanding.
> . . . (pp. 237-38)

The relationship subsequently, and predictably, ends in a
restaurant when Naipaul abandons the bellicose Sikh, who had
started a fight with some Dravidians.
    It is with a high level of anticipation and anxiety
that Naipaul seeks out the village of his grandfather, the
village of the Dubes. His first impressions are striking:

> A boy came out. His thin body was naked save for
> his dhoti and sacred thread. He looked at me
> suspiciously . . . but when the IAS officer who was
> with me explained who I was, the boy attempted
> first to embrace me and then to touch my feet. I
> disengaged myself and he led us through the
> village. . . .
>   A year before I might have been appalled by what
> I was seeing. But my eye had changed. This
> village looked unusually prosperous; it was even
> picturesque . . . [The men] unlocked the grilled
> doors and showed me the images, freshly washed,
> freshly dressed, marked with fresh sandalwood
> paste, the morning's offerings of flowers not yet
> faded. My mind leapt years, my sense of distance
> and time was shaken: before me were the very
> replicas of the images in the prayer-room of my
> grandfather's house. (pp. 268-69)

He hears from Jussodra (who had also been to Trinidad) the
full story of his grandfather's indentureship, and he
studies old photographs taken in Trinidad. His colonial
prudence prevailing, he refuses the hospitable offer of not
only water but food. Back at the hotel, Naipaul receives an
uncomfortable visit from Ramandra Dube, the patriarch of the
Dubes, and an invitation to return to the village. However,

306

the second visit is even more discomfiting as Ramandra,
after a strenuous effort at communication, indicates that he
wishes Naipaul's financial assistance with a new land
litigation. The interpreter explains:

> It is about your grandfather's land, the land that
> produced the rice he gave you. That is why God
> sent you here. You grandfather's land is now only
> nineteen acres, and some of that will be lost if he
> can't get this new litigation started. If that
> happens, who will look after your grandfather's
> shrine? (p. 276)

Repulsed by the circular discussion and the request, Naipaul
leaves, without managing even a courteous wave. "So it
ended, in futility and impatience, a gratuitous act of
cruelty, self-reproach and flight." "It was a journey,"
Naipaul admits, "that ought not to have been made; it had
broken my life in two" (pp. 280-81). To most Indians, both
in India and abroad, it was also a journey about which he
never should have written.

Indians have traced the root of anger in this book to
Naipaul's background, that is, to his preconceived,
romanticized idea of India and his Brahmin and Western
sensibility. Noting that the Trinidadian-born writer
romanticized India from what he had heard as a child and
subsequently sought to realize that dim, vague image in what
he saw when he came to India, P. C. David wrote:

> We cannot help feeling that Naipaul continually
> tries to impose his personalised, romanticised
> image of India on the reality, and when the reality
> militates against his preconceived notions, he
> allows his narrative to slip into an exercise in
> banter, unwarranted moralising and misplaced
> criticism of the actuality. . . . Naipaul weaves a
> myth of India in his imagination and this myth
> falters and eludes his grasp when he fails to find
> its parallel in the reality. Hence a tension
> between imagination and reality is a strong feature
> of Naipaul's An Area of Darkness. Such a tension
> would perhaps be a valid artistic device in any
> other form of writing but it wreaks havoc in a
> travelogue which is expected to be a fairly
> faithful reproduction of verifiable experience.[9]

Although David mentioned that the first chapter in An Area
of Darkness points to a sort of ambivalence in attitude
towards India, he stressed Naipaul's "romantic reverie which
cannot stand the glare of the day."[10] However, K. S.
Ramamurti, who did not classify Naipaul's visit as a
disillusionment (since disillusionment implies destruction

of favorable impression), concluded that Naipaul never had
any favorable impressions of India: "Though India lay about
him during the years of childhood in a hundred things, in
the people around him, in family customs, festivals and
ceremonies, in dress and food habits, it had made no
impression on him which was palpable or favourable."[11]
Ananda Thota saw in Naipaul's attitude towards India
neither ambivalence nor rejection but a confused cultural
stance stemming from harboring Indian myths in a
Western-oriented background. He explained further: "The
coalescence of two cultures in Naipaul, one nurtured by his
family about India, and the other by the Western
misconception about India shaped his susceptibilities about
India to such a degree that he became incapable of
confronting Indian reality of the twentieth century." To
Thota, Naipaul's childhood impression of Hinduism and caste,
however vague, formed the writer's Brahmin ego and made him
incapable of examining with "tolerant interest" the Hinduism
of India.[12] H. H. Anniah Gowda, noting Naipaul's
confessions of childhood prejudices, also blamed the
writer's "puritanical, Brahminical blood."[13] Finally, in
his study of Naipaul's background as a caricature of Indian
Hindu society, K. I. Madhusudana Rao appeared to hold a
similar view: "The restlessness of Naipaul as a historical
recorder of the cultural scene, whether in India or in the
West Indies or in England, may be traced partly to its
inheritance, his acquired western attitudes of mind and
temperament."[14] Naipaul has been unfavorably compared to
the Indian Raja Rao, who, residing outside India, has
cherished it as a source of spiritual sustenance. The
conclusion is that the vision of the insider who is outside
is more authentic than that of the outsider who is
inside.[15] In short, then, Indian critics agree that
Naipaul's cultural stance is a hindrance to sound
investigative writing on India.
It is interesting to note that Western reviewers argue
that Naipaul's ethnic affinity and at the same time his
cultural distance place him in the advantageous position of
both an insider and outsider. The reviewer for the Times
noted that Naipaul is "uniquely placed" and that the
"comprehensive imprecision" achieved in An Area of Darkness
could not have been possible by either an Indian or an
Englishman.[16] The Times Literary Supplement also drew
attention to Naipaul's privileged status: "From the
beginning of his travels he experienced the tension between
belonging and not belonging, between identification and
alienation, and it is this that gives his report of his
year's sojourn its extraordinary poignancy."[17] Even Paul
Theroux, who dubbed Naipaul a "complete stranger" instead of
a "returning son," concluded that "in special ways,
Naipaul's behaviour is that of an Indian; and briefly he

belongs to the country," even though he assumes a tone of
remoteness when he discusses Indian attitudes.[18]
Regardless of Naipaul's Indianness or his privileged
position, however, some Western scholars have agreed with
their Indian counterparts in tracing the angry tone in An
Area of Darkness to Naipaul's Brahmin and Western
tradition. In his full-length study, V. S. Naipaul, William
Walsh, referring to Naipaul's "general Western distaste for
the crude ways of a rural people," wrote: "He [Naipaul]
brought to bear upon the Indian scene a refinement of that
superior, detached Brahmin tradition drawn from India
itself."[19] D. J. Enright is equally severe in calling
Naipaul "something of an aesthete, an aristocrat . . . [who]
has the sensibility of a brahmin."[20] These two Westerners
are more or less exceptions.

Indian critics have pointed to Naipaul's prejudice and
strong personality which run through An Area of Darkness,
making the book difficult to be placed in any one genre,
especially the travelogue. C. D. Narasimhaiah, who has
written one of the strongest and most popular attacks on
Naipaul's work, suggested that the book defies classification: [It] is too good to be called a mere hit-and-run
kind of traveller's diary and too often obtrusively personal
. . . to be called a fictionalized autobiography."[21] P.
C. David argued that a travelogue writer should be
prejudiced only in favor of reality; Naipaul falls short
since he has a "prejudice for some personal vision of
India." David further suggested that despite its "chatti-
ness," An Area of Darkness is structurally a travelogue,
which mixes with the technique of the novel to suit the
writer's convenience and advantage.[22] Santha Rau noticed
another type of blend: a travelogue mixed with a series of
vignettes.[23] Other critics have encouraged a strictly
autobiographical classification. For example, T. R. S.
Sharma claimed that it is a mistake of critics to read the
work as a travel book since it is "deeply, disturbingly
autobiographical," while H. H. Anniah Gowda branded it as a
cold, unsympathetic, personal testament filled with
prejudice.[24] Finally, K. S. Ramamurti formulated a description which accommodates almost all possible suggestions:
"It is a personal history which combines the modes of
travelogue with techniques of fiction and is personal in the
sense that it is an exploration of the self through a
virtual exploration of a land which had remained an area of
darkness in his [Naipaul's] consciousness."[25] A few
Westerners have also seen An Area of Darkness as colored by
Naipaul's own personality and have agreed that the work is
more about Naipaul than about India. However, in spite of
the personal element, they are generally not apt, as are
Indian critics, to dismiss or refute Naipaul's general
findings or specific complaints.[26]

Naipaul's specific statement about being faceless and undistinguishable in India has puzzled and angered Indians. C. D. Narasimhaiah, noting that Naipaul's ego was hurt when no "special quality of response" came, concluded that Naipaul "had to fight for self-preservation, well, by looking down upon Indians if necessary. Which means to understand India, one must understand Mr. Naipaul. Hardly the way to understand a country."[27] I. K. Masih also theorized that Naipaul's anger stems from his failure to be treated in a unique manner: "In his failure to accept the fact that he was no diffrent [sic] from an Indian student staying in Europe too long lies his ordeal. Why does difference matter so much to him?"[28] This is the same question posed by Nissim Ezekiel, whose angry rebuttal to Naipaul's book matches Narasimhaiah's:

> What, in God's name, is there to be upset about that, unless he has abandoned humility altogether? . . .
>
> This fear, this anxiety, this feverish insistence on being different, this frequent assertion of what and where he had been 'made', this irrational urge to 'impose' and the rage at being unable to do so, this constitutes the mirror Mr Naipaul holds up to India. This is the source of his curses, the cause of his raving and ranting. . . . Mr. Naipaul's book has the moral authority of hysteria, the interest and value of a suffering impotence.[29]

Indian critics have not tried to understand Naipaul's uneasiness at being regarded as a part of this troubling society and, thus, his wish to disengage himself from it. They insist that it is his need for distinction which causes his anger.

Indian commentators have criticized the lengthy description of the frustration Naipaul experiences in recovering the two opened bottles of liquor (he was told that he stood a better chance in passing customs inspection if the bottles were opened). Wondering why Naipaul tried circumventing the law instead of obeying it, Narasimhaiah is amazed and angered: "And six pages to recover from the customs the two bottles surreptitiously brought in! We are of course a thoroughly inefficient lot but why should they who know better add to our inefficiency and call us names?"[30] H. H. Anniah Gowda pointed out that bureaucractic incompetence exists in all countries and is certainly not characteristic of India only.[31] On the whole, Indians do not question the veracity of Naipaul's difficulty with the Indian bureaucracy, but they think that he made too much of his experience in retrieving his bottles.

In other cases, Naipaul is criticized for his misrepre-
sentation and mistreatment of characters and incidents in
order to make a preconceived point. Indians often argue
that it is odd that in his one year sojourn in India,
Naipaul met no acceptable Indian but only caricatures and
the "dull-witted." K. Natwar-Singh sarcastically called
that failure a "unique achievement."[32] Nissim Ezekiel
attributed it to Naipaul's personality:

> He keeps running into obtuse, unsympathetic
> Indians, bland, silly and incapable of
> understanding his simplest problems. It may be
> true, but somehow one feels that Mr Naipaul's
> aloof, sullen, aggressive manner contributed to his
> difficulties, accentuated them. . . .
> Most of the persons . . . were grotesque,
> contemptible or pathetic creatures. He writes
> about them at great length as though they are
> important illustrations of his argument.[33]

Ezekiel criticized Naipaul's condescending treatment of Mrs.
Mahandra (who is "craze for foreign") and Mr. Butt and Aziz
at the Kashmir hotel. About Naipaul's other characters,
Ezekiel has many questions and serious doubts. "In
Naipaul's India, 'the clerk will not bring you a glass of
water even if you faint'. In my India, a clerk will do
virtually anything for you if he is treated humanely."[34]
The stories of the stenographer Ramnauth, the supervisor
Maholtra, and the engineer Malik are equally questionable:

> In my India, stenographers type out the letters
> dictated to them. . . . There are so many
> questions I would like to ask about it [the story].
> . . .
> There was undoubtedly some misunderstanding. . .
> . A young Englishman of my acquaintance in Bombay
> used to speak bitterly to me about his Indian
> office assistants, claiming that they invariably
> misinterpreted his simplest instructions . . . so
> clipped and jerky was his manner of speech. . . .
> He [Naipaul] has swallowed Maholtra's story as he
> swallowed many others. These stories enabled him
> to believe what he wanted to believe. . . .
> Malik's story too is suspect in my eyes. . . . In
> my India, engineers trained abroad, provided they
> have what it takes, advance rapidly, buy a car
> before they can afford it . . . land superior jobs
> even if they don't have a car. . . . Malik failed
> to get a better job because his personality and
> abilities did not measure up to his
> qualifications. They explain their failures in
> many ways. Malik believes it is because he has no

car, though he could easily buy one and sail over
the alleged obstacle.[35]

Ezekiel contended that his objections have to do with
Naipaul's mode and habit of "falsifying examples." For
instance, he agreed with Naipaul that Indians are reluctant
to perform physical labor, considered a degradation, but
doubted that train passengers hesitate to roll out their
bedding.[36]

Other critics are more explicit in their charge that
Naipaul deliberately exaggerates or fabricates his
characters to suit his purpose. P. C. David, for example,
quoting from Naipaul's description of Gold Teeth Nanee, who
in her greed mistakenly drinks flanco fluid, made this point:

> His characters which he would have us believe to be
> real are absurd caricatures. In order that they
> may sound real and also perhaps effective, he would
> make them grotesque. Usually we find him alighting
> on some trivial aspect of his personages and
> exaggerating it out of all proportions until they
> defy credibility. . . . Her [Gold Teeth's] greed
> is exaggerated to the extent of vulgarity. . . .
> She is too outlandish to be an inhabitant of any
> real world. . . .
> The element of caricature detracts heavily from
> the authenticity and solidity of Naipaul's
> personages. We suspect that this distortion is
> deliberate and arises from the perversity of not
> wanting to see human beings in their normal human
> dimensions.[37]

David saw the same type of deliberate exaggeration in
characters such as Mrs. Mahindra and Ramon.[38]
Narasimhaiah, directly accusing Naipaul of inventing for
certain effects, commented on the descriptions of Jivan and
Vasant:

> 'Well written,' one would say but would add,
> 'difficult to swallow though.' . . . It is not
> surprising that the writer who invented Jivan and
> Vasant with such impunity should not have gone to
> any of our hundreds of sober hotel and unromantic
> government-subsidized guest-houses but chosen to go
> into the most unrepresentative--one in ten
> thousand, if any--Indian home of that fictional
> character, Mrs Mahindra. . . .[39]

However, Western reviewers have not raised the question of
the authenticity of Naipaul's characters; instead, they
admire the novelistic technique of <u>An Area of Darkness</u> and

share Michael Thorpe's view that it is through the
characters that the "abstraction 'India' acquires life."[40]
     On a number of other specific points, Indians have
complained of Naipaul's lack of good judgment in selecting
his subjects. His frequent references to the Indian habit
of openly defecating prompted the British critic William
Walsh to write that "one sometimes feels that to Naipaul,
India consists of nothing but people at stool."[41] Ezekiel
did not elaborate on the subject, which he stated Indians
spurn as unpleasant for discussion.[42] However, Gowda
questioned Naipaul's taste, fact, and emphasis:

> Naipaul is obsessed with it [public defecation].
> . . . His horror is purely a kind of cultural
> reaction; it is not inspired by any ideal of public
> health; and in its frequency this reference to
> defecating is a flagrant breach of good taste, if
> not of fact. . . .
>   While in Madras, having lost himself in
> describing defecation, he has not one word for the
> lovely beach which faces and gives a majestic
> background to the building on the Marina. Naipaul,
> in his personal reminiscences, has chosen to shut
> his eyes to the India which is not defecating.[43]

Similarly, Indians are enraged by Naipaul's poor taste in
his unpleasant description of South Indians eating. K. S.
Ramamurti called it a "horrifying 'tale'" and predicts that
Dravidians will be tempted "not only to hate the Aryan
Naipaul but to think seriously in terms of reviving the
hobby-horse of anti-Aryanism which is now old and
tired."[44] Narasimhaiah, a South Indian himself, vented his
anger:

> I envy Mr. Naipaul that he at least has been able
> to capture the entire labyrinthine act of our
> eating in such impeccable English--his English is
> throughout most remarkable, but the feelings? And
> considering the passage in its context, I cannot
> help wondering from what celestial region has this
> archangel strayed into our poor planet and my
> wonder grows when I see him snigger, perched as it
> were, on a tree-top, not wanting to come down for
> fear of contamination by this sub-sub-standard
> species gobbling its filthy fodder.[45]

To Indians, Naipaul not only exercises poor taste in his
selection of details but also assumes a tone of arrogance
and superiority.
     Naipaul's alleged superciliousness, along with his lack
of understanding, is at the core of most negative criticisms

of <u>An Area of Darkness</u>. Santha Rau criticized the emphasis
on Indian poverty: "Had it never occurred to . . .
[Naipaul] that most of the world's population lives in
adject poverty?"[46] Masih, equally impatient, wrote:

> He will not see the fact that poverty is no excuse
> for charity but an inherent character of Indian way
> of life. . . . He builds up a disgusting picture
> of the land of his ancestors forgetting to
> appreciate the fact that in spite of the assault of
> the British for hundreds of years, Indians have not
> broken down.[47]

Masih also claimed that Naipaul misses the point on Indian
mimicry, a trait which is an exception, not the rule.[48]
Others have concluded that no matter what Indians do,
Naipaul is determined to be quarrelsome. For example,
Ezekiel noted, "[Bunty] speaks English fluently, which
maddens Mr Naipaul. If he had spoken it badly, Mr Naipaul
would have despised him."[49] Narasimhaiah arrived at a
similar conclusion: "He blames us as much for being only
Indians as for not being wholly Indian."[50] Robert Hammer,
an American critic, disagreed with Narasimhaiah's
conclusion: "There is no real contradiction. Naipaul is
selective in his condemnations. He dislikes customs which
retard growth and cause public nuisances. . . and he
disapproves the adoption of meaningless forms and
affectations."[51] To Indians, however, Naipaul is
hopelessly irascible. To them, he comes expecting to see
the wrong things; he is prejudiced against all the East (the
"farther away from Europe the more hellish"); he harbors a
morbid obsession with filth; he briefly refers to Gandhi
only to indict India; he speaks of the condition of Indian
public lavatories as the "visitor's nightmare"; he is easily
irritated by the "Indian" question "Where did you come
from?"; he is not interested in Hinduism but in the <u>Kama
Sutra</u> from which he quotes; he delights in half-truths and
generalizations; he fails to praise Kashmir's impressive
scenery or the grandeur of the Himalayas; he does not enter
the cave of Amarnath because he is impious; he makes no
effort to appreciate Indian sculpture or South Indian
paintings and judges Indian architecture by Western
standards; finally, he finds fault in everyone and with
everything, even the Taj Mahal. Naipaul criticizes
everything in India, and Indians do not hesitate to do the
same with <u>An Area of Darkness</u>.[52]
  It is, however, the last episode, the climactic visit
to the Dubes, which Indian readers find the most
unsettling. It is of no surprise to them that Naipaul's
hope for a resuscitation of his childhood feeling for
mythical India is dashed (they had been well prepared for
the scene). It is the coldness of the meeting which

confounds them. Narasimhaiah selected quotations which he
thinks reveal Naipaul's lack of sympathy:

> The worst of all his sins of commission is his
> heartlessness in his encounter with his (country)
> cousin and earlier, his wife 'who seized my feet, in
> all their Veldschoen, and began to weep. She wept
> and would not let go'. He desisted from giving them
> any help ostensibly to prevent them from starting a
> litigation. Or would he say to conquer the feeling
> he had experienced before: 'How easy it is to feel
> power in India!' But the fact remains that 'the
> ugliness was all mine'.[53]

D. V. K. Raghavacharyulu passed a similar judgment: "Naipaul
finds himself incapable, in the situation, of even the
dubious, patronising civility of an affluent cousin from a
distant land towards his origins. He is in fact much too
baffled by his own lack of sympathy to pursue his homecoming
any further."[54] T. R. S. Sharma's conclusion that the
scene is written "more in pain, self-affliction than in
arrogance or lack of humility" is not shared by his fellow
nationals.[55] Interestingly enough, however, Western
reviewers tend to ignore the encounter or to share Naipaul's
revulsion.[56] For example, in reviewing _An Area of Darkness_
for _Commentary_, John Mander, who predicted that the
description of the visit will receive a high place in any
anthology of English writing about India, wrote from
Naipaul's stance:

> The village and its Brahmin community are not quite
> as he [Naipaul] and his Trinidad family had been
> brought up to believe. A traditional welcome is
> laid on: but it is soon apparent that this
> prodigal's return is seen as a financial oppor-
> tunity not to be missed. It is the final humilia-
> tion. The shameless beggary of India. . . .[57]

The overall difference between Indian and Western reviews,
despite one or two exceptions, is noticeable.
   This difference surfaces more clearly in reaction to the
Kashmir interlude, which remains every Western reviewer's
favorite section.[58] John Mander, who saw the strength of
the book in the "novelist's ear for talk, in his shrewd,
observant eye for detail," noted that the Kashmir
descriptions are done with a "sureness that is equal to
anything in his [Naipaul's] fiction."[59] The _Spectator's_
judgment is that the portrayal of the hotel personnel matches
the "comic vividness and completeness of the characters in
The Mystic Masseur" without the "farcical exaggeration."[60]
Finally, even D. J. Enright, whose opinions on _An Area of
Darkness_ generally coincide with those of Indian commenta-

tors, called the idyll the "most charming section of the book."[61]   Except for Narasimhaiah's brief passing phrase about the "justly praised section," Indians are strangely silent about any merit the scene might have.[62]   Instead, there are regrets about Naipaul's neglect of the Kashmir scenery and his emphasis on the hotel staff, whom he is thought to have treated with impertinence.[63]

An examination of Indian response, then, reveals the tendency of each critic to call attention to and challenge specific episodes or observations which he thinks are distasteful or incorrect and to proceed to make a general denunciation of the entire book.   Nonetheless, even the staunchest Indian critics of An Area of Darkness concede-- though grudgingly--that what Naipaul says of India is substantially true. Narasimhaiah, who stated that Naipaul is "largely correct in his observations of life on the surface," admitted the writer's charges:

> Our failings are so many and so varied that the most patriotic of us cannot defend them. Our love of symbols and labels rather than of action, our adolescent pride in real and imaginary achievements in our past; our love of the past without cultivating it to make it continuous; our neglect of our great art and literature unless they are approved by Europe scholars and critics; our celebration of festivals without knowing their significance; our prolific production of politicians and speeches, our imbecile intellectuals, our double-talk and double-think, our tedious films, infantile textbooks and our endless mimicry--all these have been diligently pointed out by Mr. Naipaul and we shall own them and not be angry though irritation is our first reaction.[64]

Gowda also agreed that "there is an element of truth in the observation that Indians lack the ability to see what is obvious, but are given to a philosophy of despair, leading to passivity, detachment and acceptance."[65]   Even Ezekiel offered his list of concessions: "I am not doubting in fact his [Naipaul's] veracity . . . All that he says against the grossness and squalor of Indian life, the routine ritualism, the lip-service to high ideals, the petrified and distorted sense of cleanliness, and a thousand other things, all this is true."[66] If Naipaul is essentially correct, why, then, the outburst of angry reaction, the tendency to explain the book away as a personal whim and to quickly discredit specific details?

To answer the question, most Indians return to the problem of Naipaul's personality and stance. They often cite his "callousness," "perversity," "nagging, irritable manner," "detachment."[67] Ezekiel admitted, "My quarrel is that Mr Naipaul is so often uninvolved and unconcerned . . . he shows little humility, spiritual or other."[68] T. R. S. Sharma is the only one who takes exception. Disagreeing with Ezekiel, he claimed that an uninvolved person could not even pose Naipaul's question about Indians being able to read their history without pain.[69] To K. S. Ramamurti the detachment contributes to a keener insight, but there are serious problems:

> There is no doubt a clarity of vision, a detachment, an objectivity in Naipaul's writing which makes it exceedingly interesting and authentic, but the total effect is disastrous. . . . What Naipaul brings to bear on the India of his study is an attitude of heartlessness, of unsympathetic sneer and a readiness to attack in a mood of anger. He is not moved by the suffering, misery and poverty that he sees everywhere, but is visibly angered by the dirt, filth and squalor. . . . What we find in him is a kind of arrogance arising from a sense of racial superiority, an arrogance which makes him scoff at the black Dravidians of the South, at the South Indian 'monkeys', makes him realize his kinship with the 'Noble' Aryans and share 'the colour prejudice' of his Sikh fellow-travellor.[70]

Some of the blame inevitably is shifted back to Naipaul's inner conflict and cultural displacement as a "Brahmin East-Indian-West-Indian-Englishman."[71] To Masih, Naipaul fails to realize that he too is a Dube--a "Yahoo," a "Chip of the same block"; instead, he uses a western Kaleidoscope to examine India.[72] Generally, there is the rejection of the pompous, cold outsider, who thinks he is qualified to report authoritatively on India.

Equally irritating to Indians is what they see as Naipaul's strong penchant for accentuating only the ugly aspects of Indian life. Gowda, while conceding that an artist is not obliged to highlight the complete picture, condemned the book's one-sidedness and the author's blind spot.[73] Similarly, in her chapter on Naipaul, Prema Nandakumar (who agreed that An Area of Darkness records truth) argued that the author deliberately "chose to see" only a certain side and ignored other things "which his observant eye shouldn't have missed."[74] What disturbs Indians is Naipaul's inability to adopt a positive attitude in the midst of darkness. Narasimhaiah contrasted Naipaul's attitude to that of a Canadian who, observing naked children playing, remarked that at least they enjoy a united family and are blessed with good health, while in affluent societies one out of every ten is a mental case.[75]

Finally, some readers have examined <u>An Area of Darkness</u>
as a work which is of no value to the image of India. India,
it is argued, needs no "prophets of doom."[76] In his review
for the <u>Canadian Forum</u>, K. Gupta, while admitting that no
honest Indian could deny Naipaul's sordid details, voiced his
concern about the country's international image:

> Mr. Naipaul's mind has always been a land shrouded
> in eternal darkness from which there is no
> escape. . . . Perhaps Mr. Naipaul was acting with a
> certain missionary zeal to expose the perversities
> in the Indian social structure, but how does that
> help? . . . It is likely to misrepresent India
> abroad--one need hardly mention the damage that was
> done by Katherine Mayo's "Mother India" and Beverly
> Nichols' "Verdict on India"--secondly, it is
> perversion of the truth which Mr. Naipaul seems so
> much after. The fact is that today's India is
> undergoing a change which is unprecedented in its
> history. . . .[77]

It is interesting to note that the <u>Times Literary Supplement</u>
reviewer, like a number of other Western commentators,
predicted Indian hostility to <u>An Area of Darkness</u>: "Mr.
Naipaul, like Mrs. Mayo a generation or two back, will anger
progressive Indians." The reviewer, noting that Indians may
quite rightly say that Naipaul is one-sided, warns against
castigating Naipaul, who has successfully revealed important
socio-psychological problems which trouble progressives.[78]
    In contrast to Indians, Western commentators place stress
on Naipaul's investigative and literary skill rather than on
the distatesful, unpleasant truths or patronizing air in <u>An
Area of Darkness</u>. Whatever the approach, the conclusion is
generally the same: praise for Naipaul. Thus, to the
<u>Spectator</u> Naipaul finds little to love in India, whereas to
the <u>New York Times</u> he disguises his love for India--the
former commends his honesty; the latter excuses his violent
reaction.[79] Everyone has pointed out Naipaul's brutal
details, but the feeling is that though the writer may be
offensive, he has deep insight and understanding. In fact,
the blurb on the book captures the flavor of Western
reaction: "With a few swift and beautifully calculated
strokes, Mr. Naipaul brings the essence of a social situation
so vividly to life that one begins to wonder whether all the
sociologists, anthropologists and political scientists who
have tried to explain India have not laboured in vain."[80]
To Indians, however, there is no other document in which
"India is . . . so completely misunderstood.[81]
    In concluding <u>An Area of Darkness</u>, Naipaul reports that
whatever he wrote about India, it "exorcised nothing."
India, in fact, continued to possess and haunt his imagina-

tion. Shortly after the publication of the book, he reportedly said that he would like to try to live in India.[82] In Kingston, Jamaica, in 1970 Gowda met Naipaul, who indicated that he was impressed with India's progress, and in 1971, he confessed to Narasimhaiah that he was Indian in his feeling and sensibility and that "two generations don't make all that difference."[83] Not surprisingly, then, in spite of his first disenchanted trip, Naipaul continued to make frequent visits to India (three in thirteen years after that). He has published a few short occasional, mainly repetitious, pieces (eventually collected in The Overcrowded Barraccoon [1972]) and India: A Wounded Civilization (1977), the latter a result of his journey from August 1975 to October 1976, the time of Indira Gandhi's Emergency rule. Serialized in the New York Review of Books prior to publication, India, while more mellow than An Area of Darkness, is almost as provocative and has drawn mixed reviews from Indians.

Repeating some of Naipaul's earlier impressions, India, which is less personal and more analytical than An Area, consists of a Preface and three parts--"A Wounded Civilization," "A New Claim on the Land," and "Not Ideas, but Obsessions." Although the Times Literary Supplement reviewer called the structure loose,[84] each section is unified by the theme of inquiry about the Emergency, an inquiry which Naipaul contends must extend beyond the political to Indian attitudes and civilization. He reflects on his ambivalence towards India as he sets the tone of the book:

> India is for me a difficult country. It isn't my home and cannot be my home; and yet I cannot reject it or be indifferent to it. . . . I am at once too close and too far. . . .
> India, which I visited for the first time in 1962, turned out to be a very strange land. A hundred years had been enough to wash me clean of many Indian religious attitudes; and without these attitudes the distress of India was--and is--almost insupportable. It has taken me much time to come to terms with the strangeness of India. (p. ix)

It is apparent that any inquiry has to begin with Naipaul himself because in him "there survive, from the family rituals . . . phantasmal memories of old India which for me outline a whole vanished world" (p. x).

"Sometimes old India, the old, eternal India many Indians like to talk about does seem just to go on." Part one opens with the idea of that continuity, a point illustrated in Naipaul's description of the old ruined Hindu kingdom of Vijayanagar and a temple where pilgrims, who have accepted the present ruin as the magical continuation of the old,

still flock. The Hinduism of Vijayanagar has degenerated
into barbarism. Naipaul sees the ruin as a metaphor for all
India and its "wounded" civilization:

> What happened in Vijayanagar happened, in varying
> degrees, in other parts of the country . . . at
> Vijayanagar, among the pilgrims, I wondered whether
> intellectually for a thousand years India hadn't
> always retreated before its conquerors and whether,
> in its periods of apparent revival, India hadn't
> only been making itself archaic again, intellec-
> tually smaller, always smaller, always vulnerable.
> . . . The crisis of India is not only political or
> economic. The larger crisis is of a wounded old
> civilization that has at last become aware of its
> inadequacies and is without the intellectual means
> to move ahead. (pp. 9-10)

Naipaul then examines India through R. K. Narayan's casual
1961 statement that "India will go on." In Narayan's Sampath
(1949), the aimless hero Srivinas, answers the pivotal
question "Why bother about anything?" with withdrawal; to him
Gandhism has already become "nondoing, noninterference,
social indifference." It is a philosophy connected with the
dangerous concept of karma, "the Hindu killer, the Hindu
calm, which tells us that we pay in this life for what we
have done in past lives: so that everything we see is just
and balanced, and the distress we see is to be relished as
religious theater" (p. 17). Srivinas' quietism, which is
"compounded of karma, nonviolence, and a vision of history as
an extended religious fable," parasitically leaves action to
others. Narayan's The Vendor of Sweets (1967) repeats the
theme of eventual withdrawal and acceptance, as Jagan (whose
son rebels against tradition) seeks religious retreat in the
jungle--just like the pilgrims among the ruins of
Vijayanagar. Trivial gestures of rebellion are interpreted as
rejection of piety, rejection of karma. Significantly, Mrs.
Gandhi had warned (and Naipaul apparently agrees) that while
Indians must know their past, they must strive towards the
future.

Naipaul traces the deep-seated root of the breakdown,
which prompted the Emergency, to Independence. "A multitude
of Jagans . . . had worked to undo that Independence. Now
the Jagans had begun to be rejected, and India was discovering that it had ceased to be Gandhian" (p. 41). Gandhi's
simplicity threatened to make poverty holy, and bonded labor
was accepted as karma. Naipaul refers to Vijay Tendulkar's
play The Vultures which essentially reiterates the theme of
The Vendor, that is, "the end of reverences, the end of the
family, individuals striking out on their own, social chaos"
(p. 45). However, although Tendulkar also sees the need for
aloofness, religion provides no relief. In another of his

plays, <u>Sakharam Binder</u>, the low caste hero who rejects all faith and community ties, is totally destroyed. Thus, Naipaul concludes this section with an assault of Hinduism: "Gandhism has had its great day . . . Hinduism hasn't been good enough for the millions. . . . It has enslaved one quarter of the population and always left the whole fragmented and vulnerable . . . if has stifled growth" (p. 50).

Part two begins with a telling picture of poverty and overcrowding in Bombay. Beggars, once a demonstration of the operation of Karma, have now become too numerous to be neatly accommodated within the system. A family is fortunately "established" if, regardless of size, it occupies a chawl room, that is, a single room connected to a central corridor, with lavatories and facilities. The less fortunate have created squatter's settlements (low mud huts) for themselves, evolving a new religion and affiliating with Shiv Sena, the xenophobic army of Shiva (Shivaji, a seventh century Maratha guerrilla leader). Naipaul takes a firsthand look at one such settlement and the workings of the several Sena Committees. He notices that the members of the group are small, averaging five feet—"generations of undernourishment had whittled away bodies and muscle" (p. 65). Hearing the committee leader's apologetic remark that since it is Sunday, the municipal sweepers have not come, Naipaul muses:

> Again! Sweepers, the lowest of the low . . . some sections of the settlement . . . there were as yet no Committees. Through these sections we walked without speaking, picking our way between squits and butts and twists of human excrement. It was unclean to clean; it was unclean even to notice. It was the business of the sweepers to remove excrement, and until the sweepers came, people were content to live in the midst of their own excrement. (pp.67-68)

Naipaul is even more repulsed by the sight of two women trying to huddle into hiding two street cows "who had been tethered, churning up excrement with their own." That evening, hearing a journalist speak on the subject of Indian identity, Naipaul thought of the Sena men, "unaccommodated men making a claim on their land for the first time. . . . For them the past was dead; they had left it behind in the villages (pp. 71-72).

The next visit takes Naipaul to a cooperative irrigation project on the Deccan plateau. He observes that Old India "requires few tools, few skills, and many hands." The images are arresting: "The street-sweeper in Jaipur City uses his fingers alone to lift dust from the street into his car (p. 75). Naipaul narrates his tour to a Maharashtran village near Pune, a tour guided by the <u>sarpanch</u>, chairman of the village <u>panchayal</u>, or council. The <u>sarpanch</u> was regarded as

blessed and powerful, but the Patel, the biggest landowner in
the village, was a grander master, controlling the fate of
several families. Naipaul gets an insider's look at the
house of the Patel: "It was a house of plenty, a house of
grain. . . . Electric light, ready water, an outhouse: the
Patel was the only man in the village to possess them all"[99]
(pp. 82-88). With the oppressive rule of the Patel and his
attendants, it is impossible that laws about minimum wage,
abolition of untouchability, and rural indebtedness could be
enforced. People are trapped:

> All the way from Poona . . . it was dotted with
> sodden little culsters of African-like huts: the
> encampments of people in flight from the villages,
> people who had been squeezed out and had nowhere
> else to go, except here, near the highway, close to
> the town, exchanging nullity for nullity: people
> fleeing not only from landlessness but also from
> tyranny, the rule in a thousand villages of men like
> the Patel and the sarpanch. (pp. 91-92)

Some of these humiliated people are forced to form criminal
communities. In fact, one such revolutionary movement, led
by communists, began in 1968, north of Bengal in a district,
Naxalbari. However, the "Naxilite" movement, as the group
was called, lacked the intellectual ability and understanding required. "But the alarm has been sounded. The
millions are on the move. Both in the cities and in the
villages there is an urgent new claim on the land. . . . The
poor are no longer the occasion for sentiment or holy
almsgiving (pp. 96-97).

Part three begins with Naipaul's most controversial
essay, "A Defect of Vision," which discusses the Indian ego.
Quoting from Gandhi's autobiography, The Story of My
Experiments with Truth, Naipaul points out that the landscape and the outward are saliently missing, something true
of many other Indian autobiographies: "The inward concentration is fierce, the self-absorption complete. . . . No
London building is described, no street, no room, no crowd,
no public conveyance. . . . The outer world matters only in
so far as it affects the inner" (pp. 102-6). To prove his
point that this attitude is typically Indian, Naipaul quotes
approvingly from Dr. Sudhir Kakar, a psychotherapist at
Jawaharlal Nehru University in New Delhi:

> The Indian ego is "undeveloped," "the world of magic
> and animistic ways of thinking lie close to the
> surface", and the Indian grasp of reality
> "relatively tenuous." "Generally among Indians" . .
> . there seems to be a different relationship to
> outside reality, compared to one met within the
> West. In India it is closer to a certain stage in

322

childhood when outer objects did not have a
separate, independent existence but were intimately
related to the self and its affective states. . .
." (p. 107)

According to Kakar, the underdeveloped Indian ego is
controlled by a strictly regulated social and religious
structure and never allowed to grow. Naipaul explains: "Men
do not actively explore the world; rather they are defined by
it." This attitude is the key in understanding the condition
of India which now "has little to offer the world except its
Gandhian concept of holy poverty and the recurring crooked
comedy of its holy men, and which, while asserting the
antiquity of its civilization . . . is now dependent in every
practical way on other, imperfectly understood civilizations"
(pp. 109-10). U. R. Anantamurti's novel Samskara, which
portrays a barbaric civilization crippled by rules and magic,
corroborated Kakar's thesis. The tragedy is that "when men
cannot observe, they don't have ideas; they have
obsessions." Naipaul comments on India's current state of
affairs:

> India is poor: the fact has only recently begun to
> be observed in India . . . until the other day
> [poverty] was regarded by everyone else as a fact of
> Indian life, and holy, a cause for pious Gandhian
> pride. . . .
> Individual obsessions coalesce into political
> movements . . . Many of these movements look back
> to the past, which they reinterpret to suit their
> needs. Some, like the Shiv Sena . . . have positive
> regenerating effects. Others, like the Anand Marg .
> . . asserting caste and violence and sexual laxity .
> . . are the grossest kind of Hindu cult. . . .
> Hinduism can decline into barbarism. (pp. 120-21)

Naipaul next attacks the India "lover," particularly a
woman who lied about the reality of India:

> She spoke with passion, but she didn't believe what
> she said. The poor of Bombay are not beautiful,
> even with their picturesque costumes in low-caste
> colors. In complexion, features and physique, the
> poor are distinct from the well-to-do: they are
> like a race apart, a dwarf race, stunted and
> slow-witted and made ugly by generations of
> undernourishment; it will take generations to
> rehabilitate them. The idea that the poor are
> beautiful was, with this girl, a borrowed idea. (p.
> 125)

In order to avoid the trap of sentimentality and to come to
terms with the poor, Indians are forced to look outside their

country; however, they are intellectually confused by imported ideas. Efforts at intermediate technology have circled back to the past--the spinning wheel, the bullock cart. Old India, which "continues," thrives on borrowed ideas, as seen in various disciplines and skills. The National Institute of Design at Ahmedabad in Gujarat, continually redesigning tools for peasants, is an imported institution, which is out of touch with reality. Thus, the problem is that India's "past was too much with it, was still being lived out in the rituals, the laws, the magic" (p. 138). Under compulsion from the government, the press, which reflects a limited vision and spirit of inquiry, has now turned to social issues, instead of political ones. But the law, because of its conflict with _dharma_, can resist change. Naipaul concludes that the Emergency "dramatizes India's creative incapacity, its intellectual depletion, its defenselessness, the inadequacy of every Indian's idea of India" (p. 144).

Naipaul is disgusted by Indians who surrender to the enjoyment of wallowing in self-pity. A number of leaders in the opposition to Indira Gandhi's Emergency offer different shades of Gandhianism, mostly revolution without ideas. Mr. Desai's distorted version included the "old Indian attitudes of defeat, the idea of withdrawal . . . a sinking back into the past, the rediscovery of old ways, 'simplicity'" (p. 153). Naipaul observes that Mahatma Gandhi "took India out of one kind of _Kal yug_, one kind of Black Age; his success inevitably pushed it back into another" (p. 165). To Naipaul, Gandhi's failure is that he left India without an ideology and with an intellectual vacuum:

> If he had projected onto India another code of survival, he might have left independent India with an ideology, and perhaps even with what in India would have been truly revolutionary, the continental racial sense, the sense of belonging to a people specifically of India, which would have answered all his political aims, and more. . . . (p. 190)

Gandhi's worshippers became vain. Vinoba · Bhave, his successor, who distorted and parodied his master, has made religion "a kind of barbarism; it would return men to the bush. It is the religion of poverty and dust" (p. 177). The Emergency, which dismantled borrowed institutions, left India with the "blankness of its decayed civilization," a civilization in which men are fettered by _dharma_. Thus, Naipaul's main thesis about India is that this intellectually depleted country is doomed unless the Indian mind becomes free of obsession with Hinduism--"the only hope lies in further swift decay" (p. 191).

The maturity and mellowness of India, in comparison to An Area of Darkness, perhaps account for the mixed reaction from Indian critics.[85] Again, familiar questions have been raised about Naipaul's qualifications and about his capacity for the objectivity required to conduct a sound study of India. Western reviewers often comment on Naipaul's dual perspective as the outsider and insider. For example, the National Review saw Naipaul as "especially well situated to mediate between the Indian and the Westerner," and to both Listener and the Christian Science Monitor, the Trinidadian scene gave the writer the impartial eye of a stranger.[86] Indian critics, however, are divided. Riaz Hussain, agreeing with Westerners, argued that Naipaul as a Trinidadian has "retained a basic understanding of the Indian way of thinking. He is a visitor to India but his roots are there; he is both an insider and a foreigner."[87] T. R. S. Sharma noted that since Naipaul enjoys the position of an expatriate writer who is not "committed," he has the license to write unpalatable truths, even if they are unsuitable for genteel taste.[88]

These opinions on Naipaul's position, however, have been challenged by some Indians who blame the "misconceptions" contained in India on the expatriate's inability to understand Indian cultural values. H. H. Anniah Gowda theorized that since Naipaul has lived in several societies, he has been robbed of an inner vision. Accusing the writer of approaching India with only the knowledge of "a handful of naturalistic novels" written for foreigners, Gowda sarcastically wrote: "Perhaps in the latter half of the twentieth century, it is fashionable to pass off as a cultural relativist by judging a society by standards which manufacture best-selling fodder.[89] Dilip Chitre, whose blistering refutation of India is popular, is even more acerbic than Gowda. Chitre censured Naipaul for turning away from the Caribbean identity and for identifying himself with "upper-class English" and with the literary and intellectual traditions of England. Chitre suggested that Naipaul is "psychologically an émigré, an atavist though inverted," who aspires to Anglo-Saxon culture and spurns his "ethnic identity and native nationality." Speculating on the reason why Naipaul found India difficult, Chitre raged:

> Naipaul's difficulty is shared, in some familiar way, by Indian migrants to various countries. They cannot do anything about their ethnic visibility; nor is cultural integration easy, swift, and complete anywhere in the world. . . . A certain paranoid schizophrenia is likely to persist. . . . Why should he compulsively return to India and produce two books—more than twelve years apart—to vehemently reject a country as if it were some fetish of his own? Is Naipaul carrying the burden

of some guilt for being brown, for having had Hindu
ancestors, for having been born in a tiny island
colony like Trinidad, for being physically and very
visibly like any other wog? Does his English
conditioning and English ambition conflict with a
subconscious sense of inferiority--both ethnic and
cultural?[90]

This anger goes beyond Naipaul's cultural background.
    Apart from the praise of Naipaul's language in the
description of Bombay,[91] Chitre has found everything wrong
with India. He questioned the very foundation of Naipaul's
approach and listed the following as common intellectual
traps into which the writer falls: "the stereotypes, the
generalizations, the simplifications, the fallacies arising
out of partial insights, the temptation selectively to
present to oneself only evidence that supports one's
assumptions and biases."[92] To Chitre, India is the
antithesis of a tourist brochure and just as selective.
Reading Naipaul's comments on the Sena Committee members'
height as an example of Gulliveran fantasy, Chitre snapped:
"I believe Mr. Naipaul himself, in terms of physical size, is
not much different from the average North Indian. . . .
Would Naipaul looking at the size of Japanese or the Chinese
draw similar conclusions?" Chitre argued that in the visit
to the House of Patel, Naipaul looks only for the kind of
detail which fits into his preconceived notion, failing to
see that the Patels, no longer vulnerable, are becoming
democratized.[93] Naipaul is also accused of making sweeping
generalizations based on R. K. Narayan's fictional characters:

    To say that Jagan's 'ultimate Hindu retreat' from
    reality signifies "the death of a civilization, the
    final corruption of Hinduism" is to make an
    attractively bold intuitive assertion. . . . A
    reading of Bengali, Urdu, Punjabi, Marathi, Hindi,
    Gujarati or Kannada fiction and short fiction
    produced during the last four decades may reveal
    something else.[94]

In his review of India, Gowda likewise blamed Naipaul's
dependence on "stories" and his failure to see that India is
neither a "story" nor a "fable" but a "living country."[95]
    It is, however, the conclusions on the Indian ego and
Gandhi that have excited the greatest interest. Chitre,
refuting the section on Indians' inability to observe
external reality as evident in Gandhi's autobiography, My
Experiment, angrily charged that Naipaul deliberately ignores
the fact that the book was written forty years after the
events it describes. Chitre continued:

And he [Naipaul] ignores that Gandhi's autobiography
is an attempt to analyse his own moral development.
It is not meant to be some sort of nostalgic or
juicy memoirs; nor does it attempt to recollect,
forty years later, seasons, places and people for
their own sake. . . .
      While one does not deny the possibility that
Gandhi's apathy towards the external world is, as
alleged by Naipaul, a consequence of his Hindu
upbringing and obsessions, there could be other
explanations. . . . Gandhi, to make an under-
statement, was a unique individual even by Hindu
standards.[96]

In article for the Indian Book Chronicle Mohindar Singh
justified Gandhi's omission of the external by placing My
Experiments in a special category, more aligned with the
genre of St. Augustine's than with other autobiographies.
Gandhi's autobiography, according to Singh, describes the
man's "moral and spiritual itinerary rather than historical
chronology," and there "isn't room enough for lengthy
discursive accounts of people and places except those which
have a direct bearing on the formation of personal values and
principles, and the activity involved in pursuit of the
same." Singh further speculated that Gandhi was probably
discouraged by the wealth of material from which to
choose.[97] Of Naipaul's comments about the undeveloped
Indian as evident in Gandhi's and other Indian's autobiographies, Chitre retorted: "On the basis of what bibliography has Naipaul arrived at this conclusion? . . . When
Naipaul talks of the 'the Indian way experience' and glibly
refers to 'many Indian autobiographies' he is covering up his
lack of preparation with a smooth, reassuring, assertive
style."[98] Gowda is disturbed more by Naipaul's criticism
of Gandhi: "This clever man [Naipaul] is trying to be too
clever. Of late, it has become a fashion with some of our
writers living in the West . . . to denigrate Gandhi . . .
He is unfair to Gandhi and to his immense efforts in
propounding a political ideology beyond the comprehension of
Naipaul."[99] Still, some Indians, both inside and outside
the country, have ended up endorsing Naipaul's interpretation of Gandhi's legacy. For example, although Sharma
doubted that Gandhi's obsessions should be ascribed to
Hinduism, he conceded that many of Naipaul's statements on
the leader are indisputable.[100] Srinivasa Sastry wondered
what specifically Naipaul had in mind when he accuses Gandhi
of leaving "no code of survival" and no "continental racial
sense"; however, the reviewer admitted that Naipaul's
analysis of the character and contribution of Gandhi is both
"perceptive and understanding."[101]
      Perhaps because of national pride, strong Indian
nationalists expect unfavorable reviews of any book critical

of Gandhi or of India. Ramlal Agarwal noted this expectation
but refused to conform:

> Under the circumstances, if an Indian reviewer does
> not brand Naipaul's book as anti-Indian and there-
> fore totally untrue and undependable, he is likely
> to be called a renegade, a brown sahib. Even so,
> there is no gainsaying the fact that _India_ . . . is
> an astonishingly accurate analyst of Indian
> character.[102]

A surprising number of Indian reviewers have agreed with this
evaluation. To Riaz Hussain, for example, this worthwhile
book is a "searching enquiry into the Indian mentality and
presents the Indian scene as it really is."[103] But the
most detailed confirmation of the validity of Naipaul's
thesis, especially as it relates to attitudes about the past,
comes from K. Narayan Kutty, whose article is published next
to Chitre's in the same issue of _New Quest_. Although
acknowledging that _India_ contains serious flaws, he welcomed
the book which he predicted will infuriate "intellectually
touchy" nationals.[104]

Kutty lauded _India_ as an invigorating work, superior to
the hollow and "mindless adulation India receives from
sentimental and self-indulgent Western visionaries."[105]
Praising Naipaul for crushing existing myths and for not
becoming consumed with India's spirituality, Kutty agreed
that Indians have used the past as an excuse for isolation,
indifference, inaction, and parasitism. He analyzed the
problem:

> Most Indians are unwilling to change their age-old
> ways of life; change is anathema to them; they
> accept anarchy as order and instability as perma-
> nence. Because of their fear of change, Indians
> cling to their past. . . . But this past is a dead
> past; it lives on only in its ruins; it has nothing
> to offer by way of a cure for the many ills of
> contemporary India. Indians have to liberate
> themselves from the intellectually stultifying past;
> its meaningless rituals and destructive traditions
> have stymied the progress of India as a nation. . .
> . Naipaul is not asking Indians to reject their
> past . . . he is only asking them to liberate
> themselves from its lethal and enervating
> influences. More importantly Naipaul is asking
> Indians not to retreat into the past when the
> present appears chaotically unmanageable.[106]

According to Kutty, the fictional characters to whom Naipaul
alludes have dangerously retreated into archaism and rituals.
Impatient with this Indian dependence on piety and

spirituality (a characteristic which permits India simply to
"go on"), Kutty called for the elimination of Karma and he
saw Ramrajya as "sheer fantasy" which impedes India's
progress: "As Naipaul says, no amount of pious talk about
Ramrajya, about ancient village panchayats, and about the
purity of the self is going to change anything in India."
Kutty suggested that a radical change, in the modern
direction in the attitudes of Indians, will effect the much
needed social, economic, and cultural revolution. Finally,
he underscored the point that the real past, used
advantageously, can become an important part of the present
and can prompt Indians to act, to live well, not to flee or
merely "exist."[107]
    Other reviewers appear to be willing to strike a
compromise with Naipaul's recommendation concerning the
past. Srinivasa Sastry wondered: "True, the past is dead;
but it is deadening? . . . Is it not possible and/or
worthwhile to achieve a relationship to the past through an
awareness of what it is and what its worth is for us
today?"[108] Similarly, interpreting Naipaul's comments as a
call for total rejection of the past, Sharma argued:

> But to deny one's past completely is to reject one's
> history. Naipaul's statement therefore is
> incomplete. He doesn't answer the question, after
> rejecting the past, what next? . . . [Indians
> should] pick examples from their own past where
> there was a far more egalitarian usage, and say, ah,
> this is what we are talking about, it's not really
> so remote from us . . .
>   Well, that's how perhaps a dialogue should
> begin between the present and the past.[109]

Sharma contended that the Hindu attitude leaves no room for
"new morality," and he agrees with Naipaul on the irration-
ality of the caste system which shows no sign of being
dismantled. As an escape from the squalor and the moral and
physical dereliction, Indians turn to religion, and according to Sharma, Naipaul simply exposes this defense mechanism
and reflex.[110]
    Perhaps it is unwise to generalize about Western
reception of India, but a glance at the several reviews shows
that despite some questions about Naipaul's thesis, the book
has enjoyed a higher rating in the West than in India. To
Joseph Lelyveld, Naipaul holds impossible standards and
treats Gandhi unfairly, but the work is "indispensable for
anyone who wants seriously to come to grips with the
experience of India"; to Nicholas Mosley he makes
generalizations which are not peculiar to India only, but he
presents "a tough, sharp-witted, brightly illuminating book",
nonetheless; to Paul Scott he labels Indians unfairly as a

separate group, but the book is a "fine collection of
beautifully modulated and thought-out essays" from the pen
of a "front novelist" and a "first-rate journalist"; to the
reviewer for Economist he presents an unbalanced Indian
truth, but his pessimism is persuasive; finally, to Peter
Berger Naipaul supposes Western superiority but writes with a
"surgical eye."[111] Apart from these reservations and apart
from complaints from the reviewers for America and American
Historical Review that Naipaul is biased against Indira
Gandhi's opposition and against Hinduism, no other Western
critic expresses any major concerns.[112] The rest have
given unqualified praise; to them India, written with "great
insight," is an "incredibly intelligent, passionate and even
brilliant book," with an "instinct for home truth."[113] The
mere fact that the New York Times Book Review selected India
as one of the best books published in 1977 in the non-fiction
category speaks of the book's standing in the West.

However, in India, despite the few favorable reviews and
the admission of at least some truth in Naipaul's analysis,
India is largely dismissed as the work of an unfeeling
Western-oriented stranger who cannot understand the country.
Sharma made the point that Indians are angry because they
perceive Naipaul as an outsider and they "want to deny him
the right to use an insider's knowledge, a knowledge which in
our honest moments we recognise as truth."[114] Sharma
compared the attitude of Indian critics to that of the
protagonist in Achebe's A Man of the People, Odili, who
rebukes an American driving him around the slums of Lagos:
"Your accusation may be true but you have no right to make
it."[115] However, Kutty strongly believed that what India
really needs is "positive response to constructive criticism,
however harsh and from whatever source, and he hoped that
Naipaul will generate some disgust:

> Acceptance of Naipaul's serious criticism of India
> may make at least some Indians disgusted with the
> squalid and undignified lives of the Indian masses.
> Disgust with the way things are, that is what
> Indians need to feel today. Disgust will replace
> complacency and apathy. Disgust will open their
> eyes to the abjectness of the lives of nearly
> three-quarters of the great Indian population.
> Disgust will lead to a new consciousness of the
> realities of Indian life, which, in turn, will lead
> to the conviction that they should demand more for
> themselves and from themselves.[116]

However, this hope, as we learn from Naipaul himself, has
been dashed.

In 1979 conversation with Robert Boyers and Bharati
Mukherjee, Naipaul, reiterating his main thesis, not only

condemned the sympathetic approach to India but also
expressed regret that his books have landed on deaf ears in a
country urgently in need of self-analysis. He was blunt:

> N: They've [Indians] had too much sympathy, don't you
> think? They've had too many lovers of India loving
> them for their wretchedness and their misery and
> their slavery and their wish to keep others trapped.
>
> BM: But no one I know wants to encourage that kind of
> Indophile.
>
> N: What do you want? You see, I'm not sure you know.
> What I want is for India to regard itself as a big
> country. It should be doing something in the
> world. It should have high standards of
> achievement. A country with 600 to 700 million
> people which is now offering the world nothing but
> illegitimate holy men should be ashamed of itself. .
> . . For a time I hope my little proddings might
> start something. But clearly they're not going to
> start anything at all.[117]

In fact, Naipaul has arrived at the conclusion that Asiatics
are a people who, at any rate, do not read for the sake of
inquiry or curiosity. Their religion has filled their world
completely for them, thus their dependence solely on "magic"
and on holy books, sacred hymns, wisdom books, materials
which will do them "good."[118] In an interview with
Elizabeth Hardwick, having again complained of being tired of
"India-lovers," he issued the same provocative statement: "I
do not write for Indians, who in any case do not read. My
work is only possible in a liberal, civilized Western country.
It is not possible in primitive societies."[119]

Naipaul's prognosis of India, then, articulated in _An
Area of Darkness_ and _India_ is as blistering as his prognosis
of the Caribbean seen in the West Indian books. In both of
these regions of which Naipaul writes with so much rage--and
concern--he is greeted with the expected denial and repu-
diation. The protests of Indian critics--about Naipaul's
Brahmin upbringing and Western sensibility, his expatriate
lack of understanding and one-sidedness, his superiority
complex and cold detachment--are familiar ones already echoed
in the Caribbean. No doubt in his stubborn insistence on
focusing primarily on the brutal and the repulsive in a
compassionless and unsympathetic manner, Naipaul courts and
provokes the type of response his works have generated. Had
he transmitted the same ideas but applied a more tactful and
a less uninhibited approach, perhaps his reception in the
Third World might have been different. But to demand this
approach of Naipaul is to open a Pandora's box of questions
about the obligation, responsibility, and freedom of the
writer.

Notes

1 V. S. Naipaul, <u>An Area of Darkness</u> (London: André Deutsch, 1964; rpt. New York: Vintage Books, 1981), pp. 29-44. All further references to this work appear in the text.

2 Shyam M. Asnani, "Quest for Identity Theme in Three Commonwealth Novels," in <u>Alien Voice</u>, ed. Avadhesh K. Srivatava (Lucknow, India: Print House, 1981), pp. 128 ff; K. I. Madhusudana Rao, "The Complex Fate," in <u>Alien Voice</u>, pp. 194 ff.

3 Prema Nandakumar, <u>The Glory and the Good</u> (New Delhi: Asia Publishing House, 1965), pp. 267 ff.; Satendra Nandan, "The Immigrant Indian Experience in Literature," in <u>Awakened Conscience</u>, ed. C.D. Narasimhaiah (New Delhi: Sterling Publishers Pvt. Ltd., 1978), pp. 354-55.

4 M. K. Naik, "Irony as Stance and as Vision," <u>The Journal of Indian Writing in English</u>, 6, No. 1 (Jan. 1978), 1-13; D. V. K. Raghavacharyulu, "Naipaul and Narayan," in <u>Awakened Conscience</u>, pp. 210 -20; C. N. Srinath, "Crisis of Identity," <u>The Literary Criterion</u>, 14, No. 1 (1979), 33-41; K. S. Ramamurti, "Patterns of Distinctiveness in the Language of Commonwealth Fiction," <u>The Literary Half-Yearly</u>, 22, No. 2 (July 1981), 85-100.

5 Satyanarain Singh et al., eds., <u>Osmania Journal of English Studies</u> (Hyderabad, India: Osmania University, 1982).

6 Raghavacharyulu, "Naipaul and Narayan," p. 219; Srinath, p. 34.

7 Eric Stokes, "The High-caste Defector," rev. of India, <u>Times Literary Supplement</u>, 21 Oct. 1977, p. 1229; V. S. Naipaul, <u>India</u> (New York: Alfred Knopf, 1977; rpt. New York: Vintage Books, 1978), p. xi. All further references to this work appear in the text.

8 Paul Theroux, <u>V. S. Naipaul</u> (New York: Africana Publishing Co., 1972), p. 90; Landeg White, <u>V. S. Naipaul</u> (London: Macmillan Press, 1975), p. 21.

9 "Between Two Stools," in <u>Alien Voice</u>, pp. 230-31.

10 "Between Two Stools," p. 230.

11 "Areas of Darkness and Light," <u>Journal of the Madras University</u>, 54, No. 1 (Jan. 1982), 2.

12 "V. S. Naipaul and the Confused Hindu Sensibility," in Osmania Journal of English Studies, pp. 39-44.

13 "Naipaul in India," The Literary Half-Yearly, 11, No. 2 (July 1970), 166.

14 "The Complex Fate," p. 197.

15 Ramamurti, "Areas of Darkness and Light," p. 9.

16 "West Indian Writer Visits Homeland of his Ancestors," rev. of An Area of Darkness, The Times (London), Sept. 17 1964, p. 17.

17 "Mr. Naipaul's Passage to India," rev. of An Area of Darkness, Times Literary Supplement, 24 Sept. 1964, p. 881.

18 Theroux, p. 98.

19 V. S. Naipaul (Edinburgh: Oliver and Boyd, 1973), p. 23

20 "Who is India?" rev. of An Area of Darkness, Encounter, 23 (December 1964), 61.

21 "'Somewhere Something Has Snapped,'" Indian Horizons, 21, No. 4 (Oct. 1972), 39-40.

22 David. pp. 233-34.

23 "Two Descriptions of the Elephant," rev. of An Area of Darkness, Reporter, 9 Sept. 1965, p. 42.

24 Sharma, p. 29; Gowda, "Naipaul in India," p. 163.

25 "Areas of Darkness and Light," p. 2.

26 Orville Prescott, "The Land of His Ancestors," rev. of An Area of Darkness, New York Times, 16 April 1965, p. 27; Robert Hamner, V. S. Naipaul (New York: Twayne Inc., 1973), p. 225; Enright, "Who is India?" p. 60; William Walsh, V. S. Naipaul, p. 26; Michael Thorpe, V. S. Naipaul (London: The British Council/Longmans, 1976), p. 23.

27 "'Somewhere Something has Snapped,'" p. 44.

28 "India: Theirs and Mine," in Osmania Journal of English Studies, p. 129.

29 "Naipaul's India and Mine," in New Writing in India, ed. Adil Jussawalla (Baltimore, Maryland: Penguin, 1974), pp. 75-76.

[30] "'Somewhere Something Has Snapped,'" p. 41.

[31] "Naipaul in India," p. 165.

[32] "Unhappy Pilgrim," rev. of An Area of Darkness, New York Times Book Review, 11 July 1965, p. 35. See alo K. Narayan Kutty, "Naipaul and India 1," New Quest (India), 9 (May-June 1978), 173.

[33] "Naipaul's India and Mine," pp. 75, 85.

[34] "Naipaul's India and Mine," p. 77.

[35] "Naipaul's India and Mine," pp. 78-81.

[36] "Naipaul's India and Mine," p. 84.

[37] David, pp. 231-32.

[38] David, p. 232.

[39] "'Somewhere Something Has Snapped,'" pp. 42-43.

[40] Thorpe, p. 24. See also Eric Stokes, p. 1229.

[41] V. S. Naipaul, p. 23.

[42] Ezekiel, p. 87.

[43] "Naipaul in India," pp. 166-67.

[44] "Areas of Darkness and Light," p. 7.

[45] "'Somewhere Something Has Snapped,'" p. 37.

[46] "Two Descriptions of the Elephant," p. 40.

[47] Masih, "India," p. 129.

[48] Masih, pp. 128-30.

[49] Ezekiel, p. 82.

[50] "'Somewhere Something Has Snapped,'" p. 44.

[51] Hamner, V. S. Naipaul, p. 26.

[52] Ramamurti, "Areas of Darkness and Light," pp. 5-6; Narasimhaiah, "'Somewhere Something Has Snapped,'" p. 46; Ezekiel, pp. 83-84; K. Natwar-Singh, "Unhappy Pilgrim," p. 35; Gowda, "Naipaul in India," p. 166.

334

53 "'Somewhere Something Has Snapped,'" p. 49. See also Gowda, "Naipaul in India," p. 165.

54 "Beyond Exile and Homecoming," in _Alien Voice_, p. 33.

55 Sharma, p. 30.

56 One exception is Theroux, who thinks that Naipaul is impatient and easily fatigued, p. 100.

57 "The Anglo-Indian Theme," rev. of _An Area of Darkness_, _Commentary_, 39 (June 1965), 96.

58 In addition to the sources cited in this paragraph, see also V. S. Pritchett, "Back to India," rev. of _An Area of Darkness_, _New Statesman_, 11 Sept. 1964, pp. 361-62; "Mr. Naipaul's Passage to India," p. 881.

59 Mander, p. 96.

60 Henry Reed, "Passage to India," rev. of _An Area of Darkness_, _Spectator_, 2 Oct. 1964, p. 452.

61 "Who is India?" p. 61.

62 "'Somewhere Something Has Snapped,'" p. 45.

63 Rau, p. 42; Gowda, "Naipaul in India," p. 167; Ezekiel, p. 85.

64 "'Somewhere Something Has Snapped,'" pp. 38-39.

65 "Naipaul in India," p. 170.

66 Ezekiel, pp. 75-84.

67 Ezekiel, p. 74; Narasimhaiah, "Somewhere Something Has Snapped,'" p. 48.

68 Ezekiel, pp. 74-77.

69 Sharma, p. 29.

70 "Areas of Darkness and Light," pp. 5-7.

71 "Areas of Darkness and Light," p. 7; Rao, "The Complex Fate," p. 198; Masih, p. 128.

72 Masih, pp. 126-27.

73 Gowda, "Naipaul in India," pp. 163-4. See also Thota, "Naipaul and the Confused Sensibility," p. 37.

[74] The Glory and the Good, p. 267.

[75] "'Somewhere Something Has Snapped,'" p. 48.

[76] Ramamurti, "Areas of Darkness and Light," p. 10.

[77] Rev. of An Area of Darkness, Canadian Forum, 45 (June 1965), 70.

[78] "Mr. Naipaul's Passage to India," p. 881. See also Reed, p. 453 and Prescott, p. 27.

[79] Reed, p. 453; Prescott, p. 27.

[80] "Mr. Naipaul's Passage," p. 881.

[81] Raja Rao, "Out of Step with Shiva," rev. of An Area of Darkness, Book Week, 29 Aug. 1965, p. 14.

[82] K. Natwar-Singh, p. 35.

[83] H. H. Anniah Gowda, rev. of India, Ariel, 10, No. 1 (Jan. 1979), 99; C. D. Narasimhaiah, "Report on the Conference. . . ." The Literary Criterion, 10, No. 2 (Winter 1971). 4.

[84] Eric Stokes, p. 1229.

[85] Both Sharma, p. 30 and Kutty, p. 173 noted that India is more relaxed and less angry than An Area of Darkness. Western reviewers agree, except Martin Amis, "In a State of Emergency," rev. of India, New Statesman, 21 Oct. 1977, p. 543.

[86] Linda Bridges, "Books in Brief," rev. of India, National Review, 26 May 1978, p. 667; Nicholas Mosley, "In Place of Taboos," rev. of India, Listener, 3 Nov. 1977, p. 591; and Henry S. Hayward, "Naipaul Presents an India both Changing, Unchanging," rev. of India, Christian Science Monitor, 20 June 1977, p. 23.

[87] Riaz Hussain, rev. of India, Best Sellers, 37 (Aug. 1977), 153.

[88] Sharma, p. 26.

[89] Rev. of India, p. 100.

[90] Dilip Chitre, "Naipaul and India 2," New Quest (India) 9 (May–June), 176–80. Sudha Rai's book, V. S. Naipaul (New Delhi: Arnold-Heinemann Publishers Ltd., 1983), attempts to refute Naipaul's theses on India in all his Indian works and examines his complex sensibility as a crucial factor that accounts for his misunderstandings.

[91] Chitre, pp. 182-83.

[92] Chitre, p. 177.

[93] Chitre, pp. 183-84.

[94] Chitre, p. 181.

[95] Rev. of India, p. 100.

[96] Chitre, pp. 184-85.

[97] "Gandhi and 'A Defect of Vision,'" Indian Book Chronicle, 4, Nos. 1 & 3 (Jan. 1979), 34.

[98] Chitre, p. 185.

[99] Rev. of India, pp. 100-01.

[100] Sharma, p. 31.

[101] "Naipaul on India," Cross Currents, 27, No. 4 (1977-78), 479.

[102] Rev. of India, World Literature Today, 52 (Spring 1978), 343.

[103] Hussain, p. 153.

[104] "Naipaul and India 1," New Quest (India), 9 (May – June 1978), 167-73.

[105] Kutty, p. 169.

[106] Kutty, pp. 168-69.

[107] Kutty, p. 171.

[108] Sastry, p. 480.

[109] Sharma, p. 35.

[110] Sharma, p. 33.

[111] Joseph Lelyveld, "For Naipaul a Difficult Country," rev. of India, New York Times Book Review, 12 June 1977, pp. 10, 44; Nicholas Mosley, pp. 591 -92; Paul Scott, "India's Collective Amnesia," rev. of India, Guardian Weekly (London), 17 July 1977, p. 18; "Defect of Vision," rev. of India, Economist, 5 Nov. 1977, p. 132; Peter Berger, rev. of India, The New Republic, 9 July 1977, pp. 31-32.

112 Jermiah Novack, rev. of India, America, 25 June 1977, p. 570; Edward Haynes, rev. of India, The American Historical Review, 83 (Oct. 1978), 1079-80.

113 Rev. of India, Book World (Washington Post), 14 May 1978, p. G 6. Tomas Massey, "China, India, and Me," rev. of India, The Washington Monthly, 10 (March 1978), 44; Shernaz Mollinger, rev. of India, Library Journal, 102 (July 1977), 1478.

114 Sharma, p. 34.

115 Sharma, p. 34.

116 Kutty, p. 173.

117 Bharati Mukherjee and Robert Boyers, "A Conversation
with V. S. Naipaul," Salmagundi, 54 (Fall 1981), 20.

118 Mukherjee and Boyers, p. 5.

119 Elizabeth Hardwick, "Meeting V. S. Naipaul, New York Times Book Review, 13 May 1979, p. 36.

Bibliography

I. Primary Sources

A. Books

Naipaul, V. S. Among the Believers: An Islamic Journey.
New York: Alfred Knopf, 1981; rpt. New York: Vintage
Books, 1981.

_____. An Area of Darkness. London: André Deutsch,
1964; rpt. New York: Vintage Books, 1981.

_____. A Bend in the River. New York: Alfred Knopf,
1979; rpt. Vintage Books, 1980.

_____. Finding the Center: Two Narratives. New
York: Alfred Knopf, 1984.

_____. A Flag on the Island. Harmondsworth, England:
Penguin, 1967; rpt. New York: Penguin Books, 1982.

_____. Guerrillas. London: André Deutsch, 1975;
rpt. New York: Vintage Books, 1980.

_____. A House for Mr Biswas. Londòn: André
Deutsch, 1961; rpt. New York: Penguin Books, 1982.

_____. In a Free State. London: André Deutsch,
1971; rpt. New York: Penguin Books, 1982.

_____. India: A Wounded Civilization. New York:
Alfred Knopf, 1977; rpt. New York: Vintage Books, 1978.

_____. The Loss of El Dorado. London: André
Deutsch, 1962; rpt. New York: Penguin Books, 1981.

_____. The Middle Passage: Impressions of Five
Societies--British, French and Dutch--in the West
Indies and South America. London: André Deutsch,
1962; rpt. New York: Vintage Books, 1981.

_____. Miguel Street. London: André Deutsch, 1959;
rpt. New York: Penguin Books, 1981.

340

_____. The Mimic Men. London: André Deutsch, 1967; rpt. New York: Penguin Books, 1981.

_____. Mr Stone and the Knights Companion. London André Deutsch, 1963; rpt. New York: Penguin Books, 1981.

_____. The Mystic Masseur. London: André Deutsch, 1957; rpt. London: Heinemann Educational Books Ltd., 1978.

_____. The Overcrowded Barracoon. London: André Deutsch, 1972; rpt. New York: Penguin Books, 1976.

_____. The Return of Eva Peron with the Killings in Trinidad. New York: Alfred Knopf, 1980; rpt. New York: Vintage Books, 1981.

_____. The Suffrage of Elvira. London: André Deutsch, 1958; rpt. New York: Penguin Books, 1981.

B.   Articles--Those items reprinted, for example, in The Overcrowded Barracoon, A Flag on the Island, In a Free State, and The Return of Eva Peron will not be mentioned.

"Bennett Award Acceptance Speech, 1980." Hudson Review, 33, No. 4 (Winter 1980-81), 481.

"Caribbean Medley." Vogue, Nov. 15, 1959, pp. 90, 92-93.

"Comprehending Borges." New York Review of Books, 19 Oct. 1972, pp. 3-4, 6.

"A Country Dying on Its Feet." New York Review of Books, 4 April 1974, pp. 21-23.

"Critics and Criticism." Bim (Barbados), 10, No. 38 (Jan.-June 1964), 74-77.

"The Documentary Heresy." Twentieth Century, 173 (Winter 1964), 107-08.

"Et in America Ego!" Listener, 4 Sept. 1969, pp. 302-04.

"Grenada: An Island Betrayed." Harper's Magazine, March 1984, pp. 61-72.

"Honesty Needed in West Indian Writing." Sunday Guardian (Trinidad), 28 Oct. 1956, p. 29.

"India's Cast-Off Revolution." <u>Sunday Times</u> (London), 25 Aug. 1963, p. 17.

"Introduction," in <u>East Indians of the Caribbean</u>: <u>Colonialism and the Struggle for Identity</u>. Papers presented to a Symposium of East Indians in the Caribbean, University of the West Indies, June 1975.

"Letter to Maria." <u>New Statesman</u>, 5 July 1958, p. 14.

"The Little More." <u>The Times</u> (London), 13 July 1961, p. 13.

"Living Like a Millionaire." <u>Vogue</u>, 15 Oct. 1961, pp. 92-93, 144, 147.

"Prologue to an Autobiography." <u>Vanity Fair</u>, 46, No. 2 (April 1983), 51-59, 138-56.

Rev. of <u>Of Age and Innocence</u>, by George Lamming. <u>New Statesman</u>, 6 Dec. 1958, pp. 826-27.

"Speaking of Writing." <u>The Times</u> (London), 2 Jan. 1964, p. 11.

"Tea With an Author." <u>Bim</u> (Barbados), 9, No. 34 (Jan.-June 1962), 79-81.

"They are Staring at Me." <u>Saturday Evening Post</u>, 10 April 1965, 82-84.

"Trinidad." <u>Mademoiselle</u>, 59 (May 1964), 187-188.

"A West Indian Culture?" <u>The Illustrated Weekly of India</u>, 30 May 1965, p. 23.

"What's Wrong with Being a Snob?" <u>Saturday Evening Post</u>, June 3, 1967, pp. 12, 18.

"Writing 'A House for Mr. Biswas.'" <u>The New York Review</u>, 24 Nov. 1983, pp. 22-24.

II. Secondary Sources

A. Book Reviews

1. <u>An Area of Darkness</u> (1964)

Benda, Harry J. <u>Yale Review</u>, 55 (Autumn 1965), 121-23.

342

Biswas, Robin. "Exhaustion and Persistence." <u>Tamarack
    Review</u>, 35 (Spring 1965), 75-80.

<u>Booklist</u>, 15 May 1965, pp. 897-98.

Bram, Joseph. <u>Library Journal</u>, 15 April 1965, p. 1904.

Dathorne, O. R. <u>Black Orpheus</u>, 18 (Oct. 1965), 60-61.

Delaney, Austin. "Mother India as Bitch." <u>Transition</u>, 26
    (1966), 50.

Enright, D. J. "Who is India?" <u>Encounter</u>, 23 (Dec. 1964),
    59-62; rpt. in <u>Man is an Onion</u>. Ed. D.J. Enright.
    London: Chatto & Windus, 1972.

Gupta, K. <u>Canadian Forum</u>, 45 (June 1965), 70.

Hitrec, Joseph. "A Disenchanted Journey." <u>Saturday Review</u>,
    1 May 1965, p. 42.

Mander, John. "The Anglo Indian Theme." <u>Commentary</u>, 39
    (June 1965), 94-97.

"Mr. Naipaul's Passage to India." <u>Times Literary Supplement</u>,
    24 Sept. 1964, p. 881.

Muggeridge, Malcolm. <u>Esquire</u>, 64 (Oct. 1965), 28.

Naim, C. M. <u>Books Abroad</u>, 2 (Spring 1966) p. 230.

Natwar-Singh, K. "Unhappy Pilgrim." <u>New York Times Book
    Review</u>, 11 July 1965, p. 35.

Oberbeck, Stephen. "Angry Young Indian." <u>Newsweek</u>, 16
    April 1965, pp. 103-04.

Prescott, Orville. "The Land of His Ancestors." <u>New York
    Times</u>, 16 April 1965, p. 27.

Pritchett, V. S. "Back to India." <u>New Statesman</u>, 11 Sept.
    1964, pp. 361-62.

Pryce-Jones, A. <u>New York Herald Tribune</u>, 20 April 1965,
    p. 25.

Rao, Raja. "Out of Step with Shiva." <u>Book Week</u>, 29 Aug.
    1965, pp. 4, 14.

Rau, Santha Rama. "Two Descriptions of the Elephant."
    <u>Reporter</u>, 9 Sept. 1965, pp. 40-43.

Reed, Henry. "Passage to India." Spectator, 2 Oct. 1964, pp. 452-53.

Sheehan, Edward R. F. "Cities of the Dreadful Night." Nation, 14 March 1966, pp. 300-02.

Time, 23 April 1965, pp. 109-10.

"Too Great a Burden." Economist, 12 Dec. 1964, p. 1257.

Walcott, Derek. "Mr. Naipaul's Passage to India." Sunday Guardian (Trinidad), 20 Sept. 1964, p. 4.

Walsh, William. "Meeting Extremes." Journal of Commonwealth Literature, No. 1 (Sept. 1965), 170-72.

"West Indian Writer Visits Home of His Ancestors." The Times (London), 17 Sept. 1964, p. 17.

2.   A Flag on the Island (1967)

Barker, Paul." Fiction of the Week." The Times (London), 14 Sept. 1967, p. 11.

Buchan, William. Spectator, 22 Sept. 1967, pp. 328-29.

Coleman, J. "Mr. Naipaul's Other Island, Observer, 10 Sept. 1967, p. 22.

Hartman, John W. Best Sellers, 15 April 1968, p. 29.

Kirkus, 1 Jan. 1968, p. 25.

McInnis, Raymond G. Library Journal, 1 March 1968, p. 1021.

Mac Namara, Desmond. "Flayed Skin." New Statesman, 15 Sept. 1967, p. 325.

Marsh, Pamela. "Fiction-Concentrate," Christian Science Monitor, 29 March 1968, p. 13.

Miller, Karl. "Naipaul's Emergent Country." Listener, 28 Sept. 1967, pp. 402-3.

"Movietone." Times Literary Supplement, 14 Sept. 1967, p. 813.

Panton, George. "West Indian Satirist." Sunday Gleaner (Jamaica), 3 Dec. 1967, p. 4.

Plant, Richard. "Potpourri of the Antilles." Saturday
     Review, 8 June 1968, p. 52.

Price, R. G. G. Punch, 27 Sept. 1967, p. 484.

Pritchett, V.S. "Crack-up." New York Review of Books,
     11 April 1968, pp. 10, 12-14.

Publishers' Weekly, 15 Jan. 1968, p. 83.

Wain, John. "Characters in the Sun." New York Times Book
     Review, 7 April 1968, p. 4.

3. Guerrillas (1975)

Ackroyd, Peter. "On Heat." Spectator, 13 Sept. 1975, p.
350.

Adams, P. L. Atlantic Monthly, Jan. 1976, p. 98.

Broyard, Anatole. "The Author vs. His Characters." New York
     Times, 25 Nov. 1975, p. 39.

Choice, March 1976, p. 72.

DeMott, Benjamin. "Lost Words, Lost Heroes." Saturday
     Review, 15 Nov. 1975, pp. 23-4.

Epstein, Joseph. "Nowhere Men." Book World (Washington
     Post), 16 Nov. 1975, pp. E11-E12.

Gosine, Vishnu R. "Shades of Abdul Malik in Naipaul's
     Guerrillas." Trinidad Guardian, 3 Oct. 1975, p. 4.

Gray, Paul. "Burnt-Out Cases." Time, 1 Dec. 1975, p. 84-86.

Hamner, Robert D. Library Journal, 1 Oct. 1975, p. 1846.

Jefferson, Margo. "Misfits." Newsweek, 1 Dec. 1975, pp.
     102, 104.

Jones, D. A. N. "Little Warriors in Search of a War," Times
     Literary Supplement, 12 Sept. 1975, p. 1013.

Knickerbocker, Brad. "The Caribbean: Setting for Contempo-
     rary Story of Unrest." Christian Science Monitor, 24
     Dec. 1975, p. 23.

Larson, Charles R. "Watching the Revolution Go By."
     Nation, 13 Dec. 1975, pp. 627-28.

Lewis, Warner Maureen. Caribbean Quarterly, 23, Nos. 2 & 3
    (June-Sept. 1977), 103-05.

Miller, Karl. "In Scorn and Pity." New York Review of
    Books, 11 Dec. 1975, p. 3.

Mellors, John. "Mimics into Puppets: The Fiction of V. S.
    Naipaul." London Magazine, 15 (Feb.-March 1976),
    117-20.

New Yorker, 22 Dec. 1975, p. 95.

Pantin, Raoul. "The Wasteland of Naipaul." Caribbean
    Contact, 3, No. 8 (Nov. 1975), 3, 8.

Reedy, Gerard C. America, 1 May 1976, p. 385.

Spurling, John. "The Novelist as Dictator." Encounter,
    Dec. 1975, pp. 73-6.

Theroux, Paul. "An Intelligence from the Third World:
    Guerrillas." New York Times Book Review, 16 Nov. 1975,
    pp. 1-2.

Thorpe, Michael. "Naipaul Again." The Literary Half-Yearly,
    17, No. 1 (Jan. 1976), 123-26.

"West Indian Guerrillas." Sunday Gleaner (Jamaica), 23 Nov.
    1975, p. 23.

Wyndham, Francis. "Services Rendered." New Statesman, 19
    Sept. 1975, pp. 339-40.

Yale Review, 65 (Spring 1976) XIV-V.

4. A House for Mr Biswas (1961)

Bagai, Leona B. Books Abroad, 36 (Autumn 1962), 453.

Balliet, Whitney. New Yorker, 4 Aug. 1962, p. 70.

Carr, Bill. "A House for Mr. Naipaul." Public Opinion
    (Jamaica), 20 March 1964, pp. 8-10.

Chapin, Louis. Christian Science Monitor, 19 July 1962,
    p. 11.

Cruttwell, Patrick. Hudson Review, 15 (Winter 1962-63),
    591-92.

346

Eimerl, Sarel. "A Trinidadian Dickens." <u>Reporter</u>, 19 July
    1962, 56–57.

Fuller, John. <u>Listener</u>, 19 Oct. 1961, p. 621.

Gilbert, Morris. "Hapless Defiance." <u>New York Times Book
    Review</u>, 24 June 1962, p. 30.

"High Jinks in Trinidad." <u>Times Literary Supplement</u>, 29
    Sept. 1961, p. 641.

Jacobson, Dan. "Self-Help in Hot Places. <u>New Statesman</u>,
    29 Sept. 1961, pp. 440–41.

Keown, Eric. <u>Punch</u>, 25 Oct. 1961, p. 621.

Krikler, Bernard. "V. S. Naipaul's <u>A House for Mr Biswas</u>."
    <u>Listener</u>, 13 Feb. 1964, pp. 270–71.

<u>Kirkus</u>, 1 March 1962, p. 249.

Lamming, George. "A Trinidad Experience." <u>Time and Tide</u>,
    5 Oct. 1961, p. 1657.

MacInnes, Colin. "Caribbean Masterpiece." <u>Observer</u>, 1 Oct.
    1961, p. 31; rpt. "A House for Mr. Biswas." <u>Bim</u>, Vol.
    9, No. 35 (July–Dec. 1962), 221–23.

Mann, Charles W. <u>Library Journal</u>, 15 May 1962, p. 1917.

Mitchell, Julian. "Everyman's Island." <u>Spectator</u>,
    6 Oct. 1961, p. 472.

"New Fiction." <u>The Times</u> (London), 5 Oct. 1961, p. 16.

<u>New York Herald Tribune Books</u>, 24 June 1962, pp. 6–7.

Owens, R. J. <u>Caribbean Quarterly</u>, 7, No. 4 (April 1962),
    217–19.

Panton, George. "West Indian Writing Comes of Age." <u>Sunday
    Gleaner</u> (Jamaica) 3 Dec. 1961, p. 14.

Ramchand, Kenneth. "The World of A House for Mr. Biswas."
    <u>Caribbean Quarterly</u>, 15, No. 1 (March 1969), 60–72;
    rpt. in <u>The West Indian Novel and its Background</u>. New
    York: Barnes and Noble Inc., 1970.

Rogers, W. G. <u>Saturday Review</u>, 9 June 1962, p. 37.

<u>Time</u>, 22 June 1962, p. 96.

Times Weekly Review (London), 12 Oct. 1961, p. 10.

Wyndham, Francis. London Magazine, 1, No. 7 (Oct. 1961),
   90-93.

5. India: A Wounded Civilization (1977)

Adams, P. L. Atlantic, 240 (July 1977), 87.

Agarwal, Ramlal. World Literature Today, 52 (Spring 1978),
   343.

Amis, Martin. "In a State of Emergency." New Statesman,
   21 Oct. 1977, pp. 543-44.

Berger, Peter L. The New Republic, 9 July 1977, pp. 30-32.

Booklist, 15 May 1977, p. 1393.

Book World (Washington Post), 14 May 1978, p. G6.

Bridges, Linda. National Review, 26 May 1978, p. 667.

"Defect of Vision." Economist, 5 Nov. 1977, p. 132.

Ezekiel, Nissim. "Wounded and Doomed?" Debonair, 5 May
   1978, pp. 68-9.

Gordon, Leonard A. "The Marginal View." Nation, 2 June
   1977, pp. 26-27.

Gowda, Anniah H. H. Ariel, 10, No. 1 (January 1979), 98-101.

Grigg, John. "Expatriate." Spectator, 22 Oct. 1977, p. 23.

Haynes, Edward S. The American Historical Review, 83 (Oct.
   1978), 1079-80.

Hayward, Henry S. "Naipaul Presents an India Both Changing,
   Unchanging." Christian Science Monitor, 20 July 1977,
   p. 23.

Hussain, Riaz. Best Sellers, 37 (April-March 1977), 153.

"India's Tragic Flaws." Newsweek, 6 June 1977, p. 84.

Kiernan, Victor. Journal of Contemporary Asia, 8, No. 3
   (1978), 379-80.

Kirkus Review, 1 April 1977, p. 399.

Lelyveld, Joseph. "For Naipaul a Difficult Country."
    New York Times Book Review, 12 June 1977, pp. 10, 44.

Massey, Thomas. "China and India and Me." The Washington
    Monthly, 10 (March 1978), 46-7.

Mollinger, Shernaz. Library Journal, 102 (July 1977), 1478.

Mosley, Nicholas. "In Place of Taboos." Listener, 3 Nov.
    1977, pp. 591-92.

New Yorker, 6 June 1977, p. 136.

Novack, Jeremiah. America, 25 June 1977, pp. 570-71.

Paton, David. "Suffering Subcontinent." Times Educational
    Supplement, 2 Dec. 1977, p. 24.

Progressive, 41 (Sept. 1977), 44.

Publishers' Weekly, 28 March 1977, p. 70.

Publishers' Weekly, 7 Nov. 1977, p. 82.

Sastry, Srinivasa. "Naipaul on India." Cross Currents, 28,
    No. 4 (1977-8), 477-80.

Scott, Paul. "India's Collective Amnesia." Guardian Weekly,
    17 July 1977, p. 18.

Singh, Mohindar. "Gandhi and 'A Defect of Vision.'" Indian
    Book Chronicle, 16 Jan. 1979, pp. 33-36.

Stokes, Eric. "The High-caste Defector." Times Literary
    Supplement, 21 Oct. 1977, p. 1229.

Smith, William. "Lest the Past Kill." Time, 20 June 1977,
    pp. 86-89.

Towers, Robert. New York Review of Books, 14 June 1977, p.
    6.

Van Praagh, David. "The New India?" Pacific Affairs, 52
    (Summer 1979), 315-18.

6. The Loss of El Dorado (1969)

Adams, Phoebe. Atlantic Monthly, 225 (May 1970), 132.

Booklist, 1 Sept. 1970, p. 34.

Book World (Washington Post), 21 June 1970, p. 11.

Book World (Washington Post), 6 Dec. 1970, p. 22.

Borome, Joseph A. Library Journal, 1 April 1970, p. 1367.

Bryden, Ronald. "Between the Epics." New Statesman, 7 Nov. 1969, pp. 661-62.

Carnegie, J. A. "Rediscovery from Outside." Savacou (Jamaica), 5 (June 1971), 125-28.

Cheuse, Alan. "The Realms of Gold." Nation, 5 Oct. 1970, pp. 311-12.

Elliott, J. H. "Triste Trinidad." New York Review of Books, 21 May 1970, 25-27.

"The Failings of an Empire." Times Literary Supplement, 25 Dec. 1969, p. 1471.

Greene, Graham. "Terror in Trinidad." London Sunday Observer, 26 Oct. 1969, p. 34.

Hosein, Clyde. "Naipaul's Latest Called a Novel About History." Sunday Guardian (Trinidad), 14 Dec. 1969, p. 20.

Innes, Hammond. "For God and Profit." Spectator, 8 Nov. 1969, pp. 647-48.

Kirkus Review, 15 Feb. 1970, p. 224.

Lask, Thomas. "Brave New World." New York Times, 20 June 1970, p. 27.

Marshall, Peter. American Historical Review, 76, No. 3 (June 1971), 848.

May, Derwent. "A Black Tale." The Times, (London) 1 Nov. 1969, p. V.

Millar, Neil. "Slavery's High Cost." Christian Science Monitor, 28 May 1970, p. 13.

Miller, Karl. "Power, Glory and Imposture." Listener, 13 Nov. 1969, pp. 673-74.

Noel, Jesse A. "Historicity and Homelessness in Naipaul." Caribbean Studies, 11, No. 3 (Oct. 1971), 83-87.

Observer, 16 Sept. 1973, p. 18.

350

Observer, 23 Sept. 1973, p. 33.

Paterson, James H. "Hot Little Offshore Island." Sunday Guardian (Trinidad), 16 Nov. 1969, p. 5.

Plumb, J. H. "A Nightmare World of Fantasy and Murder." Book World (Washington Post), 19 April 1970, pp. 1, 3.

Publishers' Weekly, 2 Feb. 1970, p. 86.

Rabassa, Gregory. "The Dark, Obverse Side of the Shining Myth." New York Times Book Review, 24 May 1970, pp. 7, 22.

Rodman, Selden. "Three on Latin America." National Review, 6 Oct. 1970, pp. 1064-65.

"Slave Colony." Economist, 8 Nov. 1969, pp. 64, iv.

"To Dream No More." Time, 25 May 1970, pp. 105-06.

Updike, John. "Fool's Gold." New Yorker, 8 Aug. 1970, pp. 72-76.

Wade, C. Alan. "The Novelist as Historian." The Literary Half-Yearly (Mysore), 11, No. 2 (1970), 179-84.

7. The Middle Passage (1962)

Allen, Walter. "Fear of Trinidad." New Statesman, 3 Aug. 1962, pp. 149-50.

Bedford, Sybille. "Stoic Traveler." New York Review of Books, 14 Nov. 1963, pp. 4-5.

"Book Reviews: The Middle Passage." Bim (Barbados), 9, No. 36 (Jan.-June 1963), 290-93.

Bryden, Ronald. "New Map of Hell." Spectator, 3 Aug. 1962, p. 161.

Carr, Bill. "The Irony of W. I. Society." Sunday Gleaner (Jamaica), 27 Jan. 1963, pp. 14, 24.

di Giovanni, Norman Thomas. "Return of a West Indian." Nation, 26 Oct. 1963, pp. 262-63.

Dolbier, Maurice. New York Herald Tribune, 3 Sept. 1963, p. 19.

Encounter, 19 Sept. 1962, p. 84.

Hearne, John. "Book Reviews." Caribbean Quarterly, 8, No. 4
    (Dec. 1962), 65-66; rpt. "Unsentimental Journey with
    V. S. Naipaul." Sunday Guardian (Trinidad), 3 Feb.
    1963, pp. 3-4.

Jabavu, Noni. "Return of an Insider." New York Times Book
    Review, 22 Sept. 1963, p. 14.

Johansson, Bertram B. "Caribbean Counterpoint." Christian
    Science Monitor, 30 Oct. 1963, p. 9.

Lucie-Smith, Edward. Listener, 16 Aug. 1962, pp. 254-55.

Malan, Harrison B. Library Journal, 15 Oct. 1963, pp. 3842-
    43.

Marshall, Harold. Bim (Barbados), 9, No. 36 (Jan.-June
    1963), 290-92.

New Yorker, 12 Oct. 1963, pp. 213-14.

Nicholson, Geoffrey. "Passage to the Indies." Manchester
    Guardian Weekly, 9 Aug. 1962, p. 10.

"On and Off Miguel Street." The Times (London), 2 Aug. 1962,
    p. 13.

Panton, George, "Slavery's Greatest Damage." Sunday Gleaner,
    (Jamaica), 9 Sept. 1962, p. 14.

Poore, Charles. "A Native's Return to the Caribbean World."
    New York Times, 7 Sept. 1963, p. 17.

Punch, 8 Aug. 1962, p. 213.

"The Re-Engagement of Mr. Naipaul." Times Literary Supple-
    ment, 10 Aug. 1962, p. 578.

Walcott, Derek. "History and Picong." Sunday Guardian
    (Trinidad), 30 Sept. 1962, p. 9

8. Miguel Street (1959)

Booklist, 1 July 1960, p. 654.

Coleman, John. Spectator, 24 April 1959, p. 595.

Collymore, Frank A. Bim (Barbados), 8, No. 29 (June-Dec.
    1959), 67.

Malone, Robert M. Library Journal, 15 May 1960, p. 1938.

352

McMichael, George. "A Gallery of Rogues Along Trinidad's
    Miguel Street." San Francisco Sunday Chronicle, 22 May
    1960, p. 26.

Moore, Gerald. Black Orpheus, 9 (June 1961), 66–67.

"Naipaul Does it Again." Sunday Guardian (Trinidad), 17 May
    1959, p. 22.

New Yorker, 27 Aug. 1960, pp. 98–100.

"New Fiction." The Times (London), 23 April 1959, p. 15.

Observer, 15 Aug. 1971, p. 18.

Panton, George. "Let's Laugh at Ourselves." Sunday Gleaner
    (Jamaica), 1 Nov. 1959, p. 14.

Payne, Robert. "Caribbean Carnival." Saturday Review,
    2 July 1960, p. 18.

Poore, Charles. New York Times, 5 May 1960, p. 33.

Richardson, Maurice. New Statesman, 2 May 1959, p. 618.

Rodman, Selden. "Catfish Row, Trinidad." New York Times
    Book Review, 15 May 1960, p. 43.

Shrapnel, Norman. "Moves on a Racial Chessboard." Manches-
    ter Guardian Weekly, 24 April 1959, p. 10.

"Street Scene." Times Literary Supplement, 24 April, 1959,
    p. 237.

Time, 30 May 1960, p. 79.

Wickenden, Dan. "Stories Told Under the Sun of Trinidad."
    New York Herald Tribune Book Review, 22 May 1960, p. 10.

Wood, Percy. "Echoes of 'Cannery Row' in a Novel of
    Trinidad." Chicago Sunday Tribune Magazine of Books,
    15 May 1960, p. 6.

Wyndham, Francis. London Magazine 6, No. 9 (Sept. 1959),
    80–81.

9. The Mimic Men (1967)

Beloff, Max. "Verandahs of Impotence." Encounter, 29
    (Oct. 1967), 87–88.

Blackburn, Sara. "Book Marks." Nation, 9 Oct. 1967, pp. 347-48.

Boston, Richard. "Caribbean and Aegean." The Times (London), 27 April 1967, p. 16.

Carr, Bill. "Excess of Skill: A View of Naipaul's The Mimic Men." New World Quarterly (Jamaica), 1, No. 1 (1969), 34-39.

Corke, Hilary. Listener, 25 May 1967, p. 693.

Curley, Arthur. Library Journal, 15 Sept. 1967, p. 3057.

Gray, Simon. New Statesman, 5 May 1967, pp. 622-23.

Kirkus, 15 July 1967, p. 831.

Lask, Thomas. "Shadow and Substance." New York Times, 16 Dec. 1967, p. 39.

Maloff, Saul. New York Times Book Review, 15 Oct. 1967, p. 55.

Miller, Karl. "V. S. Naipaul and the New Order." Kenyon Review, 29 (Nov. 1967), 685-98.

Moore, Gerald. Bim (Barbados), 12, No. 46 (Jan.-June 1968), 134-36.

Nancoo, Joseph. "Magnificent 'Mimic.'" Trinidad Guardian, 25 Aug. 1967, p. 14.

Panton, George. "The West Indian Scene." Sunday Gleaner (Jamaica), 18 June 1967, p. 4.

Plant, Richard. "Caribbean Seesaw." Saturday Review, 23 Dec. 1967, pp. 32-33.

Pritchett, V. S. "Crack-Up." New York Review of Books, 11 April 1968, pp. 10, 12-14.

Price, R. G. G. Punch, 10 May 1967, p. 696.

Pryce-Jones, David. London Magazine, 7, No. 2 (May 1967), 82-4.

Publishers' Weekly, 10 July 1967, p. 176.

Rao, K. S. Narayana. Books Abroad, 42, No. 1 (1968), 167.

Rickards, Colin. Books and Bookmen, Oct. 1967, p. 47.

354

Roach, Eric. "As Naipaul Sees Us." Trinidad Guardian, 15
    May 1967, p. 7 and 17 May 1967, p. 9.

Seymour-Smith, Martin. "Exile's Story." Spectator, 5 May
    1967, p. 528.

"Suburbia in the Sun." Times Literary Supplement, 27 April
    1967, p. 349.

Thorpe, Michael. English Studies, 49 (June 1968), 272-73.

Wain, John. "Trouble in the Family." New York Review of
    Books, 26 Oct. 1967, pp. 33-35.

Walcott, Derek. "Is V. S. Naipaul an Angry Young Man?"
    Sunday Guardian Magazine (Trinidad), 6 Aug. 1967, pp.
    9-10.

Wilson, Agnus. "Between Two Islands." London Sunday
    Observer, 30 April 1967, p. 27.

10. The Mystic Masseur (1957)

Balliet, Whitney. New Yorker, 30 May 1959, p. 101.

Baro, Gene. "Ganesh's Beguiling Exploits." New York Herald
    Tribune Book Review, 7 June 1959, p. 6.

Bayley, John. Spectator, 24 May 1957, p. 688.

Bryden, Ronald. Listener, 30 May 1957, p. 890.

Collymore, Frank A. Bim (Barbados), 7, No. 26 (Jan.-June
    1958), 119-20.

"Ganesh in the Years of Guilt." Sunday Guardian (Trinidad),
    16 June 1957, p. 23.

"Huckster Hindu." Time, 6 April 1959, p. 99.

Levin, Martin. "How the Ball Bounces Down Trinidad Way."
    New York Times Book Review, 12 April 1959, p. 5.

"The 'Mystic Masseur.'" Sunday Gleaner (Jamaica), 19 May
    1957, p. 12.

"New Fiction." The Times (London), 23 May 1957, p. 15.

Nyren, Karl. Library Journal, 1 May 1959, p. 1533.

"Out of Joint." <u>Times Literary Supplement</u>, 31 May 1957,
    p. 333.

Quinton, Anthony. <u>New Statesman and Nation</u>, 18 May 1957,
    p. 649.

<u>Time</u>, 22 June 1962, p. 96.

Wood, Percy. <u>Chicago Sunday Tribune Magazine of Books</u>, 12
    July 1959, p. 5.

11. <u>The Overcrowded Barracoon</u> (1972)

Bryden, Ronald. "The Hurricane." <u>Listener</u>, 9 Nov. 1972,
    p. 641.

<u>Choice</u>, June 1973, p. 610.

"The Editor's Column." <u>Queen's Quarterly</u>, 80, No. 3 (Autumn
    1973), 496-97.

Figueroa, John. "<u>The Overcrowded Barracoon</u> and Other
    Articles by V. S. Naipaul." <u>Caribbean Studies</u>, 13, No.
    4 (Jan. 1974), 135-40.

Green, Martin. "Naipaul's Burden." <u>Guardian Weekly</u>, 4 Nov.
    1972, p. 21.

"Harrison, Tony. "Fantasia-Asia." <u>London Magazine</u>, 12, No.
    5 (Dec. 1972-Jan. 1973), 135-40.

In Search of Another Country." <u>Times Literary Supplement</u>,
    17 Nov. 1972, p. 1391.

<u>Kirkus Reviews</u>, 1 Feb. 1973, p. 171.

L[indo], C[edric]. "All About Naipaul." <u>Sunday Gleaner</u>
    (Jamaica), 5 Nov. 1972, p. 39.

Mac Innes, Colin. "Not Just for Today but Long Tomorrows."
    <u>Sunday Guardian</u> (Trinidad), 12 Nov. 1972, p. 6.

Mukherjee, Bharati. "Colonies Caste Adrift." <u>Book World</u>
    <u>(Washington Post)</u>, 18 March 1973, pp. 4, 8.

<u>New York Times Book Review</u>, 16 Sept. 1973, p. 18.

Pantin, Raoul. "The Ultimate Transient." <u>Caribbean</u>
    <u>Contact</u>, 2, No. 2 (Jan. 1973), 4, 23.

356

Parker, Dorothy. <u>Christian Science Monitor</u>, 14 March 1973,
    p. 13.

Potter, Dennis." The Writer and his Myth." <u>The Times</u>
    (London), 4 Dec. 1972, p. 6.

<u>Publishers' Weekly</u>, 22 Jan. 1973, p. 62.

Roach, Eric. "Naipaul's Death Wish is not Our Bag."
    <u>Trinidad Guardian</u>, 1 Feb. 1973, p. 4.

12. <u>The Return of Eva Peron</u> with <u>The Killings in Trinidad</u>
    (1980).

"An Army that Marches on its Fantasies." <u>The Times</u>
    (London), 4 May 1982, p. 8a.

Amis, Martin, "More Bones." <u>New Statesman</u>, 4 July 1980,
    pp. 19-20.

Beatty, Jack. <u>New Republic</u>, 12 April 1980, pp. 36-39.

"Bizarre Political Lives." <u>Progressive</u>, Oct. 1981, p. 61.

<u>Booklist</u>, 1 June 1980, p. 1390.

<u>Book World</u> (<u>Washington Post</u>), 29 March 1981, p. 12.

Breslin, Patrick. "Naipaul and the Empire of Discontent."
    <u>Book World</u> (<u>Washington Post</u>), 30 March 1980, pp. 1, 6.

<u>Choice</u>, September 1980, p. 92.

Didion, Joan. "Without Regret or Hope." <u>The New York Review
    of Books</u>, 12 June 1980, pp. 20-21.

Garebian, Keith. "False Redeemers." <u>Canadian Forum</u>, 60
    (Nov. 1980), 33.

Gornick, Vivian. "Terror and Rhetoric in Hot Places."
    <u>Esquire</u> (April 1980), 22.

Hunter, Frederic. "V. S. Naipaul Wanders the Post-colonial
    World." <u>Christian Science Monitor</u>, 10 March 1980, p.B2.

<u>Guardian Weekly</u>, 20 Jan. 1980, p. 22.

<u>Guardian Weekly</u>, 4 May 1980, p. 18.

<u>Kirkus Reviews</u>, 1 Feb. 1980, p. 196.

Kramer, Jane. "From the Third World." New York Times Book Review, 13 April 1980, pp. 1, 30-2.

Listener, 26 June 1980, p. 835.

Marnham, Patrick. "Half-made." Spectator, 5 July 1980, p. 18.

Mc Tair, Roger. "Critical Response to Naipaul." Caribbean Contact, 8, No. 6 (Oct. 1980), 3, 14.

Newsweek, 31 March 1980, p. 73.

New Yorker, 19 May 1980, pp. 158-60.

Observer, 13 July 1980, p. 29.

Observer, 29 June 1980, p. 28.

Observer, 7 Dec. 1980, p. 27.

Observer, 11 Oct. 1981, p. 32.

Publishers' Weekly, 23 Jan. 1981, p. 123.

Rodman, Selden. "The Bush Moves Closer." National Review, 14 Nov. 1980, p. 1406.

Rose, Phillis. "Of Moral Bonds and Men." Yale Review, 70, No.1 (Oct. 1980), 149-56.

Said, Edward W. "Bitter Dispatches from the Third World." The Nation, 3 May 1980, pp. 522-24.

Sheppard, R. Z. Time, 7 April 1980, pp. 89-90.

Spectator, 12 Dec. 1981, p. 25.

Times Educational Supplement, 14 May 1982, p. 30.

Windrich, Elaine. Library Journal, 1 March 1980, p. 615.

13. The Suffrage of Elvira (1958)

Newby, P. H. London Magazine, 5, No. 11 (Nov. 1958), 84.

"New Fiction." The Times (London) , 24 April 1958, p. 13.

Panton, George. "Satire on Trinidad." Sunday Gleaner (Jamaica), 22 June 1958, p. 11.

358

"Tropical Heat." <u>Times Literary Supplement</u>, 2 May 1958,
    p. 237.

B. Books and Articles

Adams, Robert Martin. "V. S. Naipaul." <u>The Hudson Review</u>,
    33, No. 3 (Autumn 1980), 474-80.

Allis, Jeannette B. <u>West Indian Literature</u>: <u>An Index to
    Criticism, 1930-1975</u>. Boston, Massachusetts: G. K.
    Hall & Co., 1981.

Amis, Kingsley. "Fresh Winds from the West." <u>The Spectator</u>,
    2 May 1958, pp. 565-66.

"An Area of Brilliance." <u>Weekly Observer</u> (London), 28 Nov.
    1971, p. 8; rpt. <u>Trinidad Guardian</u>, 5 Dec. 1971, p. 5.

Anderson, Linda R. "Ideas of Identity and Freedom in V. S.
    Naipaul and Joseph Conrad." <u>English Studies</u>, 59, No. 6
    (Dec. 1978), 510-17.

Angrosino, Michael. "V. S. Naipaul and the Colonial
    Image." <u>Caribbean Quarterly</u>, 21, No. 3 (Sept. 1975),
    1-11.

Argyle, Barry. "Commentary on V. S. Naipaul's 'A House for
    Mr Biswas': A West Indian Epic." <u>Caribbean Quarterly</u>,
    16, No. 4 (Dec. 1970), 61-69.

Augier, F. R. et al. <u>The Making of the West Indies</u>. London:
    Longmans, Green Co. Ltd., 1960.

B., M. "An Explanation for Naipaul's Attitude." Letter.
    <u>Trinidad Guardian</u>, 18 Dec. 1981, p. 8; rpt. <u>Trinidad
    Express</u>, 21 Dec. 1981, p. 5.

Bahadoorsingh, Krishna. <u>Trinidad Electoral Politics</u>: <u>The
    Persistence of the Race Factor</u>. London: Headley
    Brothers Ltd., 1968.

Bates, David. "V. S. Naipaul." (London) <u>Sunday Times
    Supplement</u>, 26 May 1963, pp. 12-13.

Baugh, Edward. "Toward a West Indian Criticism." Rev. of
    <u>The Islands in Between</u>, ed., Louis James. <u>Caribbean
    Quarterly</u>, 14, Nos. 1 & 2 (March-June 1968), 140-44.

Belitt, Ben. "The Heraldry of Accommodation: A House for
    Mr. Naipaul." <u>Salmagundi</u>, 54 (Fall 1981), 23-42.

359

"The Bennett Award, 1980" (Announcement). The Hudson Review, 33, No. 3 (Winter 1980-81), 321.

Blodgett, Harriet. "Beyond Trinidad: Five Novels by V. S. Naipaul." South Atlantic Quarterly, 73, No. 3 (Summer 1974), 388-403.

Boxill, Anthony. "The Concept of Spring in V. S. Naipaul's Mr. Stone and the Knights Companion." Ariel, 5 (Oct. 1974), 21-28.

_____. "Mr Biswas, Mr. Polly and the Problem of V. S. Naipaul's Sources." Ariel, 8, No. 3 (July 1977), 129-41.

_____. "The Little Bastard Worlds of V. S. Naipaul's The Mimic Men and A Flag on the Island." International Fiction Review, 3, No. 1 (Jan. 1976), 12-19.

_____. "The Paradox of Freedom: V. S. Naipaul's In a Free State." Critique: Studies in Modern Fiction, 18, No. 1 (1976), 81-91.

_____. V. S. Naipaul's Fiction. Canada: York Press, 1983.

_____. "V. S. Naipaul's Starting Point." Journal of Commonwealth Literature, 10, No. 1 (Aug. 1975), 1-9.

Boyers, Robert. "V. S. Naipaul." The American Scholar, 50 (Summer 1981), 359-67.

Brathwaite, L. Edward. "Jazz and the West Indian Novel." Bim (Barbados), 11, No. 44 (Jan.-June 1967), 275-84; Bim, 12, No. 45 (July-Dec. 1967), 39-51; Bim, 12, No. 46, (Jan.-June 1968), 115-25.

_____. "Roots." Bim, 10, No. 37 (July-Dec. 1963), 10-21.

_____. "West Indian Prose Fiction in the Sixties: A Survey." Critical Survey, 3, No. 3 (Winter 1967), 169-74.

Brereton, Bridget. A History of Modern Trinidad, 1783-1962. London: Heinemann Educational Books, Inc., 1981.

_____. Race Relations in Colonial Trinidad. London: Cambridge University Press, 1979.

Brown, John L. "V. S. Naipaul: A Wager on the Triumph of Darkness." World Literature Today, 57, No. 2 (Spring 1983), 223-27.

360

Brown, Wayne. "The First Generation of West Indian
    Novelists." Sunday Guardian (Trinidad), 7 June 1970,
    p. 6.

_____. "On Exile and the Dialect of the Tribe."
    Sunday Guardian (Trinidad), 8 Nov. 1970, p. 19.

Calder, Argus . "World's End: V. S. Naipaul's The Mimic
    Men." In Commonwealth Writer Overseas. Ed. Alastair
    Niven. Bruxelles: Librarie Marcel Didier S.A., 1976.

Campbell, Elaine. "A Refinement of Rage: V. S. Naipaul's
    Bend in the River." World Literature Written in
    English, 18, No. 2 (Nov. 1979), 394-406.

"The Caribbean Mixture." Times Literary Supplement, 10 Aug.
    1962, p. 578.

Carr, W. I. "Reflections on the Novel in the British
    Caribbean." Queen's Quarterly, 70, No. 4 (Winter
    1963), 585-97.

_____. "The West Indian Novelist . . . A Footnote."
    Sunday Gleaner (Jamaica), 23 April 1961, pp. 14, 20.

_____. "The West Indian Novelist: Prelude and
    Context." Caribbean Quarterly, 11, Nos. 1 & 2
    (March-June 1965), 71-84.

Carthew, John. "Adapting to Trinidad: Mr Biswas and Mr
    Polly Revisited." Journal of Commonwealth Literature,
    13, No. 1 (Aug. 1978), 58-64.

Cartey, Wilfred. "The Knight's Companion--Ganesh, Biswas,
    and Stone." New World Quarterly (Jamaica), 2, No. 1
    (1965), 93-98.

Chitre, Dilip. "Naipaul and India 2: For him a Difficult
    Country." New Quest (India), 9 (May-June 1978), 175-86.

Collymore, Frank A. "Writing in the West Indies: A Survey."
    Tamarack Review, 14 (Winter 1960), 111-24.

Cooke, John. "A Vision of the Land: V. S. Naipaul's Later
    Novels." Journal of Caribbean Studies, 1, Nos. 2 & 3
    (1980), 140-61.

Coombs, Orde, ed. Is Massa Day Dead? New York: Anchor
    Press, 1974.

Coulthard, G. R. "The Literature of the West Indies." In
    The Commonwealth Pen. Ed. Alan L. McLeod. Ithaca,
    N.Y.: Cornell University Press, 1961.

Cudjoe, Selwyn. "Revolutionary Struggle and the Novel." *Caribbean Quarterly*, 24, No. 4 (Dec. 1979), 1-30.

_____. "Trying to Understand Naipaul: The Hindu in Search of Self." *Sunday Express* (Trinidad), 30 May 1982, pp. 41, 51.

Dathorne, Oscar R. ed. *Caribbean Narrative: An Anthology of West Indian Writing*. London: Heinemann, 1966.

Davies, Barrie. "The Personal Sense of a Society--Minority View: Aspects of the 'East Indian' Novel in the West Indies." *Studies in the Novel*, 4, No. 2 (Summer 1972), 284-95.

Derrick, A. C. "Naipaul's Technique as a Novelist." *Journal of Commonwealth Literature*, 7 (July 1969), 32-44.

Despres, Leo. *Cultural Pluralism and Nationalist Politics in British Guiana*. Chicago: Rand McNally & Co., 1967.

Doerksen, Nan. "*In a Free State* and *Nausea*." *World Literature Written in English*, 20, No. 1 (Spring 1981), 105-13.

Dopson, Andrew. "I'll Stop Writing for Less." *Trinidad Guardian*, 12 Dec. 1971, p. 18.

Drayton, Arthur. "The European Factor in West Indian Literature." *The Literary Half-Yearly* (Mysore), 11, No. 1 (July 1970), 71-95.

_____. "West Indian Fiction and West Indian Society." *Kenyon Review*. 25, No. 1 (Winter 1963), 129-41.

Erapu, Lakan. "V. S. Naipaul's *In a Free State*." *Bulletin of the Association for Commonwealth Literature and Language Studies*, 9 (March 1972), 66-84.

"An Exile Returns." *Trinidad Guardian*, 25 Sept. 1960, p. 7.

Eyre, M. Banning. "Naipaul at Wesleyan." *South Carolina Review* 14, No. 2 (Spring 1982), 34-47.

Ezekiel, Nissim. "Naipaul's India and Mine." In *New Writing in India*. Ed. Adil Jussawalla. Baltimore, Maryland: Penguin, 1974.

Fanon, Frantz. *Black Skin, White Masks*. Trans. Charles Lam Markmann. New York: Grove Press, Inc., 1967.

362

Fido, Martin. "Mr. Biswas and Mr. Polly." Ariel, 5 (Oct. 1974), 30-37.

Figueroa, John J. "Introduction--V. S. Naipaul: A Panel Discussion." Revista/Review Interamericana, 6, No. 4 (1976-77), 554-63.

_____. "Some Provisional Comments on West Indian Novels." In Commonwealth Literature. Ed. John Press. London: Heinemann, 1965.

Fraser, Fitzroy. "A Talk with Vidia Naipaul." Sunday Gleaner (Jamaica), 26 Dec. 1960, p. 14.

Froude, James Anthony. The English in the West Indies. London: Charles Scribner's Sons, 1888; rpt. New York: Negro Univ. Pres, 1969.

Freedman, Richard. "Three by Naipaul." Book World (Washington Post), 10 Oct. 1976, p. E5.

Furnivall, J. S. Colonial Policy and Practice. New York: New York University Press, 1956.

Garebian, Keith. "V. S. Naipaul's Negative Sense of Place." Journal Commonwealth of Literature, 10, No. 1 (Aug. 1975), 23-25.

Gary, M. "Naipaul--Snob, Provocative Artist, or What?" Letter. Express (Trinidad), 28 Dec. 1981, p. 5.

Glasgow, Roy Arthur. Guyana: Race and Politics Among Africans and East Indians. The Hague: Martinus Nijhoff, 1970.

Gomes, Albert. Through a Maze of Colour. Trinidad: Key Caribbean Publications Ltd., 1974.

Goodheart, Eugene. "Naipaul and the Voices of Negation," Salmagundi, 54 (Fall 1981), 44-58.

_____. "V. S. Naipaul's Mandarin Sensibility." Partisan Review, 50, No. 2 (1983), 244-56.

Gowda, Anniah H. H. "India in Naipaul's Artistic Conscious-ness." The Literary Half-Yearly (Mysore), 16, No. 1 (Jan. 1975), 27-39.

_____. "Naipaul in India." The Literary Half-Yearly (Mysore), 11, No. 2 (1970), 163-70.

Grant, Lennox. "For Naipaul There is a Challenge of Faith."
(Interview with Gordon Rohlehr.) Tapia (Trinidad), 13
July 1975, pp. 6-7.

_____. "Naipaul Joins the Chorus." (Interview with
Gordon Rohlehr.) Tapia (Trinidad), 6 July 1975, pp.
6-7.

Guinness, Gerald. "Naipaul's Four Early Trinidad Novels."
Revista/Review Interamericana, 6, No. 4 (Winter
1976-77),
564-73.

Gurr, A. J. "The Freedom of Exile in Naipaul and Doris
Lessing." Ariel, 13, No. 4 (1982), 7-18.

_____. "Third World Novels: Naipaul and After."
Journal of Commonwealth Literature, 7, No. 1 (June
1972), 6-13.

_____. Writers in Exile: The Identity of Home in
Modern Literature. Sussex: The Harvester Press Ltd.,
1981.

Gussow, Mel. "V. S. Naipaul: It is Out of This Violence
I've Always Written." New York Times Book Review, 16
Sept. 1984, p. 45.

_____. "Writer Without Roots." New York Times
Magazine, 26 Dec. 1976, pp. 8-9, 18-19, 22.

Hackett, Jeff. "Why Vidia Naipaul's Vision is Limited."
Trinidad Guardian, 3 March 1983, p. 17.

Hackett, Winston. "The Writer and Society." Moko
(Trinidad), 13 Dec. 1968, p. 4.

Hamish, Keith. "The Ridiculous Panic Behind Vidia Naipaul.
Trinidad Guardian, 29 Nov. 1973, p. 9.

Hamner, Robert D., ed. Critical Perspectives on V. S.
Naipaul. Washington, D.C.: Three Continents Press,
Inc., 1977.

_____. V. S. Naipaul. New York: Twayne
Publishers Inc., 1973.

_____. "V.S. Naipaul: A Selected Bibliography."
Journal of Commonwealth Literature, 10, No. 1 (Aug.
1975), 36-44.

Hardwick Elizabeth. "Meeting V. S. Naipaul." New York Times
Book Review, 13 May 1979, pp. 1, 36.

Harris, Michael. "Naipaul on Campus: Sending Out a Plea for Rationality." _Tapia_ (Trinidad), 29 June 1975, p. 2.

Harris, Wilson. _Tradition, the Writer & Society_: _Critical Essays_. London: New Beacon Publications, 1967.

Hearne, John. "The Snow Virgin: An Inquiry into V. S. Naipaul's 'Mimic Men.'" _Caribbean Quarterly_, 23, Nos. 2 & 3 (Jan.-June 1977), 31-7.

Hemenway, Robert. "Sex and Politics in V. S. Naipaul." _Studies in the Novel_, 14, No. 2 (Summer 1982), 189-202.

Herdeck, Donald E., ed. _Caribbean Writers_: _A Bio-Bibliographical-Critical Encyclopedia_. Washington, D.C. Three Continents Press, Inc., 1979.

Hill, Errol. "The West Indian Artist." _The West Indian Review_, 9 Aug. 1952, pp. 13-14.

Howe, Irving. "A Dark Vision." Rev. of _A Bend in the River_. _New York Times Book Review_, 13 May 1979, pp. 1, 37.

_____. "Irving Howe Replies." Letter. _New York Times Book Review_, 24 June, 1979, p. 45.

Jagan, Cheddi B. _The West on Trial_. London: Michael Joseph Ltd., 1966.

James, C. L. R. "The Artist in the Caribbean." In _The Future in the Present_. Connecticut: Lawrence Hill & Co. Publishers, Inc., 1977.

_____. "The Disorder of Vidia Naipaul." _Trinidad Guardian Magazine_, 21 Feb. 1965, p. 6.

_____. "Home is Where They Want to Be." _Trinidad Guardian Magazine_, 14 Feb. 1965, pp. 4-5.

J., G.R. "Was John Hearne Inspired by Professional Jealousy?" _Sunday Guardian_ (Trinidad), 17 Feb. 1963, p. 3.

James, Louis ed. _The Islands in Between_: _Essays on West Indian Literature_. London: Oxford University Press, 1968.

Jayawardena, Chandra. _Conflict and Solidarity in a Guianese Plantation_. London: The Athlone Press, 1963.

John, George R. "In Defense of Naipaul." _Trinidad Guardian_, 22 Aug. 1982, p. 8.

Johnson, Andrew. "Gunga Din of Caribbean Literature."
    Trinidad Express, 3 July, 1982.

Johnstone, Richard. "Politics and V. S. Naipaul." Journal
    of Commonwealth Literature, 14, No. 1 (Aug. 1979),
    100-08.

Jones, J. Joseph. "ACLALS: Conference at Kingston." World
    Literature Written in English, 19 (April 1971), 14-16.

Kakutani, Michiko. "Books of the Times." New York Times,
    17 Jan. 1983, p. C20.

King, Bruce. The New English Literatures. New York: St.
    Martin's Press, 1980.

_____, ed. West Indian Literature. London: The
    Macmillan Press, Ltd., 1979.

King, Lloyd. "The Trauma of Naipauland." Trinidad Guardian,
    24 Sept. 1967, pp. 16, 19.

Klass, Morton. East Indians in Trinidad. New York:
    Columbia University Press, 1961.

Kutty, K. Narayan. "Naipaul and India 1: A Case of Will-
    lessness." New Quest (India), 9 (May-June 1978),
    167-73.

Lacovia, R. M. "The Medium is the Divide: An Examination
    of V. S. Naipaul's Early Works." Black Images, 1, No.
    2 (1972), 3-6.

La Guerre, John, ed. Calcutta to Caroni: The East Indians
    of Trinidad. London: Longman Group Ltd., 1974.

Lamming, George. The Pleasures of Exile. London: Michael
    Joseph, 1960.

Lane, M. Travis. "The Casualties of Freedom: V. S.
    Naipaul's In a Free State." World Literature Written
    in English, 12, No. 1 (April 1973), 106-10.

Lee, R. H. "The Novels of V. S. Naipaul." Theoria, 27
    (Oct. 1966), 31-46.

Lewis, Gordon K. The Growth of the Modern West Indies. New
    York: Monthly Review Press, 1968.

Lima, Emma E. de Oliveira Fernandes. "Now Tell Me Who You
    Are!" Estudos Anglo-Americanos. Nos. 3-4 (1979-80),
    98-102.

366

Linfors, Bernth. "The West Indian Conference on Common-
    wealth Literature." World Literature Written in
    English, 19 (April 1971), 9-13.

Lockwood, Bernard. "V. S. Naipaul's The Middle Passage."

Revista/Review Interamericana, 6, No. 4 (1976-77), 580-86.

Lopez de Villegas, Consuelo. "Identity and Environment:
    Naipaul's Architectural Vision." Revista/Review Inter-
    americana, 10, No. 2 (1980), 220-29.

_____. "Matriarchs and Man-Eaters: Naipaul's
    Fictional Women." Revista/Review Interamericana, 7
    (1977-78), 605-14.

_____. "The Paradox of Freedom: Naipaul's Later
    Fiction." Revista/Review Interamericana, 6, No. 4
    (1976-77), 574-79.

Lord, Rudolph. "Naipaul's Article on Black Power Criti-
    cised." Moko (Trinidad), 23 Oct. 1970, p. 3.

Lovelace, Earl. "Poor Naipaul: He Has Become His Biggest
    Joke." Express (Trinidad), 26 Oct. 1970, p. 10.

Lowenthal, David. West Indian Societies. London: Oxford
    University Press, 1972.

Lowenthal, David and Lambros Comitas, eds. The Aftermath of
    Sovereignty: West Indian Perspectives. New York:
    Anchor Press, 1973.

_____. Consequences of Class and Color. West
    Indian Perspectives. New York: Anchor Press, 1973.

Macdonald, Bruce F. "The Birth of Mr. Biswas." Journal of
    Commonwealth Literature, 11, No. 3 (1977), 50-54.

_____. "Symbolic Action in Three of V. S.
    Naipaul's Novels." Journal of Commonwealth Literature,
    9, No. 3 (April 1975), 41-52.

Maes-Jelinek, Hena. "The Myth of El Dorado in the Caribbean
    Novel." Journal of Commonwealth Literature, 6, No. 1
    (June 1971), 113-28.

Maharajh, Mahabir. "The Deeper Meaning of Naipaul's 'bush.'"
    Letter. Trinidad Guardian, 13 Jan. 1982, p. 8.

_____. "Failure to Understand Naipaul." Letter.
    Trinidad Guardian, 30 Aug. 1982, p. 8.

367

Mahood, M. M. The Colonial Encounter: A Reading of Six
     Novels. New Jersey: Rowman and Littlefield, 1977.

Malik, Yogendra. East Indians in Trinidad: A Study in
     Minority Politics. London: Oxford University Press,
     1971.

McColgan, Kathleen. "Born Yesterday." The West Indian
     Review, May 16, 1953, p. 17.

McSweeney, Kerry. "V. S. Naipaul: Sensibility and
     Schemata." Critical Quarterly, 18, No. 3 (Autumn
     1976), 73-79.

Medwick, Cathleen. "Life, Literature, and Politics: An
     Interview with V. S. Naipaul." Vogue, 171 (Aug. 1981)
     129-30.

Mentus, Ulric. "Is There Something Called Black Art?":
     Ulric Mentus Interviews Rex Nettleford on Statements by
     Derek Walcott and Vidia Naipaul. Caribbean Contact, 3,
     No. 11 (Feb. 1976), 7, 17.

Michener, Charles. "The Dark Visions of V. S. Naipaul."
     Newsweek, 16 Nov. 1981, pp. 104-15.

Mills, Therese. "The House of Mr. Biswas." Trinidad
     Guardian, 28 Jan. 1973, p. 11.

Milne, Anthony. "In Defense of V. S. Naipaul." Trinidad
     Express, 4 Jan. 1982, p. 21.

Modern Fiction Studies (Purdue University), Special Issue on
     V. S. Naipaul, 30, No. 3 (Autumn 1984).

Mooke, Robert A. Chee. "The Middle Passage of Naipaul--a
     Passage to Nowhere." Sunday Express (Trinidad), 16 May
     1982, p. 6.

Moore, Gerald. The Chosen Tongue: English Writing in
     the Tropical World. London: Longmans, Green and Co.
     Ltd., 1969.

_____. "East Indians and West: The Novels of V.
     S. Naipaul." Black Orpheus: A Journal of African and
     Afro-American Literature, 7 (June 1960), 11-15.

Morley, Patricia A. "Comic Form in Naipaul's Fiction."
     Bulletin of the Association for Commonwealth Literature
     and Language Studies, 9 (March 1972), 49-65.

Morris, Mervyn. "Some West Indian Problems of Audience."
     English, 16, No. 94 (Spring 1967), 127-31.

Morris, Robert K. <u>Paradoxes of Order</u>: <u>Some Perspectives on the Fiction of V. S. Naipaul</u>. Columbia, Missouri: Missouri Press, 1975.

Mukherjee, Bharati and Robert Boyers. "A Conversation with V. S. Naipaul." <u>Salmagundi</u>, 54 (Fall 1981), 4-22.

Muro, Ian, et al. "Writing and Publishing in the West Indies." <u>World Literature Written in English</u>, 19 (April 1971), 17-22.

Murray, Peter. "<u>Guerrillas</u>: A Prefatory Note." <u>Journal of Commonwealth Literature</u>, 14, No. 1 (Aug. 1979), 88-9.

Nachman, Larry David. "The Worlds of V. S. Naipaul." <u>Salmagundi</u>, 54 (Fall 1981), 59-76.

Naik, M. K. "Irony as Stance and as Vision: A Comparative Study of V. S. Naipaul's <u>The Mystic Masseur</u> and R. K. Narayan's <u>The Guide</u>." <u>The Journal of Indian Writing in English</u> (India), 6, No. 1 (Jan. 1978), 1-13. This article is reprinted with minor changes in "Two Uses of Irony: V. S. Naipaul's <u>The Mystic Masseur</u> and R. K. Narayan's <u>The Guide</u>." <u>World Literature Written in English</u>, 17, No. 2 (Nov. 1978), 646-55.

"Naipaul is the Literary Curiosity." <u>Sunday Guardian</u> (Trinidad), 10 Nov. 1968, p. 4.

"Naipaul Wins UK's Top Literary Award." <u>Trinidad Guardian</u>, 26 Nov. 1971, p. 1.

"Naipaul's Principles of Literary Criticism." <u>Sunday Gleaner</u> (Jamaica), 1 Dec. 1963, p. 3.

Naipaul, Seepersad. <u>The Adventure of Gurudeva</u>. Foreword. V. S. Naipaul. London: André Deutsch Ltd., 1976.

_____. <u>Gurudeva and Other Indian Tales</u>. Trinidad: Trinidad Publications, 1943.

Naipaul, Shiva. <u>Love and Death in a Hot Country</u>. Great Britain: Hamish Hamilton Ltd., 1983, rpt. New York: Penguin Books, 1985.

Nandakumar, Prema. <u>The Glory and the Good</u>. New Delhi: Asia Publishing House, 1965.

Narasimhaiah, C. D., ed. <u>Awakened Conscience</u>: <u>Studies in Commonwealth Literature</u>. New Delhi: Sterling Publishers Pvt. Ltd., 1978.

_____. "Report on the Conference of Commonwealth
    Literature Held in Kingston, Jamaica (West Indies) in
    January 1971." The Literary Criterion, 10, No. 1
    (Winter
    1971), 1-9.

_____. "'Somewhere Something Has Snapped.'"
    Indian Horizons, 21, No. 4 (Oct. 1972), 37-50.

Nath, Dwarka. A History of Indians in British Guiana.
    London: Thomas, Nelson & Sons Ltd., 1950.

Nazareth, Peter. "The Mimic Men as a Study of Corruption."
    East Africa Journal, 7, No. 7 (July 1970), 18-22.

Neill, Michael. "Guerrillas and Gangs: Frantz Fanon and V.
    S. Naipaul." Ariel, 13, No. 4 (1982), 21-62.

Nettleford, Rex. "Caribbean Perspectives: The Creative Po-
    tential and the Quality of Life." Caribbean Quarterly,
    17, Nos. 3 & 4 (1971), 114-27.

New, William. Among Writers: An Introduction to Modern
    Commonwealth and South African Fiction. Canada,
    Ontario: Press Porcepic, 1975.

Ngai, Mbatau Kaburu Wa. "The Relationship Between Lit-
    erature and Society and How It Emerges in the Works of
    C. [sic] Lamming, V. S. Naipaul and W. Harris."
    Busara, 8, No. 2 (1976) 53-67.

Niehoff, Arthur and Juanita Niehoff. East Indians in
    Trinidad. Wisconsin: Milwaukee Public Museum
    Publications in Anthropology #6, 1960.

Niven, Alastair. "Crossing the Black Waters: N. C.
    Chadhure's A Passage to England and V. S. Naipaul's An
    Area of Darkness." Ariel, 9, No. 3 (July 1978), 21-36.

_____. "V. S. Naipaul's Free Statement."
    Commonwealth Literature and the Modern World. Papers
    Delivered at a Conference, University of Liege, April
    2-5, 1974. Ed. Hena Maes-Jelinek. Brussels: Didier,
    1975.

"The Novelist V. S. Naipaul Talks About His Work to Ronald
    Bryden." Listener, 22 March 1973, pp. 366-67.

"The Novelist V. S. Naipaul Talks to Nigel Bingham About His
    Childhood in Trinidad." Listener, 7 Sept. 1972, pp.
    306-07.

Nunez-Harrell, Elizabeth. "Lamming and Naipaul: Some
    Criteria for Evaluating the Third World Novel."
    Contemporary Literature, 19, No. 1 (1978), 26-47.

Ormerod, David. "In a Derelict Land: The Novels of V. S.
    Naipaul." Wisconsin Studies in Contemporary
    Literature, 9 (Winter 1968), 74-90.

_____. "Theme and Image in V. S. Naipaul's A
    House for Mr. Biswas." Texas Studies in Literature and
    Language, 8, No. 4 (Winter 1967), 589-602.

Oxaal, Ivar. Black Intellectuals Come to Power. Cambridge,
    Mass.: Schenkman Pub. Co., Inc., 1968.

_____. Race and Revolutionary Consciousness: A
    Documentary Interpretation of the 1970 Black Power
    Revolt in Trinidad. Cambridge, Mass.: Schenkman Pub.
    Co., 1971.

Pantin, Raoul. "Portrait of an Artist: What Makes Naipaul
    Run." Caribbean Contact, 1, No. 6 (May 1973), 15,
    18-19.

Panton, George. "V. S. Naipaul: The Most Famous West Indian
    Writer." Sunday Gleaner (Jamaica), 22 June 1975, pp.
    23, 31.

Parrinder, Patrick. "V. S. Naipaul and the Uses of Liter-
    acy." Critical Quarterly, 21, No. 2 (Summer 1979), 5-13.

Patterson, John. "Challenging CLR and the Naipauls."
    Sunday Guardian (Trinidad), 18 Oct. 1970, pp. 7, 10.

Peach, Ceri. West Indian Migration to Britain. London:
    Oxford University Press, 1968.

Powrie, Barbara. "The Changing Attitude of the Coloured
    Middle Class Towards Carnival." Caribbean Quarterly,
    4, No. 3 (1956), 224-32.

Ragahavacharyulu, D. V. K. ed. The Critical Response.
    Madras: The Macmillan Company of India Ltd., 1980.

Rai, Suhda. V. S. Naipaul: A Study in Expatriate
    Sensibility. New Delhi: Arnold-Heinemann Publishers
    Ltd., 1983.

Ramamurti, K. S. "Areas of Darkness and Light." Journal of
    The Madras University, 54, No. 1 (Jan. 1982), 1-10.

_____. "Patterns of Distinctiveness in the Language of Commonwealth Fiction--A Comparative Study of the Language of Achebe, Naipaul, Narayan and Nagarajan."

The Literary Half-Yearly, 22, No. 2 (July 1981), 85-100.

Ramchand, Kenneth. "Concern for Criticism." Literary Half-Yearly, 11, No. 2 (July 1970), 151-61.

_____. "In-Between." (Review of The Islands in Between: Essays on West Indian Literature, ed., Louis James.) Journal of Commonwealth Literature, No. 9. (July 1970), 126-27.

_____. "Partial Truths: A Critical Account of Naipaul's Later Fiction." MS., n.d.

_____. "V. S. Naipaul and West Indian Writers." Kenneth Ramchand Speaks with Selwyn Cudjoe, Antilia (Univ. of the West Indies), 1 (1983), 9-20.

_____. "West Indian Literature as the Expression of National Cultures." Lecture, Johns Hopkins Univ., November 9, 1983.

_____. The West Indian Novel and Its Background. New York: Barnes and Noble Inc., 1970.

_____. "The West Indies." In Literature of the World in English. Ed. Bruce Alvin King. London: Routledge and Kegan Paul, 1974.

Ramraj, Victor. "Sly Compassion: V. S. Naipaul's Ambivalence in 'A Christmas Story.'" Commonwealth, 6, No. 1 (Autumn 1983), 61-70.

_____. "V. S. Naipaul's Identity in Fact and Fiction." Paper given at the European Association for

Commonwealth Literature and Language, Barcelona, Spain, April 1984.

_____. "V. S. Naipaul: The Irrelevance of Nationalism." World Literature Written in English, 23, No. 1 (1984), 187-96.

_____. "Voice in V. S. Naipaul's Fiction and Non-fiction." Item 117, MLA Convention, New York. 28 Dec. 1983.

Rao, K. I. Madhusudana. "V. S. Naipaul's Guerrillas: A
Fable of Political Innocence and Experience." Journal
of Commonwealth Literature, 14, No. 1 (Aug. 1979),
90-99.

Razdan, B. M. "Settembrini in the Tropics." New Quest, 26
(March 1981), 121-25.

Richardson, R. K. "Majority Power Would be Better."
Trinidad Guardian, 26 March 1970, p. 10.

Riis, Johannes. "Naipaul's Woodlanders." Journal of Commonwealth Literature, 14, No. 1 (Aug. 1979), 109-15.

Roach, Eric. "Fame a Short-Lived Cycle, Says Vidia."
Trinidad Guardian, 4 Jan. 1972, pp. 1-2.

_____. "Merciless in Aim for Perfection." Rev.
of In a Free State. Trinidad Guardian, 30 Dec. 1971,
p. 7.

Rohlehr, Gordon. "Character and Rebellion in A House for Mr
Biswas." New World Quarterly, 4 (1968), 66-72.

_____. "Predestination, Frustration and Symbolic
Darkness in Naipaul's 'A House for Mr. Biswas.'"
Caribbean Quarterly, 10, No. 1 (March 1964), 3-11.

Rothfork, John. "V. S. Naipaul and the Third World."
Research Studies, 49, No. 3 (Sept. 1981), 183-92.

Rouse, Ewart. "Naipaul: An Interview with Ewart Rouse."
Trinidad Guardian, 28 Nov. 1968, p. 9, 13.

Rowe-Evans, Adrian. "The Writer as Colonial." Transition,
40 (1971), 56-57; rpt. Quest (India), 78 (Sept.-Oct.
1972), 47-55.

Ryan, Selwyn D. Race and Nationalism in Trinidad and Tobago:
A Study of Decolonization in a Multiracial Society,
Toronto: University of Toronto Press, 1972.

Sachs, William. "V. S. Naipaul and the Plight of the Dispossessed." Christian Century, 17 Nov. 1982, pp.
1167-69.

Sandall, Roger. "'Colonia' According to Naipaul." Commentary, 76, No. 6 (Dec. 1983), 77-81.

Sertima, Ivan Van. Caribbean Writers: Critical Essays.
London: New Beacon Books, Ltd., 1968.

Seymour, A. J. "The Novel in the British Caribbean." Bim, 12, No. 44 (Jan.-June 1967), 238-42.

Shenfield, Margaret. "Mr. Biswas and Mr. Polly." English, 23, No. 117 (Autumn 1974), 95-100.

Sherlock, Philip M. West Indies. London: Thames and Hudson, Ltd., 1966.

Singh, H. B. "V. S. Naipaul: A Spokesman for Neo-colonialism." Literature and Ideology, 2 (Summer 1969), 71-85.

Singh, Satyanarain, et al., ed. Osmania Journal of English Studies: V. S. Naipaul, Special Number. Hyderabad (India): Osmania University, 1982.

Smith, M. G. The Plural Society in the British West Indies. Los Angeles: University of California Press, 1965.

Smith, Raymond. British Guiana. London: Oxford University Press, 1962.

Srinath, C. N. "Crisis of Identity: Assertion and Withdrawal in Naipaul and Arun Joshi." The Literary Criterion, 14, No. 1 (1979), 33-41.

Srivastava, Avadhesh K. ed. Alien Voice: Perspectives on Commonwealth Literature. Lucknow, India: Print House, 1981.

Subramani. "The Historical Consciousness in V. S. Naipaul." Commonwealth Quarterly, 4, No. 13 (Dec. 1979), 3-22.

Sudama, Trevor. "Defending CLR and the Naipauls." Sunday Guardian (Trinidad), 1 Nov. 1970, p. 5.

_____. "Walcott-Naipaul: The People in Our Society Can be Likened to Migratory Birds." Trinidad Guardian, 20 Aug. 1967, p. 9.

Swinden, Patrick. Unofficial Selves: Character in the Novel from Dickens to the Present Day." New York: Macmillan Press, Ltd., 1973.

Taylor, Mac Donald Celestin. "A Little Scrutiny of Naipaul's Honesty." Letter. Trinidad Guardian, 12 Jan. 1982, p. 8.

_____. "For Naipaul--a Literary Milestone." Letter. Trinidad Guardian, 17 March 1982, p. 8.

_____. "Naipaul: T'dad Has Gone Back to the Bush." Letter. Trinidad Express, 10 Dec. 1981, p. 5.

374

_____. "Understand Naipaul, Don't Blame Him. . . ."
Letter. Trinidad Guardian, 20 Aug. 1982, p. 8.

Thelwell, Michael M. "African Views." Letter. New York
Times Book Review, 24 June, 1979, p. 45.

Theroux, Paul. V. S. Naipaul: An Introduction to His
Work. New York: Africana Publishing Co., 1972.

Thieme, John. "'Apparitions of Disaster': Bront·an Parallels in Wide Sargasso and Guerrillas." Journal of
Commonwealth Literature, 14, No. 1 (Aug. 1979), 116-31.

_____. "Authorial Voice in V. S. Naipaul's The
Middle Passage." Prose Studies, 5, No. 1 (May 1982),
139-50.

_____. "V. S. Naipaul's Third World: A Not So
Free State." Journal of Commonwealth Literature, 10,
No. 1 (Aug. 1975), 10-22.

Thorpe, Marjorie. "The Mimic Men: A Study in Isolation."
New World Quarterly, 4, No. 4 (1968), 55-59.

Thorpe, Michael. V. S. Naipaul. Writers and Their Works
Series, No. 242. London: The British Council/Longman
Group Ltd., 1976.

Tiffin, Helen. "V. S. Naipaul's 'Outposts of Progress.'"
World Literature Written in English, 22, No. 2 (1983),
309-19.

"Unfurnished Entrails - The Novelist V. S. Naipaul in Conversation with Jim Douglas Henry." Listener, 25 Nov. 1971,
p. 721.

"University News." The Times (London), 21 Feb. 1983, p. 12.

"UWI to Honour Naipaul." Sunday Guardian (Trinidad), 29
June 1975, p. 1.

"V. S. Naipaul in Paris." (Interview). Manchester Guardian
Weekly, 26 July 1981, p. 13.

Walcott, Derek. "The Achievement of V. S. Naipaul." Sunday
Guardian (Trinidad), 12 April 1964, p. 15.

_____. "At Last! Now Hope for Exiled Artists."
Sunday Guardian (Trinidad), 21 Aug. 1960, p. 4.

_____. "Interview with V. S. Naipaul." Sunday
Guardian (Trinidad), 7 March 1965, p. 8

_____. "Is V. S. Naipaul an Angry Young Man?" Sunday Guardian Magazine (Trinidad), 6 Aug. 1967, p. 9.

_____. "Naipaul's New Book." Rev. of Mr Stone and the Knights Companion. Trinidad Guardian, 7 July 1963, p. 15.

Walsh, William. Commonwealth Literature. London: Oxford University Press, 1973.

_____. "Necessary and Accommodated: The Work of V. S. Naipaul." Lugano Review, 1, Nos. 3-4 (1965), 169-81.

_____. V. S. Naipaul. Edinburgh: Oliver Boyd, 1973.

_____. "V. S. Naipaul." The Literary Criterion, 10 (Summer 1972), 23-37.

_____. "V. S. Naipaul," in A Manifold Voice: Studies in Commonwealth Literature. New York: Barnes & Noble Inc., 1970.

_____. "V. S. Naipaul: Mr. Biswas." Literary Criterion, 10, No. 2 (1972), 27-37.

Warner-Lewis, Maureen. "Cultural Confrontation, Disintegration and Syncretism in 'A House for Mr. Biswas.'" Caribbean Quarterly, 16, No. 4 (Dec. 1970), 70-79.

Weatherby, W. J. "Naipaul's Prize?" The Sunday Times (London), 21 Sept. 1980, p. 32.

White, Landeg. V. S. Naipaul: A Critical Introduction. London: Macmillan Press, 1975.

"Why Wayne Brown Chose Edna Manley." Trinidad Guardian, 11 Jan. 1976, p. 10.

Wickham, John. "West Indian Writing." Bim (Barbados), 13, No. 50 (Jan.-June 1970), 68-80.

Williams, Eric. History of the People of Trinidad and Tobago. New York: Frederick A. Praeger, 1962.

Wood, Donald. Trinidad in Transition. London: Oxford Univ. Press, 1968.

Woodcock, George. "Two Great Commonwealth Novelists: R. K. Narayan and V. S. Naipaul." Sewanee Review, 87, No. 1 (1979), 1-28.

_____. "V. S. Naipaul and the Politics of
     Fiction." Queen's Quarterly, 87, No. 4 (Winter 1980),
     679-92.

Wyndham, Francis. "V. S. Naipaul." Listener, 7 Oct.
     1971, pp. 461-62.

_____. "Writing is Magic." Trinidad Guardian, 15
     Nov. 1968, p. 12.

Wynter, Sylvia. "Reflections on West Indian Writing and
     Criticism." Jamaica Journal, 2, No. 4 (Dec. 1969),
     22-32.

_____. "Novel and History, Plot and Plantation."
     Savacou (Jamaica), 5 (June 1971), 95-105.

_____. "Strangers at the Gate: Caribbean Novel-
     ists in Search of Identity." Sunday Gleaner (Jamaica),
     18 Jan. 1959, p. 14.

DATE DUE